Exploring
Human Resource
Management

Exploring
Human Resource Management

Christine Porter
Cecilie Bingham
David Simmonds

McGraw-Hill
Higher Education

London Boston Burr Ridge, IL Dubuque, IA Madison, WI New York San Francisco
St. Louis Bangkok Bogotá Caracas Kuala Lumpur Lisbon Madrid Mexico City
Milan Montreal New Delhi Santiago Seoul Singapore Sydney Taipei Toronto

Exploring Human Resource Management
Christine Porter, Cecilie Bingham and David Simmonds
ISBN-13 978-0-07-711102-1
ISBN-10 0-07-711102-8

**McGraw-Hill
Higher Education**

Published by McGraw-Hill Education
Shoppenhangers Road
Maidenhead
Berkshire
SL6 2QL
Telephone: 44 (0) 1628 502 500
Fax: 44 (0) 1628 770 224
Website: www.mcgraw-hill.co.uk

British Library Cataloguing in Publication Data
A catalogue record for this book is available from the British Library

Library of Congress Cataloguing in Publication Data
The Library of Congress data for this book has been applied for from the Library of Congress

Commissioning Editor: Rachel Gear
Senior Marketing Manager: Alice Duijser
Head of Production: Bev Shields
Head of Development: Caroline Prodger

Text Design by Jonathan Coleclough
Cover design by SCW
Printed and bound in Spain by Mateu Cromo Artes Graficas S.A.

ISBN-13 978-0-07-711102-1
ISBN-10 0-07-711102-8

Brief Table of Contents

Detailed Table of Contents

PART 1 Introduction

PART 2 Strategic aspects

Preface

The book is aimed at those who are seeking to understand the application of human resource management (HRM) concepts in the workplace. We believe that it will be extremely useful to you not only in your studies, but also in your future organisational life.

The book covers the main areas of HRM activity utilised to achieve organisational objectives and analyses how these activities might be carried out by both line managers and human resource specialists in order to help organisations meet their objectives in the most effective manner. As international markets have developed and employees with specialist skills have become more scarce, and therefore more expensive to employ, so the function of HRM has increased in importance. Whether you are working in management or in a specialist function, therefore, you are likely to find that what you can achieve within the organisation will be highly dependent on an in-depth understanding of HRM. HRM is also increasingly important in the not-for-profit sector in order to make the best use of scarce resources.

There are certain aspects of HRM that we discuss in the book and wish to draw your attention to. These can be summarised as follows:

◆ HRM policies and procedures are not implemented as ends in themselves but as a means of achieving a certain set of objectives. We need to ask ourselves what our objectives are as a first question in relation to any HRM issue.

◆ The overall strategy of an organisation needs to be designed bearing in mind the realities of the human resource situation.

◆ HRM is an integrated activity: each HRM policy ideally needs to be integrated both with organisational objectives, with organisational policies in other areas and with each other HRM polices.

◆ HRM needs to be carried out in an ethical manner, bearing in mind the environment and moral obligations towards employees and other interested parties.

◆ HRM is not just the responsibility of the human resource (HR) department, but of all managers within an organisation.

The book has been divided into **SECTIONS** and **CHAPTERS** that reflect the overall structure of HRM as identified in the following model

An integrated model of HRM
© 2006 Porter, Bingham and Simmonds

HOW TO USE THIS BOOK

We have tried to make the book as practical as possible by including a number of helpful elements in it for you and your tutor.

It is not a novel so do not be tempted to sit down and try to read it from beginning to end. Instead you should *read Chapter One* to give you an overview of the subject and then make use of the **CONTENTS** and **INDEX** sections to find your way round the various sections and chapters. Since the book is presented as an integrated study, you might well find, say, 'Induction training' discussed in several different areas.

We have attempted to make the page layout as attractive as possible. The white space is there deliberately for you to add your own notes, thoughts and reflections. The more you interact with the text, the more you will learn and remember.

In each **CHAPTER** there are a number of special elements to help you in your studies.

♦ Firstly, it's important to remember that separate chapters have been written by different authors. They each have a different style and approach to the various areas. We hope this helps you to see how HRM is both a diverse and yet integrated area for study.

♦ At the start of each chapter, you will find a list of **LEARNING OUTCOMES.** These are what you should be able to do as a direct result of having studied the elements in that chapter. To find out how well you are progressing, you should regularly consult these learning outcomes and ask yourself: 'Can I do this?'

♦ Also included at the beginning of each chapter is a short **OUTLINE** of its purpose and content. This should give you an idea of what is to be covered. By the end of each chapter you should return to this statement and reflect by enquiring: 'Has all this been covered? Do I understand it all?'

♦ Each chapter is divided into smaller parts by **HEADINGS** and **SUB-HEADINGS** to help you focus on specific areas in your studies. Ask yourself: 'How do these parts fit together? Can I see the links?'

♦ The **MODELS**, **TABLES** and **DIAGRAMS** have been inserted in order to illustrate various points in the text. But don't just look at them. Engage with each illustration by asking yourself: 'What does this mean? How does it apply?'

♦ There are a number of **EXERCISES** for you to complete on your own or in a group. Discuss your findings with your tutor and other students, and ask yourself: 'How does this exercise help me to understand the point being made in the text? Does this kind of thing happen in any organisations that I know about?'

♦ Short **SCENARIOS** and **WINDOWS INTO PRACTICE** are provided as examples of HRM practice in different organisational settings, sometimes based on interviews with human resource practitioners. Use these to enquire: 'What is happening here, and why? Would it happen in other organisations?'

♦ **CASE STUDIES** are also provided. There is one case study, Warbings, that is referred to throughout the text and about which there are more details below. In addition, there are a number of smaller chapter-specific case studies. These are also usually based on actual problems that have been identified in real situations. Like the scenarios and windows into practice identified above, the organisations on which they are based are not always identified in order to respect confidentiality. Use these to practise diagnostic skills, to identify the problems and their causes, and suggest solutions for overcoming these appropriate to the case situation.

♦ The **PAUSE FOR THOUGHT** questions have been deliberately placed throughout the text to help you to stop reading and to start thinking reflectively. Take time to think through your responses; write them down; discuss them in a group; ask your tutor for feedback; perhaps you could use an electronic discussion board to pursue your ideas.

♦ The **FURTHER READING** list is to guide you towards other books and articles to help you as you develop your understanding of the various aspects of HRM.

♦ The **REVIEW QUESTIONS** at the end of the chapter will help you to summarise your understanding. This will give you confidence in what you have learned from your studies. Check your answers with others on your course.

♦ **USEFUL WEBSITES** can also be found at the end of each chapter. These indicate where you may wish to explore further.

♦ The **GLOSSARY** gives a definition for words that the authors have identified as being part of a specialist HRM vocabulary.

WARBINGS – A major focus of this book is the use of a large case study throughout the text. Each chapter has questions presented as Exercises or Pauses for Thought for you to apply different areas of study to the same organisation. This will help you to appreciate the integrative nature of HRM. You need constantly to ask yourself how different sections and chapters relate together. Using the WARBINGS case will help you in this. You can find the case study on page xxiii.

The W for Warbings logo [seen here] is repeated in the book wherever the activity refers to the WARBINGS case.

Guided Tour

Learning Objectives

Each chapter opens with a set of learning objectives, summarising what readers should learn from each chapter.

Learning outcomes

By the end of this chapter, you should be able to:

◆ Identify the potential contribution of HRM to the achievement of organisational objectives;
◆ Explain the role that the HR department can play in relation to the line manager;
◆ Identify HR practitioners' perspectives about the role that they need to play in an organisation;
◆ Explain the backgrounds of line managers, the likely impact of these backgrounds on the management of employees and the action that needs to be undertaken in order to make managers more effective;

Pause for Thought

Throughout the book these quick activities give you opportunities to test your learning and also your reasoning around HR issues.

pause for thought

What activities can you think of that are carried out by organisations for legal, so political reasons?

Window on Practice

Brief vignettes and examples throughout the text bring the book to life and help you understand how human resource management (HRM) works in practice.

window into practice

At a healthcare trust in the UK it emerged at formal disciplinary proceedings that was a pattern of similar types of failings in patient care, serious enough to warran ciplinary action, including dismissal. The existence of the pattern was reported committee responsible for monitoring clinical governance. This enabled that comm to make a strategic intervention to try and determine the causes of these shortcor and ensure appropriate remedial action was taken and that the strategic 'plan altered accordingly.

Chapter summary

This briefly reviews and reinforces the main topics you will have covered in each chapter to ensure you have acquired a solid understanding of the key topics.

Summary

The role of HRM in an organisation is intended to help the organisation ensure that it meets its corporate objectives by the effective management of its employees. Both HR specialists and line managers carry out this role. HR specialists would need to help ensure that line managers are selected when they have both the desire and the skills to carry out their managerial activities. The practice of HRM is subject to many fashions and fads and it is important when applying HRM techniques to remember the importance of diagnosing accurately the causes of problems in an organisation in order that the most appropriate technique can be adopted. In addition, it is also important that the HRM technique adopted fits with the culture of the organisation.

Most HRM techniques are based on a unitary perspective. That is to say, they are based on the assumption that management and employees' objectives are the same. However, this is

Review Questions

These questions encourage you to review and apply the knowledge you have acquired from each chapter. They are pitched at different levels.

Review Questions

You may wish to attempt the following as practice examination style questions.

1.1 How do you think HRM contributes to the achievement of organisational objectives?

1.2 In what ways do HR managers in the public sector differ in their perceptions of their role from those HR managers in the private sector?

1.3 What HR skills do line managers need to make their work more effective?

1.4 Is HRM culturally dependent? Why did you give this answer?

Mini Case Studies

The book includes case studies designed to test how well you can apply the main techniques learned. Each case study has its own set of questions.

Mini case study: Recruitment and selection in a UK Bank

A large clearing bank in the UK decided to change its recruitment policies in response to changes in the market place. The bank had an HR department but the lead function within the organisation was banking and there was little or no emphasis on the importance of HRM in helping the organisation to achieve its objectives. Rather, it was felt that the organisation would be most effective by concentrating on banking specialists, who were very skilled in banking but largely untrained in managing people.

Previously banks had concentrated on the protection of their clients' deposits but after deregulation of the financial services sector it became possible to enter into other fields of financial activity, including the provision of mortgages and insurance policies. In addition, deregulation of financial services meant that building societies and overseas banks were able to operate in the same fields as UK banks. The UK clearing bank, along with others, therefore decided to put much more emphasis on sales and marketing in an effort to compete.

The traditional approach to recruitment and selection in the bank had been to create long

Warbings Case Study

As explained on page xiii a running case study on the fictional Warbings company helps to show the integrative nature of HRM. To read the introductory material on the case, go to page xxiii.

CASE STUDY

Warbings Office Systems Plc

Background

References, Further Reading and Weblinks

Extra resources listed at the end of chapters help you find useful and current sources of information – a starting point for researching your assignment or essay.

Further Reading

Leopold, J. (ed.) (2002). *Human Resources in Organisations*, FT/Prentice Hall.

Useful Websites

www.cipd.co.uk/search/default.aspx?q=hr%20strategy – links to the Chartered Institute of Personnel and Development resources relating to HR strategy

www.dti.gov.uk – links to Department of Trade and Industry information on ethics and corporate and social responsibility. Also links to other sites identified by DTI as being of

www.humanresourcemanagement.co.uk – publishes articles and news releases about HR surveys, employment law, HR research and related books and other publications

www.btinternet.com/~alan.price/hrm – a free source of worldwide HRM information

www.hrmguide.co.uk – publishes articles and news releases about HR surveys, employment

Visit www.mcgraw-hill.co.uk/textbooks/porter today

Online **Learning** Centre

Online Learning Centre (OLC)

After completing each chapter, log on to the supporting Online Learning Centre website. Take advantage of the study tools offered to reinforce the material you have read in the text, and to develop your knowledge in a fun and effective way.

Resources for students include:

♦ *Learning Objectives*

♦ *Glossary*

♦ *Self-test questions*

♦ *Weblinks*

Also available for lecturers:

♦ *Questions for study and discussion*

♦ *Power Point presentation*

♦ *Additional case studies*

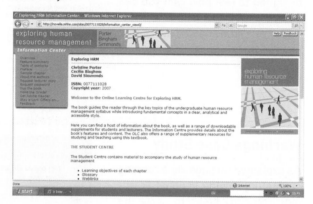

 EZTEST

EZTest, a new computerised testbank format from McGraw-Hill, is available with this title. EZTest enables you to upload testbanks, modify questions and add your own questions, thus creating a testbank that's totally unique to your course! Find out more at: **http://mcgraw-hill.co.uk/he/eztest/**

The test bank created for this title contains a wide variety of questions for use in assessment or exams. There are over 30 questions for each chapter of the book.

Lecturers can obtain a copy of the testbank by contacting their McGraw-Hill representative. To locate your rep, go to www.mcgraw-hill.co.uk/he/rep_locator.

Custom Publishing Solutions: Let us help make our content your solution

At McGraw-Hill Education our aim is to help lecturers find the most suitable content for their needs and the most appropriate way to deliver the content to their students. Our **custom publishing solutions** offer the ideal combination of content delivered in the way which suits lecturer and students the best.

The idea behind our custom publishing programme is that via a database of over two million pages called Primis, **www.primisonline.com**, the lecturer can select just the material they wish to deliver to their students:

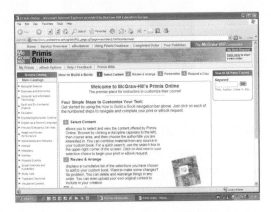

Lecturers can select chapters from:

◆ textbooks

◆ professional books

◆ case books – Harvard Articles, Insead, Ivey, Darden, Thunderbird and BusinessWeek

◆ Taking Sides – debate materials

Across the following imprints:

◆ McGraw-Hill Education

◆ Open University Press

◆ Harvard Business School Press

◆ US and European material

There is also the option to include material authored by lecturers in the custom product – this does not necessarily have to be in English.

We will take care of everything from start to finish in the process of developing and delivering a custom product to ensure that lecturers and students receive exactly the material needed in the most suitable way.

With a **Custom Publishing Solution**, students enjoy the best selection of material deemed to be the most suitable for learning everything they need for their courses – something of real value to support their learning. Teachers are able to use exactly the material they want, in the way they want, to support their teaching on the course.

Please contact your local McGraw-Hill representative with any questions or alternatively contact Warren Eels at **warren_eels@mcgraw-hill.com**.

Acknowledgements

Thank you to all students past and present who have contributed to the knowledge distilled in this book. Thank you also to the chapter authors for their forbearance and likewise to our families.

We are also indebted to Moira King for her support, to Graham Macklin who wrote the Glossary, and to David Rees and Katy Ward for technical advice.

Christine Porter
Cecilie Bingham
David Simmonds
June, 2007

The publishers would also like to thank the reviewers for their constructive and helpful comments at various stages of the text's development, from the initial book proposal to draft manuscript. Their feedback has been invaluable in shaping the book. The reviewers were:

Shirley Barrett, University of Ulster
Guy Brown, Northumbria University
Shelagh Cauwood, Newcastle University
Gill Christy, Portsmouth University
Nicolina Kamenou, Heriot Watt University
Kirsten Krauth, Coventry University
Stephen Leybourne, Plymouth University
Margaret Masson, Glasgow Caledonian University
John Mendy, University of Lincoln
Lyn Nicholl, University of Gloucestershire
Joe O'Mahoney, Cardiff University
Eileen O'Neill, University of Paisley
Jasmine Pidduck, Kingston University
Maureen Royce, Liverpool John Moores University
Peter Samuel, Nottingham University

Contributors

Cecilie Bingham is a Senior Lecturer at Westminster Business School, University of Westminster, specialising in employee relations and diversity. She is course leader for the MA in human resource management and is an active part of the diversity research cluster attached to the School. Prior to her academic career she was commissioning editor for *Managing Best Practice* (The Industrial Society) and senior research officer on both Incomes Data Services Report and Brief.

Anton Bradburn is a Research Fellow at Westminster Business School, University of Westminster. He is currently conducting a research programme into trust and risk in online transactions. His previous research work includes an empirical study of knowledge management in large UK service organisations in the private, public and voluntary sectors. He has a background of employment in both public and private sector organisations.

Kevin Dalton has a background in public sector management, including action research and organisational development. In recent years he has been Director of the Seychelles Institute of Management and Senior Lecturerin Organisational Behaviour and Management Development. His research interests are in organisational story-telling; ideology, power and politics and management in Eastern Europe.

Liz Kennedy For the first 12 years of her career Liz worked in Personnel Management for pharmaceutical companies and hospitals both in England and Canada, and then as Personnel Manager at the National Theatre. She joined the University of Westminster in 1979, lecturing in Human Resource Management. She has an extensive consultancy practice advising organisations on Human Resource issues in the public, private and voluntary sectors. Clients include the BBC, local authorities, Sadlers Wells, Unilever and London Fire Brigade. Liz is a Fellow of the Chartered Institute of Personnel and Development (CIPD) and an Associate Advisor for the Industrial Society, specialising in Reward Management and has contributed to several of their publications.

Julie Lister has worked as a Human Resource Practitioner for many years, in both private and public sector organisations of varying size and culture. She is currently HR Policy and Planning Manager for City University, London. A former graduate of the Westminster Business School, University of Westminster, she returned as a Visiting Lecturer on the MA in Personnel and Development programme.

Angela Mansi is a Chartered Organisational Psychologist, Director of WorkLife Management Ltd. and is an active member of the BPS Special Group of Coaching Psychologists. Her specialist areas of consultancy, and research, are in senior management 'derailment', development and training; recruitment and selection, career and stress counselling. She works with senior managers to help them through career development and transitions, and coaches on the 'dark side' of personality at work.

Lisa Matthewman is a Principal Lecturer in Occupational and Organisational Psychology at the Westminster Business School, University of Westminster. She is a Chartered Occupational Psychologist and Associate Fellow of the British Psychological Society. She is currently responsible for teaching and facilitating group work in all aspects of personal and professional development to both undergraduates and postgraduates. Currently, Lisa is writing and publishing work on mentoring relationships, personal and professional development, and work psychology.

Sue Miller is a Principal Lecturer at Westminster Business School, University of Westminster. She started her working life as a graduate management trainee with the Department of Employment Group, and worked in a variety of roles within the Manpower Services Commission, and the Equal Opportunities Branch of the Department of Employment. She is currently Course Leader for Westminster Business School's MA in Public Services

Management and teaches a range of postgraduate and undergraduate human resource and organisation behaviour modules, including equality and diversity in employment.

Christine Porter is Head of the Department of Human Resource Management at Westminster Business School, University of Westminster and a Fellow of the Chartered Institute of Personnel and Development (CIPD). The Department itself is a CIPD-recognised Centre of Excellence and is one of the largest centres for human resource management teaching in the UK with 500 students taking postgraduate qualifications in the area at any one time. Christine has extensive experience in Management Education in both the UK and overseas and is currently researching the internationalisation of educating HR professionals. She is the co-author of *The Skills of Management*, Thomson Learning, 6th edition (forthcoming) – a text of HR skills for line managers.

Keith Porter is a Senior Lecturer in the Human Resource Management Department of Westminster Business School, University of London, course leader for the MA in Personnel and Development and a Fellow of the Chartered Institute of Personnel and Development (CIPD). He also works as an independent HR consultant, specializing in helping managers to develop into a coaching role. A registered Investors in People advisor, he has helped many organizations to achieve the Standard and has worked extensively as a performance management consultant.

He is the lead author of a popular HR text (Porter K., Smith P. and Fagg, R. 2006. *Leadership and Management for HR Professionals*, 3rd edition, Butterworth-Heinemann).

Patricia Price is a Principal Lecturer at the Westminster Business School, University of Westminster, with many years of experience, specializing in employment law for HRM specialists at postgraduate and professional levels. She regularly advises on and draws up policy on employment law, particularly for voluntary sector organisations. She has undertaken case work for managers covering all aspects of employment law, as well as representing clients in resolution of conflict within the workplace.

Amanda Rose is a Principal Lecturer in occupational and organisational psychology at the University of Westminster. Her research interests are in the areas of women and work and the ethical aspects of business practice. She has worked as a consultant in the public sector in the field of equal opportunities and assessment at work.

Sue Shortland is a Principal Lecturer in International Human Resource Management at London Metropolitan University where her research interests include gender diversity within international assignments. She has written extensively on expatriation and international HRM and is a Chartered Fellow of the CIPD. Her latest book, authored with Stephen Perkins, is entitled *Strategic International Human Resource Management: Choices and Consequences in Mutinational People Management*, published by Kogan Page in 2006.

David Simmonds has over 30 years' experience in training, learning, education and development in the public, private and voluntary sectors. He teaches on postgraduate programmes, helping managers to learn about learning, and has a passion to improve standards and quality of training and is a Fellow of the Chartered Institute of Personnel and Development (CIPD). He is also the author of a popular CIPD text, *Designing and delivering training*, CIPD, London, 2003.

Paul E Smith is a Principal Lecturer in Human Resource Management and is Head of the HR Subject Group at the University of Hertfordshire School of Business. He is the author of a number of books in the field of HRM and is a Fellow of the CIPD.

Bill Spear is a Principal Lecturer in Human Resource Management and is course leader of MA Strategic HRM and leader of two MA-level modules – Strategic People Management and Development, and Strategic Personnel and Development. Bill has had extensive experience both as a line manager and HR Director in the public sector, in addition to a number of academic posts in further and higher education.

Gill Sugden has more than 25 years of lecturing experience in higher education and 12 years experience of leading and managing a university department. She now lectures in e-business and strategies for information management. Her research is in the areas of knowledge management, and assessment, in particular formative assessment in Higher Education.

Kieran Williams is a Senior Lecturer in Organisation Behaviour, Diversity and Change Management at Westminster Business School, University of Westminster and freelance training consultant specialising in the management of people, teams and diversity in the public and voluntary sector. She teaches courses on culture, change and diversity to postgraduate students at Westminster and is a qualified flying instructor.

Angela Wright is a Senior Lecturer in Human Resource Management at Westminster University, Business School of Westminster. She is a Fellow of the Chartered Institute of Personnel & Development (CIPD) and has research interests in several aspects of pay and reward including employee benefits, as well as in diversity and equal opportunities. During her careerin the pay/remuneration field,

she has worked for the public sector pay review bodies, as their Remuneration Specialist/ Adviser; and she led the pay research team at Industrial Relations Services, following a research role at Incomes Data Services.

She is the author of a CIPD (2004) text – *Reward Management in Context*.

Carol Wood is a Senior Lecturer in Human Resource Management at Westminster Business School, University of Westminster, teaching on a range of courses including staff development on the PGCHE. She joined the University after 20 years' experience in the telecommunication, financial and retail sectors as a business analyst and in HRM. Her interest and writing about work-life balance issues developed as a result of her experiences of portfolio working, juggling a number of part-time roles in the private sector and in higher education including Birkbeck College, University of London.

Warbings Office Systems Plc

Background

Warbings Office Systems is a small but rapidly growing company, focusing on delivering and supplying office-based products to a target market of small businesses in the UK and, increasingly, Europe. As the trend for homeworking continues, much of their new business is in supplying office materials to individuals working from home. Currently offering some 18,000 different product lines in store and 39,000 via catalogue ordering, it intends to double its product turnover in the next three years by increasing its web-based ordering capabilities. With the marketing strapline 'you need it, we've got it', Warbings aims to make office supply shopping as easy as possible for customers. Priding itself on being a 'thoroughly modern company with old traditions', Warbings has used technology to evolve into a customer-focused business, striving to give each customer a 'personal service second to none', with a variety of different, but easily accessible, ways of ordering and receiving products tailored to their individual needs. The more cynical of their staff occasionally reflect that the customers even dictate the lavatory breaks and bedtimes of the Warbings' employees. Graffiti on one of the depot walls, that intriguingly reappears every time it is removed, says 'you need it, we bleed it' and occasionally 'Wosp stings'.

The Warbings CEO is passionate about delivery and customer care and he is convinced that the way in which customers are treated is the key to repeat business. The Warbings mission statement reflects this philosophy, stating that:

> 'Our mission is to cost-effectively supply both the professional and home office with a complete range of supplies, including stationery, filing equipment, office equipment, computer consumables and cleaning materials. To do this, the Warbings team is committed to meeting the needs of each and every customer by delivering competitively priced quality products, with innovative functionality and modern design. We help design, provide, advise on and deliver the right products to you, for you. Our daily objective is to ensure that our customers, wherever they are, whoever they are, whether they purchase in one of our shops, through our direct sales department or over the internet, receive the same level of care, courtesy, helpful service and respect to which they are entitled. It is this service from our people that makes the essential difference.'

The company sees no need for a values statement, insisting that everything necessary is contained within the mission statement.

Evolving from a nineteenth-century printing shop in the East End of London, Warbings has been formed over the years by acquisition and merger. (At one stage it considered further growth by expanding to supply goods to office supplies distributors, but decided against this and, for the short term anyway, is now intent on consolidating rather than expanding its present base.) Based in East London, it has a warehouse and driver depot in Basildon and an additional two warehouses in Leeds and Manchester. As well as its delivery service it has three out-of-town retail superstores (Farnham, Marchington and Lewis), a European office in Ulm (West Germany), together with a call centre and a small copying and printing service attached to its head office in Bow, East London. Around 600 employees work in the company, of whom 210 are part time and based in the three superstores. (See organisation chart at the end of the case study.)

Business and personnel climate

As the business has grown and become geographically diverse, the company faces a growing challenge of cohesion. Communicating between the divisions is becoming more and more difficult as the company tries to achieve uniformity in vision, performance and delivery of information to all employees in a timely and efficient way. The IT department has become crucial in this, and is in the process of organising and replacing the business PCs – which are reaching the end of their life cycle – with a system that supports Warbings' expanding product and customer base, while still delivering an intranet interface which is efficient, user-friendly and less prone to break down under the pressure of use.

The directors at the head office are delighted with the way in which the new system is becoming embedded and enthuse about the ways in which they can access performance data at the drop of a hat, spot buying trends in the market and yet still use the same system to communicate new targets and schemes instantly to the workforce. There are plans to introduce a monthly electronic newsletter for all staff, discussing the virtues of new product lines, showing which divisions are exceeding targets, explaining any changes to the company, and perhaps highlighting the top salesperson for that month. 'E-updating by unobtrusive drip feeding' is part of the thinking behind this. A monthly competition to 'guess the quickest route' is likely to be incorporated, as the CEO says he knows that this will 'keep the drivers on their toes'; he has suggested that lunch with him will be a suitable prize. The HR manager, who has been told that he will have to co-ordinate and produce this experimental missive, was reputed to have been overheard muttering something along the lines of, 'I'll have a guess the weight of the CEO competition.'

A number of the staff see the shift to electronic communication as a necessary evil, increasing the ease of communicating with customers but reducing telephone or face-to-face contact between employees. There is an additional degree of unrest because the information system is also used as a way of recording details about staff performance – sales staff and call centre employees in particular are now required to input data about their daily activities, expected calls and actual calls. Many regard this increasing level of surveillance as indicative of the impersonal way in which Warbings regards them as a means to a profitable end. Indeed, the lack of consultation about the type of computers to install and their potential use so infuriated two of the sales team that they left, moaning about the ways in which their jobs had become unrecognisable, and the fact that they were supposed to adapt to the new ways without comment. Among the remaining staff, comments such as 'no one asked us, yet we are the people who have to use this system; it is such a waste of time' and 'when everything goes wrong, as it probably will, we will be the ones who have to work harder just to stand still' are commonplace. Ironically, the system that was supposed to make things easier may, in some instances, be making them worse.

The constant pressures to hit targets, increase sales, improve the portfolio of products and increase points of sale, while decreasing the time it takes to process goods through the system, has resulted in a rather frenetic culture where there is little time for reflection, where strategic decision making comes a poor second to reaction to the market place, and where supervisors and managers feel obliged to push their teams to the limit. Absence levels have gone up by a third over the last quarter and six people have had their contracts terminated because they were taking extended sick leave due to stress. The union (Unite) representatives have, on a number of occasions, brought up health and safety issues linked to increasing workloads and shorter delivery times. The company is therefore aware that the drivers in some of the divisions are members of Unite but it tries to have as little to do with the union as possible. Indeed, part of the determination to keep outside forces at bay is epitomised by its attitude to the Road Haulage Association. It acknowledges that this sets national pay rates, but is unsure whether or not these apply to Warbings and does not want to 'find out for sure' in case the knowledge commits the company to delivering terms and conditions out of line with the regionally based ones it currently offers. A number of lost tribunal cases, coupled with numerous lengthy and unsettling calls to the Advisory, Conciliation, and Arbitration Service (ACAS) helpline, resulted in the CEO rather grudgingly, and some would say belatedly, appointing the new human resource (HR) director and her assistant. He is confident that these two can 'tidy up' the way in which the company operates, and has set them a target of six months to 'iron out any controversy' and phase in any procedures they feel appropriate.

Training in all sections is *ad hoc*, given when necessary and usually delivered in-house by an already proficient member of the team. It rarely, if at all, follows from a systematic review of performance and training needs by a line manager. A similar approach is taken with regards to recruitment and selection. Outline job descriptions are produced but recruitment and selection of staff is fairly informal and there is a lack of consistency between sites. The most popular selection methods are an application form, interview (which often takes the form of an informal chat) and references. The main recruitment methods used are the local paper, word of mouth and specialist agencies.

The CEO makes a point of delivering a 'state of the nation' pep talk to all divisions during the slacker summer period. The HR manager feels these talks are possibly counterproductive but has enough to do firefighting and coping with the additional paperwork generated by bi-monthly board meetings without jeopardising his career by interfering and offering the CEO 'helpful' suggestions. Since it has become known that he is to rationalise the ways that each division works, he has received at least 30 emails a day from a range of individuals demanding changes to a variety of things and seeking clarification on others. Typically, these missives cover such topics as:

- The shift system
- Overnight allowances
- On-site chiropody
- Flexible working
- Different ways of complaining
- Abolition of staff monitoring
- Heavy-handed line management
- Health and safety
- Holiday pay
- Training
- Quality of cleanliness, soap and lavatory paper in the washrooms
- The introduction of a faith room
- Different ways of setting and communicating targets.

The state of business and employee relations in each of the firm's main units

The sections below outline the situation for each main unit.

East London-based sections: head office, call centre and printing division

In an effort to achieve greater integration of the total business, the directors have increased the role of head office in developing financial and administrative procedures (particularly those associated with IT) that can be applicable throughout the organisation.

The personnel function has been strengthened by the appointment of a full-time HR manager and assistant, whose tasks will be to impose uniform procedures on the currently chaotic areas such as pay, disciplinary and grievance policies and manpower returns. They are expected to produce a new staff handbook and ensure essential compliance with the law by the end of the year. This task is unenviable. Even where there are uniform procedures, they are not always followed consistently, and some are capable of being interpreted in a variety of ways.

The call centre operators and admin/clerical staff are mostly local people, and labour turnover is very low. The new computer system has engendered a lot of muttered discontent (in the main because changes were imposed and not discussed). Sickness levels have risen by 12 per cent since its introduction.

The sales team are young, male and rely on commission to maintain their income levels. The two members of the sales team who covered Wales and the South of England, respectively, left the organisation within the last six months, see above, and have not been replaced.

The technical staff based on this site regard themselves as essential to maintaining Warbings' market position, but the CEO regards them as an increasing cost to the company, even though some of their salaries are below the national average. Although morale seems high, there is nevertheless a relatively high level of turnover of representatives and technical support staff, most of whom are young, ambitious and highly marketable in a very competitive market.

Overall at head office Warbings faces difficulties in attracting sufficient applicants for many vacancies and there are currently a number of unfilled posts.

Basildon warehouse and driver depot

Because the business is expanding, and the company has increased its market share in the London/Europe area, this division is extremely busy. Drivers are now routinely expected to deliver in Europe as well as at home, and this means that they have to, on occasion, spend several days abroad at short notice. The CEO is aware that driving for long periods can be a health and safety risk, but it is one he is prepared for his drivers to undertake, assuming they will be extra vigilant when they think of the additional overtime payments. Wages and salaries are higher than in the other divisions, but staff turnover is quite high too.

Leeds warehouse and driver depot

Business here is rather static and the company is struggling to maintain market share. Wages and salaries are lower than in the other divisions and staff morale is low, but labour turnover over the last year has been unexpectedly static.

Manchester warehouse and driver depot

This is an extremely busy division, with drivers and depot workers frequently expected to work overtime with little or no notice. Pay is below average for the region, turnover high and union membership increasing.

The depots recruit drivers primarily through word of mouth; when vacancies occur the drivers are asked if they know of anyone who might be interested and would be suitable. Only if this doesn't produce enough applicants are other recruitment methods used – primarily a specialist agency. So far this approach has seemed to work reasonably well in filling vacancies.

Three superstores

These are maintaining sales in the face of fierce competition from high street franchise operations. The workforce is mostly female and part time, and the employees are generally older than in other divisions. The rates of pay and holidays vary across the stores and reflect regional variations. Posts are usually filled quickly, but turnover is also relatively high and resignations often peak around school holidays, something that has become a source of bleak humour among the longer-serving staff.

Ulm

The German office is staffed mostly by local employees, with the exception of the director and four ex-pat sales staff. Pay is higher than average and the ex-pat staff are paid an additional number of supplements, including a 'working abroad bonus', housing allowance, any school fees, and health insurance. Turnover is low and staff recalled to the UK tend to resent their loss of supplementary benefits and often suggest that they should return to Germany in a coaching capacity.

Current strategy

Key strategic targets include:

♦ Rationalise staff processes;

♦ Increase the competitiveness of every decision in every division;

♦ Speed up the introduction of computerised systems;

♦ Reduce costs in relation to sales/output by necessary restructuring, even if this means compulsory redundancies;

♦ Increase the European market share.

Warbings Office Systems Plc

East London (HQ)
CEO, Managing Director, Finance Director, Purchasing Director, her assistant and a team of 5 buyers, IT Director, Web-master and 6 IT programmers and support staff, Administration Manager, HR Manager and assistant, Marketing and Sales Director, with a sales team of 18 and 25 admin/clerical staff, respectively, and two security staff.

Ulm office serving Europe
European Director, his PA and a sales team of 12.

East London call centre
Director of Services, Head Floor Supervisor and deputy, with their 3 PAs and 30 call operators who work a 10 days on, 4 days off shift system.

East London copying and printing
Chief Print Manager, Head Engineer, 7 skilled machine operatives and their manager, 20 production staff, including 2 supervisors, plus 3 admin staff.

Basildon warehouse and driver depot
Divisional Manager, plus 4 clerical/admin staff, 13 store hands, 5 security staff and 34 drivers. The majority of the drivers are in the TGWU section of Unite.

Leeds warehouse and driver depot
Divisional Manager, plus 4 clerical/admin staff, 16 store hands, 5 security staff and 41 drivers. The majority of the drivers are in the TGWU section of Unite.

Manchester warehouse and driver depot
Divisional Manager, plus 4 clerical/admin staff, 12 store hands, 5 security staff and 36 drivers. The minority of the drivers are in the TGWU section of Unite.

Farnham superstore
General Manager, his secretary, 93 floor staff and 4 security staff.

Marchington superstore
General Manager, his secretary, 87 floor staff and 4 security staff.

Lewis superstore
General Manager, his secretary, 102 floor staff and 4 security staff.

PART 1
Introduction

Part contents

CHAPTER 1

What is Human Resource Management?

By Christine Porter and Ania Przwieczerska

Chapter outline

Human Resource Management (HRM) is a philosophy of people management based on the belief that human resources are uniquely important to sustained organisation success, and the notion that an organisation gains competitive advantage[1] by ensuring that its employees are able to make use of their expertise and ingenuity to meet clearly defined corporate objectives (Price, 1997). The purpose of this chapter is twofold. Firstly, it seeks to outline the various roles that HRM plays within the organisation both at policy and practitioner level. The organisational problems that emerge in carrying out this role will be identified, with particular emphasis on the role of the line manager and the problems faced by the HR function in interfacing with line managers. Secondly, the chapter will serve as an introduction to the rest of the book, indicating the areas that are covered in the chapters that follow.

Learning outcomes

By the end of this chapter, you should be able to:

- Identify the potential contribution of HRM to the achievement of organisational objectives;
- Explain the role that the HR department can play in relation to the line manager;
- Identify HR practitioners' perspectives about the role that they need to play in an organisation;
- Explain the backgrounds of line managers, the likely impact of these backgrounds on the management of employees and the action that needs to be undertaken in order to make managers more effective;
- Explain the cultural basis of HRM and the extent to which changes may need to be made in the adoption of HRM tools to fit with different cultures;

---

[1] In not-for-profit organisations, a more relevant objective would be that of improving organisational effectiveness by achieving 'value for money'.

◆ Explain the contingency approach to the application of HR strategy and techniques;
◆ Identify the basis of conflict at work and the need for this to be taken into account when managing employees.

Introduction

HRM is a multidisciplinary activity based on ideas and theories drawn, for example, from sociology, law, psychology and economics. The subject has developed over the last 25 years to encompass fields of study that include organisation behaviour, personnel management and employee relations. It is viewed as involving all managers, especially general managers, and is therefore seen by many as broader in perspective than the subject matter of, say, personnel management. The extent to which this perception is founded on reality is discussed later in this chapter.

The term 'HR function' itself is a little ambiguous since it could relate to the activity of HR (or personnel management) throughout the organisation – wherever it is practised – thus including the activities of line managers as well as HR managers. It could also, however, just relate to the activities of the HR department. While the design of HR policies should be a joint effort involving both the HR specialists and line managers in an organisation, the implementation of human resource policies will be divided between the HR function and line management. There may be some difficulties in identifying the boundaries between these two sets of players and the extent to which either party are interested and willing to take responsibility for certain tasks. Much emphasis has been placed in the recent past on the strategic role of the HR department and HR practitioners do indeed need to take a corporate role and play an important part in the creation of organisational strategy, at least in relation to the extent to which the availability of skilled human resources will affect the achievement of these objectives.

The HR practitioner is part of the management team and their activities will impact on the relationship between the organisation and its employees. Despite interest in the extent to which HR is involved in the creation of strategies, HR practitioners also have an important role to play in administration and in the welfare of employees, although not necessarily as a buffer activity between management and unions. The relationship with line management and the need for line managers to be involved in the HR function is an important one and will be examined in greater detail in this chapter.

Historical perspective

HR began as a welfare and establishment function known as 'personnel management'. Personnel management was conceived of as being the practice of those in a specific department in the organisation. It was the duty of the personnel department to ensure that employees' health and safety needs were catered for. They also had to keep records of the numbers employed, dates of employment, holiday entitlement, rate of pay and training received. These aspects of the function are still important, in addition to the strategic approaches that HR could and should take and the need and desire for HR to be more involved in decision making at a corporate or strategy-making level.

The HR function has grown in importance with the growth of global competition. The increased pace of globalisation has meant that private sector organisations face far greater competition than in the past and one way of ensuring that they remain competitive has been to concentrate on their workforce. The need for skilled employees has increased, along with competition in the market place and the acquisition, retention and replacement of suitable employees has in itself become an even more skilled activity than in the past. Organisations are much more likely to recruit internationally than in the past but employees are therefore more likely to view the job market as global. As demand for skilled labour in the private sector has increased so has demand for skilled labour in the public sector. Both sectors require employees who are flexible and willing to respond to the ever-changing demands that organisations place on them. The public sector, non-governmental and quasi non-governmental organisations have all been under pressure. Public sector organisations have been required to make more effective use of their employees as the pubic expectations of service provisions have risen in excess of the financial resources available to meet these expectations.

The importance of the HR function has also increased in the UK with membership of the European Union, which has resulted in a plethora of statutes and directives that impact on the employment relationship (Ambler et al., 2004). UK government intervention in the workplace has also increased but much of this has been related to EU initiatives.

> 'The personnel function in firms has grown dramatically in recent years to cope with the expansion of regulation. The membership of the Institute of Personnel Management was 12,000 in 1979, and even as late as 1990 it was only 40,000. Today the grandly renamed Chartered Institute of Personnel and Development has around 120,000 members.'
>
> (Shackleton, 2005: 128–129)

The interventions in the employment relationship are also a response to changes in social norms about the protection of employees and the need, sometimes, for free enterprise to be restricted in order to promote the welfare of employees. Legislation has also increased the cost of employing people, therefore requiring the more efficient utilisation of human resources. This is in addition to the need for employers to be briefed about the details of legislation not just in order to avoid falling foul of the law, but because many of the provisions in employment statutes indicate levels of good practice that it is necessary for the employer to observe as a means of managing the workforce effectively.

The pace of economic change has quickened so that there is forever the problem of matching stock of skills with the requirements.[2] As this chapter is being written, Ernst & Young report that the UK economy is booming (*Sunday Times*, 2007), and there are low levels of unemployment. Despite the frequent scarcity of highly skilled employees in some areas, there is still a tendency among managers to treat employees as if they were the least significant and most easily malleable or

---

[2] Kersley et al. (2006: 107) suggest that skills are 'an increasing priority in British workplaces'. They also suggest that there is a large proportion of over-skilled employees and that these employees might be better utilised. This is backed up by research conducted between 1986–2001 (Felstead et al., 2002).

manipulated aspect of any change programme and for their needs and views on a situation not to be taken into account (see ACAS, 2004 for an analysis of the volume of case referrals).

Although the incidence of collective disputes has declined markedly since the peak of union recognition in 1979, the Workplace Employment Relations Survey (WERS) team point out (Kersley et al., 2006) that the focus has shifted to 'unorganised and individualised expressions such as grievances, Employment Tribunal claims and management-led sanctions including dismissals' (p. 207). Employees have increasingly higher expectations of their employers and may, if working in an area of skills shortage, be able to take their skills to another organisation. Their increased expectations partly relate to changes in education but also to increased expectations in terms of quality of life and a heightened view of themselves as 'the customer' and their importance in the market place (often encouraged by the marketing policies of the companies for whom they work). This increase will manifest itself in terms of negative attitudes towards authoritarian management, a desire for participation in decision making (particularly when they are subject to a programme of change), a need for improved physical working conditions and pressure for increases in pay and other rewards.

The move in the UK from a manufacturing to a service economy has meant that there is a greater than ever need for workers with a different skill base. The service economy has had to adapt to the requirement of a 24/7 service. With the rise in flexible working patterns, facilitated in some cases by new technology, has come further demand for services to be provided around the clock.

The HR function itself has in the past been slow to adapt to computerisation and to take advantage of the opportunities provided. However, that is changing with the increasing use of software to support HR activities in-house. Kettley and Reilly (2003) report that there is little independent evidence on the take-up of e-HR, which they describe as 'the application of conventional, web and voice technologies to improve HR administration, transactions and process performance'. According to IRS (2004a, 2004b), 90 per cent of organisations are using some form of e-recruitment packages to manage the process from advertising vacancies, through candidate applications to initial short-listing. Other software supports human capital management: this covers payroll, absence monitoring, staff development and providing data for human resource planning. Packages are also available to support employee learning and development needs via self-managed learning.

Models of human resource management

Globalisation and the greater need for organisations to be competitive on a global basis have meant that greater emphasis has been placed on the human resource. Delery and Shaw (2001) point out that human capital may be a source of competitive advantage. The advent of the knowledge worker has also meant that the human resource has been more valued. This led in the early 1980s to the development of models of HRM that emphasised the link with organisational objectives. It has always been the case that personnel (or HR) managers need to take into account organisational objectives when deciding on a package of employment policies. Similarly, organisations have always needed to consult with HR when devising corporate objectives, in order to ensure that their plans were feasible from the

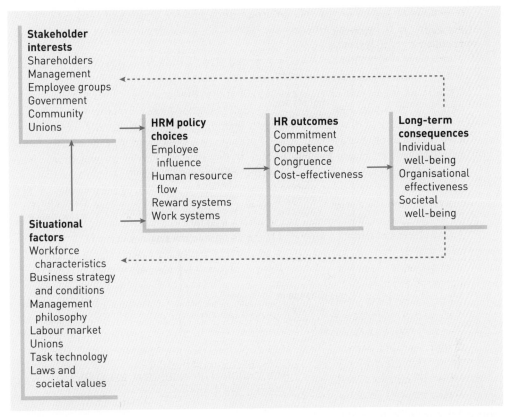

Figure 1.1 Map of HRM territory
Source: Beer et al. (1984: 16)

perspective of the labour resource. However, models of HRM written about in the 1980s were put forward as an innovative approach to managing people: an example of a repackaged idea, common in this area.

There were many models of HRM developed between 1984 and 1995. Two sub-divisions of models of HRM are emphasised – the 'hard' and 'soft' versions (Storey, 1992). Hard HRM emphasises employee costs and head count. Soft HRM emphasises employee participation, organisational capability and training and development.

A useful model for identifying the different interest groups within organisations is that of Beer et al. (1984), based at that time at Harvard University. As can be seen, the model of HRM reproduced as Figure 1.1 identifies the stakeholders and situational factors that will impact on the implementation of the HRM policies that an organisation devises and which therefore need to be taken into account. The model has the advantage that it appears to recognise that not all stakeholders will share the same interests and that because of this there could be conflict in implementing HRM practices. The model also encourages consideration of the need for policies and practices to be congruent with one another and for long-term consequences to take into account individual and societal well-being as well as organisational effectiveness.

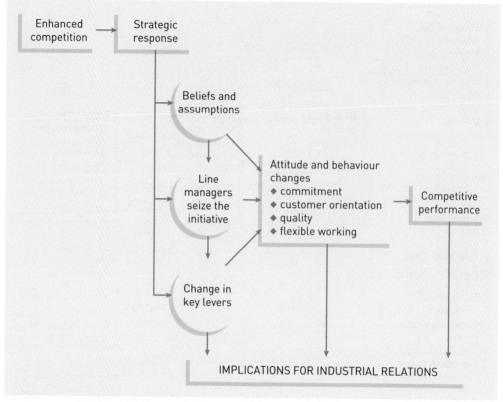

Figure 1.2 A model of the shift to HRM
Source: Storey (1992: 38)

Storey (1992) researched the transformation of organisations to the use of HRM instead of personnel management practices. From this research he created a model of the transformation, although he refers to it as an 'ideal type' – meaning that he has exaggerated the conception of how organisations have been transformed in order to make a point (see Figure 1.2). He identified 27 points of difference between the two terms human resource management and personnel management – these are summarised in Table 1.1.

Whether HRM exists as a separate approach to personnel management is open to debate. It is certainly true that many of the differences that are attributed to HRM (e.g. integration of HR with organisational strategy) can be identified as existing in organisations before HRM began to be discussed as a distinctive model.

Practitioners' perceptions of human resource management

As indicated above, despite the work of Storey and others, for some time academia (and to a lesser extent industry) has engaged in a debate on the differences, if any,

Table 1.1 Twenty-seven points of difference

Dimension	Personnel and IR	HRM
Beliefs and assumptions		
1 Contract	Careful delineation of written contracts	Aim to go 'beyond contract'
2 Rules	Importance of devising clear rules/mutuality	'Can-do' outlook; impatience with 'rule'
3 Guide to management action	Procedures	'Business need'
4 Behaviour referent	Norms/custom and practice	Values/mission
5 Managerial task *vis-à-vis* labour	Monitoring	Nurturing
6 Nature of relations	Pluralist	Unitarist
7 Conflict	Institutionalised	De-emphasised
Strategic aspects		
8 Key relations	Labour management	Customer
9 Initiatives	Piecemeal	Integrated
10 Corporate plan	Marginal to	Central to
11 Speed of decision	Slow	Fast
Line management		
12 Management role	Transactional	Transformational leadership
13 Key managers	Personnel/IR specialists	General/business/line managers
14 Communication	Indirect	Direct
15 Standardisation	High (e.g. 'parity' and issue)	Low (e.g. 'parity' not seen as relevant)
16 Prized management skills	Negotiation	Facilitation
Key levers		
17 Selection	Separate, marginal task	Integrated, key task
18 Pay	Job evaluation (fixed grades)	Performance-related
19 Conditions	Separately negotiated	Harmonisation
20 Labour management	Collective bargaining contracts	Towards individual contracts
21 Thrust of relations with stewards	Regularised through facilities and training	Marginalised (with exception of some bargaining for change models)
22 Job categories and grades	Many	Few
23 Communication	Restricted flow	Increased flow
24 Job design	Division of labour	Teamwork
25 Conflict handling	Reach temporary truces	Manage climate and culture
26 Training and development	Controlled access to courses	Learning companies
27 Foci of attention for interventions	Personnel procedures	Wide-ranging cultural, structural and personnel strategies

Source: Storey (1992: 38). Reproduced by kind permission of Blackwell Publishers.

between 'human resource management' and 'personnel management'. The central discussion revolves around whether these terms represent practices and approaches that are qualitatively different, or are merely alternative labels for applied principles that are fundamentally the same. Rarely, however, has this discussion sought to take account of actual HR/personnel practitioners' understandings of these issues and how, if at all, they describe what they do.

HRM/personnel management – the debate

Unpublished preliminary findings from research conducted by Przwieczerska in 2003 suggest that, notwithstanding the niceties of the academic debate, for some practitioners, HRM and personnel management are largely interchangeable terms, with the former representing little more than an Americanisation of the latter. However, others perceive a more substantive difference, with personnel management seen as denoting a more reactive set of activities, primarily concerned with the administration of employment and provision of employee welfare, while HRM is seen as more proactive, strategically driven people management, with the emphasis on eliciting performance. HRM is seen as a way of enhancing the profile and role of an otherwise low-status and misunderstood function. What often comes across is uncertainty about what the term entails and how it could be incorporated in an organisation's future development. Instead, it is not regarded in as much high esteem as other departments as its contributions are viewed as merely administrative, concerned with immediate workforce concerns rather than long-term plans.

Senior versus junior practitioners

Przwieczerska's research findings indicate that the terms HRM and personnel management seem to have different meanings for senior and junior practitioners. Senior practitioners emphasise HRM and its associated strategic role – that is, managing the performance of human resources in order to achieve the organisation's strategic goals. More junior practitioners, while recognising the theoretical distinctiveness of HRM, perceive what they are doing as primarily personnel management – the routine administration of pay, recruitment, appraisal, grievances and redundancy – without any evident sense of strategic purpose. In organisations where HRM does not appear to be regarded as highly as other departments, new HR managers are not allowed to put into practice their ideas and initiatives, and instead are pigeon-holed into what was previously titled personnel management roles. One very visible casualty of this restricted role is the training versus organisational development debate, discussed further in Chapters 15, 16 and 17.

Public versus private sector

The research conducted by Przwieczerska revealed signs of differences between the public and private sectors. Private sector practitioners appear to perceive their role more in terms of HRM, with an emphasis on strategy and performance, whereas public sector practitioners perceive their role more in terms of old-style personnel management, with a continuing emphasis on bargaining and employee welfare. It could be argued that this difference reflects the way the private and public sectors function.

Do you think that these perceived private/public sector distinctions described above will affect the potential for employee job satisfaction?

What were the reasons for you coming to this conclusion?

Models of HRM indicate the need to have HR practices that do not conflict with one another. For example, the simultaneous existence of practices such as performance-related pay that is based on an individual's performance and teamworking that obviously promotes the value of the team can be conflicting and therefore counter-productive. The lack of involvement of HR practitioners at board level very often militates against the development of strategy that takes account of the human resource realities in terms of the capacity of the organisation to undertake certain activities as the following example illustrates.

window into
practice

A London-based children's charity decided to take over a number of nurseries in an ambitious programme of expansion. The charity did not involve the HR director in the decision to expand in this way and was therefore unaware that the employees in these other organisations had employment rights that made it difficult to make them redundant. The charity also lacked the managerial expertise to run a larger organisation. Before long they found themselves in severe financial difficulties and were lucky not to become bankrupt.

The extent to which strategic HRM is practised will vary from one organisation to another, and also from one country to another. There is, for example, far greater involvement of the function in Japanese and North American organisations. Japanese organisations in particular may have HR specialists who have worked for many years with the same company and are therefore very knowledgeable about the organisation. Any board member will need to have an understanding of the whole business in order to make a useful contribution to strategy development. For this reason, the professional examinations that HR professionals take to achieve chartered status include a strong general management component.

If HR directors have come from other organisations there may be a problem with adapting what worked in those organisations to the new situation. HR directors and other managers will need to take a contingency approach to the situation in which they find themselves.

window into
practice

The HR function has to earn its place on the board of directors

The new director of human resources at a well-established and respected research institute was pleased to be appointed to this job, especially since the role had been upgraded to a director level position. Previously he had worked for six years for a firm of management consultants who operated mainly in the private sector. His predecessor at the research institute had operated in what had been in reality an old style 'establishments'

continued

department making sure that all the records were kept up to date and ensuring that everyone got paid on time. The predecessor had not been professionally qualified, unlike the new director.

The main problem that the new HR director identified was the over-involvement of the professional staff in the detailed work of their various units. Their loyalty appeared to be just to their discipline and not to their colleagues in other departments or the institute as a whole. He saw the professional staff as not being very deferential to authority and with a weak sense of corporate identity.

The HR director did not integrate with the organisation and became increasingly frustrated in his attempts to develop a modern human resource management function, which he thought was necessary to support the organisation in both the accomplishment of its strategic objectives and day-to-day operational effectiveness. He sought to implement a range of techniques that he saw as being 'best practice' but without identifying whether they fitted in with the culture of the institute. No attempt was made by him to identify the problems that line managers faced and when there was a real problem he was nowhere to be seen.

Eventually the HR director's post was down-graded since he was not perceived as contributing to organisational effectiveness.

The role of the HR manager

The role of the HR manager is seen to have changed over the years from that of a 'clerk of works' (Tyson and Fell, 1986) to that of 'strategic business partner' (attributed to Ulrich, 1998). A more strategic input for HR managers is seen as being an advance in the status of the profession. However, many of the roles identified still need to be undertaken simultaneously with that of a strategic input if organisations are to function effectively.

In 2003, Caldwell attempted to test out two models of the 'personnel manager's role' (that of Storey, 1992 and Ulrich, 1997) to identify the extent to which roles had changed now that 'HRM has increasingly become part of the rhetoric and reality of organisational performance' (Caldwell, 2003: 983). Storey (1992) draws on case-based research to inform his model that identified four different roles for HR managers: Advisors, Handmaidens, Regulators and Changemakers. These four roles were identified along two axes: *intervention* versus *non-intervention* and *strategy* versus *tactics* (see Figure 1.3).

HR managers as Advisors offer expertise and advice to line managers while operating in an essentially non-interventionist manner. Handmaidens provide specific services to management and, like those playing an Advisor role, are seen by Storey as being reactive. Regulators are interventionist, formulating policy and monitoring the implementation of it. Storey saw Changemakers as interventionists with a strategic agenda looking at the hard realities of business performance as well as the HR interventions designed to enhance employee commitment and motivation.

Ulrich's model, published five years later, also defines four roles along two axes. The two axes he calls *strategy* versus *operations* and *process* versus *people*. The four roles that he identified are: Strategic Partners to help successfully carry out

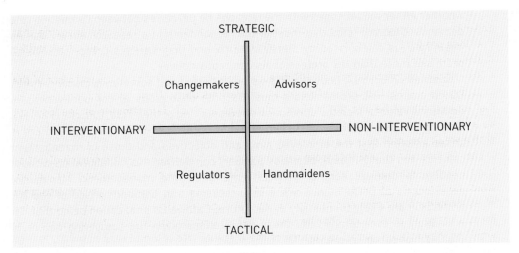

Figure 1.3 Storey's four roles of personnel managers
Source: Caldwell (2003: 986)

organisational objectives; Administrative Experts to constantly improve organisational efficiency by re-engineering the HR function and other work processes; Employee Champions to maximise employee commitment and competence; and Change Agents to deliver organisational transformation and cultural change (see Figure 1.4).

Caldwell (2003) comments that Ulrich's model is prescriptive and not based on research but is nevertheless a systematic framework for 'capturing the emergence of new roles'. The role definitions provided by Storey and Ulrich are useful in identifying the range of activities that HR professionals undertake. Caldwell sets out to identify changes in roles and contrasts Storey's typology with that of Ulrich to ascertain

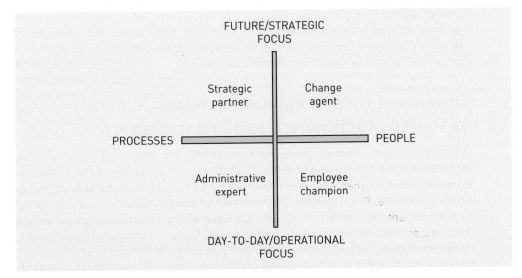

Figure 1.4 Ulrich's four roles of HR professionals
Source: Caldwell (2003: 987)

whether either model copes with the tensions he perceives between competing role demands. Caldwell finds that most of the respondents in a research survey had no 'main role' as categorised by Storey's matrix and that 'Ulrich's prescriptive vision promised more than HR professionals can really deliver'.

Caldwell (2003: 987) finds Ulrich's vision 'inspiring and sometimes disconcerting'. Ulrich claims 'HR professionals must become champions of competitiveness in delivering value or face the diminution or outsourcing of their role' (Ulrich, 1997: 17). As Caldwell points out (p. 1003), Ulrich's view of the HR role is unitary, i.e. there is an assumption that the employee aims and objectives and those of management coincide and that HR as a 'business partner' can deliver this collaboration without needing to manage conflict between employees and management. Managerial expectations of performance are ever increasing and demands made of the HR profession are likely to intensify in the future; Caldwell's implication being that HR is unlikely to ever totally fulfil these expectations given the competing nature of organisational requirements.

Some observers perceive a need for HR to be a presence within the workforce and to concentrate on guaranteeing 'employee well-being and satisfaction and work-life balance for all employees' (Francis and Keegan, 2006: 243). Francis and Keegan see the HR department as being 'guardians of employee well-being . . . who will ensure consistency of organisational justice for all employees.'

They comment that:

> 'the devolution of transactional HR work to the line combined with its relocation to service centres as well as the fact that business partners are largely oriented towards strategic issues means that employees are increasingly losing day-to-day contact with HR specialists and relying on line managers who have neither the time nor the training to give HR work the priority it needs.'

The following discussion is based on the assumption that HR exists to ensure that line managers take responsibility for employees by trying to ensure that those selected as line managers have the potential to take employees into account when carrying out their managerial role, giving managers the training and development necessary to ensure that they develop the skills to do this and setting up structures so that managerial performance can be monitored.

Division of responsibilities between human resource practitioners and line managers

As indicated above, some thought needs to go into the division of responsibilities between the HR department and the line manager. In this respect the distinction between 'manager' and 'supervisor' may not be a particularly useful one, so the following can be taken to refer to both managers and supervisors.

Problems in the division of responsibilities are incurred because of either line managers' unwillingness to carry out responsibilities or members of the HR department intervening in operational tasks, thus usurping the role of the line manager. In some organisations, problems will occur where the HR department is seen as perpetually thwarting the line management function in its efforts to carry out the operational role. Sometimes, line managers do need to be advised of the likely ill consequences of their decisions. HR practitioners may need to use their influencing skills to bring pressure to bear on a manager who persistently refuses to take advice and then leaves the HR department to sort out the ensuing situation. However, if HR professionals are able to show that much of the time they are there to facilitate the smooth running of the organisation, then they can be seen as making an overall positive contribution to the achievement of organisational objectives.

Areas where line managers have responsibility will include the following:

- **Human resource planning** – line managers would need to be involved in discussions on the development of their function. As discussed in Chapter 3, the HR department would need to advise on the human resource implications of any organisation development. As far as staffing levels for current and future activities are concerned, line managers would be in a position to know whether they are able to deliver a satisfactory service given their current staffing levels but would need to justify this in budgetary terms.

- **Organisational and job design and development in order to meet unit and departmental objectives** – HR professionals should have specialist skills and advice to give on organisational development and job design. They would need to work in close co-operation with line management over this. Chapter 17 discusses the organisational development issues from the perspective of the HR function.

- **Recruitment and selection** – the role of the HR department in relation to recruitment and selection is discussed in Chapter 7. HR should ensure that line managers have the necessary skills to draw up job descriptions and person specifications and carry out a selection interview, with due regard to equal opportunities legislation. Those in the HR department would be able to give guidance on legislative requirements and, together with line managers, can draw up a suitable advertising campaign.

- **Implementing equal opportunities** – HR practitioners would be involved in not only giving specialist advice about the state of legislation in this area but would also be able to indicate a range of policies that could be adopted in order to create an equal opportunities environment. However, the line manager would be involved in implementing these policies and ensuring that staff within their department adhere to them.

- **Performance management** – this includes objective setting and appraisal, both formal and informal. As is pointed out in Chapter 8, performance management is very much an integral part of the day-to-day responsibilities of the line manager. In a formal sense, performance management can be seen as an integrated system that is aligned with the corporate objectives, although performance management should occur in all organisations – whether they have adopted a formal, integrated system or not. The role of the HR manager in relation to performance management would be to participate in the development of any formal systems and to ensure that the line managers in the organisation have been developed in the skills of setting departmental and individual work objectives and of conducting appraisals.

- **Remuneration** – it is essential that line managers understand the basis on which the people in their department are being remunerated. If there are any queries about pay, the line manager will need to ensure that a good explanation can be given about the calculation of pay. It is also useful to know, when wanting to allocate work, exactly what impact this might have on actual remuneration. Similarly line managers may have to be involved if there are claims for upgrading; if nothing else, the manager needs to be aware of the impact on the rest of the department if an increase in pay is given. The actual reward structure will probably be designed by HR professionals, hopefully in discussion with line management. Chapter 9 explains the issues that the HR function will need to bear in mind, as well as trends in employee remuneration.

◆ **Training/coaching/mentoring** – HR professionals would be involved in creating an environment in which staff development needs could be identified, e.g. via a formal system of appraisal. The line manager and the individual employee would undertake the identification of staff development needs. HR practitioners might be in a position to give advice on the likely applicability of externally run programmes or deliver certain formal training programmes themselves. However, much of the day-to-day staff development will either be undertaken by the line manager in the role of coach or by the employee themselves, developing new skills on the job. Chapter 15 has a discussion on training and development and Chapter 19 on coaching.

◆ **Employee relations** – as explained in Chapter 12, those in the HR department will need to draw up procedures either unilaterally or in conjunction with staff representatives where these exist. These procedures will need to cover sickness absence, capability, discipline, grievance, disputes, health and safety, and redundancy. HR will need to ensure that line managers have knowledge and understanding of the procedures and an ability and willingness to implement them. Line management will undertake discussions with staff representatives on a day-to-day basis. Even if the board of the organisation is involved in deciding on pay increases without negotiation, there may be many negotiations taking place on a daily basis between the line managers and individual employees.

◆ **Disciplinary handling** – as is discussed in Chapter 12, the practice of handling disciplinary issues is often necessary to ensure that employees' behaviour matches that required to meet organisational objectives. As an HR manager you would need to ensure that managers have the skills not only to handle disciplinary issues themselves, but also to coach supervisors who report to them in how to handle discipline. If supervisors understand their role in dealing with problems before they escalate, then disciplinary issues can be dealt with at an early opportunity. By coaching supervisors rather than dealing with issues themselves, the manager can avoid acting down and undermining the supervisor. (For a more in-depth explanation of the role of the line manager in disciplinary handling, refer to the disciplinary pyramid in Rees and Porter, 2001: 296.)

HR managers have a major role in taking the lead in developing strategies related to the above areas that reflect the needs of the organisation as well as the values that the employees wish to aspire to. HR also has a role in ensuring that line managers have skills regarding the above (see Chapter 16 for a discussion on management development). Line managers will need to have access to 'bouquets' as well as 'brickbats'. Very often it is first line managers who have to hand out unpleasant tasks, reprimand staff or take awkward decisions. This is probably as it should be, since if these responsibilities are taken away from them the line structure could be undermined. However, they also need to be given the opportunity to hand out any 'goodies' that are available such as bonus payments or promotions or staff development opportunities (which are often seen in this light).

When implementing new policies and procedures, it is essential that HR and line managers work closely together. If they do not work together, new policies may be implemented that do not meet organisational needs and do not fit with the organisational culture.

window into practice

One UK organisation introduced a system of job evaluation. Assuming that the technique was extremely robust, there was a lack of line manager input into the outcomes of the scheme. This resulted in some employees who had 'talked up' their jobs being over-promoted, leading to a sense of dissatisfaction among other employees who had not been promoted but felt that their jobs were equally demanding. This led to a large increase in the costs of employing people with no discernible improvements for organisational effectiveness. A similar result occurred in the UK's National Health Service, when doctors were asked to describe their jobs and on the basis of this were given increases in pay for no increase in service or productivity. Under a contract negotiated between the UK's Department of Health and the British Medical Association (which represents doctors in the UK), general practitioners received an uplift in pay of nearly 23 per cent on average in 2006 compared with 2003–04 for no apparent increase in services offered (*The Times*, 2007).

exercise

Make a presentation showing, with examples, the areas of the HR line manager's responsibilities and indicating what might happen if these are not aligned to organisational effectiveness.

The background of managers

The day-to-day responsibility for staff will rest with the line manager. It is also very often the case that the line manager will be implementing HR policies. Guest, writing about HRM in 1989, placed considerable emphasis on the role of the line manager as one of the central aspects of his model. This may have been a useful opportunity to emphasise the importance of line management, however, as McGovern (1999) points out, there is little empirical evidence that line managers' responsibilities have changed where HRM has been adopted compared with their role in organisations where models of 'personnel management' more reflect the norm.

For human resources to be effectively managed, the line manager needs to be willing to take responsibility for various aspects of staff management as well as have the skills and training to handle these situations. The background of many managers, particularly in the professions, is such that they either do not want to take on staff management activities or do not have the skills or training to undertake these activities effectively. However, in order to achieve departmental objectives they will need to devote more and more of their time to managing the people in their department, not just to implement HR policies as an end in themselves but in order to

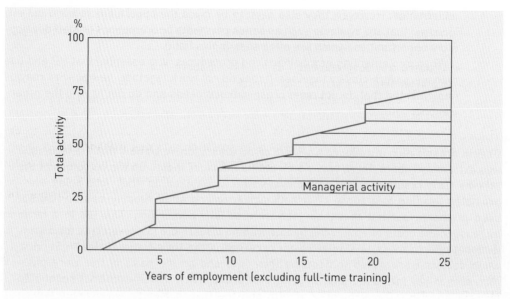

Figure 1.5 The managerial escalator
Source: Rees and Porter (2001: 5)

ensure that the human resources for whom they are responsible are effectively managed. The common path into management is illustrated by the so-called Managerial Escalator (Rees and Porter, 2001) – see Figure 1.5.

Looking at the above diagram (Figure 1.5), the horizontal axis gives an approximation of the amount of time that a manager will have been in management and the vertical axis indicates the percentage of working time that a manager at stages in his or her career is likely to need to spend on managerial activities. Many managers will have entered their chosen profession out of a sense of vocation and may be loathe to spend their time on activities that they do not perceive as related to their skills, expertise and training. Most managers in the professions will have had many years training related to their profession. However, the amount of training that they may have received to carry out what may be the greater part of their responsibilities could be counted in days, if not hours.

The HR department will need to help ensure that managers are effective in their jobs by observing four key action points:

◆ **Use of accurate role definitions and job titles** – very often managers are recruited to jobs that do not bear the name 'manager', nor are they given a job description that indicates the key areas of responsibility. Managerial jobs that do not bear the name manager include engineer, chief architect, nursing sister, head teacher, dean (of a university faculty) and bishop.

◆ **Recruitment and selection** – even if an accurate job description exists, managers are frequently recruited on the basis of spurious criteria that do not relate to the requirements of the job. For example, a head teacher may be appointed to manage a school on the basis that they were excellent at teaching. Once in post the new manager will find that his or her time will not be spent doing the activities on the basis of which they were promoted. This is not so problematic if the new post holder (a) also possesses the skills or the potential to develop the skills that are needed and (b) is willing to spend less of their time doing their previous job. Unfortunately, this is not always the case.

◆ **Training and development** – as mentioned above, the amount of training that a manager has received by the time of taking on the managerial duties may be very little and the post holder may find that the demands of their new job are such that they are reluctant to take time away from the office in order to develop these new skills. Nevertheless, some managerial development is likely to be necessary. If time is not available to spend on a formal management training course, then other techniques such as coaching and mentoring could be used to help the individual manager be as effective as possible in staff management. A deeper discussion on management development can be found in Chapter 16 and on coaching and mentoring in Chapter 19.

Developing the supervisor: Trouble in store

Fred Larkins is a forklift truck driver who has been with the company where you are warehouse manager for nine months. Fred's supervisor, Walter Smith, comes to see you towards the end of the working day and complains that he told Fred three hours ago to load a particular vehicle ready for the following morning. Walter further explains to you that when he had just asked Fred why he had not done as he had been asked, he had explained that he had been busy on other jobs and had not appreciated the urgency of the request. Walter added that Fred had failed to appreciate the urgency of a previous instruction about six weeks ago, which had led to a delivery crew getting away late and being caught in the morning rush hour traffic.

1. What would your objectives be in this situation, as the warehouse manager?

2. How would you seek to achieve these?

3. What impact might there be if you decided to speak to Fred yourself?

◆ **Monitoring and evaluation** – senior managers will need to monitor the performance of the more junior managers, and offer guidance where necessary if organisational objectives are not being met. The HR department will need to ensure that a system is set up so that this is carried out effectively, as well as being on hand to offer advice to management generally.

Write an email to the board of Warbings explaining why and how the four action points discussed above should be implemented.

Problem solving in human resource management

HRM is often the victim of fads as employers seek to find answers to their current problems, or rush to adopt a technique just because it is fashionable. Very often there is a lack of diagnosis of the causes of problems faced by the organisation

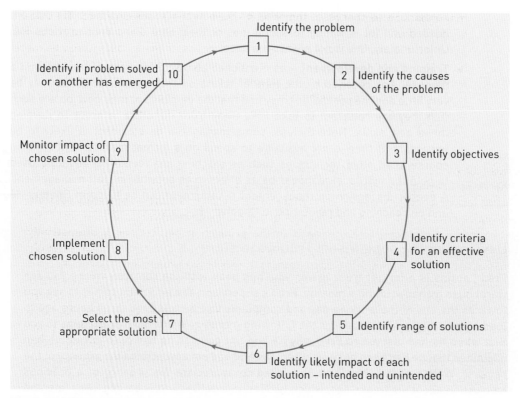

Figure 1.6 The problem-solving cycle
Source: Rees and Porter (2001)

(Watson, 2004). This lack of diagnosis may result in the adoption of inappropriate techniques. This can unfortunately mean that the problem besetting the organisation is not solved, although time, energy and organisational credibility will have been consumed, often resulting in a loss of face for the HR function. One way of overcoming this is to adopt a more structured approach to problem solving, as illustrated in Figure 1.6.

When problems are identified, the natural reaction is to implement a solution as quickly as possible. The problem-solving cycle puts more emphasis on diagnosing the causes of problems and of setting up criteria by which the chosen solution be judged. The latter stages of the cycle emphasise monitoring and evaluation, which may lead to the identification of further problems, and thus the need to continue with the problem-solving process. In analysing problems, a distinction needs to be drawn between symptoms and causes. It is also necessary to prioritise problems, since not all problems will be as important as others in terms of their impact.

Systems approach

When trying to identify the likely employee problems that may arise, managers may find it useful to take a systems approach. This emphasises the interconnectedness of organisational activity and the possibility that a change made in one area may impact on another area, sometimes known as the 'knock-on effect'. The impact of these decisions on employees may be more successfully identified if the HR manager is involved in the decision-making process. In many cases it may be more important for the HR manager to have a good understanding of the interrelationship between various functions of the organisation than to have an understanding of the fine points of strategy development. In any case it is important for the HR manager to understand the phenomenon of the 'knock-on effect' (Rees and Porter, 2001: 338–340).

exercise

Read the following case study then make two lists, the first delineating the problems and the second saying how you think these problems might have been rectified.

In a local evening newspaper, technological developments made it apparently possible to replace the former full-time print production staff with relatively unskilled part-time staff. While this reduced labour costs in the production department, it dramatically increased problems in the advertising department. This was particularly because of the loss of accumulated knowledge of customers' needs in the production department.

The consequences of this included the loss of customers. It also meant that the advertising staff had to spend a significant amount of time with the remaining customers for rectification work and dealing with customer complaints, thus cutting into the time available for selling advertising space to new customers. This in turn affected the commission payments made to advertising staff causing high labour turnover when the staff left for more lucrative jobs. The newspaper depended on advertising revenue for about 80 per cent of its income (Rees and Porter, 2006).

pause for thought

Can you identify any cases of organisations implementing new policies without thinking through the consequences?

Conflict at work

One aspect of HRM that is frequently overlooked is that, to improve organisational effectiveness, there may be a conflict with employee objectives. Many models of HRM do not make any allowances for employee representation and make assumptions that employees will automatically accept and co-operate with whatever changes management wish to make.

Managers' and employees' objectives in employee relations can be identified as shown in Table 1.2. There are two ways of examining the relationship between employers and employees: the unitary and pluralist perspectives. If the manager takes a unitary perspective this assumes that there is no difference between the objectives of management and employees. However, an examination of Table 1.2 demonstrates that managements' and employees' needs are often in conflict: managers wish to minimise unit labour costs and control change, whereas employees want to maximise the terms under which they are employed and also control change. A pluralist approach will take account of the likely conflict that may occur

Table 1.2 Management and employee objectives

Management objectives	Employee objectives
◆ Cost-effective performance ◆ Control of change ◆ Avoidance of stoppages and other sanctions	◆ Maintenance and, where possible, improvement of terms and conditions of employment ◆ Job security ◆ Control of change ◆ Avoidance of stoppages and other sanctions

Source: Rees and Porter (2001: 315)

when change is implemented, especially if it is likely to result in a worsening of terms and conditions of employment. This does not mean to say that employees must be allowed to dictate to management what change happens and what change does not, but it does mean that management will be more successful in implementing change if they think through the likely impact and make plans to deal with it. Further discussion about the impact of managerial styles on employee relations. can be found in Chapter 12

Conflict is often seen in this context as being a negative concept. The term is often seen as being synonymous with strike action. However, a strike, or application of other sanctions, will only occur as a means of trying to resolve the conflict when negotiations have broken down. Because of changes in the labour market, some employees have far less ability to impose sanctions than when there was a seller's market for labour. Changes that have affected certain employees' abilities to impose sanctions have included high levels of unemployment in some regions and occupations; a far lower level of trade union membership; a continuing diminution in trade union ability to impose sanctions; new technology – creating a buyer's labour market overseas; and more peripheral and part-time jobs.

However the ability of management to impose change, without consultation in some instances, still needs to take into account the importance of getting 'buy in' from the workforce and the likelihood that the implementation of new work practices is likely to be more effective if they have taken into account employee expertise.

Global applicability of human resource management techniques

HRM is generally conceived as if the principles on which it is based are universally valid. Additionally, HR textbooks often refer to HRM techniques as if they should be adopted by each and every organisation, within the UK as well as elsewhere, and that not to do so will automatically mean that a particular organisation will be deficient in some respect, not making the most effective use of its human resources. The concept of 'best practice' is often adopted to underline the message that there is one best way in which to manage human resources. However, the proposition that the practice of HR is converging around a common set of principles is not supported by all. Some HR practitioners are of the opinion that different techniques need to be adopted in different situations. Since organisations tend to reflect the societies in which they operate, it is necessary to be familiar with local conditions in order to identify the techniques appropriate for the situation in which they are operating.

A study carried out by Triandis (1994) indicates that 90 per cent of behavioural theories on which systems of HRM are based are derived from the US and UK. Frederick and Rodrigues (1994) point out that differences in culture exist not only between different societies but also between those operating in different economic systems, between different hierarchical levels within an organisation and between different types of organisations. This could mean that countries, which may be at different stages in their development, may have different requirements in terms of the HR policies that they will find useful and need to adopt. Employment systems reflect the context in which they operate. These contexts have historical, legal, socio-political/cultural dimensions.

Can you think of any overseas organisations that have had problems because they tried to impose the managerial culture of their 'homeland' on a UK-based part of their organisation?

pause for thought

Those who argue against the convergence thesis will point to the impact of history, legal system and laws, socio-political climate and societal culture upon organisations, resulting in differing organisational climates and HR requirements. Proponents of the convergence thesis will point to the impact of globalisation – technology; media; build up of global markets/trading blocs; and global travel – to back up their proposition that countries are becoming more and more alike.

An analysis of the assumptions on which HRM tools is based will indicate that not all HRM tools are appropriate for every situation. An analogous situation would be that of a physician who advocated a certain range of medicines without first conducting a diagnosis of the patient's condition. Legge (1978) points out that a physician will not only conduct a diagnosis as part of a professional approach to a patient but will also be on the look out for any symptoms that may indicate the onset of further bodily dysfunction and will advise the patient on lifestyle choices that could help to avoid future problems. She advocates such an approach among HR professionals and refers to the need for a contingency or best fit approach (Legge, 1978; Kinnie et al., 2005). A contingency approach will involve the HR practitioner analysing the situation in which they find themselves, diagnosing the causes of the problems they seek to address and proposing some solution that takes into account the dynamics of the situation and the actual causes of the problem. There is a further discussion regarding the appropriateness of 'best fit' compared with 'best practice' approaches in Chapter 3 of this book. Watson (2004) has an interesting discussion tracing the development of analysis in HRM and lamenting the quantity of normative and prescriptive thinking, which is relevant to this discussion.

In analysing the assumptions on which HRM is based, it is interesting to examine the cultural basis of HRM. It has been estimated that more than 90 per cent of the theories of how individuals think and behave in organisations reflect Western perspectives, primarily British and North American (Triandis, 1994). If the values underpinning the practice of HRM in various countries are analysed, however, it is clear that there is a great variation in the extent to which they match with the under-pinning values of the UK and the US. Students from other countries may therefore be studying the subject from a UK or a US perspective and find that they are unable to recognise the premises on which the subject is based.

In the West, the management of human resources is second to the aim of achiev-ing and maintaining the ultimate economic survival of an organisation. This has resulted in the US and the UK in the development of models of HRM to encourage a concentration on business objectives and the need for organisations to develop human resource policies which help the organisation to deliver those objectives. This contrasts with other, more paternalistic, cultures where the emphasis in the practice of HRM is not so much on the economic well-being of the company but to a greater extent on issues concerned with perceived obligations to individual employees, albeit often tempered by a fairly autocratic management style. In this context it is appropriate to mention that HRM in the US and the UK is much more likely to be based on a pluralist perspective, whereas in many developing countries both employers and employees take a unitary perspective: the assumption is made that organisational and employee objectives are the same (see Fox, 1974).

As well as differing views about organisational objectives, there are also differ-ing expectations of the State. In EU countries there is an enhanced role for the State compared with the US. In PR China, for example, the role of the State is even more pronounced, as would be expected given the historical preponderance of State-owned enterprises. The role of the State in some economies is such that certain Western policies and procedures as used in the US or the UK are unlikely to be appropriate. For these and other reasons it is appropriate to take a contin-gency approach when implementing HR practices, rather than assuming that the techniques that are currently in favour in other countries will immediately be appro-priate in another culture.

The future for HR across the world looks as if it will maintain its current import-ance. New markets are being created as previous dormant nations become eco-nomically more active. These markets include China, India and the former Soviet bloc countries in Central and Eastern Europe. As these economies expand, so will global competition become more intense and the need for skilled staff available as and when required become ever more important.

Current and future trends in HRM

Since HRM is concerned with delivering organisational effectiveness, it is likely that directors of organisations will continue to explore the extent to which the HR input in an organisation can most effectively contribute to this. The current debates about HR as a business partner, its contribution to the 'bottom line' and the extent to which this function can be outsourced will therefore continue. New labels may be invented to give added impetus to the debate but the concepts will be of a similar nature.

HR specialists will nevertheless continue to be called upon to reflect the concerns of society at large. For example, debates relating to societal well-being and the environment may have added impetus as the developed world takes on board the need to act as custodian of limited resources. The debate relating to ethics and HRM is continued in Chapter 2.

Summary

The role of HRM in an organisation is intended to help the organisation ensure that it meets its corporate objectives by the effective management of its employees. Both HR specialists and line managers carry out this role. HR specialists would need to help ensure that line managers are selected when they have both the desire and the skills to carry out their managerial activities. The practice of HRM is subject to many fashions and fads and it is important when applying HRM techniques to remember the importance of diagnosing accurately the causes of problems in an organisation in order that the most appropriate technique can be adopted. In addition, it is also important that the HRM technique adopted fits with the culture of the organisation.

Most HRM techniques are based on a unitary perspective. That is to say, they are based on the assumption that management and employees' objectives are the same. However, this is not always the case. HR techniques introduced to address organisational problems may have adverse consequences from an employee perspective. HR specialists and line managers therefore need to understand the employee perspective if they are to manage effectively and help employees realise their full potential in terms of the contribution they make to the organisation.

Review Questions

You may wish to attempt the following as practice examination style questions.

1.1 How do you think HRM contributes to the achievement of organisational objectives?

1.2 In what ways do HR managers in the public sector differ in their perceptions of their role from those HR managers in the private sector?

1.3 What HR skills do line managers need to make their work more effective?

1.4 Is HRM culturally dependent? Why did you give this answer?

References

ACAS (2004). Coming to the table with ACAS: from conflict to cooperation, *Employee Relations*, Vol. 26, No. 5, pp. 510–513.

Ambler, T., Chittenden, F. and Obodovski, M. (2004). *Are Regulators Raising Their Game? UK Regulatory Impact Assessments in 2002/3*, London: British Chambers of Commerce.

Beer, M., Spector, B., Lawrence, P.R., Quinn Mills, D. and Walton, R.E. (1984). *Managing Human Assets*, New York: Free Press.

Caldwell, R. (2003). The changing roles of personnel managers: old ambiguities, new uncertainties, *Journal of Management Studies*, Vol. 40, No. 4, pp. 983–1004.

Delery, J.E. and Shaw, J.D. (2001). The strategic management of people in work organisation: review, synthesis and extension, *Research in Personnel and Human Resource Management*, Vol. 20, pp. 165–197.

Felstead, A., Gallie, D. and Green, F. (2002). *Work Skills in Britain 1986–2001*, Nottingham: DfES Publications.

Fox, A. (1974). *Beyond Contract: Work, Power and Trust Relations*, London: Faber & Faber.

Francis, H. and Keegan, A. (2006). The changing face of HRM: in search of balance, *Human Resource Management Journal*, Vol. 16, No. 3, pp. 231–249.

Frederick, W.R. and Rodrigues, A.F. (1994). A Spanish organisation in Eastern Germany: culture shock, *Journal of Management Development*, Vol. 13, No. 2, pp. 42–48.

IRS Employment Review 792a (2004a). Recruiters March in Step with Online Recruitment, 23 January, pp. 44–48.

IRS Employment Review (2004b). Answering the Recruitment Call Online, 7 May, pp. 46–48.

Kersley, B., Alpin, C., Forth, J., Bryson, A., Bewley, H., Dix, G. and Oxenbridge, S. (2006). *Inside the Workplace: Findings from the 2004 Workplace Employment Relations Survey*, London, Routledge.

Kettley, P. and Reilly, P. (2003). *eHR: An Introduction*, Institute of Employment Studies Report 398, Brighton: IES.

Kinne, N., Hutchinson, S., Purcell, J., Rayton, B. and Swart, J. (2005). Satisfaction with HR practices: why one size does not fit all, *Human Resource Management Journal*, Vol. 15, No. 4, pp. 9–29.

Legge, K. (1978). *Power, Politics and Problem Solving in Personnel Management*, London: McGraw-Hill.

McGovern, P. (1999). *Strategic Human Resource Management*, Oxford: Oxford University Press.

Price, A.J. (1997). *Human Resource Management in a Business Context*, London: International Thomson Business Press.

Rees, W.D. and Porter, C.M. (2001). *The Skills of Management*, London: Thomson Learning.

Rees, W.D. and Porter, C.M. (2006). Corporate Strategy Development: the case for the incremental approach, Part 2 – implications for learning and development, Industrial and Commercial Training, Vol. 38, No. 7, pp. 354–359.

Shackleton, J.R. (2005). Regulating the labour market, in P. Booth (ed.) *Towards a Liberal Utopia*, pp. 128–143, Part 1, London: Institute of Economic Affairs.

Storey, J. (1992). *Developments in the Management of Human Resources*, Oxford: Blackwell.

Sunday Times (2007). *Booming Britain heads 'onwards and upwards',* 21 January. *The Times* (2007). *Doctors' anger over plan to limit pay*, 20 January.

Triandis, H.C. (1994). Cross-cultural and organisational psychology, in H. C. Triandis, M. Dunette and L. Hough, *Handbook of Industrial and Organisational Psychology*, pp. 103–172, Palo Alto, CA: Consulting Psychologists' Press.

Tyson, S. and Fell, A. (1986). *Evaluating the Personnel Function*, London: Hutchinson.

Ulrich, D. (1997). *Human Resource Champions*, Boston: Harvard University Press.

Ulrich, D. (1998). A new mandate for human resources, *Harvard Business Review*, Vol. 76, pp. 124–134.

Watson, T.J. (2004). HRM and critical social analysis, *Journal of Management Studies*, Vol. 41, No. 3, pp. 447–467.

Further Reading

Boxall, P. and Purcell, J. (2003). *Strategy and Human Resource Management*, Basingstoke: Palgrave.

Leopold, J. (ed.) (2002). *Human Resources in Organisations*, London: FT/Prentice Hall.

Purcell, J. and Astrand, B. (1994). *Human Resource Management in Multi Division Companies*, Oxford: Oxford University Press.

Redman, T. and Wilkinson, A. (2002). *The Informed Student Guide to Human Resource Management*, London: Thomson Learning.

Useful Websites

www.cipd.co.uk – the official website of the Chartered Institute of Personnel and Development – the lead body for HR professionals

http://www.cipd.co.uk/subjects/maneco/general/rolefrntlinemngers.htm?IsSrchRes=1 – examines the role of the front-line manager in enacting and delivering HR processes

www.dti.gov.uk – the official website of the Department of Trade and Industry. A department of the UK government, the DTI collects and disseminates information and statistics relating to business and industry within the UK

www.humanresourcemanagement.co.uk – gives human resource information relating to both employers and employees

www.btinternet.com/~alan.price/hrm – a free source of worldwide human resource management in formation

www.hrmguide.co.uk – publishes articles and news releases about HR surveys, employment law, human resource research and related books and other publications

CHAPTER 2

Ethics and Human Resource Management

By Amanda Rose

Chapter outline

Standards, values, morals and ethics have become increasingly complex in a postmodern society where absolutes have given way to tolerance and ambiguity. This particularly affects managers in human resource (HR), where decisions will affect people's jobs and their future employment. This chapter explores some of the ethical dilemmas encountered in the workplace, discussing ethical behaviour and values that relate to HR. It looks at relevant ethical tools, such as utilitarianism and relativism in order to examine current practices in the workplace and their links to corporate social responsibility.

Learning outcomes

By the end of this chapter, you should be able to:

◆ Critically explore and evaluate the ethical nature of human resource management (HRM);

◆ Identify and define current ethical and moral issues confronting HR managers;

◆ Compare, contrast and critically appraise a range of approaches to ethical analysis;

◆ Critically appraise the relevance and usefulness of philosophical analysis to HR practice.

Introduction

HRM is a business function that is concerned with managing relations between groups of people in their capacity as employees, employers and managers. Inevitably, this process may raise questions about what the respective responsibilities and rights of each party are in this relationship, and about what constitutes fair treatment. These questions are ethical in nature, and this chapter will focus on debates about the ethical basis of HRM.

The ethical nature of human resource management

'All HR practices have an ethical foundation. HR deals with the practical consequences of human behaviour'.

(Johnson, 2003)

'The entire concept of HRM is devoid of morality'.

(Hart, 1993: 29)

Despite these moral appreciations of HRM, there is a strong tradition in business that insists that business should not be concerned with ethics. As Milton Friedman, a vociferous proponent of this position, has put it: *'The social responsibility of business is to its shareholders. . . . The business of business is business'* (1970).

The core concern of business – proponents of the market economy argue – is in attempting to secure the best possible return on any investment. Any dilution of this focus will lead to the corruption of what is a finely balanced system. Businesses that seek to be 'ethical' as well as profitable will probably fail economically, following which the whole community may suffer. Rather, let the *invisible hand* guide the market and all will prosper. Like some evolutionary force, the best will always survive. Wealth will trickle down from successful enterprises, and humanity will be best served. Any constraint on the freedoms of the market – be they motivated by ethical angst or vote-seeking government policy – will just mess everything up.

Notwithstanding the appeal of this position, a critique of business practice has continued to accumulate and assert itself, and to challenge the notion that business and morality have no meeting point. Concern has surfaced from a variety of sources: from consumer groups, political groups, religious and charitable organisations. Entrepreneurs, for example, Anita Roddick of The Body Shop (2000), academics and researchers (Winstanley and Woodall, 2000; Greenwood, 2002) and management professionals (Brown, 2003) have all expressed the view that standards of behaviour within business need to be evaluated, and improved.

A case can be made that negative consequences flow from poor ethical standards:

◆ While short-term goals may be achieved through the cut-throat tactics of free market principles, in the long run business will survive better if good standards of conduct are maintained;

◆ Ethical business creates a positive environment in which to buy and sell, as corruption, poverty and lack of respect for the environment generate problems for the business community in the long term;

◆ Finally, people neither hold moral values nor have religious beliefs to guide the conduct of their lives. Why should the area of business be exempt?

pause for thought Do you think that ethical behaviour is relevant in today's business world? Why did you reach this conclusion?

Much of the recent focus on business ethics has been directed against financial corruption, especially a concern with accounting standards. The scandals involving Enron Corp. and WorldCom are two recent examples. But concern has been raised over a very broad range of issues, for example:

♦ Abuse of the world's physical resources, and the global ecological balance (Esso);

♦ Abuse of human rights (Shell/Nigeria);

♦ Animal rights (KFC, McDonald's);

♦ Aggressive treatment of competitors (Wal-Mart);

♦ Exploitative and unscrupulous marketing (Philip Morris) (Klein, 2000).

exercise

What other examples of unethical business practice have you heard about?

What have you experienced in an organisation known to you?

What is the difference between being fair and acting appropriately?

The unethical practice of HRM itself has also hit public attention:

♦ Off-shoring and exploiting 'cheap' labour markets;

♦ Using child labour;

♦ Reneging on company pension agreements;

♦ Longer working hours;

♦ Increasing work stress;

♦ The use of disputed and dubious practices in hiring and firing personnel.

It has been shown that just as consumers' perception of the ethics of a company can affect sales, so the views of its investors will affect its share price. Similarly, it has been suggested that poor standards of conduct emanating from the top management affect employee motivation and commitment to organisational goals (Schramm, 2004).

Ethics in the business environment

Concern with standards must be seen in the current context of business processes. We live in a complex society, which is both morally and culturally diverse.

Key drivers and features of this complexity can be identified:

♦ Globalisation of markets and labour forces ('McDonalidisation');

♦ Intensification of both competition and monopolies ('Coca Colonisation');

♦ Paradigmatic changes in technology and the application of ICT, creating new opportunities, but also new dilemmas over communication, surveillance and privacy;

♦ Rapidly increasing rates of product innovation, obsolescence and demand;

♦ Aggressive marketing and the use of celebrities by the media;

♦ An escalation of materialist values and the commodification of everything, even education;

- Increased isolationism, individuality and world-weariness, often demonstrated by cynicism, sarcasm and mockery, with a disregard for traditional values and any form of authority;
- A rise in secular concerns – but also a concern with a loss of spirituality.

Against this background, management style and management ideology has undergone great change. New organisational forms and new ways of managing, including the emergence of more flexible working patterns, have come into force. During this era, HRM has become more strategically focused and more concerned with facilitating the achievement of organisational goals.

Winstanley and Woodall (1996) highlight a number of ethical concerns about standards of HR practice, arising from this strategic focus. These include:

- Increased job insecurity – arising from 'flexible' work practices; short-term and temporary conditions of employment; fear of job loss due to outsourcing and off-shoring; increased stress; and a widening imbalance of power between management and workforce;
- Increase in surveillance and control – this ranges from the use of psychometric tests to electronic surveillance of work patterns through the application of ICT;
- Deregulation – freedom of the market place has been imposed by global regulators such as the World Trade Organizationl (WTO), and has led to what Storey (1993) has termed: 'impatience with rule' and 'can-do outlook' among line managers, which in practice may be seen to push HR into compromising 'good' practice, for business needs. In professional services organisations, for example, fee-earners may be challenged to decide between 'doing good' and 'doing well';
- Aligned to this is a decline in management integrity, leading to accusations of recourse to rhetoric and deceit among HR professionals. For example, the current emphasis on managing organisational culture and commitment of employees can be contrasted with a highly instrumental approach to the supervision of the employment contract.

In this current context, it becomes most relevant to examine the ethical dimension of HRM practice. In what ways can HRM be ethical and/or unethical? Are there guidelines and principles that all HR professionals ought to follow and adhere to? How can we judge what a good course of action might consist of in a specific situation?

However, it is simplistic to consider HRM as a coherent and unitary set of principles and practices. It varies from organisation to organisation, from culture to culture, and can be diverse both within and between industries and sectors. It has evolved in complex historical, economic and social contexts.

The current global operation of business creates extraordinary interactions of values and practice. HRM is a feature of both the public, private and voluntary sectors, and management practice differs accordingly. It is argued (Winstanley and Woodall, 2000) that HRM holds the moral 'stewardship' of organisations. It is interesting therefore to consider the special role of HRM in the generation of an ethical and moral climate in organisations in general.

Ethics and values

Organisations are bound by law to treat the people they employ fairly and not to discriminate against identified groups. Legislation is a codification of accepted moral principles, and acts to moderate standards within a community – 'the greatest good of the greatest number'.

But, conformity to all legal requirements does not necessarily ensure the best treatment of employees. The law itself may not be fair; it may not cover all eventualities; and it may not always offer a clear guide to action.

How far do you agree with the following list of HR objectives?

◆ In recruitment and selection: ensure that all assessment measures are fair and just.
◆ In reward management: ensure fairness in allocation of pay and benefits.
◆ In promotion and development: ensure equal opportunities and equal access.
◆ Ensure a safe working environment for all employees.
◆ Ensure that procedures are not unduly stressful, and that the needs of employees' work-life balance are not compromised.
◆ When redundancies occur, to be fair and just in handling job losses.
◆ Deal effectively with all forms of bullying and harassment.
◆ In outsourcing and offshoring: ensure that contractors, consultants and franchisees are fair and honest in their dealings with employees, clients and customers.

Ethics is a key branch of philosophy, concerned with analysing what is right or wrong in people's behaviour or conduct. Ethics and morality are terms that are often used interchangeably in discussions of good and evil. The term 'ethics' is usually applied to persons (ethics comes from the Greek *ethos*, meaning character) – and 'morality' to acts and behaviour (moral comes from the Latin *moralis*, meaning customs or manners).

Philosophy presents us with suggestions about the nature of morality and ethics. It also offers us a set of tools for analysing and exploring morality. Some main issues and approaches will now be discussed:

◆ Relativism and absolutism;
◆ Consequentialist approaches (e.g. utilitarianism);
◆ Non-consequentialist approaches (deontological or 'duty' ethics);
◆ The ethics of human rights;
◆ Virtue ethics;
◆ The *stakeholder* approach.

Cultural relativism

One core distinction when analysing morality is the issue of *relativism* – the idea that morality varies with culture, time and circumstances. The opposite position is that of *absolutism*, the notion that there are universal truths in morality that apply at all times and in all circumstances. In a global business world, this aspect becomes significant. When businesses operate globally, how far should they adapt company rules to local circumstances? Situational ethics can become problematical for organisations wishing to expand into new international markets.

exercise

The ethical concerns of personnel managers

A survey of over 1,000 US personnel managers (Danley et al., 1991) found that the most common areas causing ethical concern were: favouritism in hiring, training and promotion; sexual harassment; inconsistent disciplinary measures; not maintaining confidentiality; sex discrimination in promotion, and pay; and non-performance factors used in appraisals.

◆ How far do you feel these are culturally specific?

◆ Why did you reach this conclusion?

◆ Would personnel managers in different cultures agree with this list? Give reasons for your answer.

Consequentialist approaches (utilitarianism)

This approach was developed by Jeremy Bentham (1748–1832) and John Stuart Mill (1806–1873). Its main premise suggests that the morality of an act is determined by its consequences: people should do that which will bring the greatest *utility* (which is generally understood to mean whatever the group sees as good) to the greatest number affected by a given situation.

exercise

A company needs to make savings to survive a recession. They have a number of plants in the Yorkshire area, some of them in areas of above-average unemployment. All plants are equally profitable.

◆ Which plant should they close?

◆ Should they make their decision on purely economic grounds? Why?

◆ What if financial analysis doesn't produce an obvious choice?

◆ What should they then decide to do?

For example, military contractors may be faced with ransom demands for kidnapped employees. The UK government was embroiled in such a situation in 2004 in the case of a UK citizen who was taken hostage in Iraq. His captors demanded economic and political concessions to win his release. His family pleaded with the prime minister to meet these demands. The government argued that to do so would jeopardise the lives of many more UK subjects in Iraq and globally. In doing so, the government was appealing to utilitarian arguments.

Critics suggest that in practice it is very difficult to accurately determine what the maximal *utility* would be for all affected by a situation. People may not have the necessary information. The notion of utility is very vague. Are we thinking of the short or long term? These perspectives may lead to different conclusions. People may vary in their perceptions and requirements. What is the 'majority'? Can we accept a situation where the benefits of the majority might mean the exploitation, and suffering, of the minority? In this system, vast income disparity, or even slavery, might be condoned on the grounds that it maximised the benefits of the majority. Some very morally repugnant acts might be condoned on the grounds of utilitarianism.

Non-consequentialist or deontological approaches

This approach, associated with Immanuel Kant (1724–1804), is sometimes referred to as 'duty ethics'. Kant's aim was to establish a set of absolute moral rules, developed through the application of *reason*. He also put forward an acid test for evaluating the quality of moral rules and this is termed: the *categorical imperative*. This states that: 'I ought never to act except in such a way that I can also will that my maxim should become a universal law.' In other words, moral rules should follow the principle of *reciprocity*: do as you would be done by. This premise can be found in the moral principles of many religious systems, including Islam, Christianity, Judaism and Buddhism.

Kant further stated: 'Act in such a way that you always treat humanity . . . never simply as a means, but always at the same time as an end.' The defining characteristics of this approach are the universal *applicability* of principles to all humanity, and basic respect for humans.

A key notion for Kant was that of *intentionality*. It might well be that the outcome of an act leads to very bad consequences for people – for example, the closure of a site and subsequent job losses – but if one's aims and intentions are good, then the act is a moral one. It's all about motivation and meaning.

Goodpaster (1984) has attempted to develop a set of rules along Kantian lines for business practice:

1. Avoid and prevent harming others.

2. Help those in need.

3. Do not lie or cheat.

4. Respect the rights of others.

5. Keep promises or contracts.

6. Obey the law.

7. Be fair.

8. Encourage others to follow these principles.

Examine the rules of business practice developed by Goodpaster and the CIPD code of professional conduct, which can be found at the following site: www.cipd.co.uk/about/profco.htm.

◆ Which of these rules would you find:

– easiest to follow?

– hardest to follow?

Outline the reasons for your answer.

The SHRM code of ethical and professional standards in HRM

Core principles

As HR professionals we are responsible for adding value to the organisations we serve and contributing to the ethical success of those organisations. We accept professional responsibility for our individual decisions and actions. We are also advocates for the profession by engaging in activities that enhance its credibility and value.

- As professionals we must strive to meet the highest standards of competency and commit to strengthen our competencies on a continuous basis.

- HR professionals are expected to exhibit individual leadership as a role model for maintaining the highest standards of ethical conduct.

- As human resource professionals we are ethically responsible for promoting and fostering fairness and justice for all employees and their organisations.

- As HR professionals we must maintain a high level of trust with our stakeholders. We must protect the interests of our stakeholders as well as our professional integrity and should not engage in activities that create actual, apparent or potential conflicts of interests.

- HR professionals consider and protect the rights of individuals, especially in the acquisition and dissemination of information while ensuring truthful communications and facilitating informed decision making.

The development of codes of good or ethical practice within organisations and professional associations stems from the deontological approach. However, the approach has been seen to present problems in its implementation, as follows:

- How do you judge that a rule is a good one?
- What, in the final analysis, is fair?
- Can we all agree?
- How should we proceed in cases where principles compete?
- And what about situations when avoiding harm to one person means harming another or where keeping a contract with one person or group leads to breaking it with another?

Hart (1993) has suggested that current HR practice falls short of Kant's categorical imperative. In tough business contexts, policies seem to support the premise that: 'We should behave towards our fellow human beings with the over riding objective of extracting added value' (p. 29).

Human rights

Another very influential view stems from seeing people as having basic *human rights*. In this view, there is recognition of a core set of human rights. Where a human right exists, there must also be a duty or *responsibility* to recognise, support and acknowledge that right.

John Locke (1632–1704) was one philosopher who emphasised and elaborated an ethics based upon human rights. He argued that it is not so much the application of reason to acts that is important to morality, but an *appreciation* of the fair and equal treatment of all people, enshrined in the recognition of basic human rights. For Locke, the key rights included freedom, and rights to property.

There have been many attempts to codify and elaborate human rights, including the declaration of the *Rights of Man* (1789), the *Universal Declaration of Human Rights* (1948) and the *European Convention on Human Rights* (1950). Recently, the UK has passed the *Human Rights Act* (1998) in an attempt to codify rights within British law. The full implications of this act for the business and employment arenas are currently being explored through case law and, undoubtedly, this will have major implications for HR practice.

Virtue ethics

Virtue ethics is an approach that is seen to originate with Aristotle (384–322 BC). It has recently regained prominence through the work of the philosopher Alasdair Macintyre (1981). Aristotle was not concerned to identify the qualities of good acts, or principles, but of good people. Acting as a 'good person,' Macintyre suggests, 'is the state of being well and doing well . . . a complete human life lived at its best' (pp. 148–149). For Aristotle, the virtuous man has to know that what he does is virtuous; a good man has to 'judge to do the right thing in the right place at the right time in the right way' (p. 150). This is not just the simple application of rules. The virtues include both intellectual and character virtues. Macintyre includes the need to *feel* that what one is doing is good and right; to have an *emotional* as well as a *cognitive* appreciation of morality is an essential component of virtue.

A key distinction between this approach and others is that it focuses on the issue of *agency* in ethical conduct. It suggests that neither good intentions nor outcomes, codes and the recognition of basic rights will necessarily ensure 'goodness'. In the final analysis, the effectiveness of an ethical system depends on the nature of the people who employ it. And are people essentially good or bad?

Stakeholder analysis

This approach has emerged from the area of applied business ethics, and proponents include Freeman (1998) and Weiss (1994). As discussed earlier, free market economics accords rights only to shareholders in the business enterprise. Stakeholder analysis offers an alternative view.

Stakeholder analysis sees morality as evolving within a community of equals, where rights and needs are recognised as residing within all individuals and groups that partake in business life. Organisations consist of many interwoven webs of relationships, rights and responsibilities. Many individuals and groups have a 'stake' in how an organisation performs, apart from just the shareholders and members of the board. Employees, customers, suppliers and the wider community should all be considered when decisions are made, and they should be consulted accordingly.

exercise

Have a look at the Warbings case study.

Who are the various stakeholders in the organisation?

What rights and duties do you think they have concerning the activities of the company?

How could their concerns be raised and dealt with?

Winstanley and Woodall (2000) argue that this is a very useful approach for analysing ethical issues in HRM. Jones (1995) has presented evidence to suggest that companies that follow a stakeholder approach are actually more profitable. Greenwood (2002) finds this an underused approach in analysing the ethical aspects of HRM. She feels that it provides a framework which brings into relief both the macro (ideology) and micro (specific policy) aspects of HRM.

However, there are a number of practical problems with this approach. Firstly, companies must identify relevant stakeholders – and this is not always an obvious matter. Secondly, when stakeholders are identified, an organisation has a moral obligation to discover their views. This is not always easy. For example, 'the community' is a very vague term – who is included here? Will everyone in the 'community' have the same views? Can they all realistically be consulted? A company may, with the best of intentions, obtain a partial view of the wishes of its stakeholders that does not acknowledge the voices of several relevant diverse groups.

Corporate social responsibility and human resource management

Crowe (2002) defines CSR as, 'all the ways in which a company relates to society from purchasing to product disposal, from human resources to human rights'. The concept is generally used in management literature to refer to the responsibilities and relations between an organisation and the community within which it operates. This focuses attention away from individual practices and procedures, to the strategic direction and mission of the corporation as a whole.

One approach that companies can take to CSR is to include a 'social audit' in their annual reports. This was first recommended by Medawar (1978), and shows not just the financial performance of a company, but also details of its impact on both the environment and the community. It was reported in 2003 that 132 of the FTSE 250 companies now report their environmental performance, and 100 also report on social and ethical issues.

CSR can affect a company through the message it signals to potential recruits. Research conducted by Duncan Brown of the CIPD (2003) suggests that companies that adopt a policy of social responsibility tend to fare better in attracting new recruits – a key concern for UK companies in the current labour market. Eighty-eight per cent of participants surveyed said concordance of individual and organisational values was a key component in job choice.

Current CSR policies include an attempt to involve employees in voluntary community work. One-third of companies based in the City of London have community and volunteering programmes, covering an estimated 27,000 staff and providing charitable support worth an estimated £337 million (Heart of the City, 2002). Examples of companies that have implemented such schemes through the Business in the Community initiative include Walkers Snack Foods and IBM. Potentially, CSR can usefully form part of an employee development programme, and may benefit the community, employees and the organisation itself.

Corporations are unelected and unmonitored, and their involvement in charitable enterprises could be seen to compromise people's right to self-determination. Social critics, such as Klein (2000), have argued that corporations that involve themselves in community projects may be accused of promoting their own self-interest.

Tesco has spearheaded a 'Computers for Schools' campaign that gives shoppers in their stores tokens which can be exchanged for much needed IT equipment for schools. Many schools publicise this to parents – effectively asking them to shop at Tesco. This moral pressure is in Tesco's interests, and while the outcome may be positive and therefore applauded from a utilitarian point of view, it cannot be viewed as ethical from a non-consequentialist perspective. A similar discussion took place in the book and film *The Constant Gardener*, which explored the practice of a pharmaceutical company that killed healthy African adults in its clinical trials.

From a stakeholder perspective, CSR initiatives might seem to be the right approach, where companies acknowledge their responsibilities to their surrounding environment and community. But the critics of the approach would caution that a clearer analysis of the needs and interests of respective stakeholders needs to be undertaken in order to establish whether these are always beneficial, and ethically laudable. Employees and community members alike may be exploited through such initiatives. Both parties might benefit more from greater corporate governance in collaboration with national and international agencies or charities in the provision of social services. It might be better for companies to simply pay higher taxes.

Summary

Ethical conduct in business practice and HR procedures is no longer a matter of choice for UK companies. In 2000, the European Union included a requirement for social and environmental reporting in its fourth company law directive. The EU also voted in May 2000 to develop a label to endorse products made by companies that can demonstrate commitment and respect for human and trade union rights.

The current government strategy in the UK supports voluntary action, rather than legal requirement. The Department for Trade and Industry strategy is to encourage companies to sign up to best practice in CSR. The Confederation for British Industry has lobbied for this approach.

The DTI would seem to promote an approach of stakeholder analysis in recommending that company directors should consider the interests of multiple stakeholders in their strategy and action, including employees, customers, suppliers, the wider society and the physical environment.

There are a number of codes of practice to choose from:

• *The Global Compact*, launched by the United Nations in July 2000, encourages companies to incorporate nine human rights into their strategies and business dealings, and to consider a broad range of stakeholders in setting strategy;

- *The International Labour Organisation (ILO)* has prepared a Declaration of Fundamental Principles and Rights at Work (1998). This focuses on eliminating forced labour, child labour, freedom of association and the right to work free from discrimination;

- *The Organization for Economic Co-operation and Development (OECD) Guidelines for Multinational Corporations* cover standards of behaviour in employment and industrial relations; environmental impact; combating bribery; consumer interests; science and technology; competition and taxation.

Website addresses for these organisations can be found at the end of this chapter.

A deontological position would caution that if people are just mechanically following a guide, if they have no intention to act well, then their behaviour isn't strictly ethical. This is as true of the employee following company guidelines as of the management who devise them. For example, consider the role of both employees and directors in recent railway disasters in the UK.

A virtue analysis would suggest that the effectiveness of these codes depends on the goodness of the people who try to apply them.

HRM has a key interest in codes of behaviour, as it will most likely be the department called upon to implement and monitor them. A basic problem resides in the wider context. No matter how far HRM may work to improve the behaviour of professionals and aid in the implementation of codes of conduct that affect all employees, if businesses show little respect for any ethical or even legal considerations over and above the generation of profit, then the pursuit of an ethical HRM is essentially futile.

Review Questions

You may wish to attempt the following as practice examination style questions.

2.1   What is 'ethics'? How does it differ from 'morality'?

2.2   What is 'moral relativism'? Give an example from a business context.

2.3   'Corporate social responsibility without HR is just PR.' Do you agree? Why? Why not?

2.4   What is 'utilitarianism'? Give an example of a utilitarian argument in HRM.

2.5   List some human rights that are relevant to the work context.

2.6   What is the 'stakeholder' approach? List the key stakeholders in a typical work organisation.

2.7   Give an example of an ethical code of conduct? What are the key characteristics of a *good* code? How can they improve standards of behaviour?

2.8   What mechanism does HR have to ensure stakeholder participation in organisational decision making?

References

Brown, D. (2003). From Cinderella to CSR, *People Management*, Vol. 9, No. 16, p. 21.

CIPD (2003). *A Guide to Corporate Social Responsibility*, July.

Crowe, R. (2002). *No Scruples*, London: Spiro Press.

Danley, J., Harrick, E., Strickland, D. and Sullivan, G. (1991). HR ethical situations, *Human Resources Management*, Vol. 26, pp. 1–12.

Freeman, R.E. (1998). A stakeholder theory of the modern corporation, in Hartman L.P. (ed.) *Perspectives in Business Ethics*, pp. 171–181, Chicago: McGraw-Hill.

Friedman, M. (1970). The social responsibility of business is to increase its profits, *New York Times Magazine*, 13 September.

Goodpaster, K.E. (1984). *Ethics in Management*, Boston: Harvard Business Books.

Greenwood, M.R. (2002). Ethics and HRM: a review and conceptual analysis, *Journal of Business Ethics*, Vol. 36, No. 3, pp. 261–278.

Hart, T.J. (1993). Human resource management: time to exercise the militant tendency, *Employee Relations*, Vol. 15, No. 3, pp. 29–36.

Heart of the City (2002). Corporate social responsibility – City firms lead the way, at: http://theheartofthecity.com/html/news:htm.

Johnson, R. (2003). HR must embrace ethics, *People Management*, Vol. 9, No. 1, p. 10.

Jones, T.M. (1995). Instrumental stakeholder theory: a synthesis of ethics and economics, *Academy of Management Review*, Vol. 20, No. 2, pp. 404–437.

Klein, N. (2000). *No Logo*, Hammersmith: Flamingo.

Macintyre, A. (1981). *After Virtue*, London: Duckworth.

Medawar, C. (1978). *The Social Audit Consumer Handbook*, London: Palgrave Macmillan.

Roddick, A. (2000). *Business as Usual. The Triumph of Anita Roddick: The Body Shop*, London: Thomsons.

Schramm, J. (2004) Perceptions on ethics, *Human Resources*, Vol. 49, No. 11, p. 176, Society for Human Resource Management.

Storey, J. (1993). The take-up of human resource management by mainstream companies, *International Journal of Human Resource Management*, Vol. 4, No. 3, pp. 529–555.

Weiss, J.W. (1994). *Business Ethics: A Managerial Stakeholder Approach*, Belmont, CA: Wadsworth.

Winstanley, D. and Woodall, J. (1996). Business ethics and human resource management, *Personnel Review*, Vol. 25, No. 6, pp. 5–12.

Winstanley, D. and Woodall, J. (eds.) (2000). *Ethical Issues in Contemporary Human Resource Management*, Basingstoke: Macmillan.

Further Reading

Goodstein, J.D. (2000). Moral compromise and personal integrity: exploring the ethical issues of deciding together in organisations' business, *Ethics Quarterly*, Vol. 10, No. 4, pp. 805–819.

Legge, K. (2000). The ethical context of HRM: the ethical organisation in the boundaryless world, in Winstanley, D. and Woodall, J. (eds.) *Ethical Issues in Contemporary Human Resource Management*, pp. 23–39, Basingstoke: Macmillan.

McIntosh, M., Leipziger D., Jones, K. and Coleman, G. (1998). *Corporate Citizenship: Successful Strategies for Responsible Companies*, London: FT/Pitman.

Werther, W.B. and Chandler, D. (2006). *Strategic Corporate Social Responsibility Stakeholders in a Global Environment*, London: Sage.

Work Foundation (2002). *Corporate Social Responsibility: Managing Best Practice*, No. 98.

Useful Websites

www.dti.gov.uk – links to Department of Trade and Industry information on ethics and corporate and social responsibility. Also links to related sites identified by DTI

www.ilo.org – the International Labour Organisation (ILO) gives information about rights at work and social issues related to the workplace

www.globalcompact.org – The Global Compact is a United Nations initiative to identify and promulgate ethical business principles

www.bitc.org.uk – this is the website of Business in the Community, a network of 700 companies committed to operating on ethical business lines

www.tuc.org.uk – this is the official website of the UK Trade Union Congress. The website gives advice on ethical approaches to employment, welfare and society and work-life balance

www.businesslink.gov.uk – Business Link gives advice to business about corporate and social responsibility

http://www.csr.gov.uk – the UK government's site advising on corporate and social responsibility

www.nottingham.ac.uk/business/ICCSR/research/paperseries.html – link to research papers produced by University of Nottingham's International Centre for Corporate and Social Responsibility

PART 2
Strategic aspects

CHAPTER 3

Strategic Human Resource Management

By Christine Porter and Bill Spear

Chapter outline

This chapter is concerned with the concept of strategic human resource management (SHRM), the process of strategic planning in organisations and the impact of various HR practices on the achievement of organisational objectives. Therefore, the chapter starts with a discussion of the concept of strategic HRM. This is followed by an overview of some of the different approaches to strategy formulation. The chapter discusses the best practice and contingency approaches to integrating HR practices and explores some of the techniques that organisations can use when strategic planning. The chapter concludes with a discussion of the obstacles to integrating organisational strategy and strategic HRM and discusses the relevance of the strategy literature to the public sector and other not-for-profit areas of the economy.

Learning outcomes

By the end of this chapter, you should be able to:

◆ Identify the key features of SHRM;

◆ Explain the relationship between HRM and organisational strategy;

◆ Differentiate between the different approaches to organisational strategy and to SHRM;

◆ Identify the obstacles to the involvement of HR functions in strategic decision making.

Introduction

Senior managers in organisations very often do not take into account the HR perspective when planning the strategic direction of their organisation. Many HR departments (and also some teaching programmes) concentrate solely on the operational aspects of human resources. Very often there is too much thought of HR techniques as ends in themselves rather than as needing to mesh with broader objectives in organisation terms. However, strategic planning needs to take into account the human dimension: for example, organisational capacity, cultural issues and the interaction between the employees and the technical basis of the organisation. This chapter seeks to explain the relationship between corporate objectives and HR strategics, both in terms of the way that corporate objectives need to be set taking into account the HR realities as well as the contribution that 'bundles' of particular HR techniques can make to the achievement of organisational objectives.

Strategic human resource management

The purpose of strategic SHRM is to ensure that organisational objectives are adopted that reflect the reality of HR capability within an organisation and that human resources are managed in such a way that organisational objectives are met. The debate about the relationship between corporate and staffing decisions is not new. It has, in theory, however taken on increased significance as scarce resources have to be more tightly controlled and markets have become more competitive. As Tyson points out (1995: 15), 'the management of labour [with which SHRM concerns itself] is a fundamental process [from a societal point of view] because it creates the kind of society in which people live.'

The key feature of strategic HRM is the integration (or strategic fit) of HRM policies and practices with organisational strategy, ensuring that HRM is fully integrated into strategic planning at a senior level. There are numerous definitions of strategic HRM. Schuler (1992: 4) defines it as, 'all those activities affecting the behaviour of individuals in their efforts to formulate and implement the strategic needs of the business', and Bratton (in Bratton and Gold, 2003: 37) as, 'the process of linking the HR function with the strategic objectives of the organisation in order to improve performance'. Armstrong and Baron (2002) identified the main features of strategic HRM as:

- Integrating business and HR strategies;
- Contributing to the achievement of competitive advantage;
- Commitment to the organisation's mission and values;
- Culture of trust and commitment;
- People seen as an investment not a cost;
- Top management driven;
- HR policies and practices are mutually supportive;
- Line managers are responsible for implementing HR policies and practices;
- Unitarist employee relations.

While these features may be useful as an aide-memoire and help to give a basic understanding of the concept of strategic HRM, they merely represent a list of ideal criteria that in practice will be difficult to achieve simultaneously. In any case, SHRM is concerned with strategic choices that are very often not used uniformally with an organisation but may vary from one employee group to another within the same organisation.

There is often confusion between HRM and strategic HRM. Some writers see the two terms as synonymous (Mabey et al., 1998); others do not. Golding (2004) suggests that the confusion arises because embedded in the HRM literature is the notion of strategic integration of HRM with organisational objectives. It appears however that the discussion about whether HRM and SHRM mean the same thing is largely academic. It is the difference between the rhetoric of policy statements and the reality of action that is important. Senior HR professionals need to be involved from the beginning in board-level discussions which might have HR implications. HRM policies need to fit across policy areas and across departments. As mentioned in Chapter 1, line managers also need to follow appropriate HRM practices as part of their everyday work.

The evolution of strategic human resource management

The potential contribution of strategic HRM has been well documented from early academic theories of US business schools such as Harvard (Beer et al., 1984) and Michigan (Fombrun et al., 1984) to recent key texts such as that by Boxall and Purcell (2003).

While the HRM literature emphasises a strategic theme, some critical evaluation demonstrates that in practice HRM lacks integration with the objectives of the organisation. In 1989, Guest concluded that strategic HRM seemed to have had little or no impact on improving organisational performance. There appeared to be no increase in boardroom representation and little evidence of 'soft' HRM, although there was some evidence of increased line manager involvement in the management of people. Storey (1992), in a survey of 15 UK organisations, found that extensive change in people management practice was under way, driven by non-personnel specialists and focused on organisational restructuring, quality and culture. However, his findings revealed that despite the widespread adoption of some strategic HRM features that are essentially unitarist, many of the organisations in his survey retained their pluralist perspective. Legge (1995) suggests that while some changes have taken place in people management processes, this largely reflects the pragmatic response to opportunities and constraints in the environment rather than the implementation of coherent employment policies. The evidence of Marginson (1993) and Millward et al. (2000), referring to the lack of board-level representation, supports this. As one of the researchers noted at the time:

> 'if one of the defining characteristics of human resource management is the explicit link with corporate strategies, then this survey has failed to find it for the majority of companies'.
>
> (Marginson, 1993: 71)

The 2004 Workplace Employee Relations Survey (Kersley et al., 2006) used three indicators to ascertain whether employers are becoming more strategic in their approach to managing people. The three indicators are: (1) evidence of workplace strategy covering employee development; (2) strategy not covering employee development; and (3) no strategy. They found that 'across the economy as a whole there was little change [since 1998] in the percentage of workplaces incorporating employee development in their strategic business plans'. 'Furthermore [they continue], HR managers were less likely to be involved in the preparation of strategic plans in 2004 than in 1998, a trend discernible across all sectors of the economy [in the UK]' (Kersley et al., 2006: 67–68). Similar, if not even more profound, doubts about the strategic importance place by organisations on HR as a competitive tool across the EU generally were identified by Stavrou et al. (2004).

Despite the positive findings of some research (Guest et al., 2000a, 2000b; Boxall and Purcell, 2003), the reality appears to be that whereas many chief executives subscribe in principle to the concept of strategic HRM, the evidence of the practical implementation of SHRM is somewhat sketchy. A key reason for this gap between rhetoric and reality may be the difficulty that many organisations experience in being able to demonstrate a direct causal link between the implementation of strategic people management practices and the achievement of organisational objectives. It is very difficult to demonstrate that HR benefits organisational profits for a number of reasons: for example, a company may be very profitable simply because it is operating in a growing market. In the public sector there may be few worthwhile measures of an organisation's effectiveness, despite examples in the UK of where governments have attempted to do this – e.g. by drawing up league tables of schools and hospitals.

Nevertheless, the ethos behind this chapter is that planning and strategy are essential to the effective delivery of organisational objectives, which accepts the findings of research such as that by Koch and McGrath (1996) which showed that:

> 'Labour productivity . . . tend(s) to be better in firms that both formally plan how many and what kinds of labour they will need, as well as where employers systematically evaluate their recruitment and selection portfolios and practices . . .' (p. 350).

pause for thought   What else is important for determining whether an organisation achieves its objectives other than its management of labour?

The interface between human resource management and organisational strategy

To understand the interface between organisational strategy and SHRM, it is necessary to analyse the responses made by an organisation to the context within which it operates, as well as to examine the way in which the HRM techniques are employed. Such techniques are (a) likely to impact on the delivery of organisational strategy and (b) have the potential to have a negative impact on other aspects of HRM, as the following case study seeks to illustrate.

Mini case study: Recruitment and selection in a UK Bank

A large clearing bank in the UK decided to change its recruitment policies in response to changes in the market place. The bank had an HR department but the lead function within the organisation was banking and there was little or no emphasis on the importance of HRM in helping the organisation to achieve its objectives. Rather, it was felt that the organisation would be most effective by concentrating on banking specialists, who were very skilled in banking but largely untrained in managing people.

Previously banks had concentrated on the protection of their clients' deposits but after deregulation of the financial services sector it became possible to enter into other fields of financial activity, including the provision of mortgages and insurance policies. In addition, deregulation of financial services meant that building societies and overseas banks were able to operate in the same fields as UK banks. The UK clearing bank, along with others, therefore decided to put much more emphasis on sales and marketing in an effort to compete.

The traditional approach to recruitment and selection in the bank had been to create long career ladders, engaging most employees when they left school or university. An individual employee would then work their way up the organisation, as far as it was deemed that their capabilities would allow. Employees had been recruited using criteria related not only to whether they were numerate but also related to diligence and caution.

The new environment, however, required that employees were needed who were more extrovert, less cautious and more creative, willing to push the sales and marketing agenda. Not only did the recruitment policies change, but so did staff development and career planning. As priorities changed within the organisation senior employees with new skills profiles related to sales were brought in at higher levels in the organisation than previously. Unfortunately, this had a knock-on effect since these new employees had not worked their way through the various departments and therefore had less organisational knowledge than those who had followed the more traditional career paths. Not only did this mean these new employees were less effective in some senses, due to lack of organisational knowledge, there was also some resentment among the employees who had not been given the opportunity to leap over the heads of others.

To reinforce the new organisational objectives, a payment by results reward management system was introduced. In addition, employees were required to work in teams and small groups in a way that had not been felt to be appropriate before. Unfortunately, the individually based payment system did not fit easily with teamworking and it was some while before management realised the conflict between individual incentives and teamworking. The individual incentive scheme also had an adverse effect on client relationships, since employees were not being encouraged to spend time with people who simply had queries rather than wanted to purchase a mortgage or insurance policy.

The bank was restructured partly to take advantage of the new ways of working made possible by advances in information technology that enabled customers to carry out their own banking online or through Automatic Telling Machines (ATMs). Many branches of the bank were closed resulting in massive redundancies. Some long-standing employees were pleased to leave the bank's employment, however, because they felt that the new ways of working were not to their liking. Unfortunately, the bank subsequently discovered that too many people had been allowed to leave, thus resulting in public embarrassment for the bank as well as the loss of many long-serving and talented employees.

exercise

From the above case study, identify:

- the impetus for changes being introduced into this banking organisation.
- the impact of the changes on HRM practices.
- the contradictions that resulted and which could be attributed to an absence of SHRM.
- For what reasons might directors of this organisation not have wanted to adopt a strategic approach to HRM?

The banking case gives an example of a situation where a strategy was devised and implemented without discernible input from HR specialists. It also illustrates the role that HR can play in helping the organisation to achieve its objectives as well as the need to employ a range of HR techniques that complement one another. The emphasis in an organisation, at least as far as HRM is concerned, needs to be not just on the effectiveness of a particular technique at micro level but in the interaction between the 'bundles' of HR practices and their contribution to the achievement of organisational objectives.

Delivering strategic objectives

As well as being involved in devising strategy, the HR department can help the organisation achieve its objectives by advising on, and designing, a range of policies and practices. The banking organisation, in the case study above, used its recruitment process and redundancy packages as tools for changing the profile of the employees in the organisation, in response to changes in the statutory environment that altered the market place in which the organisation was operating. The bank could have also considered a programme of HR development, not only to develop the employees who were already 'on the books' but also to develop the management function and to ensure that the HR practices that were implemented, worked as effectively as possible. A stronger HR department could also have advised the organisation about the likely interplay between the various practices. For example, an individually based payment scheme means that individuals are encouraged to enhance their own performance. If employees perceive that an enhanced group or team performance potentially has a negative effect on their own pay, this may militate against them supporting the team effort. The simultaneous use of individually based payment by results systems and teamworking are therefore usually counterproductive.

The banking case study above illustrates how the following range of key HR techniques – HR planning, recruitment, redundancy, HR development and training and reward management – can help to deliver organisational strategy. They are explained in greater detail in the following chapters of this book.

What is organisational strategy?

Organisational strategy deals with fundamental issues that affect the future of the organisation, seeking to answer fundamental organisational questions such as:

Where are we now? Where do we want to be? How do we get there? Ideally, strategy matches internal resources with the external environment, involving the whole organisation and covering the range and depth of its activities.

The origins of strategy have a military connection going back hundreds of years. From the organisational perspective, strategy has taken an increased role in planning since the end of the Second World War. Chandler (1962: 7) provides a definition of organisational strategy as, 'the determination of the basic long term goals and objectives of an enterprise, and the adoption of courses of action and the allocation of resources necessary for carrying out these goals'. Organisational strategy means that an organisation will seek to organise both its *tangible* resources in the form of the core competencies of its staff, physical assets and finance, and also its *intangible* resources such as brand, image, reputation and knowledge, in order to deliver long-term added-value to the organisation.

Vocabulary of strategy

Strategy is a rather imprecise subject and the terminology used is very inconsistent in everyday operations and academic literature. Johnson et al. (2005) have offered general guidelines for the terms associated with strategy:

- **Mission** – overriding purpose and direction of the organisation in line with the values or expectations of the stakeholders.
- **Vision** – a desired future state; the aspirations of the organisation.
- **Objective** – statement of what is to be achieved and when (quantifiable if possible).
- **Policy** – statement of what the organisation will and will not do.
- **Strategic capability** – resources, activities and processes. Some will be unique and provide competitive advantage.

Features of strategy

Lynch (2003) suggests that the strategic decision-making process consists of a number of key elements that relate primarily to an organisation's ability to add value and compete in the market place. It should be:

- **Sustainable** – for the long-term survival of the organisation, it is important that the correct strategic decisions are made to ensure that the strategy is sustainable.
- **Deliverable** – strategy is at least partly about how to develop organisations, helping them evolve towards their chosen purpose.
- **Competitive** – a sustainable strategy is more likely to be achieved if it delivers competitive advantages for the organisation over its actual or potential competitors. There are many different ways in which this can be achieved, including differentiation (unique product); low costs; niche marketing (narrow market segment); superior quality or service; high performance; and culture, leadership and style of an organisation.
- **Exploit linkages between the organisation and its environment** – links that cannot easily be duplicated contribute to superior performance. The strategy has to

exploit the many linkages between the organisation and the external environment, including suppliers, customers, competitors and government.

- **Visionary** – the long-term survival of the organisation depends on the ability of senior management to move the organisation forward beyond the current environment. This may involve the development and implementation of innovative strategies that could focus on growth or competition or a combination of both.

pause for thought

Think of an organisation you perceive as visionary. What is it that makes it a visionary organisation?

The strategic planning process

There are three aspects to the strategic planning process – strategic analysis, strategic development and strategic implementation:

- **Strategic analysis** is an assessment made by management of the current position of the organisation – *where are we now?* It includes the impact of the external environment on strategy – the political, economic, social, technological, legal and environmental issues; the identification of resources available to the organisation – physical, human, financial, and intangible assets such as knowledge, brand and image; expectations of stakeholders; and structures of power and influence.

- **Strategic development** is an assessment of *where do we want to be?* This is achieved by the generation of different strategic options, an evaluation of those options, and the selection of the most appropriate strategy for the organisation.

- **Strategic implementation** is an assessment of *how do we get there?* This is concerned with putting strategy into action and evaluating the outcomes in practice. For the implementation stage to be successful, the organisation requires a structure designed to deliver the required performance, deployment of the necessary resources and a constant awareness of the changing circumstances of the external environment.

Approaches to strategic planning

Strategy formulation is not always a neat, sequential process. Many organisations operate in conditions of extreme uncertainty, and the opportunity to analyse, develop and implement strategy sequentially is often not undertaken. Below are four approaches to strategy formulation – planned or prescriptive, emergent, comprehensive and incremental approaches.

Planned or prescriptive

Lynch (2003) describes the planned or prescriptive approach to strategy (also called the rational or classical approach) as a sequential implementation of the three core areas of strategy – analysis, development and implementation. It is possible to use the analysis to develop a strategy that is then implemented. The strategy is *deliberately* planned in advance and is *intended to be realised*.

Key assumptions of planned strategy include strategic fit with a stable external environment, top-down control with little employee involvement, where innovation is not generally encouraged, and where training and development is task orientated. Few organisations are in circumstances that meet these criteria in full.

Emergent

The reality for many organisations is that they operate in such uncertain and un-predictable environments that their intended strategies are not realised and other unintended strategies emerge. Lynch (2003) argues that the emergent approach takes a much more experimental view of the strategy choice and its implementa-tion. It seeks to learn by trial, experimentation and discussion as strategies are developed. Strategies emerge as a pattern during the process of crafting and test-ing. There is no clear distinction in the emergent approach between the two stages of development and implementation.

Key assumptions of emergent strategy include an uncertain and unpredict-able environment; an emphasis on learning and knowledge acquisition; employee involvement; and the encouragement of innovation and experimentation. Many organisations operating today have emergent strategies because of the uncertainty that exists in the current business environment, although managers often find it difficult to create an environment where learning, innovation and experimentation are encouraged.

Comprehensive versus incremental approaches

Organisations have a choice about whether they devise a comprehensive strategy which may involve radical change or whether a more cautious incremental approach is taken. The comprehensive strategy involves more risk taking and less possibility of taking a 'strategic retreat' if the new strategy turns out to be unworkable. In large organisations, it may be much easier to take an incremental approach, giving oppor-tunities for confidence building as the strategy is implemented and greater freedom to alter course in a world where the pace of change is increasing and it may become apparent that the new strategy does not fit with the changes that are taking place (Rees and Porter, 2006).

exercise

- ◆ **How would you describe the approach to strategic HRM at Warbings Office Systems?**
- ◆ **What are the strengths and weaknesses of strategic HRM at Warbings?**

Models of strategic human resource management

Although there is some acceptance of the idea that strategic HRM should support the strategic direction of the business, there is no agreement on the best way of doing this. Two normative models epitomise the relationship between labour management and organisational strategy. The first is explored in the *best practice or universal* school. The second approach, where integration between strategic HRM and organisational strategy is an essential feature, is explored in the *contingency and configurational* schools.

Universal or best practice school

The *best practice or universal* school proposes that strategic HRM is composed of a single set of HR policies and practices that is suitable for all organisations in all circumstances. Universal or best practice HRM (also known as high-commitment or high-performance or high-involvement HRM) was originally identified in the early US models of HRM, many of which mooted the idea that the adoption of certain 'best' HR practices would lead to improved organisational performance, through improved attitudes and behaviours, lower levels of absence and turnover, higher levels of skills and, therefore, improved productivity, quality and efficiency. The models of best practice take many forms and there is no consensus on the 'correct' bundle of HR policies and practices. Furthermore it is difficult to demonstrate the link between best practice HRM and improved organisational performance.

It is difficult to accept that the universal or best practice school reflects reality because what works well in one organisation will not necessarily work well in another. HR techniques adopted may not fit the local customs, organisational or societal culture, management style or technology. The cultural basis of many techniques used in HRM was discussed in Chapter 1. Social traditions about the role of managers and their relationship with employees will determine which HR strategies are likely to be effective. Also important will be the relationship between employees, employee attitudes to work and the family and the importance of work in their lives. The interface between technology and social structures at work can also be important. Social factors may need to be taken into account at the technical design stage to avoid dehumanised working arrangements with the motivational problems that may arise as a consequence.

Contingency or best-fit school

Having learned what works and what does not work elsewhere, it is still up to the organisation to decide what may be relevant and what can be adapted to fit its own particular strategic and operational requirements. This view is consistent with the contingency or best-fit school, which advocates the need to fit HR strategy into its surrounding context. Boxall and Purcell (2003: 60) offer a view of the factors that they feel ought to be taken into account in a full assessment of the factors that can influence HR choices. These are outlined in Figure 3.1.

They point out that it is necessary to look for the 'best fit' between the organisation and the internal as well as the external environment. For this, the organisation will need to draw on the know-how of the HR professionals before making strategic decisions, as illustrated in the case study that follows Figure 3.1.

Economic and technological factors, inside and outside the firm:
- choice of sector and competitive strategy
- nature of the dominant productive technology
- size and structure of the firm and stage in the industry life cycle
- quality of business capital (well funded or under-capitalised?)
- general economic conditions

→ **Management choices in HR strategy** →

Social and political factors, inside and outside the firm:
- degree of labour scarcity
- expectations and power of employees (including union strategies, where these exist)
- managerial capabilities and politics
- labour laws and social norms
- general educational levels and vocational training systems

Figure 3.1 Major factors affecting management choices in HRM strategy
Source: Boxall and Purcell (2003: 60)

A national brewing company in the UK decided to build a large new brewery on a greenfield site in Merseyside. One reason for doing this was the government funding available for generating work in an area of high unemployment. Managers from the company's plant at Burton-on-Trent were transferred to help build and commission the new brewery. The engineering managers who were initially appointed to run the brewery were quite unused to the high degree of labour conflict that soon emerged and had great difficulty in handling it. This was because of the different regional culture in Merseyside: a key difference was the traditional antagonisms between management and employees in the area. The more amicable working relationships at Burton had not prepared the managers who had been transferred for this key aspect of their job. No one in the HR department had been consulted about the decision to make the move to Merseyside. Despite training and changes in managerial personnel, the conflict and costs persisted. When there was a need for rationalisation in the company, the new brewery, although the most modern, was the one to be closed. The labour relations issues were partly responsible for this decision (Rees and Porter, 2006: 229).

There may be a tension in balancing external and internal environments as organisations seek to meet their objectives and a need to integrate organisational and employee needs, especially in highly competitive labour markets.

Resource-based approach

The resource-based approach argues for an exclusive form of 'fit' based on the theory that an organisation's resources are the key source of competitive advantage. In this context, it may be decided that the organisation should not try to achieve strategic fit with the external environment but aim to maximise its resources to create and dominate future opportunities.

Hamel and Prahalad (1994) have explored this view of strategy and suggest that it is a process for organisations to seek new opportunities over the long term while simultaneously maintaining the capacity to out-run competitors in the short term. The ability to achieve competitive advantage rests on the uniqueness of the resources; they must have value, be rare, be impossible to copy/imitate exactly and have no close substitutes.

The resource-based approach assumes that the core competencies in the organisation are unique; people are viewed as an investment and not a cost; that learning, knowledge sharing, innovation and experimentation are encouraged, and that employees are involved in decision making.

The debate as to which approach is most effective will continue, especially between those of the 'best practice' and 'best-fit' schools of thought. However, it seems appropriate to suggest that organisations should continue to analyse their environments, especially since these are fast changing and, as seems self-evident, not all HR techniques will be appropriate over time and from one situation to another.

pause for thought

◆ **Distinguish between 'best practice' and 'best fit'.**

◆ **Which do you believe to be the most appropriate approach?**

◆ **What is your reason for coming to this conclusion?**

Human resource management-related planning tools

To some, planning may seem to entail a bureaucratic process that ossifies the organisation and is more suited to stable than dynamic environments. However, if an organisation has done some planning, then it is easier to evaluate the effects of unexpected events on the situation than if little or no planning has taken place. There are several tools available to organisations that seek to plan their HR requirements. These include techniques of human resource planning (HRP) and balanced scorecard. These two techniques are explained below.

HRP

HRP carried out effectively is inextricably linked with organisational strategy. Corbridge and Pilbeam's (1988: 33) model identifies four main components of HRP activity:

1. Investigation and analysis – both internal to the organisation and to the external environment.
2. Forecasting to determine an HR imbalance or 'people gap'.
3. Planning resourcing and retention activities.
4. Utilisation and control through HR policies, techniques and IT.

The techniques used in HRP have in the past often involved the creation of very elaborate mathematical equations, which gave a spurious accuracy to what is often a not easily quantifiable process. These techniques were probably more appropriate during periods of general labour shortages. Current problems, at least in the UK, are mainly of shortages of labour with specific skills, requiring an organisation to identify how they are going to fill these skills gaps, which may require employees to be flexible. This would especially be the case where an organisation has a superfluity of employees with skills that are no longer needed, thus indicating the need for retraining or the recruitment of people with generic skills.

A large petrochemical firm in the UK recognised the need for specialist and generic skills. Some graduates with specialist skills in petrochemical engineering were recruited to deal with the short-term needs. Graduates with a general engineering background were recruited and used in technical and managerial jobs, with a view to moving them around the organisation so that they developed a range of skills. The reasoning was that the organisation needed to be able to adapt to changes in the industry, and the latter group of generalists would more easily be able to fill the emergent jobs. This compares with the banking case study, where employees had previously only been recruited in a particular mould.

Previously referred to as manpower planning, HRP has developed from being a relatively narrow forecasting of organisational need for particular numbers of employees with particular skills to a much wider and more qualitative concern with business planning and organisational strategy.

As with strategic planning so with HRP, Boxall and Purcell (2003) have identified the need to involve all stakeholders in the process if the planning is to reflect the actual environment in which the organisation will be operating.

How would you explain the need for HR planning to be integrated into the overall organisational strategy?

Balanced scorecard

This is a managerial accounting technique developed by Robert Kaplan and David Norton, in two books (1996, 2001), that seeks to reshape strategic management. It is a process of developing goals, measures, targets and initiatives from the following four perspectives:

◆ Financial;

◆ Customer;

◆ Internal business process;

◆ Learning and growth.

Kaplan and Norton emphasise the notion that it is the strategy actually implemented that is important. Good operational systems are seen to be as important as a strategic plan. They recognise that although financial outcomes are important to shareholders, management needs to improve the organisational performance at operational level if a sound financial basis is to be created. Particular emphasis is placed on the role of HRM in helping an organisation to achieve its objectives. Boxall and Purcell (2003) criticise the model because they feel that it does not sufficiently emphasise the management of managers and the importance of team building for senior managers. They also point out that it does not recognise that some HR activities are carried out, not because they add directly to the profitability of the organisation, but for legal, social and political reasons.

pause for thought

What activities can you think of that are carried out by organisations for legal, social or political reasons?

Strategic planning as an iterative process

Strategic planning can be seen as a mechanistic process that takes place once every five years. As indicated above, however, there are other models. The development of strategy can also involve a more iterative process and be interwoven with operational issues. The following case study illustrates how contributions to strategy can occur as part of the interrelationship between the operational and the strategic.

window into practice

At a healthcare trust in the UK it emerged at formal disciplinary proceedings that there was a pattern of similar types of failings in patient care, serious enough to warrant disciplinary action, including dismissal. The existence of the pattern was reported to the committee responsible for monitoring clinical governance. This enabled that committee to make a strategic intervention to try and determine the causes of these shortcomings and ensure appropriate remedial action was taken and that the strategic 'plan' was altered accordingly.

Integrating organisational strategy and human resource management

The banking case study (p. 45) is an example of a situation where input from the HR professionals at board level would have been useful so that workable strategies were conceived. There needs to be an HR input at the start of the decision-making processes when strategic issues are being considered. Unfortunately, all the evidence points to a paucity of board membership for HR directors in the UK. The Company Level Industrial Relations Survey found that only 30 per cent of companies with a thousand or more employees had an HR director on the executive board (Marginson, 1993). The function is more usually represented by the finance director who may be the only specialist on the board.

The difficulty in devising organisational strategies that are based on HR realities is not, however, just due to the fact that HR is often not consulted or not represented on the board or equivalent decision-making body. It is also due to other features of organisational strategy making. As pointed out by Rees and Porter (2006), there is an assumption that those who develop strategy welcome the prospect of open debate. However, debate can be hindered by personality clashes, rivalries and hidden agendas. Those taking part in the debate may have conflicting interests, although it may be assumed that there are none. These potential conflicts may not be taken into account when the issues are aired: senior managers are as likely as anyone else to take a unitary perspective and want to assume that what is being proposed is in the interests of all. The failure to identify potential conflicts of interest can also lead to naïve assumptions about the extent to which different objectives can be adopted, let alone the likelihood of complete agreement between the parties if a change in organisational culture is envisaged or deemed necessary. Therefore the resulting strategies may not be as appropriate as would be the case if the conflict of interests had been identified and taken into account by the decision makers.

The involvement of HR specialists in the formulation of organisational strategy has sometimes been inhibited by certain attributes of those in the HR profession. If HR specialists are to operate at a strategic level they must understand the nature and purpose of the organisation and be able to contribute to its future plans. Without such knowledge it is not possible for HRM to devise and implement policies and practices that will help the organisation achieve its objectives. Therefore, HRM specialists operating at a senior level must have considerable commercial acumen, understanding of organisational strategy, and awareness of strategic HRM if they are to comprehend the complex set of relationships that exist. Lack of organisational awareness on the part of HR professionals may be exacerbated by the fact that many HR departments are relatively small. In order to gain promotion HR managers may need to move frequently from one organisation to another, and even from one industry to another.

All managers, whether from an HR background or not, may be susceptible to promoting the latest HR techniques, ignoring the applicability of these techniques to the context in which the organisation is operating. Techniques may also be implemented without accurate problem diagnosis on the part of those involved (either in HR or among line managers). This, together with poor implementation, may result in the adoption of HR techniques that do not aid the achievement of objectives or that 'backfire', undermining the confidence that the senior management of the organisation has in HR.

The HR department may be weighed down with administrative responsibilities or in 'fire fighting', giving little time for thought about the wider organisational issues. Sometimes the problem of gaining acceptance of proposals made by HR can be attributed to the lack of facilitation skills demonstrated by those HR managers seeking to support operational managers but who are perceived as merely 'policing' management or erecting unnecessary obstacles. This may be due to ineptness on the part of practitioners in HR but it may also be due to the difficulty that managers from other backgrounds may have in understanding or having the patience to examine the 'soft' issues with which HR concerns itself. By the term 'soft' we are referring to the types of issues which are non-quantifiable but where judgement has to be made. Usually HR managers do not come from technical backgrounds and can therefore be perceived as being outsiders when the cultures of many organisations, and the disciplines from which other senior managers come, are scientific, technical or medical.

Despite the promotion by the CIPD of HR managers as 'business partners', all too often strategy making is seen as being for 'really senior people' who do not want to share their thoughts with those whom they see as being more junior, or who have recently arrived in the organisation. Senior managers may find it more convenient to devise strategies in a vacuum rather than have 'cold water' poured on their plans by someone pointing out the shortcomings and deficiencies in their proposals.

pause for thought

What is your view of HRM? Why do you think that the HR function is not more influential in organisations?

Applicability of strategy to the public sector

One drawback of the strategy literature as far as the public and not-for-profit sectors are concerned is that the features of strategy discussed and the vocabulary employed appear to concentrate almost completely on the private sector. In some cases, the public sector (or that part of the economy that is heavily dependent on government funding for survival) will, however, have been encouraged to take a strategic approach to the management of the business. UK governments have sought to create a market, for example in the National Health Service and in educa-tion, which means that organisations in these sectors may indeed be in competition with each other for customers and the resources which follow. It is also necessary to take into account the importance of non-governmental organisations (NGOs) such as charities.

HR policies have been needed in these organisations to enable them to achieve the objectives that the new market economy has demanded. Employees in these sectors have suffered from downsizing, work intensification and a general reduction in resources per patient, per student or per client. This has been necessary to enable these organisations to be more business-like (although hospitals, schools and uni-versities are not businesses in the accepted sense of the word). Many aspects of the strategic planning process described in this chapter will therefore be relevant to such sectors, even though the stakeholders may vary and there is no requirement to produce a profit in the conventional sense. Particular features of the public sector have been the need to give value for money, the creation of performance indicators and of course the need to balance their budgets. However, while there is a need for not-for-profit organisations to be business-like they are not businesses. They often have to operate in a sensitive political environment. In addition, there is always the danger that performance indicators and targets can be manipulated to create the appearance rather than the reality of progress. There is also the danger that simplistic accountancy models mean that much energy is expended into competing with other internal units rather than developing an integrated approach that meets the needs of the organisation as a whole. Nevertheless, it is not an option not to develop a strategic approach in the not-for-profit sector, providing such dangers are recognised. These issues need to be considered before attempting to develop a strategic plan and it may be particularly appropriate for those in the HRM function to warn of the dangers of simply trying to copy the private sector.

pause for thought

How appropriate do you think the ideas in this chapter have been for public sector and other not-for-profit organisations?

What makes it difficult to adopt these ideas in such organisations?

Summary

In this chapter we have addressed the following:

- Key features of strategic HRM include integration with organisational strategy, contributing to the achievement of competitive advantage, a culture of trust and commitment, top management driven, line manager responsibility for implementing HR policies and practices, and unitarist employee relations;

- Organisational strategy deals with the fundamental issues that affect the future of the organisation. It integrates the functional areas of the organisation, covering the range and depth of its activities;

- There are three core areas of organisational strategy: strategic analysis, strategic development and strategic implementation. Although these areas are presented as occurring sequentially, they will be simultaneous in some circumstances;

- The planned approach to strategy assumes that the core areas are formulated sequentially and the emergent approach assumes that the core areas are interlinked;

- The best practice approach to HRM strategies assumes that the adoption of a core set of HR policies and practices would be suitable for all organisations. In contrast, the best fit approach advocates a contingency approach whereby policies and practices are adopted according to whether they fit the particular circumstances. The resource-based approach focuses on the organisation's resources as the basis for achieving competitive advantage;

- Features of organisational decision making that hinder the development of an appropriate strategy include the need for open debate unhindered by personality clashes, rivalries and hidden agendas;

- The lack of involvement of senior HR professionals on the board of directors together with the lack of understanding or interest in HR on the part of managers from other backgrounds will contribute to ineffective strategy formulation.

Review Questions

You may wish to attempt the following as practice examination style questions.

3.1   Consider an organisation with which you are familiar and analyse whether it has an organisation strategy. Would you say it has planned or emergent strategies or both? What has led you to this conclusion?

3.2   To what extent does the organisation strategy that you have identified concern itself with HR issues?

3.3   Is it evident that HR capacity was taken into account when the organisational strategy was developed?

3.4   What is the difference between the 'best practice' and 'best fit' approaches to strategic HRM?

3.5   What major obstacles to the integration of HR with organisation strategy can you identify?

References

Armstrong, M. and Baron, A. (2002). *Strategic HRM: The Key to Improved Business Performance*, London: CIPD.

Beer, M., Spector, B., Lawrence, P., Quinn Mills, D. and Walton, R. (1984). *Managing Human Assets*, New York: Free Press.

Boxall, P. and Purcell, J. (2003). *Strategy and Human Resource Management*, Basingstoke: Palgrave.

Bratton, J. and Gold, J. (2003). *Human Resource Management: Theory and Practice*, 3rd edition, Basingstoke: Palgrave.

Chandler, A.D. (1962). *Strategy and Structure*, Cambridge, MA: MIT Press.

Corbridge, M. and Pilbeam, S. (1988). *Employment Resourcing*, London: FT Pitman.

Fombrun, C., Tichy, N. and Devanna, M. (1984). *Strategic Human Resource Management*, Chichester: Wiley.

Golding, N. (2004). Strategic human resource management, in I. Beardwell, L. Holden and T. Claydon (eds.) *Human Resource Management*, 4th edition, London: Pearson.

Guest, D. (1989). Personnel and HRM: can you tell the difference?, *Personnel Management*, January, pp. 48–51.

Guest, D., Michie, J., Sheenan, M. and Conway, N. (2000a). *Employee Relations, HRM and Business Performance: An Analysis of the 1998 Workplace Employee Relations Survey*, London: IPD.

Guest, D., Michie, J., Sheenan, M., Conway, N. and Metochi, M. (2000b). *Effective People Management: Initial Findings of the Future of Work Study*, London: IPD.

Hamel, G. and Prahalad, C. (1994). *Competing for the Future*, Boston, MA: Harvard Business School Press.

Johnson, G. Scholes, K. and Whittington, R. (2005). *Exploring Corporate Strategy*, 7th edition, London: Pearson.

Kaplan, R. and Norton, D. (1996). *The Balanced Scorecard: Translating Strategy into Action*, Boston, MA: Harvard Business School Press.

Kaplan, R. and Norton, D. (2001). *The Strategy Focused Organisation*, Boston, MA: Harvard Business School Press.

Kersley, B., Alpin, C., Forth, J., Bryson, A., Bewley, H., Dix, G. and Oxenbridge, S. (2006). *Inside the Workplace: Findings from the 2004 Workplace Industrial Relations Survey*, London: Routledge.

Koch, M. and McGrath, R. (1996). Improving labour productivity: human resource management policies do matter, *Strategic Management Journal*, Vol. 17, pp. 335–354.

Legge, K. (1995). HRM: rhetoric, reality and hidden agendas, in J. Storey (ed.) *Human Resource Management – A Critical Text*, London: Thompson.

Lynch, R. (2003). *Corporate Strategy*, 3rd edition, London: Pearson.

Mabey, C., Salaman, G. and Storey, J. (1998). *Human Resource Management: A Strategic Introduction*, 2nd edition, Oxford: Blackwell.

Marginson, P. (1993). The multi-divisional structure and corporate control: explaining the degree of corporate coordination over decisions in labour relations, Papers in Organisation No. 12, Institute of Organisation and Industrial Sociology, Copenhagen Business School.

Millward, N., Bryson, A. and Forth, J. (2000). *All Change at Work: British Employment Relations, 1980–1998, as portrayed by the Workplace Industrial Relations Survey Series*, London: Routledge.

Pilbeam, S. and Corbridge, M. (2006). *People Resourcing – Contemporary HRM in Practice*, London: Pearson Education/Prentice Hall.

Rees, W.D. and Porter, C. (2006). Corporate Strategy Development and Related Management Development, Part I, *Industrial and Commercial Training*, Vol. 38, No. 6, pp. 226–231.

Schuler, R.S. (1992). Strategic HRM: linking people with the strategic needs of the business, *Organisational Dynamics*, Vol. 21, No. 1, pp. 18–32.

Stavrou, E., Brewster, C. and Charlambous, C. (2004). Human Resource Management as a Competitive Tool in Europe, Working Paper 0414, Henley Management College.

Storey, J. (1992). *Developments in the Management of Human Resources*, Oxford: Blackwell.

Tyson, S. (1995). *Human Resource Strategy: Towards a General Theory of Human Resource Management*, London: Pitman.

Further Reading

Leopold, J. (ed.) (2002). *Human Resources in Organisations*, FT/Prentice Hall.

Useful Websites

www.cipd.co.uk/search/default.aspx?q=hr%20strategy – links to the Chartered Institute of Personnel and Development resources relating to HR strategy

www.dti.gov.uk – links to Department of Trade and Industry information on ethics and corporate and social responsibility. Also links to other sites identified by DTI as being of related interest

www.humanresourcemanagement.co.uk – publishes articles and news releases about HR surveys, employment law, HR research and related books and other publications

www.btinternet.com/~alan.price/hrm – a free source of worldwide HRM information

www.hrmguide.co.uk – publishes articles and news releases about HR surveys, employment law, HR research and related books and other publications

CHAPTER 4

Communication

By Cecilie Bingham

Chapter outline

Communication is a process whereby individuals and groups share, swap and withhold knowledge with and from one another in a variety of ways ensuring that meaning, values and information are transferred. This chapter describes the functions and processes of communication within an organisational context: it examines the impact that different managerial styles (and philosophies) have on the ways and means of transmitting and receiving information and of sharing knowledge. The interrelationship between culture and communication is discussed and, in particular, the importance of the medium for communicating messages is examined, together with the impact that communication procedures may have on different change programmes. The development and implementation of communication strategies tied to business goals are explored.

This chapter should be read in conjunction with Chapter 5 that looks at interpersonal communication.

Learning outcomes

By the end of this chapter, you should be able to:

- Recognise the importance of communication within organisations;
- Describe different systems of communication;
- Evaluate the aptness of a variety of communication mechanisms and explain the efficacy and appropriateness of a range of processes of sharing information in a number of dissimilar circumstances;
- Analyse the impact and relative values of mechanisms for transmitting information and sharing knowledge;
- Demonstrate an awareness of different analytical models of communication;
- Determine suitable communication strategies and processes for different organisational structures;
- Outline the role of communication (and by extension the importance of communication skills) within an organisational/business context.

Introduction

Communication is essential. It is the means by which information is requested and transmitted, knowledge is disseminated and thoughts and emotions conveyed. Interpersonal communication is the bedrock of human resource management (HRM) because it is the means by which values and behaviour are transmitted. It is the way in which strategy is conveyed, enacted and modified. Communication percolates through organisations and its structures, affecting who says what, what gets said and subsequent actions. Getting it wrong can have costly repercussions, while getting it right can aid the process of change, encourage teamwork, facilitate employee involvement and commitment, and have a positive impact on productivity.

What is communication?

Communication is the means by which information and ideas are exchanged between two or more individuals or groups. It can be verbal or non-verbal and may involve written or spoken language, and verbal and non-verbal signs or symbols. Communication may be direct, when the parties deal with one another; or indirect, when a third party or intermediary, such as a trade union representative or a lawyer, acts as a conduit for the message. Similarly it may be formal and official, or informal and unofficial. The context within which the communication occurs, as well as the medium that is used to transfer information, along with the perceptions, attitudes, emotions and body language of both the receiver and sender of the information, may influence the ways in which the information is both imparted and received. Furthermore, communication is a crucial component of organisational culture because it involves the dissemination of shared sets of meanings (Hall, 1997) and is one of the ways of processing, forming, transmitting, reinforcing, enhancing and exchanging values.

Communication has been studied since the time of the Ancient Greeks, who were concerned with the art and philosophy of communication. Aristotle's first book on rhetoric, at around 330 BC, expounded the idea that clear thinking, particularly logical thinking, led to clear communication and was an essential tool for persuasion. The Greek scholars at this time however concentrated on the *imparter* of the information, rather than the *receiver*, and assumed that if the communication were clear to the originator of the message it would consequently be clear to the recipient. The Greeks thought that the receiver would automatically understand the meaning in an identical way to the communicator. This is a mistake that is not uncommon today. The receiver of the information however may not give it the same meaning as the sender. As Clampitt says, 'It is somewhat disconcerting to come to the realisation that, to a large extent, message senders are at the mercy of the interpretations of receivers. That is, regardless of the sender's actual intent, it is the receiver who will determine "the meaning" of any given utterance' (1991: 43). It is not therefore unlikely that when groups of individuals hear the same information they may interpret it in different ways. Gilbert and Mulkay (1984) have also pointed out that sometimes the same individuals will, on separate occasions, provide information that although ostensibly the same is different depending on the context in which the information is elicited.

Bulk of office staff 'baffled' by information technology (IT) jargon

Read the following article from the *Edinburgh Evening News*, Friday 23 September 2005, and then say:

1. Why you think communication is important in a business setting.
2. Whether you think jargon is an aid to communication.
3. What you think Adam Fletcher meant when he talked about 'tailoring' levels of communication?

Give reasons for your answers.

> 'Most office workers complain computer buzzwords such as Javascript and jpeg are as difficult to understand as a foreign language, according to a new survey today. The poll by recruitment firm Computer People showed that three-quarters of staff wasted more than an hour every week finding out what technical terms meant. Younger workers were just as likely to be stumped by jargon as their older colleagues. Almost two-thirds had sent emails with huge attachments which had blocked clients' systems, and one in four had to ask for help to download information. Adam Fletcher, managing director of Computer People, said: "Effective IT professionals understand the need to tailor their levels of jargon to the different groups of people they interact with."'
>
> (Source: www.scotsman.com/?id=1982752005)

Imagine that you have to write a guide on computer jargon for new recruits to your organisation. Write clear and unambiguous definitions for the following:

cookie, gigabytes, hacker, Javascript, jpeg, megabytes, PDF, spyware, Trojan horse, worm.

Definitions can be found in the appendix on page 90.

Giving and receiving messages

Communication therefore is concerned not just with the 'message' but with interpretation of the message, and consequently it is affected by a number of variables, such as:

- the ways in which the message is delivered;
- the culture of the participants;
- the context in which the message exists;
- the relationship between the parties involved.

For example, an HR director may say 'well done' to her child at home using a tone of voice and facial expression that denotes pleasure and pride, whereas the identical phrase used to a colleague at work, but accompanied by a different intonation and emphasis, coupled with a look of exasperation, would convey a completely different and rather sarcastic meaning.

When you are giving someone information, how do *you* know that they have understood exactly what you meant to impart?

Is this understanding important? Why?

Within organisations, communication is an essential part of the ways in which they operate. It is via the processes of communication that values are transferred, actions and behaviours are co-ordinated, knowledge is shared and approval or disapproval is given.

When the communicants come from different cultures, even if they are using a common language, there can be wide variations when interpreting the meaning of messages. For example, a native English person receiving a letter of welcome when starting a new job with an American company could be offended if the letter included a phrase along the lines of, 'The Corporation is quite pleased that you have chosen to join us'. The word 'quite' here has two distinct meanings: for the English reader its use implies a less than enthusiastic rather qualified welcome, while for the American its use here is equivalent to the English word 'very' (Adams, 2002). Fourboul and Bournois (1999: 211) relate how corporate communications at Unilever were different depending on the culture of the recipient. 'Unilever started to cascade a system to acquaint all employees yearly with information about how the Corporation was doing financially. For this, corporate HQ prepares a big packet full of information complete with overhead sheets and even videos. All business groups receive the same information and are expected to pass it on to their companies and eventually to all employees . . . Random checks among employees after the Cascade exercise have shown that in Eastern Europe all employees are very interested in corporate information and that "coverage" is near 100 per cent; in Western Europe coverage is "average" at some 80 per cent; but in Latin countries coverage is "difficult" at around 65 per cent because local management seems to decide that not all information is necessary or fit for their employees.'

Unspoken assumptions, particularly when the parties do not share such assumptions, can influence the ways in which messages are sent and received such that misunderstandings are almost inevitable. Misunderstandings can arise not just because of the language used, or the way a message is perceived, but may be linked to the misreading of body language, tone, facial expression or intonation. Poor interpretation and poor delivery can lead to miscommunication, misinterpretation, confusion and, even, conflict.

exercise

Look at the Warbings case study: how many examples of potential misunderstandings linked to poor communication can you find?

What implications associated with weak communication are there for Warbings? Why did you reach these conclusions?

The medium chosen for the message is important. What is wrong with this leaflet?

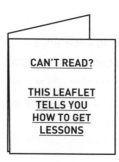

CAN'T READ?

THIS LEAFLET
TELLS YOU
HOW TO GET
LESSONS

It will have failed in its primary purpose because the medium chosen is inappropriate for the message, and the recipients. Organisations often assume that they have communicated information to their workforce and their clients but, because they have chosen the incorrect medium, the message fails to get through. For example, a company that disseminates information to employees by posting messages on the intranet may fail to communicate because not everyone will have access to it: or, as is often the case, they may lack the time, skills or inclination to look for it and then read it. Similarly, change programmes within organisations that are not backed up by adequate levels of communication are prone to failure. John Kotter (1996), in his discourse on leading change, says that without adequate amounts of appropriate communication it is not possible to get the buy-in of those affected by change. Ineffective implementation of change programmes may be the result, according to Kotter, of:

- insufficient communication from the top of the organisation despite appropriate vision;
- insufficient communication from managers in the middle of the organisation despite appropriate communication from those at the top;
- key players acting in ways that contradict the new messages thereby encouraging cynicism.

Sometimes the culture of the organisation will prevail against the messages being sent. If only bad news is ever communicated, those on the receiving end may well be cynical if 'good news' begins to be promulgated. This is often the case following redundancies: the workforce, braced for bad news, regards any new information about proposed changes with suspicion.

On occasions, of course, the culture within which the organisation is operating will have an impact upon the ways in which messages are transmitted and received. In some societies language is used just to transfer information and for ratifying and clarifying intentions, while in others language is used as a tool with which to negotiate. The various interpretations placed by different cultures on control or affiliation, on feelings or on logic, will have an impact not just on the ways in which messages are delivered but importantly upon the ways in which they are received.

Based upon earlier work by the humanist psychologist John Heron (1975), known as the Six Category Intervention Analysis, Oliver (1997: 52) has listed the main categories of business communication, shown in the box below.

Oliver's categories of business communication

- **Prescriptive** – telling people what to do and how to do it
- **Informative** – providing knowledge
- **Confronting** – challenging existing attitudes/practices
- **Cathartic** – reducing tension, dispelling emotional blockages
- **Catalytic** – accelerating the ways in which individuals think and behave about issues
- **Supportive** – affirms and recognises an individual's worth

exercise

Take 10 minutes to form a group of three people. Talk about one of the recent email messages that has been circulated by the university or from management in your organisation. During your discussion think about the ways in which you all interacted then identify and categorise the interventions used and record them in the table below.

Recording Chart

Place a tick in each box as each intervention is identified.

Category	Name		
Prescriptive			
Informative			
Confronting			
Cathartic			
Catalytic			
Supportive			

Review your findings.

Did you all interpret the messages in the same way?

What have you discovered about different ways of communicating at work?

Effective communication then requires:

- clarity of meaning;
- common understanding, despite cultural differences;
- sharing information unambiguously, using an appropriate medium.

Sometimes this process fails, as when a lecturer discusses an issue with a student who has mentally 'switched off' and is texting a friend. Sometimes this process is just one-way, as for example a company newsletter to shareholders giving recent results. At other times, it is a two-way process, as with face to face conversations; while sometimes it involves multiple interactions, as in a team meeting brainstorming the marketing strategy for a new project.

Figure 4.1 illustrates the communication process.

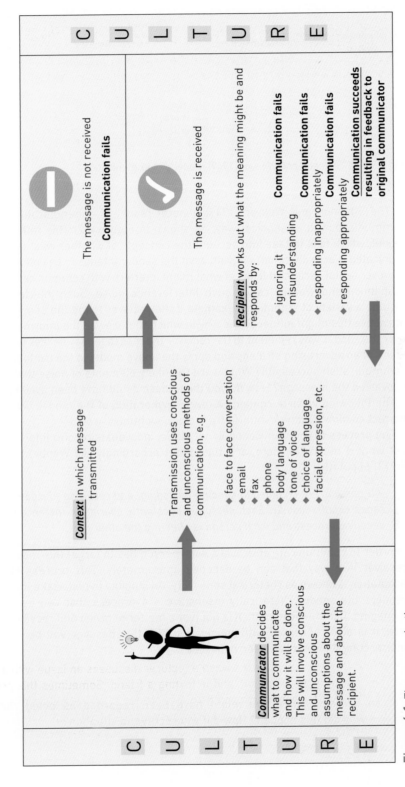

Figure 4.1 The communication process
© Bingham 2006

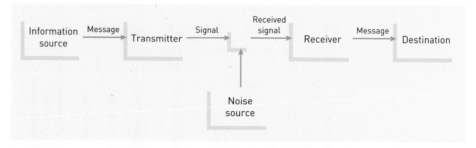

Figure 4.2 Shannon and Weaver (1949) model of communication

The Shannon and Weaver (1949) general model of communication described communication in a technical way, as shown in Figure 4.2. This rather uncritical model, which fails to take into account the concepts of whether what is being communicated is actually congruent with what the sender intends to be communicated, is however useful because it looks at what might interfere with communication patterns.

Shannon and Weaver called such interference noise. Such interference could include a variety of stimuli, for example if the receiver found the sender physically attractive this might influence the way in which they viewed the information; if however the sender was repellent to the receiver the message may be less well received. Think of an advertising strategy and apply the above model to the campaign: was the communication successful? What were the likely elements of noise that could have subverted the message? How do you think these could have been avoided?

The following website contains a useful exploration of the model: www.cultsock. ndirect.co.uk/MUHome/cshtml/introductory/sw.html.

The process of communication is not static; individuals receive information, work out what it means to them, and then react accordingly. As Wenberg and Wilmot (1973: 6) put it:

> 'All persons are engaged in sending (encoding) and receiving (decoding) messages simultaneously. Each person is constantly sharing in the encoding and decoding process and each person is affecting the other one.'

In order to communicate effectively, each person has to target the 'message' to the receiver in a way that can be decoded appropriately. This process of empathy/ adaptation is known as rhetorical sensitivity. An inability to undertake this effectively renders the sender rhetorically insensitive – a process that can be particularly damaging. Communication then is not just a matter of giving and receiving information; it is also concerned with anticipating how the message will be received and interpreting it once it has been delivered.

pause for thought

Think of an occasion when you might have been regarded as being rhetorically insensitive – why did this happen? How did you rectify the situation?

Communication approaches

Depending on the school of thought, communication processes may be regarded in different ways. Where the communication practices are mechanistic and involve the transmission of information, usually in a downward flow, this may be associated with the theories of classical management. Where, on the other hand, the purpose is to motivate and inspire the receivers, this is related to the humanistic approach. Where a communication strategy is developed in order to enhance the levels of trust between members of the organisation, to inform, motivate and involve employees in order to increase productivity and achieve organisational goals, the process is a multi-layered one of interaction and is tied strongly to HRM practices and on occasion to theories of complexity. A number of issues have led to the need to strengthen communications strategies and collaboration between managers and HRM departments:

- The rise of individualism;
- The need to encourage employee commitment;
- The requirement to ensure consistency;
- The need to avoid giving mixed messages to the workforce.

Worker involvement techniques requiring high levels of communication, such as quality circles, works councils, *kaizen*, and TQM, all have a positive impact on productivity, and have led to an awareness of the importance of communication and the burgeoning of communication training programmes.

The importance of workplace communication

Within the workplace, communication falls into a number of areas:

- **Communication from the organisation to the employees** – this communication is usually downward or may be lateral if the process goes across the organisation, for example between different departments. It may be direct or indirect. An organisation needs to communicate to those working for it so that they are able to:
  - understand the purpose, goals, values and progress of the organisation and their part in it;
  - receive feedback and praise for when they have done well;
  - be aware of what is expected of them.

  The ways that information is imparted may have both intended and unintended consequences, depending on the way it is delivered and received. For example, if information is sent to the employees about the organisation performing well, but only the CEO receives an extremely large bonus, then the message will communicate not just the success (intended) but also that the workforce is not as important as the CEO (unintended). Channels or communication pathways need to be developed so that important information is not just disseminated, but targeted to the right people in a timely way. (See Table 4.1 for examples of different communication channels.)

- **Communication from the organisation to an external audience** – such public relations and marketing will enhance the profile of the organisation, boost sales, encourage recruitment, provide information to shareholders, clients, creditors and competitors, etc. Communication in this category may also have both intended and unintended consequences; for example, when Ford changed one of its advertisements by 'whitening' the black faces of its workforce appearing in an advertisement, the consequences were the opposite of those desired: the company received adverse publicity. On occasions, of course, communications within this category will be used to troubleshoot problems and to counteract bad publicity.

♦ **Communication to the organisation from managers and employees** – this is upward communication (or, depending on the structure of the organisation and type of message, it may be lateral). It allows employees to contribute knowledge, point to problems and make suggestions. The last 20 years have seen a proliferation of ways in which employee communication has been encouraged – ranging from 360° feedback and employee surveys, to whistleblowing policies and suggestion schemes. But many of these processes, by their very structures, do not just allow employees to have a say but, subliminally, communicate the subordinate nature of their positions within the organisation and reinforce the controlling and paternalistic nature of the top management. (Some aspects of power are covered in Chapter 12.) In effect the organisation says, 'Talk to us because we are the ones who can influence your day to day activities.'

The cost of poor communication

Of the 23 million people in work in the UK, about three million have poor levels of literacy and nine million have poor numeracy. As a consequence of this, according to Etheridge (2005), most organisations in the UK will employ staff, including managers, who are not as effective as they could be. This will necessarily impact upon the ways in which organisations are run and the levels of profitability they achieve. The Confederation of British Industry (CBI) maintains that 50 per cent of employers are unhappy with their employees' basic literacy and numeracy. The Workplace Basic Skills Network estimates that UK businesses lose £10 billion each year as a direct result of low levels of these basic skills.

The following extract shows how this can have an impact on business.

Back to basics

The problem is a huge one, according to Robert Nurden of the Workplace Basic Skills Network, a national organisation based at Lancaster University. 'The construction industry alone believes that £1bn is lost every year as a result of poor basic skills. Twenty per cent of retail staff have no qualifications and lack basic skills, or have spoken-English needs. The main skills gap reported by the retail industry is in written or verbal communication – a vital skill for this or any industry,' he says.

So how can HR managers recognise whether there is a problem? Nurden believes the tell-tale signs are many and varied. He says: 'Look out for people who forget their glasses rather than admit they cannot read, or wrong or lost orders in the warehouse. Contravention of health and safety regulations because they cannot be understood is common, so too is shoddy workmanship because an employee prefers to make a "guestimate".'

(Source: *Personnel Today*, Etheridge, 2005)

Individual communication skills, while crucial, are not the only things that may have an effect on the business. Ineffective communication systems hinder businesses because they contribute towards inefficiency. Of 2,200 workers in the UK taking part in research by Microsoft, 37 per cent complained about a 'lack of team communication' and said that 'ineffective meetings' got in the way of productive working, while almost two-thirds of respondents reported that the inability to find electronic documents quickly when needed affected their productivity. This research, which in total looked at 38,000 workers worldwide, showed that poor communication led to ineffective work practices that potentially wasted two out of every five working days.

Commenting on this research, Nicola Casey, from the press office at Microsoft, said: 'Productivity is increasingly shaped by our ability to communicate and collaborate with our colleagues and less by our ability to process tasks alone. . . . The growing volume of information that workers are now expected to manage requires far greater integration than ever before. These combined changes present both a management challenge and an infrastructure challenge for all British businesses' (Thomas, 2005).

Legislation also impacts on the amount of information organisations are expected to pass on to their workforce. For example, when someone starts a new job, they receive a statement of employment giving a number of details such as the hours they are expected to work and the amount of remuneration they will receive. But more than just providing information, employers (depending on the size of the company) are legally required to consult their workforce directly (i.e. face to face) or indirectly (i.e. via workplace representatives) about a number of issues ranging from redundancy, to transfers of business ownership, to issues about health and safety.

If communication skills are poor, and the processes and mechanisms of dissemination are inadequate, then the efficacy of this information is weakened. Effective consultation cannot occur without dissemination of appropriate information; furthermore, if managers do not have the skills to impart information and if employees do not have the skills to process and discuss it, opportunities for improving the business may be lost.

The business case for better communication was made by Asif and Sargent (2000), whose research indicated that for organisations to have effective relationships with their employees, a communication culture must pervade the whole organisation and not just parts of it. Similarly, Harkness (2000) pointed out that communication within organisations was weak because it was not measured: by measuring communication, he says, companies can gauge the effectiveness of the messages they are sending out and act accordingly.

Recent research commissioned by the Department for Trade and Industry emphasises the importance of good communication for business profitability – see the example below.

The business case for information and consultation

It is expected that there will be substantial economic and social benefits from the legislation over time. Effective employee information and consultation systems are a key enabler of high performance workplaces – they can help staff feel more involved and valued by their employer, make them better aware of the business climate in which the organisation is operating, and help them be more responsive to and better prepared for change. Employers should see gains from a better informed, more motivated and committed workforce. This should lead to a greater ability to react rapidly to opportunities and threats, and lower staff turnover, thereby ultimately enhancing a company's productivity. Moreover, if employees become more willing to undertake training as a result of greater information and consultation, the result would be a more skilled workforce. Given the nature of these benefits, it is hard to quantify them. However, we estimate that they are in the order of magnitude of hundreds of millions of pounds over a ten-year period.

(Source: Department for Trade and Industry, 2004)

exercise

In an ACAS policy discussion paper, the authors say:

'Information and consultation breathe life into the employment relationship as well as being important in organisational performance and working life.'

(Source: Grell and Sisson, 2005: 1)

- ◆ What do you think this means?
- ◆ Why did you reach this conclusion?
- ◆ What is the difference between information and consultation?
- ◆ How far do you think the degree of information and consultation that an organisation adopts should be a strategic matter? Give reasons for your answer.
- ◆ How do you think additional consultation with the workforce would affect the employment relationship at Warbings? Why do you say this?

Communication pathways

The dissemination of knowledge and information within organisations is critical to their success. Galbraith (1973, 1977) showed how the way in which knowledge is channelled through an organisation is influenced by the structures within that organisation. We have already discussed upward, downward and lateral communication but within these areas there are different ways of giving and receiving messages. Where organisations operate globally, with divisions based in different countries, decision making often operates at a national rather than international level; communication patterns here are therefore complex. Information may flow horizontally or vertically throughout an organisation, sometimes in single communication lines within the organisation, and at other times via multiple lines.

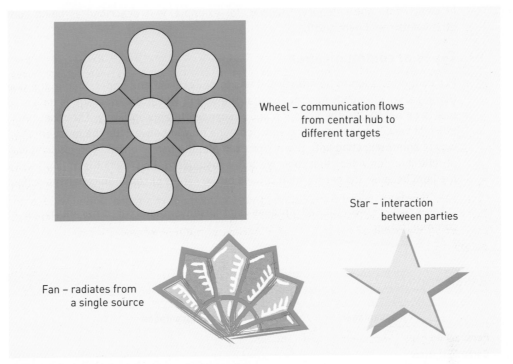

Wheel – communication flows
from central hub to
different targets

Star – interaction
between parties

Fan – radiates from
a single source

Figure 4.3 Different types of communication flow

It is possible for communication flows to be managed in a circular way; or to radiate out from a single source making a fan shape. On other occasions it may flow from a central hub out to a number of targets like a wheel. When there is interaction between the parties involved, and communication flows between a number of different parties, this can be depicted pictorially as a star with lines joining each of the points to one another (Leavin, 1972: 178–80). Of course, diagrammatically – see Figure 4.3, this is all rather two-dimensional; in reality, organisations have many layers and lines of communication, which cross and weave between and around each other. In an interesting paper examining strategic communication within large European companies, Fourboul and Bournois (1999) used the typology of Perlmutter (1969), which divides companies into four types, together with a number of in-depth case studies to discover how multinational organisations communicate and share strategic information with their employees. They found that *ethnocentrism* was present in organisations such as British Airways, where a dominant headquarters controls communication, with messages radiating out from the centre. A *polycentric* organisation, like Ericsson, had subsidiaries with a high degree of autonomy: each was responsible for its own communication. Where *regiocentrism* was evident, in organisations like LVMH, autonomy was given to regional groupings of subsidiaries: individual organisations had less communications autonomy. Where the HQ was just an integral element of a complex interrelated pattern of communications, e.g. Henkel, this fitted the pattern of *geocentrism*. Some organisations, however, did not

fit clearly into one category; Unilever, for example, was described as being both ethnocentric and geocentric.

Types of communication

For communication to be effective, it has to be received and understood in the way the imparter intended: this means that the way in which the message is delivered has to be tailored to the situation and responded to appropriately. The most time-efficient way of communicating with someone may not always be the most effective way of communicating with them. For example, the use of email is an efficient way of telling an individual that their work is substandard; however, it is an ineffective medium because the resentment caused by the *means* of communication may affect the message itself.

Table 4.1 shows the advantages and disadvantages of different types of communication.

Table 4.1 Types of workplace communication

Personal Communication type	Advantages	Disadvantages
Face to face conversation	Natural way of communicating, good for building rapport, gaining *instant* feedback, giving sensitive/bad news	Need to be physically close, appearance/gestures may obscure meaning
Meetings	Good for building rapport/instant feedback/checking understanding, knowledge sharing, widens the pool of contributions	Can be time-consuming, difficult to arrange when diary dates clash, shy people may not be heard, can be dominated by one or two assertive personalities
Email/letter/memo	Targeted to individuals, read and written at time of choice, can be referred to later, can include specific details	Can be used inappropriately when personal chat would be better, e.g. for disciplinary meeting, time-consuming, can be ignored by recipient, can be used to spread misinformation to large groups of people
Telephone	Personal, can be used over distance, instant access to feedback	Can be intrusive – can't read body language, no record of what was actually said
Video link	Used over distance, instant feedback	Not everybody happy on camera, ground rules re: interruptions, etc. have to be clear from the outset

Table 4.1 continued

	Advantages	Disadvantages
Impersonal Communication type		
Global email	Targets a lot of people simultaneously – saves time	Can be sent to those who do not need it
Road show	Creates interest, targets a mass audience, provides a focus for the message, can make people feel the organisation cares	Time-consuming to organise, simultaneously takes a lot of people from their tasks – not always sure that the intended message is received
Noticeboard	Obvious to all, simple, easy to arrange, easy to change	Not always accessible to everyone, e.g. remote workers; not always read, not always kept up to date, may be defaced/can be subject to sabotage
Mass meeting	Conveys information to large numbers of people simultaneously	Difficult to check on understanding, difficult to organise in terms of space and timing suitable for everyone
Business TV	Quick way of providing undiluted, consistent messages to large numbers, sometimes internationally	Can be expensive to set up, downward flow of information only, absent employees miss the message, usual sources of info may feel disempowered
Intranet	Easily accessed in own time, ambiguity avoided, information uniformly presented to all	Time-consuming to write and keep up to date, may not be accessed, difficult to check understanding
Newsletter	Delivers a uniform message, can be read in own time, cost-effective	Time-consuming to write, and may not be read, difficult to check understanding
Brochure	Delivers a uniform message, can be read in own time, cost-effective	Time-consuming to write, and may not be read, difficult to check understanding
Staff handbook	Delivers a uniform message, can be read in own time, cost-effective, ensures essential information imparted	Have to regularly up date, may not be read, long-serving staff may not be aware of recent changes
Electronic devices	Delivers messages instantly	Can be ambiguous or misleading. May be written without reflection May be passed on inappropriately

Examine some recent examples of communication from your own organisation – it need not be a workplace. Comment on their effectiveness.

	Comments
Face to face conversation	
Meetings	
Email/letter/ memo	
Telephone	
Video link	
Global email	
Road show	
Noticeboard	
Mass meeting	
Business TV	
Intranet	
Newsletter	
Brochure	

continued

	Comments
Staff handbook	
Electronic devices	
Others	

The Workplace Employment Relations Survey 2004 (Kersley et al., 2005: 18) looked at the incidence of nine different forms of UK workplace communication between 1998 and 2004 and found that noticeboards and the downward cascading of information were prevalent, while team meetings/briefings had increased in recent years, predominantly in the private sector. Such meetings were, in the main, structured to impart information to the workforce about production issues, future plans, training, and health and safety. Time was also set aside for employees to ask questions. Table 4.2 shows their findings.

Communication and change

Organisations are changing all the time, sometimes with small *incremental* changes that occur almost imperceptibly and at others the *transformational* change is part of a strategic programme to fundamentally alter the way in which the organisation operates. Corporate communication can ease the pain of change, aiding organisations in times of flux (Van der Waldt, 2004). Of the eight steps essential in a change programme, Kotter (1995: 59, 60) says two are concerned with the way in which the organisation informs the workforce about what is happening: one is *'creating a vision'* and the second is *'communicating the vision'*. Omitting either of these is likely to inhibit the success of the programme and possibly lead to failure. Without consistent, accurate communication, it is probable that individuals will interpret the change, and the need for change, in different ways – possibly leading to mixed and conflicting messages. Even the fact that some managers appear not to know what is going on, while others are thinking divergently not convergently, will send its own signals to the workforce. Where change occurs and the employees are left in ignorance, this has a debilitating effect on morale and can lead to rumour, mistrust and stress, with subsequent, negative, impact on productivity and labour turnover.

Ensuring that everyone knows about the change, why it is necessary and how it is to be implemented is essential because it helps them to understand not just what is required from them but why it is required. As Mintzberg (1973: 180) said: 'Managers must be able to communicate easily and efficiently and they must share a vision of the direction in which they wish to take the organisation. If they cannot agree with reasonable precision on these "plans" then they will pull in different directions and the team (or organisation) will break down.'

Table 4.2 Direct communication and information sharing, by sector of ownership, 1998 and 2004

| | % of workplaces | | | | | |
| | 1998 | | | 2004 | | |
	Private sector	Public sector	All	Private sector	Public sector	All
Direct communication						
Meetings with entire workforce or team briefings[a]	82	96	85	90	97	91
Systematic use of management chain	46	75	52	60	81	64
Regular newsletters	35	59	40	41	63	45
Noticeboards[b]	–	–	–	72	86	74
Email[b]	–	–	–	36	48	38
Intranet[b]	–	–	–	31	48	34
Suggestion schemes	29	35	31	30	30	30
Employee surveys[b]	–	–	–	37	66	42
Information disclosure over						
Investment plans	47	59	50	40	50	41
Financial position of workplace	56	82	62	51	76	55
Financial position of organisation[c]	66	67	66	51	53	51
Staffing plans	55	81	61	61	81	64

Base: All workplaces with ten or more employees.

Figures are weighted and based on responses from 2,178 managers in 1998 and 2,047 managers in 2004.

Notes

[a] Due to a number of changes in the wording of the questions in order to better identify meetings between senior managers and the workforce, and briefing groups, responses to each of these two types of meeting have been combined for comparison purposes with 1998. The single measure captures all kinds of meetings.
[b] No comparable data for 1998.
[c] Workplaces that were part of a larger organisation.

exercise

Working with someone else, look at the data in this table. Draw some conclusions about the ways in which methods of communication have changed from 1998 to 2004.

Change by its very nature imposes a different set of criteria on a situation – the processes for dealing with it may be similar but the content of the change programme will be unique. Each person will therefore need a thorough knowledge of the particular change to be implemented; the reasons why it is necessary; sensitivity to the ways in which such change may be received by those affected; and an awareness of the impact that it may have on the existing organisational culture.

Communication in practice

The managerial styles used by organisations to communicate change vary: from the *traditional* top-down and lateral flow of information throughout the organisation; through that of a more *integrative* approach where the workforce is consulted; to that of a *partnership* approach where employees not only offer suggestions as to what might happen, but are party to the decision making. Some organisations deliberately foster bottom-upwards communication channels so that employees may influence future change processes. This can range from simple suggestion schemes to more elaborate employee opinion surveys. DHL use a suggestion scheme and ensure that it works by giving publicity to those suggestions that are implemented and result in change. British Telecom has a sophisticated annual employee survey programme, *Care*, which influences the way in which the company develops and interacts with its workforce.

None of these communication styles is mutually exclusive and the same organisation may use a number of methods depending on the type and urgency of the change. These patterns of communication may be linked to Likert's (1961) descriptions of managerial styles, although his work has been criticised because it does not allow for gradations in style and differences between managers within the same organisation – see the box below.

Likert's research depicted four types of management system

- **System one** – authoritarian and exploitative, centralised decision making, downward communication, high levels of mistrust, low productivity
- **System two** – authoritarian and benevolent, major decision making centralised, management condescension towards those below them in the hierarchy, downward communication
- **System three** – consultative policy made at the top of the organisation, some decisions made lower down communication flows up and down, higher levels of trust
- **System four** – participatory goal setting, joint evaluation, unrestricted communication flows in all directions, high levels of trust, high productivity.

(Source: Andrews and Baird, 1995: 37)

The communication approach that is top down is not always exploitative as Likert suggests, but is frequently used when change has to be implemented quickly and the organisation has little choice in the direction it has to take. For example, following statutory ruling, the large US-based telecommunications company Bell adjusted its processes by implementing around 2,000 changes in the way it operated. There was no consultation with the workforce and the flow of information was top down, explaining the changes needed and instructing those in the organisation how to implement them.

A more integrated approach was taken by the energy section of Rolls-Royce when it introduced a change programme, *Better performance faster*. The company cascaded information about improvements together with new objectives down through

the organisation using 'champions', newsletters, face to face briefings, roadshows, etc. When things went well they were 'publicly celebrated'. The union representatives were consulted about the changes throughout the process and, at an individual level, once the change process was under way, a formal improvement scheme was launched. This enabled employees to submit their ideas and suggestions about how to change things.

Similarly when the supermarket Asda was acquired by Wal-Mart, it needed to change its systems to align them with the parent company. A change programme, *Breakthrough*, was introduced. This was, in the main, top down, including monthly newspapers and monthly videos shown at briefings, backed up by bulletins on in-store noticeboards. However, the process included regular listening groups to give employees the opportunity to express their feelings about the changes and to suggest further improvements.

Vertex Data Science and TXU Energi introduced more of a partnership approach when they initiated a huge change to make one core UK brand dealing with customer relationships. Initially, workshops, videos and training covered large numbers of staff to inform them of the nature and purpose of the changes. The workshops were interactive and participative, and some of the changes suggested by the employees were subsequently incorporated into the new processes: for example, face to face direct communication at the workshops resulted in suggestions to ease workloads. These were adopted: staff numbers were increased and sufficient time was allocated for tasks to be completed to a higher standard. In a similar way, Suffolk County Council has widened its communications channels with its workforce; not only does it use direct communication with employees and indirect communication via trade unions, it has introduced 45 'change champions' in an attempt to 'improve ways of involving and communicating with employees and to create a corporate culture' (Employers' Organisation for Local Authorities, 2001). These change agents are both reactive and proactive, facilitating employee discussion groups and involving employees in the processes of change.

Communication, power and managerial style

The position that an individual holds within an organisation gives them access to a lot, a little or some knowledge. The degree to which they decide to *share* or *withhold* that information from colleagues may strengthen or weaken their position within the organisation. Managerial style is important here because it will dictate the amount of information released and the way it is presented. An *authoritative* manager will cascade the minimum amount of information without discussion. A *participative* manager, on the other hand, is more likely to share information and engage colleagues in problem solving. However, Argyris (1994) made the point that where management endeavours to improve effectiveness by involving employees with initiatives such as attitude surveys and 360° feedback, it allows anonymous criticism without the communicator taking any responsibility for putting things right. This subtly creates a situation where management is seen to be the source of any problems and is therefore morally responsible for fixing them. Such a situation reinforces the power of management and the subordination of the workforce.

Where communication is controlled by one person who gathers and then transmits the message, they are called a *gatekeeper*. Harada (2003) argues that such a person often 'transforms' such knowledge before passing it on. The role of the gatekeeper, then, is not merely to transmit information; it also concerns receiving and interpreting the message. As a consequence, it is possible for messages/ knowledge to be presented or withheld in a way that may have political advantages for the gatekeeper that may not be in the best interests of the organisation. The CEO of Pan Pharmaceuticals withheld and manipulated information in this way.

In 2003, Pan Pharmaceuticals, Australia's largest contract manufacturer of complementary medicines, had to recall travel sickness and vitamin products after a number of people had become ill. It was apparent that Chief Executive Jim Selim's management style was less than inclusive. All faxes and letters, regardless of to whom they were addressed, went to him and a year later the Australian Court heard how he deliberately kept board members in the dark, deliberately playing down incidents of sickness and misreporting/falsifying test results.

There are a number of reasons why those in positions of power may choose not to pass on information:

◆ It may not occur to them to do so;
◆ They may regard it as an unwarranted dissolution of their power;
◆ They may be afraid that competitors will gain access to sensitive material;
◆ They may see it as relevant only to those at certain levels;
◆ They may not have the time;
◆ They may want to deliberately mislead their colleagues.

Where information is deliberately withheld, or only partial information is disseminated in order to maintain a position of power, then such dysfunctional behaviour will lead to high levels of mistrust. It also tends to perpetuate similar behaviour in others who become aware of their own positions and often mistakenly believe that the control of information is the best way in which to remain secure.

However, power may no longer be so easily acquired in this way, because of increasing access to knowledge via the Internet and the intranet.

Internal communication strategies

Organisations need to clearly demonstrate what they are doing, why they are doing it and how their employees fit into this picture. If this is done in a piecemeal, *ad hoc* way, then it leads to confusion, mixed messages, lack of clarity, poor motivation and a proliferation of rumour. The 'grapevine' can only exist in a communications vacuum.

The fundamental thrust behind a communications strategy is:

◆ Determine how communication will influence the organisation;
◆ Allocate appropriate resources for this to occur;
◆ Review the results.

Cochrane (1997: 28) points out that, 'a company's communication strategy needs to be derived from and intrinsically linked to the overall business goals for the organisation'.

Communications strategies need to:

- Identify which messages need to be delivered;
- Identify the purposes of the messages, e.g. to inform, to clarify, to instruct, to praise, to persuade;
- Identify the target groups for these messages and whether or not the message has to be tailored to suit the needs of different audiences;
- Introduce a system that is capable of rapidly conveying urgent information to all those who need it;
- Address the ways in which consistency is to be achieved – in particular to ensure consistency between information given to external and internal sources and between different groups within the organisation;
- Establish appropriate timescales – linked to long- and short- term objectives;
- Provide for a way of regularly evaluating the effectiveness of the communication process;
- Ensure that there are feedback loops, so that the flow of information is upward as well as downward;
- Provide robust knowledge-sharing processes, so that work is not unnecessarily duplicated;
- Institute regular communications audits;
- Establish effective communication channels for employees that go from recruitment and induction through to redeployment and retirement;
- Ensure that information sources are always up to date;
- Provide appropriate training (e.g. this could range from how to understand financial information to improving customer care or running effective team meetings);
- Endeavour to identify the intended and unintended consequences of the messages that are being disseminated.

United Utilities found to its cost that just cascading information down to employees was insufficient; its vision did not relate to the reality that the employees perceived. In 1995, when North West Water bought Norweb Plc and became United Utilities, an enormous amount of effort went into communicating with the workforce to let them know what was going on, how the company saw the future and how the changes would impact on the employees, particularly in terms of job security. To this end the company invested in promotional videos, briefing packs and newsletters. But the follow-up employee attitude surveys depicted a demoralised, under-informed, workforce. Clearly the strategy was not working and needed a rethink. It was apparent from an evaluation of the impact of the strategy that the communication methods that worked best were those where there had been face to face delivery direct to employees. A new strategy was developed, to be:

- Based around a local, decentralised method of delivery;
- Clear, directional and with a clear set of actions;
- Measurable;
- Targeted towards different groups;

- Co-ordinated so that it linked internal and external communications, ensuring messages were consistent;
- Designed to generate team participation.

Embracing all of the above, communication strategies became focused around local workplaces and were not *perceived* as coming from head office. The success of the strategy was dependant on identifying key individuals within each communication channel, and training them in communication methods, stressing the relationship between the communicator and receiver. Practices such as regular meetings, with agendas, action points and records, became the norm. The way in which communication was handled became part of the culture of the organisation and United Utilities says it has led directly to higher levels of performance and employee satisfaction, besides having a direct effect on the reputation and success of the organisation.

Imagine that you are working on a new concise 'values statement' for Warbings and would like this to use no more than 35 words. However as you want to include the company's purpose, product type, values, customers and employees, this isn't as easy as it sounds.

Write a draft statement, then ask someone else to analyse it making a list of the strengths and weaknesses. Does it:

- Appear to be clear and unambiguous?
- Communicate what you had intended it to?
- Miss out vital information?

Discuss the analysis.

Summary

Communication is a process whereby individuals and groups share information, ideas and opinions with others in a variety of ways, to ensure that meaning, values and information are transferred. This chapter has described the functions and processes of communication within an organisational context: it examined the impact that different managerial styles have on the ways and means of transmitting and receiving information and knowledge. The interrelationship between culture and communication was discussed and, in particular, the importance of the medium for communicating messages was examined. The impact that communication procedures will have on different change programmes was explored. Finally, the development and implementation of communication strategies was linked to business goals.

Review Questions

You may wish to attempt the following as practice examination style questions.

4.1   Why is accurate and appropriate communication important within organisations?

4.2   List six different ways of transmitting information and say how they would be best used.

4.3   What would you include in a communications strategy, and why?

4.4   Describe why you think communication *skills* are important within the workplace.

4.5   How would you determine whether or not a communication has been successful?

References

Adams, J.W. (2002). *US Expatriate Handbook: Guide to Living and Working Abroad*, at: www.us-expatriate-handbook.com/note.htm.

Andrews, P.H. and Baird J.E., Jnr. (1995). *Communication for Business and the Professions*, 6th edition, Madison, WI: Brown and Benchmark.

Argyris, C. (1994). Good communication that blocks learning, *Harvard Business Review*, July/August, p. 77.

Asif, S. and Sargent, A. (2000). Modeling internal communications in the financial services sector, *European Journal of Marketing*, Vol. 34, No. 3/4, pp. 299–318.

Clampitt, P.G. (1991). *Communicating for Managerial Effectiveness*, Thousand Oaks, CA: Sage.

Cochrane, L. (1997). *Influencing Communication: A practitioner's Guide to Internal Communication Consultancy*, London: Industrial Society.

Department for Trade and Industry (2004). Compendium of regulatory impact assessments, *Employment Relations Research Series* No. 41, Employment Market Analysis and Research, April.

Employers' Organisation for Local Authorities (2001) at: www.lg-employers.gov.uk/ relations/involvement/suffolk.html.

Etheridge, L. (2005). Back to basics, *Personnel Today*, 7 June.

Fourboul, C.V. and Bournois, F. (1999). Strategic communication with employees in large European companies: a typology, *European Management Journal*, Vol. 17, No. 2, pp. 204–217.

Galbraith, J. (1973). *Designing Complex Organisations*, London: Addison-Wesley.

Galbraith, J. (1977). *Organisation Design*, London: Addison-Wesley.

Gilbert, G.N. and Mulkay, M. (1984). *Opening Pandora's Box: A Sociological Analysis of Scientists' Discourse*, Cambridge: Cambridge University Press.

Grell, M. and Sisson, K. (2005). Has consultation's time come? Policy Paper No. 2 June, ACAS.

Hall, S. (1997). *Introduction to Representation: Cultural Representations and Signifying Practices*, Buckingham: Open University Press.

Harada, T. (2003). Three steps in knowledge communication: the emergence of knowledge transformers, *Research Policy*, Vol. 32, pp. 1737–1751.

Harkness, J. (2000). Measuring the effectiveness of change – the role of internal communication in change management, *Journal of Change Management*, Vol. 1, No. 1, pp. 66–73.

Heron, J. (1975). *A Six Category Intervention Analysis: Human Potential Research Project*, Guildford: University of Surrey.

Kersley, B., Alpin, C., Forth, J., Bryson, A., Bewley, H., Dix, G. and Oxenbridge, S. (2005). Inside the workplace: first findings from the 2004 Workplace Employment Relations Survey (WERS), at: www.dti.gov.uk/er/ insideWPfinalwebJune.pdf.

Kotter, J. (1995). Leading change: why transformation efforts fail, *Harvard Business Review*, March–April.

Kotter, J. (1996). *Leading Change*, Boston, MA: Harvard Business School Press.

Leavin, H.J. (1972). *Managerial Psychology*, 3rd edition, Chicago: University of Chicago Press.

Lickert, R. (1961). *New Patterns of Management*, New York: McGraw-Hill.

Mintzberg, H. (1973). *The Nature of Managerial Work*, New York: Harper and Row.

Oliver, S. (1997). *Corporate Communication Principles, Techniques and Strategies*, London: Kogan Page.

Perlmutter, H.V. (1969). The tortuous evolution of the multinational corporation, *Columbia Journal of World Business*, Vol. 4, pp. 9–18.

Thomas, D. (2005). Poor communication makes UK workers less productive, *Personnel Today*, 6 April.

Van der Waldt, De la Ray (2004). Towards corporate communication excellence in a changing environment, *Problems and Perspectives in Management*, Vol. 3, pp. 134–144.

Wenburg, J. and Wilmot, W. (1973). *The Personal Communication Process*, Chichester: Wiley.

Further Reading

Brown, A.D. and Starkey, K. (1994). The effect of organisational culture on communication and information, *Journal of Management Studies*, Vol. 31, No. 6, pp. 807–828.

Gudykunst, W.B. and Kim, Y.Y. (1997). *Communicating with Strangers and Approach to Intercultural Communication*, 3rd edition, Boston: McGraw-Hill.

Guirdham, M. (2002). *Interactive Behaviour at Work*, 3rd edition, London: FT/Prentice Hall (particularly Chapter 7).

Guirdham, M. (2005). *Communicating Across Cultures at Work*, 2nd edition, Basingstoke: Palgrave Macmillan.

Hargie, O. (2004). *Communication Skills for Effective Management*, Basingstoke: Palgrave Macmillan.

Reynolds S. and Valentine, D. (2003), *Guide to Cross-Cultural Communication*, London: Pearson.

Scoble, R. and Israel, S. (2006). *Naked Conversations: How Blogs are Changing the Way Businesses Talk with Customers*, Hungry Minds Inc.

Stanton, N. (2003). *Mastering Communication*, 4th edition, Palgrave Master Series, London: Palgrave MacMillan.

Verderber, K.S., Verderber, R.F. and Berryman-Fink, C. (2006). *Interpersonal Communication Concepts, Skills, and Contexts*, 11th edition, Oxford: Oxford University Press.

Weaver, W. and Shannon, C.E. (1949). *The Mathematical Theory of Communication*, Illinois: University of Illinois Press.

Zorn, M.T. and Violanti, M.T. (1996). Communication abilities and individual achievement in organisations, *Management Communication Quarterly*, Vol. 10, No. 2, pp. 139–167.

Useful Websites

web.cba.neu.edu – is particularly useful for students wanting to look up information about presentations, communication, teamwork and interpersonal skills. The content changes periodically, so some searching of the site may be necessary

www.mindtools.com/CommSkll/Cross-Cultural-communication.htm – offers information about cross-cultural communication, with specific relevance to those working in business organisations

www.acas.org.uk/index.aspx?articleid=674 – Students will find this booklet, intended to help and inform those involved in or affected by the processes of employee communications and consultation, helpful

Appendix

Answers to computer jargon quiz, page 67

cookie – this device enables some web pages to 'remember' your address from your visits to a site – for example, an online shopping site may use a cookie to remember which items you've placed in your online shopping basket

gigabytes – refers to a large amount of disk space

hacker – someone who illegally gains entry into your computer

Javascript – a computer programming language

jpeg – this is a compressed picture file

megabytes – the amount of disk space on a computer; sometimes it is used to measure the amount of memory a computer has

PDF – this stands for 'portable document format', which means the file is formatted in such a way that it can be read on any PC

spyware – is unwanted software that collects personal information about you and your computer use, typically without your consent, and then passes it to another

Trojan horse – following the Greek myth, this is a virus disguised as an innocent program

worm – this is a virus that continually reproduces itself until it fills all of the storage space on a drive or network

CHAPTER 5

Interpersonal Communication at Work

By Angela Mansi

Chapter outline

This is the second chapter dealing with this important topic. Whereas the previous chapter focused on the *processes* of communication, this time we will look at the *psychological aspects*, examining the importance of verbal and non-verbal communication, explaining the links between communication and personality type, culture and gender. In particular, some psychological models of communication will be described and we will examine the impact that personality differences and individual perceptions may have on communication and the impact that these will have on organisational effectiveness.

Learning outcomes

By the end of this chapter, you should be able to:

◆ Define the concept of communication;

◆ Explain effective communication styles;

◆ Outline psychological theory underpinning communication at work;

◆ Describe the adverse effects of ineffective communication;

◆ Illustrate the problems of poor communication;

◆ Demonstrate the benefits of active listening skills;

◆ Summarise the strategies for managing effective communication.

Introduction

Communication is one of the fundamental aspects of effective HR. Indeed, a key initial aim of human resource management (HRM) was 'training in interpersonal skills in order to influence, motivate and lead' (Holloway, 1992). The principle of HRM 'draws attention to the importance of the social aspects of organisation in general and the connection between communication and consultation between management and workforce' (Blyton and Turnbull, 1998). This is seen to enhance individual commitment, give greater job satisfaction, and reduce absence and turnover. Moreover, 'improved communication also affords management a greater opportunity to dispel rumours, correct "misunderstandings" and get its message across' (ibid., p. 227).

Communication and the organisation

Clear communication at the individual, group or organisational level ensures that people feel they belong and that they are included in organisational processes. Nothing arouses resentment more, or causes rumours so much, as a lack of clear information, particularly at times of change. During periods of change people feel frightened, left out, disenfranchised and threatened. It is imperative that communication at these times is functioning at its best; it must be regular, clear and inclusive.

There are many ways in which communication can be mismanaged; one way is through the model of information flow used by the organisation. Does information flow freely to all employees? Is all information filtered through one individual to all other departments? Does everyone communicate to each other or only different sections of the company? These need to be considered when planning how information is distributed to others, and how effective it will be. Hierarchical models filter information downwards so that it can often be distorted *en route*. Other models are so rigid that there is no upward flow of information, and management does not hear what the majority of the workforce is saying. Some models encourage a democratic method, whereby each employee is asked to contribute and disseminate information. This has two effects: primarily people feel involved and listened to, but more importantly, there is a plethora of information which can cause confusion and distortion, depending on individual perceptions of the information heard.

Personality differences and interpersonal and communication styles

Working with other people can often by quite stressful: we are placed in a group with strangers and expected not only to work efficiently as a team, but to understand and engage with each other. Needless to say, this gives rise to the potential for conflict due to communication style alone. Different personality types have styles of communicating that may confuse or even annoy others and can add to stress at work. Psychometric tests are increasingly used by organisations in an attempt to fit the right person to the job, the group and the corporate climate. They seek to measure, and assess, individual differences and one key individual personality difference is how we relate to others in terms of communication styles.

The Myers–Briggs Personality Type Indicator (MBTI©), Cattell's 16PF, the NEO-5 factor model (Costa and McCrae, 1992) and the Hogan Personality Inventory (HPI) are all tests that seek to measure a key component of communication, namely *interpersonal skills*. Seen variously as *team spirited*, *agreeableness*, *openness*, *friendliness* and *ability to share with others*, this will determine how someone is likely to relate to others in terms of their individual personality style.

For instance, if someone is an extrovert, based on Jungian psychology they are likely to respond to the external world more easily, share information more readily and engage with others more quickly than an introvert. Introverts are more reflective and thoughtful and take time to decide whether to engage in a conversation with others without knowing them very well. This has implications in the workplace, where extroverts might see introverts as being rather detached and cold and not responding as quickly as they would like, whereas introverts can perceive extroverts to be loud, noisy, too quick to add an opinion and overly talkative.

There are differences in the way we collect and pass on information. People who are attracted by the details of a project will prefer concrete information and evidence-based work which focuses on the minutiae that the work requires. They will prefer the data they gather with their senses (sight, smell, touch, hearing and sound). This will conflict with those who prefer to see the big picture, who grasp abstract concepts, overriding ideas of how things *could* look, rather than how they are now.

Further differences are seen in those who make decisions rationally or who base judgements on their own emotional values. These people are known, according to Jungian typology as 'Thinkers' or 'Feelers'. Feelers will make decisions based on their reactions to others; whether they like that person or not; and how much their values are in accord. Thinkers will ignore such issues, and use objective rational decision-making processes. There is often antipathy, as feelers see thinkers as being hard and uncaring, whereas thinkers see feelers as sentimental and too subjective to make fair decisions.

The MBTI© measures an aspect of personality which relates to how individuals plan and organise their time; how structured they like their lives to be. One particular area of discord is between those who plan ahead and schedule their lives according to quite specific timeframes and those who live for the moment and dislike committing to a deadline or planning too far ahead in case they feel trapped (Perceivers). This is probably the major cause of conflict at work between individual personality styles in terms of communication. Judgers like to know what they are doing several months ahead: they schedule, plan, organise and put into their diaries all their commitments and projects. They live in the future. They are highly reliable and very time conscious. Perceivers, while often seen as more fun, are considered to be less reliable as they can come across as 'scatty', are always late, have no idea of the importance of deadlines, and live very much in the moment. While this is acceptable in a social setting, at work it can significantly affect communications between colleagues, and cause confusion and resentment during projects.

Transactional analysis and communication

> 'Interpretation [in communication] is affected by both our own personality and other people.'
>
> (Berne, 1964)

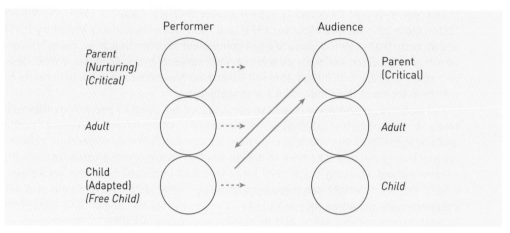

Figure 5.1 Parent–child relationships

Much research has been carried out on personality styles and communication at work. Berne (1964) and Harris (1969) found that interpersonal communication relates directly to personality type. They saw personality as having three parts: the parent, the adult and the child (see Figure 5.1). It was the interaction between these parts with other people that would determine the qualities of the relationships and the social interaction between them. For instance, if a manager is in the parent mode (P), then her personality style will cause resentment and often result in childish reactions from the employee, putting them into the child position (C), but the employee expects to be treated like an adult (A).

The ideal scenario would be for both people to communicate on the adult level, (A–A), characterised by rationality, objectivity and mutual respect and consideration. If someone talks to us in their parent role, being judgemental and moralising, fussing, criticising or micro-managing, then, Berne argues, we will be placed in the 'child' role and react accordingly. Conversely, if someone reacts as a child, we unconsciously go into our parent mode, and start to treat them like a child, which perpetuates the behaviour. Our patterns of reactions will depend on our own personality traits and which dark sides we manifest when we revert to child-like reactions.

So, instead of communicating on the basis of respect and mutuality, there is a mismatch of communication styles, which can often result in conflict, and feelings of resentment. Du Brin (1990) argued that where the styles are complementary, then the interpersonal reactions will work well.

One way organisations are addressing the problems of communication in the workplace is to ensure that developmental training includes team-building exercises, and that each person learns to understand the differences of their colleagues. Awareness of other people's personality types and styles of communicating will help with our perception of the way they communicate and allows for better working relationships.

Verbal and non-verbal communication

Communication is the symbolic interaction by which humans relate to each other (Smith, 1973) and includes more than just language. Verbal communication has various visual and auditory clues to clarify what the speaker is saying and there is, arguably, less of a problem in the transfer of information. Non-verbal communication can convey just as much, but may often be misinterpreted, hence the number of books on body language and its meaning. Non-verbal communication comprises facial expression, eye movements, the proximity of the two people, the attention given, the body language and the way they listen. People wrongly apply all sorts of misinterpretations to what are perceived non-verbal cues, when in fact the person scratching their nose might just have an itch (Furnham, 1997). That is why it is so important to clarify what is being said, to ensure that what the person meant is conveyed in as clear a way as possible.

When British Airways trains its cabin crew in safety and emergency procedures, they teach them a four-letter acronym – NITS (1995):

> N = nature of the emergency
> I = intention of the captain
> T = timescale of operation
> S = special instructions (i.e. are they just about to ditch in the Atlantic)

NITS is vital in ensuring clarity of information in an emergency situation on board the aircraft. The captain outlines all of the above and the crew are trained to repeat it back in exact fashion, to ensure they have understood, and that the captain *knows* they have understood it. This strategy is actually something that everyone could use for ensuring clarity of information when working in a stressful environment. When we are stressed, we tend to hear only key words and miss the overall content of a message, so asking people to repeat back instructions will help overcome this problem.

Indeed, something similar is already used in counselling and is seen in the active listening skill of paraphrasing, whereby the counsellor periodically summarises all that the client has said, but in their own words, to let the client know that:

- they have been following their story;

- they have understood.

Communication and cultural differences

Anything that helps us to understand and accept new information from others is effective communication, a lack of which can result in not only conflict at work but embarrassment elsewhere. A recent advertisement for HSBC proclaims that, despite their international reach, they are 'the local bank', able to understand local customs. What this shows is that communication depends not just on what is said; it also relies on individual understanding, correct interpretation and relevant context. The issue here is that communication only works if the recipient *understands* what is being conveyed.

Reassuringly, there are some non-verbal communication signals that are understood in every culture. Ekman (1980) spent many years cataloguing human expressions and found that there were seven universal facial emotional expressions which were recognised by all cultures. These seven emotions, which we all show on our faces and find it very hard to conceal, are:

◆ Anger
◆ Sadness
◆ Surprise
◆ Fear
◆ Enjoyment
◆ Disgust
◆ Contempt

However, other expressions of how we feel, such as in the HSBC advert, are culturally specific, which has implications for interpretation of meanings, and especially our individual perception.

The universal basis for emotional expression is now considered a 'pan-cultural aspect of psychological functioning' (Matsumoto, 2001). However, people will modify their expression in order to accord with their cultural norms. These norms, which Ekman (1980) called *cultural display rules*, indicate how much and how often an emotion is to be communicated, depending on the social circumstances.

Using emotional expression to convey a message is a psychological strategy which politicians use on a frequent basis. However, communication in this way is not limited to the world of politics. Customer service staff also need to convey to customers emotions they might not otherwise feel. This is called emotional labour; people are expected, as part of their role, to demonstrate an emotional state to others. Airline crew provide a good example of this; despite feeling tired, homesick, jet-lagged and possibly irritated with passengers, they are expected to be pleased to see passengers and be willing to help them, at all times. They are expected not only to smile at everyone who boards the aircraft but also 'to hold that smile for the next ten hours'.

Clearly, not all signs of communication are as they appear. The ambiguity of a smile, as a sign of communicating friendliness, is highlighted in a study by Matsumoto and Kudoh (1993), who found that it can also be used to mask emotions. Their study highlighted, also, the differences between cultures in communication styles. They showed that there is a wide gulf in how different cultures express emotions. One study reported that when viewing an unpleasant video with shocking scenes, Japanese men smiled significantly more often than American men, in order to cover their responses. A later study showed that Americans also rate smiling people as more intelligent than do the Japanese, highlighting the point that while there are universal ways to express ourselves, the communication between cultures can very easily be misconstrued.

Individual perception in communication

The manner in which we interpret verbal or behavioural communications is based on our individual perceptions and prejudices, which in turn affect our responses. Information is modified, not only by other people's perception but also by our own. We adjust what we are saying in order to sound less direct, threatening or judgemental. We want to appear more accepting, agreeable and pleasing to others. This gentle distortion means that the message we often convey is not what we really mean. We are then surprised when our message has not reached its target. Another problem is that we often hear what we want to hear, rather than what has been said or intended.

Accompanying the style of communication, we use facial expressions, tone of voice, gestures and postures which all affect the way we are heard. Some social psychologists have argued that all behaviour is communication (Miell and Dallos, 1998). If all behaviour communicates something to us, and our perceptions are coloured by our own biases, then we are prone to make judgements based on erroneous and biased perceptions. Indeed, 'all communication is coloured by perceptions of reality and if perceptions are built upon stereotypes, then communication is affected' (Smith 1973: 50). This can result in the 'horns and halo' effect, which means that, within the first few seconds of meeting a stranger, we can develop perceptions of them. This will certainly colour our communications.

Think back to the last time you were interviewed. During the first few minutes of meeting them, how did you feel about the interviewer? Why?

Now think about someone else, whom you later described as being 'Okay, once you get to know them'. What was it about them that caused you to feel there was a mismatch between what they said, and how they said it?

Communication and gender differences

'The single biggest problem in communication is the illusion that it has taken place.'

(George Bernard Shaw)

We could be forgiven for thinking that men and women do indeed come from different planets when trying to communicate with each other! Research has shown that there is a clear difference in the way that men and women communicate and when this is carried into the workplace, clashes can often occur or misinterpretations made.

Think of a time when the sex of the person you were talking to had an effect on the way in which you communicated with them.

What do you think you would have done differently had the person been of the opposite sex?

Why did you reach this conclusion?

Tannen (1986) found that misunderstandings between men and women in the workplace, due to differences in communication styles, were labelled as 'bad intentions, lack of ability, poor character and other intrapersonal qualities' *on the part of the women*. Furthermore, when styles are very different, 'it is usually women who are told to change' (Tannen, 1990: 15). She cites the example of how women request or suggest, rather than directly tell, and states that this is what causes confusion for others, who are not quite sure what is being asked. People also display different ways of communicating when trying to resolve conflict (Sheldon, 1990). Women tend to offer more listening responses such as 'mmm', 'yes' and 'okay', which indicate only that they are listening and following the conversation. Since men tend only to say 'yes' and 'okay' if they agree with the speaker, there is room for confusion. They think the woman is insincere, whereas the woman thinks she has been fully engaging in the conversation (Tannen, 1990).

Gender differences in communication styles begin early in life. Research shows that children as young as three years old show distinct differences in communication styles: ways of talking, different display dynamics in negotiating, influencing and causing conflict.

Women smile more; they laugh at other people's jokes, rather than make them; and they interrupt other people much less often than men do (Miell and Dallos, 1998). Women also apologise frequently when communicating with others. Tannen (1990) explains this as being a social convention and a way of asking for something in a polite manner. Men, however, see this as a sign of weakness or deference, and assume a mistake has been made.

Women also thank others much more than men; they see this as a way to maintain positive relationships and to show appreciation, without necessarily having received anything. And generally, they are more polite when asking for something. For example, a woman may ask, 'Would it be possible to have that report by Friday, please?', whereas a man might say, 'I need that report by Friday'. They are also seen to be more collegial and inclusive, asking others for their opinions more often as a way of building relationships. This again, if misinterpreted, is seen as someone who does not know their own mind and needs support in their decision making.

There may be a gap in understanding at times; a large study of senior managers in Fortune 250 companies said they wanted 'honest, straightforward communication' above all else in their interpersonal relationships (Peltier, 2001).

However, Hofstede (2001) found that the percentage of women managers and the presence of at least one woman in the top management team was positively correlated to openness in communication styles within the organisation. Research by Alimo-Metcalfe (2003) found that female managers valued individuals, showed empathy, communicated more openly, honestly and decisively and did not mind admitting their mistakes. Furthermore, she argued that in terms of organisational skills they showed good networking skills, focused effort, could build a shared vision internally and with external bodies, develop culture, facilitate change, and were participative and inclusive in their management style. This was confirmed by Hofstede's study, which found '. . . organizations with more women in management were found to have more open communication climates' (Hofstede, 2001: 13).

Conflict and other problems of communication

Communication problems arise when the number of people in the communication process is too large for clarity to be retained. Individual perceptions, lack of awareness, personality reactions to others, values and beliefs can all shape the process of *filtering* information, creating what is seen as 'incorrect, distorted or ambiguous messages' (McKenna, 2000: 410).

The larger the group, then, the greater the potential for discord and conflict through erroneous or distorted communication. This is seen clearly in groups which exceed a certain size. With seven–nine team members, the communication can be good; it is clear, members see each other regularly and know each other. More than seven–nine in a group can be detrimental to effective group functioning (Furnham, 1997). Should a manager find that she has a team greater than that number, then she would need to reduce the span of control by appointing two team leaders to oversee groups of a more manageable size.

Groups of between 12–18 members may experience only a very loose sense of cohesion; this is a communication vacuum, where 'the grapevine' is prevalent and misunderstandings frequently occur. When groups reach 18 plus, research shows that communication becomes unclear; rumours spread due to lack of direct information; hidden agendas develop; and resentment among members occurs due to lack of individual recognition (Furnham, 1997).

Smaller, more cohesive groups are more effective. The closer the group, then the tighter and more complex the communication that occurs. 'A single word, passed between members of an intimate group, in spite of its apparent vagueness and ambiguity, may constitute a far more precise communication than volumes of carefully prepared correspondence between two governments' (Sapir, 1931: 14).

Groupthink

Janis (1971) explained that *groupthink* is an absence of conflict, a 'mode of thinking that persons engage in when concurrence-seeking becomes so dominant in a cohesive in-group that it tends to override realistic appraisal of alternative courses of action' (p. 43). Examples of groupthink are the classic US military disasters at Vietnam, the Bay of Pigs and Pearl Harbor. Groupthink consists of a collective pattern of defensive avoidance, lack of vigilance, unwarranted optimisms, suppression of questioning and reliance on shared rationalisations (Janis, 1971). In a group, this results in an inability to accept or understand alternative views or criticism from external sources. This is seen as a threat to the overly cohesive group and impacts on rational decision making.

Interpersonal Skills

Poor interpersonal skills will almost definitely result in poor communication and may indicate someone who lacks emotional intelligence, empathy, openness and ability to relate well. One group that often needs development in this area is senior managers.

The communication skills of managers are particularly required when they need to give negative feedback. People often enjoy giving positive feedback but avoid direct, honest and constructive feedback when dealing with poor performance. People often do not know how to communicate in a way that addresses performance issues in a sensitive and direct manner. This is one reason why organisations sometimes use an external occupational psychologist or executive coach, who can give the feedback to staff on behalf of managers who lack the skills to do it themselves.

Very often managers are so busy they do not have time to listen; listening, however, is the key skill that facilitates excellent communication. Interestingly, as

Furnham and Taylor (2004) point out, senior managers have achieved their positions because they have demonstrated a facility for influencing, talking and impressing others. However, once they are promoted, opportunities to use these skills are often reduced, and they can therefore forget how to communicate well.

exercise

♦ Review the Warbings case study.

♦ Identify five separate examples of poor communication by managers.

♦ If you were the HR manager, what action would you take?

Active listening skills

Effective communication skills are 'essential tools for developing relationships and interacting' with others (Egan, 1994). One of the very best ways to communicate with someone is to just listen to them. Most of the time we are all just waiting for the person to finish speaking so that we can interject with our own opinions and comments. If we could learn to listen, actively and with attention, many conflicts at work would be minimised, and a great deal of interpersonal conflict would be resolved. Giving someone attention means to show respect for them and what they have to say. In turn, people feel appreciated and will usually reciprocate, allowing an open style of communication to occur.

The development of effective, active listening skills by HR professionals is a competency that will be useful in all areas of the workplace. Sometimes a willingness to disclose some personal information or appear vulnerable will facilitate trust, although clearly overuse of emotion in the workplace environment can be counter-productive. However, our facial expressions, voice quality and bodily postures will communicate far more than the actual words. Indeed, words contribute only 7 per cent to the impression of being liked or disliked; voice cues add 38 per cent; and facial expressions 55 per cent (Mehrabian, 1971).

Active listening skills include:

♦ Giving full attention to what is being said;

♦ Empathising with the speaker – try to see things from their point of view;

♦ Summarising what the person has told you, which clarifies this for both of you;

♦ Paraphrasing in your own words so you can demonstrate you are listening;

♦ Noting down key words only, so your attention is not diverted;

♦ Showing acknowledgement by non-verbal means during the conversation;

♦ Being open and honest;

♦ Not being afraid to say you don't know.

Gower (1987) added to this by stating the four basic rules for good communication:

Simplicity – *put things into plain language*
Brevity – *people can only remember so much at any given time*
Humanity – *try to engage with the person in a friendly, natural way*
Accuracy – *be clear in what you are saying*

Summary

As has been outlined above, good communication is the lifeblood of organisational effect-iveness and interactions with others. When handled well, communication can facilitate excellent functioning at all levels – individual, group and organisational. However commun-ication can often go wrong. Factors such as misunderstanding of what has been conveyed, perception and bias, interpersonal and individual personality styles, cultural and societal contexts and non-verbal cues all impact on what is received by the other person. Moreover, modern means of communication, such as emails and the pace of response, can alter not only the meaning but also the reception of the message by others lacking the non-verbal cues that moderate or support verbal and direct communication. Furthermore, the gender of the communicator has a significant impact on the way that communication occurs; men prefer direct, clear and simple communication whereas women generally tend to soften their language, to ask, smile and suggest more, often resulting in ambiguity at work and a mismatch of styles.

While the problems of communication are numerous, there are mechanisms for facilitating better understanding. Training in active listening skills such as paraphrasing, summarising, reflecting back to the other person what has been said; taking time before immediately replying to emails, trying to convey what the intention is directly without softening the message to the extent that the meaning is lost; being sensitive to the non-verbal cues we get from others in any interpersonal communication all aid clarity. Being sensitive is also key whenever dealing with issues of diversity, cultural differences and societal norms.

Review Questions

You may wish to attempt the following as practice examination style questions.

5.1 How do gender differences impact on the ways in which individuals communicate?

5.2 What is active listening? Make a list of the skills needed for this.

5.3 Describe how individual perceptions can influence communication for better or for worse. Why is this important within the workplace?

5.4 What is the psychological theory underpinning communication at work?

References

Alimo-Metcalfe, B. (2003). Leadership: a masculine past but a feminine future, paper presented at BPS Conference, Bournemouth, January.

Berne, E. (1964). *Games People Play: The Psychology of Human Relationships*, Harmondsworth: Penguin.

Blyton, P. and Turnbull, P. (1998). *The Dynamics of Employee Relations*, 2nd edition, Basingstoke: Macmillan.

British Airways (1995). *Safety and Emergency Procedures Manual*.

Costa, P.T. Jnr. and McCrae, R.R. (1992). Normal personality assessment in clinical practice: the NEO Personality Inventory, *Psychological Assessment*, Vol. 4, pp. 5–13.

Du Brin, A.J. (1990). *Winning Office Politics: Du Brin's Guide of the 90's*, Harmondsworth: Penguin.

Egan, G. (1994). *The Skilled Helper*, 5th edition, Pacific Grove, CA: Brookes Cole Publishing.

Ekman, P. (1980). *The Face of Man: Expressions of Universal Emotions in a New Guinea Village*, New York: Garland STPM Press.

Furnham, A. (1997). *The Psychology of Behaviour at Work: The Individual in the Organisation*, London: Psychology Press.

Furnham, A. and Taylor, J. (2004). *The Dark Side of Behaviour at Work*, Basingstoke: Palgrave.

Gower, Sir E. (1987). *The Complete Plain Words*, London: Penguin.

Harris, T.A. (1969). *I'm OK, You're OK*, London: Harper Collins.

Hofstede, G. (2001). *Culture's Consequences: Comparing Values, Behaviours, Institutions and Organizations Across Nations*, London: Sage.

Holloway, W. (1992). *Work Psychology and Organizational Behaviour: Managing the Individual at Work*, London: Sage.

Janis, I.L. (1971). Groupthink, in G.R. Miller and H.W. Simons (eds.) (1974) *Perspectives in Social Conflict*, Englewood Cliffs, NJ: Prentice Hall.

Matsumoto, D. (ed.) (2001). *The Handbook of Culture and Psychology*, Oxford: Oxford University Press.

Matsumoto, D. and Kudoh, T. (1993). American–Japanese cultural differences in attributions of personality based on smiles, *Journal of Nonverbal Behaviour*, Vol. 17, No. 4, pp. 231–243.

McKenna, E. (2000). *Business Psychology and Organisational Behaviour: A Student's Handbook*, 3rd edition, London: Psychology Press.

Mehrabian, A. (1971). *Silent Messages*, in G. Egan (1994) *The Skilled Helper*, 5th edition, Pacific Grove, CA: Brookes Cole Publishing.

Miell, D. and Dallos, R. (1998). *Social Interaction and Personal Relationships*, Thousand Oaks, CA: Sage Publications.

Peltier, B. (2001). *The Psychology of Executive Coaching*, London: Brunner-Routledge.

Sapir, E. (1931). Communication, *Encyclopacdia of the Social Sciences*, Vol. 4, pp. 78–81.

Sheldon, A. (1990). Pickle fights: gendered talk in pre-school disputes, in D. Tannen (1992) *You Just Don't Understand Me: Women and Men in Conversation*, London: Virago Press.

Smith, A.L. (1973). *Trans-racial Communication*, Englewood Cliffs, NJ: Prentice Hall.

Tannen, D. (1986). *That's Not What I Meant! How Conversation Style Makes or Breaks Relationships*, New York: Ballantine Books.

Tannen, D. (1990). You just don't understand me: women and men in conversation, in B. Peltier (2001) *The Psychology of Executive Coaching: Theory and Application*, Abingdon: Taylor and Francis.

Further Reading

Blackman, M.C. (2002). The employment interview via the telephone: are we sacrificing accurate personality judgments for cost efficiency?, *Journal of Research in Personality*, Vol. 36, No. 3, pp. 208–223.

Hargie, O. (ed.) (1996). *The Handbook of Communication Skills*, London: Routledge.

Hargie, O. and Dickson, D. (2003). *Skilled Interpersonal Communication: Research, Theory and Practice*, London: Routledge.

Leigh, A. and Maynard, M. (1993). *Perfect Communications*, London: Arrow Business.

Verderber, K.S., Verderber, R.F. and Berryman-Fink, C. (2006). *Interpersonal Communication Concepts, Skills, and Contexts*, 11th edition, Oxford: Oxford University Press.

Useful Websites

www.employer-employee.comm101.htm – useful communication tips for women at work

www.drnadig.com/listening.htm – Dr Larry Nadig's checklist for effective listening

www.gp-training.net/training/mentoring/egan.htm – explanation of Gerard Egan's skilled helper model, aimed particularly at GPs

CHAPTER 6

Knowledge Management

By Gill Sugden and Anton Bradburn

Chapter outline

This chapter introduces many of the theoretical concepts surrounding the area of knowledge management (KM) and the ways that it links to organisational learning. Readers may want to try to relate some of the ideas and examples to their own experience and to consider whether there are opportunities for development of KM activities at a local or an organisational level. Organisational systems, especially those relating to human resource management (HRM), need to provide active support for organisational knowledge. KM has to be embedded in organisations to have value and to be of benefit to them.

Learning outcomes

By the end of this chapter, you should be able to:

◆ Present a theoretical underpinning to key concepts in the KM field;

◆ Demonstrate the links between KM and the learning organisation;

◆ Consider the relationship between knowledge, intellectual capital (IC) and innovation in organisational contexts;

◆ Provide an overview of the various ways that information systems can support KM and organisational learning;

◆ Reflect on knowledge management at a personal and organisational level.

Introduction

Imagine it is the middle of the sixteenth century and you are living in Pisa, Italy. You are teaching at the University of Pisa and have been forging a career in plant science. The medicinal value of plants has been recognised for hundreds of years. But the critical barrier to disseminating this knowledge internationally has always centred on confusion and lack of agreement about identifying and naming plants. There are written descriptions and there are illustrations dating back 2,000 years, but this material is frequently unreliable because it is found to be subjective, inaccurate, and prone to errors and plagiarism. What is needed is a database of plant specimens to serve as a consistent and coherent point of reference. In your work on plants, your specimens often dry out while you are studying them. One day you realise that when plants dry out this preserves them, so you investigate the drying process and discover that it can be speeded up by pressing them. Collecting a range of plants at different stages of their growth and then pressing them, labelling them, storing them and being able to retrieve them whenever required, will enable you to build a systematic and unique archive for yourself. You now have some personal knowledge gained through a learning process, which no one else has. Would you distribute your personal knowledge by sharing it with others, or would you guard it jealously for reasons of your own? The answer to what the proto-botanist, Luca Ghini, decided is in this chapter.

Knowledge management in advanced economies

Now jump forward from the Italian Renaissance to the advanced economies of today. Land, labour and capital – the traditional inputs of industrial economies from which wealth could be created through manufacturing – are losing their importance. In post-industrial economies, knowledge is the new source of wealth. Stewart (2001) states that the earning power of manufacturing, producing and exporting tangible goods for the US economy has been overtaken by the production and exportation of knowledge. What we learn from this is that in knowledge economies, the IC residing in people is now of paramount importance: the way HRM is deployed to organisational knowledge can be a lever for organisational advantage.

Work and learning are often integral. Buckler (1998) defines learning as a process that results in changed behaviours in ways that lead to improved performance. Herbert (2000) points to knowledge being perishable so organisations must ensure that continual and preferably continuous learning occurs within the enterprise.

pause for thought	Why do you think knowledge is perishable?
	Can you think of an example of when knowledge has been lost?
	What was the impact?

Organisational learning is the process by which individuals, and whole organisations, develop and use their stock of knowledge. A learning organisation is one that both teaches and learns from itself continuously. The learning organisation can help with

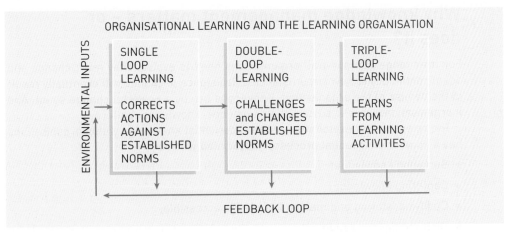

ORGANISATIONAL LEARNING AND THE LEARNING ORGANISATION

Figure 6.1 A triple-loop learning model

the turbulent environment within which modern businesses operate. A learning culture enables managers to meet the expectations of internal and external stakeholders. Harvey et al. (1998) provide a definition of a learning organisation deriving from Senge's *Fifth Discipline* (1990). They highlight several companies which have successfully become learning organisations, including Koch Industries, Ford, Skandia and National Semiconductor.

Harvey et al. (1998) identify three learning processes based on Argyris and Schon's (1978) model involving single-, double- and deutero- (or triple-) loop learning. This is illustrated in Figure 6.1. Herbert also cites Senge (1990) as a source of the term *learning organisation*. Drawing on Pedler et al. (1994) and Argyris and Schon (1978), Garrat (1986) discusses the phenomena further. In the deutero-learning state, an organisation is said to be capable of learning to learn. The single-, double- and deutero-loop model emphasises the continuous nature of learning within an organisational context. By subsequently applying that learning to the development of workforce competencies, it thereby transforms itself continuously. The concept of the learning organisation, and the extent to which such an organisation can actually exist in reality, is discussed further in Chapter 17 on Organisation Development.

In the Warbings case study, consider if there is evidence that it is a learning organisation.

 exercise

 W

Thinking of where you work, or of an organisation that you know: can you identify examples of single-, double- and triple-loop learning?

 pause for thought

Why knowledge management matters – or does it?

For their long-term survival, organisations need to evolve. They must change and adapt continually to new circumstances. Resistance to change will eventually result in the demise of the organisation. Knowledge can be a powerful change agent. And if organisations want to sustain their existence, knowledge matters.

The retention and exploitation of the experiential knowledge within organisations has a number of essential processes associated with it:

- Surfacing knowledge;
- Capturing knowledge;
- Codifying, storing and making knowledge accessible;
- Distributing knowledge;
- Leveraging knowledge;
- Measuring the value added from knowledge.

Let's return to our Italian scientist, Luca Ghini (1490–1566), a physician, botanist and teacher of medicine and herbalism. We can see that his experiential knowledge follows the first four of the six processes listed above. For us today, pressing plants as a method of preserving them seems obvious. But in those days, Ghini's solution was new. He had produced the first herbarium and according to Pavord (2005):

> '. . . the "dried garden", that Ghini pioneered, made it very much easier for scholars in different countries to agree on the correct identification and naming of plants. Drawings and paintings were good, but the real plants, if carefully pressed to preserve their essential characteristics, were even better. Everyone interested in plants quickly saw the advantages of Ghini's herbarium.'

Ghini was selfless and shared his personal knowledge by distributing it to a wider community of teachers, physicians and herbalists through personal contact, letters and publications. There is nothing to suggest Ghini ever considered ways of exploiting the commercial possibilities of his knowledge for personal gain, or of trying to measure its value.

Blumentitt and Johnston (1999) have proposed a framework in which knowledge is arranged according to its purposes so that there is:

- **Codifiable knowledge** – information;
- **Common knowledge** – routines and practices;
- **Social knowledge** – relationships and cultural matters;
- **Embodied knowledge** – experiential knowledge, embracing a lifetime's accumulation of skills, training and competencies.

Organisations need to manage knowledge effectively. This has led to the development of **knowledge management** (KM). Murray and Myers, of Cranfield School of Management, defined KM as, '. . . the collection of processes that govern the creation, dissemination, and utilisation of knowledge to fulfil organisational objectives' (1998: 14).

Allee (1997) started from the premise that knowledge represents a primary competitive tool. He states that survival depends on an organisation's ability to innovate and, to achieve this, knowledge is required to help it to learn, adjust and change. Allee offers a set of principles for KM practice. Information and communication technologies (ICT) are seen by Allee as supporting rather than driving KM. She mentions, in particular, corporate intranets, where self-directed learning is required.

Fundamental to the various threads of debate in the KM literature are discussions concerning the differences between data, information, knowledge and wisdom (Cropley, 1998). As they have different characteristics, it is possible to establish a clear boundary between them (Blumentitt and Johnston, 1999). Data may be regarded as a commodity because it is widespread and readily available.

Adding value to data

Value is added to data through attached meaning when they are *processed* into information and, in turn, information gains further value when it is *applied* in new contexts. This reuse, or recycling, is sometimes referred to as re-purposing. Re-purposing transforms information into enterprise-specific knowledge. Knowledge is also defined as information that experience, context, interpretation and reflection are added to by individuals so that it becomes a high value form of information (Davenport et al., 1998). Wisdom could be seen as knowledge employed within an ethical or values-based framework (Rowley, 2006).

Information can be retained within the organisation as organisational knowledge. Contextualised knowledge is regarded as the outcome, or product, of a learning process (Antonacopoulou, 1999; Bertels and Savage, 1999). Because it becomes owned by the organisation, such knowledge is 'sticky' in the sense that it is both localised and contextualised and therefore organisation-specific (Apostolou and Mentzas, 1999). It can be argued that organisational knowledge is socially constructed, because its added-value derives from an intra-organisational social processes of sharing.

Two forms of knowledge

There are two forms of knowledge. The first form may be labelled as domain knowledge, which can be replaced easily; the second is technical knowledge of how work is carried out and this is difficult to replace (Hildreth et al., 2000). Nonaka and Takeuchi (1995) refer to domain knowledge as *explicit* and to technical, or process, knowledge as *tacit*. Tacit knowledge is made up of experience related to work processes, which resides only within individuals. According to Platts and Yeung (2000), tacit knowledge is *knowledge in action*, indicating that tacit knowledge is that which has not been articulated, so distinguishing it from explicit knowledge, which is readily accessible from within the organisational domain.

So we can see that the knowledge base for the foundation of the organisation's core competency is composed of both explicit and tacit forms of knowledge. Tacit knowledge is embedded in the social tissue of the organisation's processes, dynamic routines and internal communication paths and provides an organisation-specific resource to sustain competitive advantage (Lei, 1997).

pause for thought

What examples of KM systems:

◆ do you regularly use?

◆ does your university regularly use?

What instances can you identify where your tacit knowledge helped you?

Why do you think some people are not prepared to share their knowledge?

exercise

W

Returning to the Warbings case study, which KM systems do you consider that the company has in operation and why have you reached this conclusion?

Organisational issues related to knowledge management

Knowledge as IC for investment and sustainable competitive advantage

Research with large UK service enterprises (Coakes et al., 2002) demonstrates that an organisational culture antagonistic towards KM is a barrier to creating value. Treating knowledge as a tangible asset allows for a value to be given to knowledge repositories. The Skandia organisation, for example, carries out an annual audit so that investors can value the business for its intellectual worth. Intellectual capital statements are intrinsic to KM, and valuations form part of the history of IC (Larsen et al., 1999). A series of Scandinavian case studies from Skandia, Ramboll, SparNord, Sparbanken and ABB demonstrate that there is no fixed model for this kind of asset accounting (Larsen et al., 1999; Van Buren, 1999).

Nine of the most frequently cited approaches in the literatures associated with KM and IC were reviewed (Coakes and Bradburn, 2005). These are shown in Table 6.1. Each of these has its advantages and disadvantages. There is no consensus about how to measure the value of such intangible assets. There are quantitative approaches, while others are primarily qualitative; still others take a blended approach.

One example of this blended approach, employing both quantitative and qualitative metrics, is a Danish company called Carl Bro (2001). This enterprise publishes an adjunct to its main annual report, which states that, 'The purpose of the Intellectual Capital Accounts is to measure the extent to which Carl Bro as a company has, and is developing, the qualifications for supplying Intelligent Solutions, and hence for ensuring future earnings.' The report explains that the company's IC accounting methods '. . . use words, numbers and images . . .' to measure how the company creates value for its various stakeholder groups.

Table 6.1 Approaches to valuing IC

Model	Attribution	Comment
Invisible balance sheet	Konrad Group (included Karl-Eric Sveiby)	Uses relative and qualitative measures
Intangible assets monitor	Karl-Eric Sveiby (1997)	Aims to measure intangible assets in a simple fashion
The balanced score card	Kaplan and Norton (1996)	Provides a means of linking an organisation's past with its present and its future
Economic value added	Introduced by New York consultants Stern Stewart	Complex and relies on historic cost rather than current valuation
The IC index		A so-called second generation practice whose purpose is to provide a comprehensive view of value creation in businesses in a single index
Technology broker		Claims to represent something of an advance on previous methodologies because it enables monetary value to be attributed to IC
Return on assets		Calculates the ratio of an organisation's average pre-tax earnings over a 3–5-year period. Has the advantage of being comparatively easy to apply and all necessary data are available in an organisation's historical financial records
Market capitalisation method		Often critiqued as a comparatively crude method because it measures an organisation's IC by simply subtracting its book value from its market value and assumes that the excess must be a market premium, which recognises the value of IC within the organisation
The direct intellectual capital method		Proceeds by identifying IC components within an organisation and then valuing them.

The growing importance of knowledge-based activities is recognised in the KM literature as an important source of innovation, particularly with those organisations specialising in knowledge-intensive business services (Miles et al., 2000). Intellectual property rights and KM strategies for innovative service firms differ from those of manufacturing companies, identifying some strategies employed by service firms to protect intellectual property and their core knowledge, namely: secrecy; short innovation cycles; making intangible products more tangible; and switching costs and entry barriers.

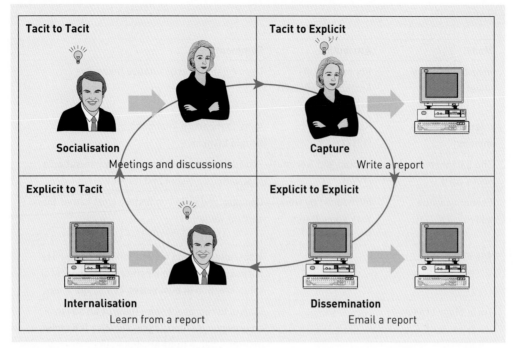

Figure 6.2 Means of converting knowledge
Source: Nonaka and Takeuchi (1995: 8)

While the potential value of tacit knowledge is widely recognised, there is a paradox in the inability of organisations to collect, store and harness the value of the experiences of their employees. Experience is seen as a fundamental form of knowledge and as such an integral part of the corporation's IC investment, which demands an effective KM system. Organisations should gather and share experience by applying techniques such as debriefing, mentoring and capturing knowledge in meetings, seminars and conferences. In the end, however, you cannot force people to part with their tacit knowledge (Geisler, 1999).

Figure 6.2 identifies a range of techniques that can be used for converting knowledge from tacit to explicit or from explicit to tacit.

KM tools

Blumentitt and Johnston (1999) state that knowledge can be created, captured and encouraged to flow around organisations. This can be facilitated by KM applications in the form of systems such as corporate intranets. Meanwhile, other investigators (McAdam and McCreedy, 1999) argue that knowledge is socially constructed and that recognising this phenomenon is critical to the continuous development of KM.

Effective KM contributes to the development of IC within organisations. IC is seen in the literature (Sullivan and Sullivan, 2000; Ordonez de Pablos, 2002; Zhou and Fink, 2003) as a combination of customer capital, organisational capital and human capital. Others (Bowonder and Miyake, 1999; Carneiro, 2000; Stewart, 2001)

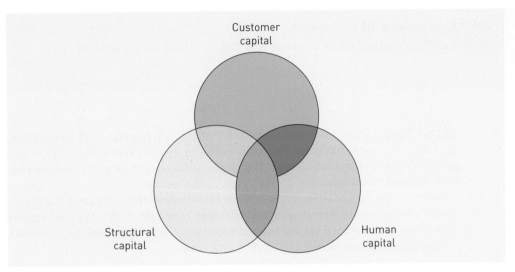

Figure 6.3 The three constituent elements of IC

argue that IC is a strategic issue, while KM is an operational issue. This means that intellectual capital is underpinned by knowledge management activities, while KM is driven by an organisation's strategic development of its intellectual capital.

Alternative approaches to surfacing and conserving tacit knowledge are linked to the role of tacit knowledge in IC's three constituent elements, which are human capital, customer capital and structural capital (see Figure 6.3).

Other writers, including Saint-Onge (1996), also consider the formation of tacit knowledge and the subsequent impact it can have on strategy development and implementation. Tacit knowledge must also be aligned to corporate and business strategies. In the Canadian Imperial Bank of Commerce, the Leadership Centre provides the organisation with systemic practices for the generation and renewal of IC. Saint-Onge (ibid.) suggests that tacit knowledge can be reshaped through participation in group sessions that draw attention to assumptions about coping with business, customers or employees. In this social process, the beliefs underlying these assumptions become transformed from tacit into explicit knowledge.

Darling (1996) also describes the Canadian Imperial Bank of Commerce as a learning organisation, before pointing out that a barrier to knowledge sharing may be the perceived threat to an individual's position in the organisation if they articulate their tacit knowledge.

Simmonds (2003) argues that attitudes are a function of beliefs and values. Fostering appropriate organisational values, attitudes, beliefs and expectations could enable a knowledge culture that might free an organisation from these mindsets. Others, like Blumentitt and Johnston (1999), discuss the advantages of corporate intranets and the use of a variety of software. While concurring with Blumentitt and Johnston, Darling (1996) additionally recommends internal websites, guides, templates and questionnaires. Darling also points to the importance for management of *walking the talk* to help transform the organisation and embed a knowledge culture within it.

What does 'walking the talk' mean?

How would you explain this to someone who had not heard the phrase before?

Lei (1997) argues that the knowledge base that lays the foundation of an organisation's core competency comprises easily replaced domain knowledge and the less easily replaced process knowledge. This easily replaced first form of knowledge has been labelled *fluid knowledge* (Coakes et al., 2003) because it is capable of flowing around an organisation. This can be achieved even more effectively when the organisation's social and technical systems are linked by means of ICT. We characterise Lei's less easily replaced second form of knowledge as *sticky knowledge*, because it is inseparable from knowing how work is processed.

Developments – the future of knowledge management and IC

Knowledge can generate organisational value through the processes of sharing and re-purposing.

Liedtka (1999) links effective communities of practice (CoPs) with competitive advantage. Businesses operating in a distributed international context secure advantage through virtual communities of practice linked by digital networks enabling them to deploy their knowledge to organisational goals. The US chemical business, Buckman Laboratories, is an example of how knowledge can be successfully leveraged through CoPs in this way for organisations to become faster and more innovative than their competitors (Graham and Pizzo, 1997).

From a study of 332 large service organisations in the UK (Coakes et al., 2004), an international charity illustrates how IC can be developed from KM to produce a range of benefits for end users. KM is concerned principally with surfacing, capturing and exploiting *sticky* knowledge, and motivating colleagues to share their experience and learning from projects. Central to the charity's KM function is a continuous concern for how IC can be stored and how it can be made accessible as widely as possible. *Fluid* knowledge is critically important to the communities of practice within the charity, and others linked to it from outside.

In the last six years, KM has become a way of working in this charity. There is a KM reference group lunchtime meeting every two months, where someone gives a prepared talk. On other occasions there may be a general discussion, during which different people will address different issues. Whatever *sticky* knowledge surfaces in these sessions is captured in real time and then posted on the charity's intranet. The discussions in these meetings, along with questions and interventions, are subsequently made available to multiple communities of practice. As a result, a local CoP has emerged, concerned with KM practices themselves.

The benefits of electronic networking enable the charity to collaborate much more closely with other like-minded charities. Policy initiatives are fed from intra-agency and inter-agency collaborations directly to a team, whose role is to lobby the World

Bank, the International Monetary Fund and the United Nations. KM and its enabling technologies are providing greater opportunities for collaboration and interaction between different countries to address issues and problems important to them.

A multinational CoP has emerged out of this charity's HIV/AIDS strategy. This community of practice comprises both specialists and non-specialists in HIV/AIDS. Through access to ICT-enabled networks, members are able to share knowledge. The charity's investment in ICT helps spread knowledge and good practice that might otherwise remain in isolated departments. Creating horizontal communication channels, rather than clinging to the hub-and-spoke model, enhances the way people get into dialogue with one another.

pause for thought

Consider whether there are groups that might usefully form COPs in an organisation known to you. Of what benefit might these be either to the organisation or to the group members?

exercise

Could Warbings effectively use CoPs in any part of their organisation?

Discuss where and how the group/s might operate.

Summary

Knowledge management can be defined as '. . . *the collection of processes that govern the creation, dissemination, and utilisation of knowledge to fulfil organisational objectives*' (Murray and Myers, 1998). The effective management of knowledge will form the basis on which an organisation is able to learn, adjust, change and thus survive.

In many public service organisations in the UK there are still resonances of an old public management ethos and associated cultural barriers. This has affected enterprise level funding decisions so that over time these organisations have become patchworks of individual initiatives. These organisations are also often strongly bureaucratic and require attitudes and ideas to be changed before KM can become part of the culture.

The cultures in private sector organisations appear to be more accepting of KM because they are often more open to change. In these organisational cultures there is often a strong sense of community and belief in the value of sharing. Silo cultures defending knowledge protectionism are usually hardly detectable.

Some of the above differences between the public and private sectors may be due to commercial imperatives and to different organisational cultures. HRM practices that encourage KM include good communication strategies, open and transparent management styles, valuing workers as individuals rather than as units of production and the creation of cultures that value the benefits to be gained from networks and interactions between individuals. HRM benefits which could accrue from KM include support for the psychological contract between employer and employee and diminution of labour turnover.

Review Questions

You may wish to attempt the following as practice examination style questions.

6.1 Explain the different types of loop learning.

6.2 List some of the key concepts in the KM field.

6.3 Explain the links between KM and learning organisations, and give some relevant organisational examples.

6.4 Describe the differences between:

(a) explicit and tacit forms of knowledge;

(b) sticky and fluid knowledge;

(c) domain and process knowledge, and say why each is important.

6.5 What is the relationship between knowledge, IC and innovation within organisational contexts?

6.6 Give a brief overview of several ways that information systems can support knowledge management and organisational learning.

. . . .

References

Allee, V. (1997). 12 principles of knowledge management, *Training and Development*, Vol. 51, No. 11, pp. 71–75.

Antonacopoulou, E.P. (1999). Individuals' responses to change: the relationship between learning and knowledge, *Creativity and Innovation Management*, Vol. 8, No. 2, pp. 130–140.

Apostolou, D. and Mentzas, G. (1999). Managing corporate knowledge: a comparative analysis of experiences in consulting firms, *Knowledge and Process Management*, Vol. 6, pp. 129–139.

Argyris, C. and Schon, D.A. (1978). *Organizational Learning: A Theory of Action Perpsective*, Wokingham: Addison-Wesley.

Bertels, T. and Savage, C.M. (1999). A research agenda for the knowledge era: the tough questions, *Knowledge and Process Management*, Vol. 6, pp. 205–212.

Blumentitt, R. and Johnston, R. (1999). Towards a strategy for knowledge management, *Technology Analysis and Strategic Management*, Vol. 11, pp. 287–300.

Bowonder, B. and Miyake, T. (1999). Japanese LCD industry: competing through knowledge management, *Creativity and Innovation Management*, Vol. 8, No. 2, pp. 77–100.

Buckler, B. (1998). Practical steps towards a learning organisation: applying academic knowledge to improvement and innovation in business processes, *The Learning Organization*, Vol. 5, No. 1, pp. 15–23.

Carl Bro Group (2001). Intellectual capital accounts: the fifth element, pp. 1–18, Glostrup (Denmark): Carl Bro ajs.

Carneiro, A. (2000). How does knowledge management influence innovation and competitiveness?, *Journal of Knowledge Management*, Vol. 4, No. 2, pp. 87–98.

Coakes, E. and Bradburn, A. (2005). What is the value of intellectual capital?, *Knowledge Management Research and Practice*, Vol. 3, No. 2, pp. 60–68.

Coakes, E., Bradburn, A. and Sugden, G. (2003). Managing and leveraging knowledge for organisational advantage, paper presented at the Knowledge Management Aston Conference, Aston University, Birmingham.

Coakes, E., Bradburn, A. and Sugden, G. (2004). Managing and leveraging knowledge for organisational advantage, *Knowledge Management Research and Practice*, Vol. 2, No. 2, pp. 118–128.

Coakes, E., Sugden, G. and Bradburn, A. (2002). Post-industrial economy and competitive positioning: the value of knowledge management and learning organizations, *OR Insight*, Vol. 15, No. 2, pp. 18–28.

Cropley, J. (1998). Knowledge management: a dilemma, *Business Information Review*, Vol. 15, pp. 27–34.

Darling, M.S. (1996). Building the knowledge organization, *Business Quarterly*, Winter, pp. 61–66.

Davenport, T.H., De Long, D.W. and Beers, M.C. (1998). Successful knowledge management projects, *Sloan Management Review*, Winter, pp. 43–57.

Garrat, B. (1986). *The Learning Organization: The Need for Directors Who Think*, London: Harper Collins.

Geisler, E. (1999). Harnessing the value of experience in the knowledge-driven firm, *Business Horizons*, Vol. 42, pp. 18–27.

Graham, A. and Pizzo, V. (1997). Competing on knowledge: Buckman Laboratories International, *Knowledge and Process Management*, Vol. 4, No. 1, pp. 4–11.

Harvey, M., Palmer, J. and Speier, C. (1998). Implementing intra-organizational learning: a phased-model approach supported by intranet technology, *European Management Journal*, Vol. 16, No. 3, pp. 341–354.

Herbert, I. (2000). Knowledge is a noun, learning is a verb, *Management Accounting*, Vol. 78, pp. 68–72.

Hildreth, P., Kimble, C. and Wright, P. (2000). Communities of practice in the distributed international environment, *MCB Journal of Knowledge Management*, Vol. 4, No. 1, p. 13.

Kaplan, R. and Norton, D. (1996). *The Balanced Scorehead: Translating Strategy into Action*, Boston, MA: Harvard Business School Press.

Larsen, H.T., Bukh, P.N.D. and Mouritsen, J. (1999). Intellectual capital statements and knowledge management: 'measuring', 'reporting', 'acting', *Australian Accounting Review*, Vol. 9, No. 3, pp. 15–27.

Lei, D.T. (1997). Competence-building, technology fusion and competitive advantage: the key rules of organizational learning and strategic alliances, *International Journal of Technology Management*, Vol. 14, No. 02/03/04, pp. 208–237.

Liedtka, J. (1999). Linking competitive advantage with communities of practice, *Journal of Management Inquiry*, Vol. 8, No. 1, pp. 4–16.

McAdam, R. and McCreedy, S. (1999). A critical review of knowledge management models, *Learning Organization Journal*, Vol. 6, pp. 91–100.

Miles, I., Andersen, B., Boden, M. and Howells, J. (2000). Service production and intellectual property, *International Journal of Technology*, Vol. 20, Nos. 1 and 2, pp. 95–116.

Murray, P. and Myers, A. (1998). Knowledge management: the current state of play, *The Antidote*, Vol. 11, pp. 14–15.

Nonaka, I. and Takeuchi, H. (1995). *The Knowledge-creating Company: How Japanese Companies Create the Dynamics of Innovation*, Oxford: Oxford University Press.

Ordonez de Pablos, P. (2002). Evidence of intellectual capital measurement from Asia, Europe and the Middle East, *Journal of Intellectual Capital*, Vol. 3, No. 3, pp. 287–302.

Pavord, A. (2005). *The Naming of Names: The Search for Order in the World of Plants*, London: Bloomsbury Publishing.

Pedler, M., Burgoyne, J. and Boydell, J. (1994). *Towards the Learning Company*, Maidenhead: McGraw-Hill.

Platts, M.J. and Yeung, M.B. (2000). Managing learning and tacit knowledge, *Strategic Change*, Vol. 9, No. 6, pp. 347–356.

Rowley, J. (2006). Where is the wisdom that we have lost in knowledge?, *Journal of Documentation*, Vol. 62, No. 2, pp. 251–270.

Saint-Onge, H. (1996). Tacit knowledge: the key to the strategic alignment of intellectual capital, *Strategy and Leadership*, Vol. 24, No. 2, pp. 10–15.

Senge, P.M. (1990). *The Fifth Discipline: the Art and Practice of the Learning Organization*, New York: Doubleday/Currency.

Simmonds, D. (2003). *Designing and Delivering Training*, London: CIPD.

Stewart, T. (2001). *The Wealth of Knowledge*, London: Nicholas Brealey.

Sullivan, P.H., Jr. and Sullivan, P.H., Sr. (2000). Valuing intangible companies: an intellectual capital approach, *Journal of Intellectual Capital*, Vol. 1, No. 4, pp. 328–340.

Sveiby, K.E. (1997). *The New Organizational Wealth: Managing and Measuring Knowledge-based Assets*, San Francisco, CA: Berrett-Koehler.

Van Buren, M.E. (1999). A yardstick for knowledge management, *Training and Development*, Vol. 53, No. 5, pp. 71–73 and 75.

Zhou, A.F. and Fink, D. (2003). The intellectual capital web: a systematic linking of intellectual capital and knowledge management, *Journal of Intellectual Capital*, Vol. 4, No. 1, pp. 34–48.

Further Reading

Drucker, P.F. et al. (1998). *Harvard Business Review on Knowledge Management*, Boston, MA: Harvard Business School Press.

Honeycutt, J. (2000). *Knowledge Management Strategies*, Microsoft.

Muller-Merbach, H. (2004). Knowledge is more than information, *Knowledge Management Research and Practice*, Vol. 2, pp. 61–62.

Nordstrom, K. and Ridderstrale, J. (2002). *Funky Business, Talent Makes Capital Dance*, London: FT/Prentice-Hall.

Scarborough, H. and Swan, J. (1999). *Case Studies in Knowledge Management*, London: Institute of Personnel and Development.

Useful Websites

www.knowledgeboard.com/cgi-bin/item.cgi?id=787&d=pg_dtl_art_news&h=0&f=0 – enables downloading of Knowledge Board Community book covering knowledge management case studies and reports on industrial practice and business modelling

www.cio.com/km/km/links.html – resources for Chief Information Officers, including research on management and technology and guidance on knowledge management strategies

www.fek.su.se/home/bic/meritum – insight into measuring intangibles to understand and improve innovation management

PART 3
Resourcing

Part contents

CHAPTER 7

Recruitment and Selection

By Paul Smith and Julie Lister

Chapter outline

This chapter introduces the theory and practice of recruitment and selection (R&S). The importance of recruitment and selection is highlighted and wider strategic and integrative issues are discussed. The psychometric approach is outlined, possible limitations of such an approach are considered and alternatives discussed. The application of theory is provided by practical examples.

Learning outcomes

By the end of this chapter, you should be able to:

◆ Describe the importance of R&S;

◆ Explain the role of R&S in relation to employee retention, and as part of a wider human resource (HR), and business, strategy;

◆ Link and integrate recruitment and selection with other areas of HRM;

◆ Analyse the contingent nature of R&S and the variety of approaches to R&S in practice;

◆ Evaluate different perspectives on the R&S process;

◆ Appraise the different methods of R&S.

Introduction

People resourcing in general, and R&S in particular, are crucial elements of HRM. It is axiomatic that organisations need people, and R&S provide the means to resource, or staff, the organisation. This chapter examines and critically evaluates R&S in the wider context of HRM and HR strategy.

Definitions

Beardwell and Wright (2004) point out that R&S are processes concerned with identifying, attracting and securing suitable people to meet an organisation's HR needs. The two terms are often used contiguously and where recruitment stops and selection begins is a moot point (Anderson, 1994). For the purposes of analysis, however, it is useful to separate the two; thus recruitment encompasses the first half of most definitions, selection the second. Recruitment is concerned with identifying and attracting suitable candidates, selection with choosing the most suitable. 'Selection represents the final stage of decision making in the recruitment process' (Cowling and Mailer, 1990: 46).

Marchington and Wilkinson (2005) argue that selection more often gets the focus of attention, particularly in relation to 'new' and 'sophisticated' selection techniques, with consequently less concern being given to recruitment or to other key aspects of resourcing such as HR planning and retention. This specificity of focus is however unjustified, given the interdependence of the different aspects of resourcing.

An examination of the different R&S methods also highlights the degree of overlap. Thus, while the drawing up of job descriptions and their use in the construction of job advertisements falls under the 'recruitment' heading, their use in formulating interview questions is part of selection. Job descriptions also play a role in wider aspects of people resourcing, such as in performance appraisal and job analysis.

Recruitment and selection: importance, links and integration

The importance of recruitment and selection (R&S) in HRM has already been alluded to: it provides the conduit for staffing and resourcing the organisation. An increasingly competitive and globalised business environment, coupled with the need for quality and customer service, has enhanced the importance of recruiting and selecting the right people and of being seen as an 'employer of choice' (Smith, in Porter et al., 2006: 19).

It can be argued that R&S form the axis on which all other HR issues turn. Dipboye (1994) argues that achieving a good fit between people and their jobs is a primary objective of HRM. As Marchington and Wilkinson (2005: 157) point out, the implications of poor selection decisions can be catastrophic for the business as a whole, in terms of the likelihood of disciplinary cases, retraining poor performers and dealing with labour turnover as a consequence. Selecting the right person or people for the task and for the organisation is paramount.

R&S and HRM

From the 1980s there were major changes in how the management of people was conceptualised and, to some extent, practised. HR became more assertive as to its role in organisations (Legge, 1995) due to an increasing awareness and evidence of the impact HR had on organisational success (Searle, 2003). The term 'Personnel Management' became increasingly subsumed by 'Human Resource Management', as explored in Chapter 1.

As part of such changes, R&S processes were recognised as critical components in successful change management (Iles and Salaman, 1995), providing a means of obtaining employees with a new attitude, as well as new skills and abilities.

In terms of models of HRM, R&S can be seen to form an important component of these. Examples include those of Beer et al. (1984), Fombrun et al. (1984), Guest (1989) and Storey (1992). Thus Beer et al.'s model has four key HR outcomes at its core: the competency of employees, their commitment, the importance of fit, i.e. congruence between the employee and the organisation's goals, and the cost-effectiveness of HR policies and practices. An organisation's R&S needed to act as enablers of these outcomes. Thus rather than *ad hoc* approaches to R&S, or methods which focused purely on the person–job fit, what was needed in a HRM approach, it was argued, were more sophisticated methods, which included consideration of prospective employee attitudes and their fit with the organisational culture.

Drawing on David Guest's work, Storey (1989: 11) provides a framework of HRM that encompasses three connecting elements: HRM aims, HRM policies and HRM outcomes. Aims would encompass high commitment, quality and flexible working for example; policies include those of selection on the basis of specific criteria using sophisticated tests.

Boxall and Purcell (2003: 85–86) point out that, in comparison with the physical, tangible assets an organisation possesses (such as plant and machinery), intangible or less tangible assets such as culture, skill and competency, motivation and social interaction are increasingly being seen as key sources of competitive advantage. 'Human resource advantage can be traced to better people employed in organisations with better processes' (ibid.). There are now many studies that seek to demonstrate this link between HRM policies and practices, including R&S, on the one hand, and performance, on the other, and these are reviewed in Marchington and Wilkinson (2005: 86–87).

Strategy and recruitment and selection

In terms of a strategic approach to the management of human resources, it is argued that R&S should form part of a wider resourcing strategy linked to organisational goals. Applying Porter's (1985) ideas on competitive strategy, Schuler and Jackson (1987) draw out the HR implications of these strategies; ideas that have been further developed by Sisson and Storey (2000). In relation to R&S, taking each of the three categories of competitive strategy, a firm adopting a cost-reduction strategy will, it is argued, have *ad hoc* methods of R&S and use agencies/subcontractors. Quality enhancement firms will show sophisticated methods of R&S, while firms in the innovation category will focus on core competences and transferable skills.

While such 'fit' models are subject to criticism, they do provide a useful reminder of the need to take contingent factors into account when deciding on relevant R&S approaches and thus form a useful alternative to best practice approaches.

HR policies and practices have also been linked to life cycle models (Schuler, 1989), i.e. matching appropriate HR to different stages of growth: Start-up, Growth, Maturity and Decline (or Renewal?). Thus, for example, during the early stages of a business, flexibility and informality are likely to be key. If and when new employees are needed, the ability to recruit and retain staff with the motivation to work long hours and engage in self-development is needed. Such a stage is likely to see formal procedures kept to a minimum.

Recruitment and selection and the small business

Andrew Ferguson is the creator of Lifeshift. He has provided training and counselling for some 8,500 career-shifters. Most of these have as a result created a self-managed or self-employed career. The following excerpt from the appropriate section of his *Lifeshift Manual* demonstrates the requirements of the single-person firm or small business person when considering expanding by recruiting.

You and whose army?

You can't hope to manage a team until you can manage yourself. And once you can do that, perhaps you won't need a team! Or not just yet . . .

Recruitment guide

Before you set off down a track that can have some hefty time and money implications, check that you really need to. Is your To Do List cluttered with things you no longer need to do? Are there more efficient ways to do the job? Do you need an extra body, or just some time management? . . .

Cost justification

If you bring this person in, how will the business benefit? What value will they bring? And what costs are involved – recruitment, selection process, induction and further training, office space, salary, etc., NI, holidays, pension, cost of management time? Corporates reckon the real cost of a manager at five times their salary! Recruitment takes faith: you can rarely see in advance how you can afford it, and have to treat every appointment as an investment . . .

Where will you find your recruit(s)?

Recruitment is mostly done by networking . . . which is also the best way to find a job (and customers). Six out of seven jobs are never advertised. Can you promote/recruit internally (this is good for morale)? Do you have a file of past applicants? Are there any other strategies available? One good way is to ask current employees if they know anyone who'd be good . . .

Initial selection

Standard approaches are written for and by people from large organisations, and assume resources and constraints you simply don't have. . . . [In an interview] ask them to tell you about themselves, what they care about, what they would bring to the job and why they want it.

continued

The paper burden

Be aware what you're taking on when you become an employer, because you are effect-ively becoming an unpaid tax inspector. According to the Federation of Small Businesses (FSB), over 99 per cent of all government revenue is collected by employers. Employers currently collect and pay tax and NI. They also pay SSP, administer SMP and fund redun-dancy payments (Ferguson, 2001: 89–93).

Mr Ferguson usefully illustrates some of the considerations regarding R&S for the small business. Is a new employee absolutely necessary? What will be the costs involved in the recruitment and selection, and with subsequent employment? Approaches are also likely to be less formalised than in a larger organisation. It is recognised that recruitment by word of mouth, by 'asking current employees if they know anyone who'd be good', carries the risk of perpetuating any gender/ethnicity imbalance that exists in the workforce and can also lead to workforce cloning, which can squeeze out new ideas and innovation (see Chapter 14). However research suggests that it leads to the recruitment of employees who stay with the company for long periods. It is thought that this is because they already have an existing knowledge of the company through friends or relatives already employed, and that this provides them with a realistic job preview. This concept is explored further in the section on 'Recruiting to retain'.

Approaches to recruitment and selection

Textbooks on the subject aimed at a management audience tend to take a normative or prescriptive approach. This does not in itself make them worthy of criticism; they provide useful practical guidance on how to recruit and select staff. The problem occurs however when such advice is taken uncritically, or is used out of context.

The psychometric approach

The dominant paradigm of the last 30 years has been that of psychometrics. This approach is based on scientific rationality, and its application (by occupational psychologists) to candidate selection in particular. Selection, and the associated assessments involved, are treated as representing problems of measurement. In simple terms, which entails measuring individual differences so that people can be objectively matched to the requirements of a job. Such approaches, seeking object-ivity and fairness in selection decisions, can be viewed as laudable. The requirement still remains however that such tests be subject to scrutiny, in relation to their con-ceptual basis, and to their application in practice, and that alternative perspectives are also given due consideration.

The psychometric approach focuses on the measurement of individual differences. To enable this to be put into practice, a number of steps are taken, in a logical order. Thus R&S may be viewed as a systematic process. The psychometric approach is also closely aligned with that of rational decision making (Redman and Wilkinson, 2001: 24); decisions are made on the basis of some kind of assessment about the suitability of individuals who might fill a vacancy.

Do you think cultural biases influence which individual differences are measured?

Central to the psychometric approach are the concepts of validity and reliability. *Validity* refers to the extent to which what one is aiming to measure is actually measured. This is most often seen in terms of subsequent job performance. *Reliability* relates to consistency, thus if a selection measure were to be repeated, would it achieve the same results? Psychometric measures seek both high validity and high reliability.

Other ways of looking at R&S include regarding selection as a process of social-isation (to the organisation) and selection as socially constructed reality, i.e. as enacted within a wider societal framework and thus subject to the power and social structures inherent in that society. It must not be forgotten that R&S is a *two-way* process involving both the employer and potential employees, rather than simply being a matter of management prerogative.

The R&S process: a systematic approach

R&S as a process is set out in Figure 7.1. The steps in this process will be reviewed below, together with some discussion as to possible difficulties and shortcomings.

HR Planning

If R&S are not to be purely reactive and last minute, they need to be based on HR planning. This involves forecasting the demand for and the supply of labour, incor-porating labour turnover and retention data (see Further Reading).

In relation to a consideration of HR planning, certain themes identified earlier in this chapter are pertinent. A competitive environment characterised by change provides a challenge for traditional planning approaches. Numbers and type of staff required may be subject to fluctuation, thus stressing the need for flexibility. Such flexibility requirements may encompass both numerical aspects (see Atkinson, 1984), i.e. hiring certain staff on atypical contingent contracts and functional, i.e. identifying prospective staff who are multi-skilled or have the ability to multi-task, or have the potential to do so.

Need requirement and job analysis

In terms of R&S *per se*, the first step is to decide whether a vacancy actually exists. When an employee leaves there may be alternative ways of filling the gap left by their departure, such as reorganisation, reassignment of tasks and automation.

The next step involves an analysis of the particular job. Job analysis refers to 'the process of collecting, analysing and setting out information about the contents of jobs' in order to determine the key tasks and roles (Armstrong, 1999: 190). Methods of job analysis include: observation of the person doing the job; getting

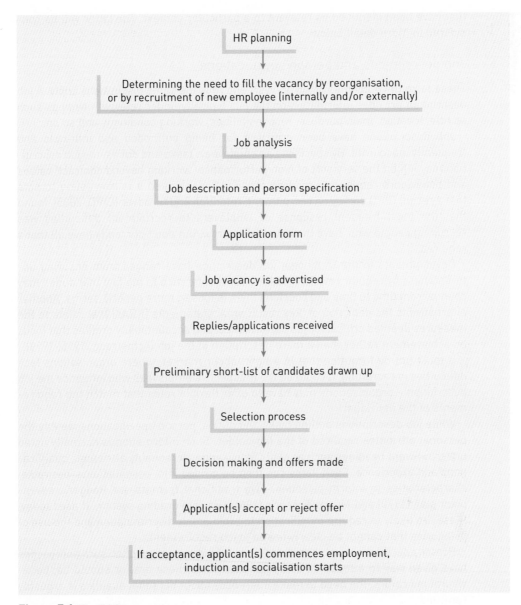

Figure 7.1 The R&S process

job-holders to record their activities in work diaries; interviewing the job-holder; questionnaires/checklists; critical incident; and repertory grid techniques (see Taylor, 2002a).

Criticisms of traditional job analysis include its focus on the job, rather than wider requirements, and that it collects information about the job as it currently exists, assuming that it will be similar in the future. Developments include future-orientated job analysis (Redman and Wilkinson, 2001), broader role analysis (Marchington and Wilkinson, 2005), and the identification of competences, i.e. behavioural indicators that have been identified as relevant to a particular context. The latter will be considered in more detail below.

Job descriptions and person specifications

These form the outcomes of job analysis and thus the same discussions apply. A job description provides information on the job, typically under relevant headings such as title, location, main purpose, responsibilities, working conditions and so on.

Job descriptions have been criticised for being outmoded and inflexible and frequently inaccurate. By specifying an employee's tasks and duties, the job description may inhibit the very sort of high performance 'working beyond contract' values and behaviours required in modern organisations. Indeed it is interesting to note that a recent CIPD survey on recruitment, retention and turnover (CIPD, 2005), found that the most frequent response of employers to recruitment difficulties was recruiting people who 'have the potential to grow, but don't currently have all that's required'.

Developments to the traditional job description have ranged from ensuring up-to-dateness by regular review, including some reference to the fact that duties may change from time to time and couching them in looser, more generic, terms. Another alternative is the depiction of 'key result area' statements (KRAs) that relate to the measures deemed critical for job performance, and accountability profiles that focus on achievement rather than a mere description of the job (Armstrong, 1995, 1999).

It must not be forgotten that in a tight labour market, where organisations face difficulties in recruiting, it could be the prospective employees who influence the job description – organisations may have to offer flexible roles that match the requirements of the individual.

While job descriptions outline tasks and duties, person specifications identify the personal attributes required of the job-holder. Such information is normally listed under relevant headings such as skills, knowledge, personality attributes, qualifications and experience. Such items can then be divided into 'essential' and 'desirable' characteristics to inform selection. Two traditional formats are Rodger's seven-point plan (1970) and Munro-Fraser's (1966) five-fold grading system. If used today, these are likely to require modification to avoid unfair discrimination and the use of categories that cannot be clearly linked to job requirements.

Person specifications rely heavily on personal judgement, so often such approaches have given way to a focus on competencies. Since these are, or should be, behavioural indicators, the need to make inferences about personal qualities is arguably removed.

Competency frameworks

Competences have been variously defined, but Roberts (in Beardwell et al., 2004: 206) has produced a definition that sees them in terms of 'the work-related personal attributes, knowledge, experience, skills and values that a person draws on to perform their job well'. Although such a broad definition encompassing such aspects as values raises the problem that the use of competences may include judgements about personal qualities and thus be subject to the same shortcomings as personal specifications, proponents argue that the focus of attention should be on the behavioural outcomes of these various characteristics.

In terms of their use in recruitment and selection, this involves the identification of a set of competences that are seen as important across an organisation or part of an organisation. Competences are person-based rather than job-based. The attributes of the top performers in the organisation are identified and profiled and the result is used to inform R&S. Commonly identified competences include: communication, achievement/results orientation, planning and organising, problem solving and teamwork. This approach has the scope for greater flexibility as it enables organisations to focus 'more on the qualities of the jobholder and the person's potential suitability for other duties as jobs change' than on the job itself (IRS, in Beardwell et al., 2004: 206).

The advantage of focusing on actual behaviour and outcomes means that there is no need to make inferences about personal qualities. However, in practice, competency approaches are often used in ways that specify not only outputs but also how these are or should be achieved (Redman and Wilkinson, 2001: 26). Generic competences on the personality or attitudinal end of the spectrum, as opposed to those that are skills-based, give greater scope for such personal judgements.

Criticisms of competency approaches include the view that they lead to an acquiescent workforce and 'cloning' (Taylor, 2002a: 106). It is also argued that they are backward looking in that they focus on past activities, and it has also been suggested that over-reliance on behavioural characteristics for recruitment or assessment purposes risks rewarding people for who they are, and not what they do.

Recruitment methods

The next step is to attract a pool of applicants from which to begin the selection process. Recruitment can be from both internal and external sources. In terms of external, the CIPD's Annual Survey (2005) estimates the average cost of filling a vacancy per employee as £3,950, rising to £4,625 if the associated costs of labour turnover are also taken into account. In total, nationally, this would run to in excess of £1 billion.

The types of recruitment methods used by organisations are listed in Table 7.1. The method chosen will be dependent on the type of vacancy and the organisation concerned. In simple terms, the method(s) used by a large well-known organisation seeking to recruit a new MD are likely to be different to those of a small business seeking an assistant to help out on Saturdays. There are also cost considerations to bear in mind and legal requirements, particularly, with regards to the latter, in the design and wording of advertisements.

---

exercise

W

At the warbings depots, drivers are primarily recruited via word of mouth. When vacancies occur, the drivers are asked if they know of anyone who might be interested and suitable. Only if this doesn't produce enough applicants are other recruitment methods used – primarily a specialist employment agency.

What are the advantages and disadvantages of such an informal word of mouth approach to recruitment?

Table 7.1 Recruitment methods

Recruitment method	% of organisations surveyed
To advertise vacancies internally:	
Intranet	70
Noticeboards	64
Team meetings	17
Staff magazine	13
To attract external applicants:	
Local newspaper advertisements	85
Recruitment agencies/search	80
Vacancies information (own website)	67
Specialist journals/trade press	59
National newspaper advertisements	55
Job centre plus	54
Speculative applications/word of mouth	52
Employee referral schemes	38
Links with schools/colleges/universities	35
Apprenticeships/work placements/secondments	32
Vacancies information (specialist website)	30
Posters/billboards/vehicles	14
Radio or TV advertisements	9
Other	7

Source: adapted from CIPD (2005)

In drawing up advertisements, the aim is to attract a reasonable number of suitably qualified applicants. Taylor (2002a: 134) refers to organisations deciding between a 'wide trawl' versus a 'wide net'. The aim of the wide trawl is to attract a large number of people – adverts are likely to be large and striking in appearance and be placed prominently. By contrast, the key aim of the net approach is to reach a relatively narrow audience and to encourage self-selection on the part of possible applicants. Advertisements in this category are likely to contain a lot of detailed information and be placed in specialist journals or on websites.

There are a number of different external agencies available that can be employed to undertake all or part of the recruitment process on behalf of employers. These include government and voluntary agents that encompass job centres, advertising and recruitment consultants, temporary employment agencies, headhunters and permanent employment agencies (Taylor, 2002a: 146).

window into practice

The recruitment consultant

David Carroll worked as a recruitment consultant before leaving to pursue postgraduate study. Here he gives a useful insight into the work of a recruitment consultant.

continued

The work of a recruitment consultant

The position of recruitment consultant can be broadly viewed as a sales role. It is typified by targeted objectives based on financial and non-financial activity to which rewards are linked, such as bonus, commission and promotion. The role is essentially focused on meeting the recruitment, and to some degree selection, needs of an external organisation in return for a pre-agreed fee. The fee is based on a percentage of a permanent salary (sometimes benefits also) or on a percentage margin of a contractor's pay rate.

A recruitment consultant's 'desk' is normally characterised by one of three areas:

♦ Firstly, on a contract/contingency basis, where the aim is meeting a short-term need of a client to cover incidents such as absence, a short-term project or an unexpected upturn in work. There is a need to fill the position quickly, normally between a few minutes and a few days. Candidates will, typically, be on the books and looking for work immediately. The placed candidate is paid by the recruitment agency/consultancy and a higher rate charged to the client.

♦ Secondly, on a permanent basis where the client's longer-term need is often due to replacing a leaver or to meet growth plans. The recruitment cycle is longer and the consultant's role will be more involved, generating fees on the basis of an agreed percentage of the basic salary/package.

♦ Thirdly, there is headhunting/campaign managed recruitment, which usually means exclusivity of business for the recruitment consultant. Positions are often at a higher level, such as director, or for specialist professional roles where there is a shortage of candidates in the market. Fees are generated at three key stages: accepting the assignment, producing a short-list for agreed interviews and on final placement. The percentage charge rate is also higher than for regular permanent recruitment fees.

Recruitment consultants are also generally specialised in niche markets and/or job types to enhance their area of expertise. This will focus their efforts towards certain types of jobs, for example secretarial/PA or architect positions and may be further focused within a geographical area and/or a market sector. The basic day-to-day key skills and competences used by a recruitment consultant include: finding positions, developing job descriptions and person specifications with the client, negotiating fees, advertising positions in selected media, resourcing, short-listing and interviewing candidates, undertaking reference and work eligibility checks, selling the client opportunity to the candidate and providing information on both the role and the company, arranging interviews, giving feedback and making offers and negotiating salary. Each of these processes has to be administered and is often performed within internal quality guidelines or by those set out by the REC.

(Information provided by David Carroll, 2005)

Electronic recruiting

Moving on from the use of external agencies, electronic recruitment methods are an increasingly important area. The use of e-recruitment is expanding, with 90 per cent of firms using some form of electronic recruitment at some stage of the process (IRS Survey, 2004). According to Marchington and Wilkinson (2005: 174), some of the main advantages of e-recruitment are:

- Reduced costs;
- Improved corporate image;
- Reduced administration;
- Wider pool of applicants;
- Shortened recruitment cycle;
- Improved overseas recruitment;
- Easier for applicants.

Among the main disadvantages are:
- Too many unsuitable applicants (because ease of application encourages speculative applications);
- Technical problems;
- Shortage of applicants;
- Expense.

And from the applicant's point of view:
- Slow feedback or follow-up;
- Insufficient job information;
- Concerns about personal security;
- Technical problems;
- Wish for human contact.

While e-recruitment is inappropriate in some circumstances (because it disadvantages certain socio-economic groups), it is likely to be the method of choice in others because candidates will perceive it as the most appropriate application method for that type of job. IT-related jobs are a good example of this. In such situations, employers can discourage more speculative applications by increasing the effort required – for example, by refusing to accept CVs and insisting on completion of online application forms.

Short-listing

Short-listing is the initial step in selection. It is done by comparing the information provided in the application form or CV with the selection criteria, as identified in the person specification. In theory, those who match the criteria will go on to the next stage of the selection process, although where there are large numbers of applicants recourse is likely to be made to the list of 'desirable' characteristics in addition to the 'essential'.

Selection

The psychometric approach aims to measure individual characteristics and match these to the requirements of the job in order to predict subsequent job performance. To achieve this, candidates who are successfully short-listed face a number of subsequent selection devices. These can be viewed as a series of hurdles to jump, with

Table 7.2 Accuracy of different selection methods (1.0 is perfect prediction)

Selection method	Accuracy
Assessment centres (promotion)	0.72
Intelligence tests *and* structured interview	0.63
Intelligence tests *and* work sampling	0.60
Ability tests	0.56
Work sample tests	0.52
Intelligence tests	0.51
Structured interviews	0.51
Personality tests	0.40
Biodata	0.35
Typical interviews	0.26
References	0.26
Years of job experience	0.18
Years of education	0.10
Graphology	0.02
Chance prediction	0.00

Source: adapted from various sources, including Smith (2002)

the 'winner' being the candidate or candidates who receive the job offer. While this analogy undoubtedly reflects the attitude of many employers, it may be considered to be somewhat out of place in an already tight labour market that is set to tighten further in the face of prevailing demographic trends. Such traditional approaches take no account of the ultimate power of the chosen candidates throughout the process to turn down the offer of employment (Dale, 1995: 160).

Various selection techniques are available; the key factors influencing the choice of these is briefly reviewed now.

Accuracy

From the psychometric perspective, selection accuracy is defined in terms of the degree of match between predictor and subsequent job performance. It encompasses the notions of validity and reliability. Table 7.2 outlines the accuracy according to research studies of different selection methods measured on the correlation coefficient between predicted and actual job performance, with 1.0 being perfect prediction and zero being pure chance.

The type of job provides 'the most significant influence on the choice of selection methods for any one vacancy' (IRS, 1997, quoted in Beardwell et al., 2004: 217). Thus, for example, assessment centres tend to be reserved for managerial and graduate posts.

Such lists should be used with caution – they vary according to the research study or studies they are based on, and according to the specific example of selection method used for each category. Accuracy will also be dependent on the selection method being used correctly in a particular context. Bearing such health warnings in mind, however, they do provide an interesting basis for comparison and discussion. Intelligence tests, when combined with another specified method, score the highest. Of techniques used on their own, work sample tests offer the highest potential for accuracy. Intuitively this may not come as a surprise, since the best way to predict whether someone can do a job is to give them the job to do. Thus Pret a Manger, for example, requires candidates to undertake a day's on-the-job experience at one of their shops as part of their selection process (Beardwell et al., 2004: 220). Other examples of work sampling are in-tray exercises and role plays.

In terms of accuracy, interviews perform better if structured and carried out by trained interviewers, while assessment centres can score reasonably high for accuracy, depending on their design and the use they are put to. References score fairly low down on the scale, while graphology and astrology are close to zero.

Cost

Cost, in terms of direct money costs and indirectly in terms of time, is a major consideration when choosing selection methods. Thus, for example, assessment centres are resource-intensive and therefore tend to be used by larger organisations and for more senior jobs or for graduate-entry, particularly where there is a number of vacancies to fill at one time.

Selection methods

Mark Cook (1993) refers to the 'classic trio' of application form, interview and references. As Taylor (2002a) points out, what is interesting is that these traditional methods continue to dominate despite evidence that other selection tools offer greater accuracy.

The interview

The interview has been described as 'a controlled conversation with a purpose' (Torrington et al., 2005: 242) and continues to be an enduringly popular part of the selection process. As Table 7.2 demonstrates, the traditional (unstructured or informal) interview has a relatively low predictive validity, yet this is markedly improved by taking a structured approach, using trained interviewers, and combining the interview with other selection methods. Two structured interview techniques are behavioural and situational interviews. Both use critical incident job analysis to determine aspects of job behaviour that are key to effective performance (see previous section on 'Need requirement and job analysis').

Testing

As can be seen from Table 7.2, tests tend to score relatively highly in terms of accuracy, particularly in combination with another selection method when considering intelligence tests. Objectivity is viewed as a key advantage of tests over other selection methods such as the interview. The relevance of the test to the job applied for needs to be carefully considered, however, and questions have also been raised concerning unfair discrimination and bias (Torrington et al., 2005: 148).

Questions surrounding the use of personality testing include whether personality is open to such measurement, whether personality is constant, and whether the tests can be faked. Another fundamental question relates to the link to job performance – many jobs could be undertaken equally successfully by people of varying person-alities. In counter-argument, certain basic personality requirements can be linked to some jobs: thus extraversion to salespeople and calmness to air traffic con-trollers. It has also been argued that, based on recent research, five basic building blocks of personality can be identified: extroversion/introversion, emotional stability, agreeableness, conscientiousness, and openness to new experiences.

Assessment centres

Assessment centres incorporate a variety of selection methods and work simula-tion, helping to potentially improve the accuracy of decisions. Job or role analysis is used to identify the behaviours and characteristics to be assessed. Assessment centres have been found to be one of the most effective means of selecting candid-ates (IRS, 2002). Drawbacks centre mainly around costs and resource issues.

Recruiting to retain

It is important not to lose sight of the ultimate business objective, which is to successfully recruit appropriately talented candidates who will continue working for the organisation for as long as the organisation wishes to retain their services. It therefore follows that strategies need to be adopted that, at best, support this objective or, at least, do not undermine it.

Central to the objective of recruiting and retaining is ensuring that the recruitment process (and the induction process) does not erode the goodwill of the chosen candidates. This is easy to do at all stages of a recruitment process that views the employer as the all-powerful party that 'awards' the job to the lucky winner. In *Successful Recruitment and Selection* (1995), Margaret Dale suggests that instilling a 'marketing' mindset in all staff involved in the recruitment process is one approach to ensuring that the favoured candidates do not de-select themselves. Every candid-ate should therefore be afforded the same courtesy given to potential clients, from the earliest stages of the process.

Taylor (2002b) stresses the importance of realistic job preview both to ensuring that the right candidate for the job is recruited, and that they stay with the organ-isation for a reasonable period of time. His approach is based on extensive research into the impact of realistic job preview conducted in the US (Wanous, 1992; Hom and Griffeth, 1995; Phillips, 1998). The concept of realistic job preview extends well beyond the obvious dangers of overselling jobs and glossing-over difficulties and disadvantages that will confront the new employee once they have joined and stresses the importance of giving candidates as realistic and complete a preview as possible – 'warts and all' – including creating opportunities for them to meet colleagues, see where they will be working and, if possible, be given an opportunity to sample the actual work.

The potential downside to this approach is readily apparent. The employment market in the UK is currently very tight, with a recent CIPD survey reporting that 85 per cent of employers are facing recruitment difficulties (CIPD, 2005). In such a competitive environment the leap of faith required to adopt such a frank and honest approach to advertising and recruitment may be seen as a step too far for many employers.

However, Taylor suggests that the advantages of realistic job preview far outweigh the disadvantages and notes that 'word of mouth' recruitment is a good way to provide this. He proposes that this is because employees have a more realistic impression of the company and the work prior to joining and that, even when they do experience disappointments, they have the support of family and friends who also work for the same employer.

Recruitment and retention at Hertfordshire County Council

A few years ago Hertfordshire County Council (HCC) took the first steps towards a new and integrated approach to recruitment and retention, an approach that culminated in them winning both the Innovation in Recruitment and Retention and the Overall Winner awards in the prestigious *Personnel Today* Awards 2003.

In common with other public sector organisations, particularly those in the South East, HCC faces significant recruitment and retention challenges – living costs are high while unemployment is low. Many local people commute to London for work. There are also national skills shortages to contend with – for teachers, qualified social workers, engineers and planners. There are approximately 2,000 permanent posts to be filled each year, and £12 million a year is currently spent on temporary staff, not including teachers. The move to a different approach to recruitment was partly in response to such challenges, but was also driven by three more specific reasons.

Firstly, HCC were then using over 150 different agencies to supply temporary staff, leading to problems in control of standards, variability in mark-up by the agencies and inconsistencies in pay rates. In addition, despite the use of so many agencies, there were still difficulties in recruiting sufficient temporary staff.

Secondly, at the time the Council was undergoing significant change. It needed a method of retraining and redeploying staff to avoid redundancies. The need for a more flexible approach to working was also recognised.

Thirdly, the HR function at the Council wanted to modernise how recruitment was done and to shorten the recruitment cycle (the time taken to fill a vacancy). E-recruitment was seen as a means of achieving this.

The Recruitment Centre opened in 2000 in partnership with Manpower plc, providing a one-stop shop 24/7 service for managers and candidates alike. Job-seekers can register onto the database for both temporary and permanent posts. Recruitment is simpler, faster and less expensive. The Recruitment Centre provides fully integrated recruitment services – advertising, provision of all temporary staff, management of permanent recruitment and redeployment. Improvements include:

- Reduction in the number of temporary staffing agencies used. Major savings made and improvement in the quality of temps;

- Launch of an interactive website. Candidates can now apply for all vacancies online. 55 per cent of all applications are now made online;

- Line managers and applicants now have a single point of contact for all recruitment activities – temporary and permanent;

- A database of people wanting to work for the Council has been set up so that vacancies, when they arise, can be filled directly;

- The redeployment service helps to retain staff in whom a significant investment has been made;

continued

♦ Improved management information provides a basis for further improvements and action;

♦ Savings of £3 million in first five years.

The setting up of the Recruitment Centre accompanied other developments that had a positive impact on recruitment and retention, including: better management information to ensure actions, such as recruitment drives, are better targeted; flexible working options; and a commitment to training and development.

(Interview with Carole Grimwood, Assistant Director of HR, Hertfordshire County Council, 1 July 2005, available at www.hertscc.gov.uk)

Summary

The prime importance of R&S in HRM has been stressed. If people really are 'our most important resource' (Smith, in Porter et al., 2006: 4), then R&S provide the key drives to resourcing the organisation from which the other HR activities flow.

Differing approaches to, and perspectives on, the R&S process can be discerned: the psychometric stresses objectivity and accuracy; yet R&S in practice is often a mix of such objective views with the pragmatic, as evidenced by the continuing popularity of the application form, interview and references as selection devices. Moves away from selecting purely for 'a job' and towards using wider criteria such as those based on the attitudinal and 'the potential to grow' (CIPD, 2005: 2) provide their own challenges for objectivity. Different situations require differing approaches, as evidenced by our case study examples and windows into practice.

exercise

Making reference to Warbings, identify the main recruitment and selection problems. Identify and justify solutions to these.

Review Questions

You may wish to attempt the following as practice examination style questions.

7.1 Is good selection an art or a science? Discuss.

7.2 How would you account for the fact that the most popular selection methods (Cook, 1993; CIPD, 2005) are not necessarily the most accurate?

7.3 What do you understand by the term 'employer of choice'? Why is it argued that being such an employer is important in today's employment market?

7.4 Reflect on the approaches to recruitment and selection that have been introduced in this chapter. Under what circumstances might you propose a particular approach, and under what circumstances might you advise against it?

References

Anderson, A. (1994). *Effective Personnel Management: A Skills and Activity-based Approach*, Oxford: Blackwell Business.

Armstrong, M. (1995). *A Handbook of Personnel Management Practice,* 5th edition, London: Kogan Page.

Armstrong, M. (1999). *Employee Reward,* 2nd edition, London: CIPD.

Atkinson, J. (1984). Manpower strategies for the flexible organisation, *Personnel Management,* August, pp. 28–31.

Beardwell, J. and Wright, M. (2004). 'Recruitment and selection', in I. Beardwell, L. Holden and T. Claydon (eds.) *Human Resource Management: A contemporary approach,* 4th edition, London: FT/Prentice Hall.

Beardwell, I., Holden, L. and Claydon, T. (2004). *Human Resource Management,* Harlow: FT/Prentice Hall.

Beer, M., Spector, B., Lawrence, P., Quinn Mills, D. and Walton, R. (1984). *Managing Human Assets,* New York: Free Press.

Boxall, P. and Purcell, J. (2003). *Strategy and Human Resource Management,* London: Palgrave.

Chartered Institute of Personnel and Development (2005). *Recruitment, Retention, and Turnover: A Survey of the UK and Ireland,* Londo: CIPD.

Cook, M. (1993). *Personnel Selection,* 3rd edition, Chichester: Wiley.

Cowling, A. and Mailer, C. (1990). *Managing Human Resources,* 2nd edition, London: Edward Arnold.

Dale, M. (1995). *Successful Recruitment and Selection,* London: Kogan Page.

Dipboye, R.L. (1994). Structured and unstructured selection interviews: beyond the best-fit model, *Research in Personnel and HRM,* Vol. 12, pp. 79–123.

Ferquson, A. (2001). *Your Lifeshift Manual,* pp. 89–93, Breakthrough Publications, at: www.lifeshift.co.uk.

Fombrun, C., Tichy, M. and Devanna, M. (1984). *Strategic Human Resource Management,* New York: Wiley.

Fraser, J.M. (1966). *Employment Interviewing,* London: Macdonal Evans.

Guest, D. (1989). Human resource management: its implications for industrial relations and trade unions, in J. Storey (ed.) *New Perspectives on Human Resource Management,* pp. 41–55, London: Routledge.

Hom, P.W. and Griffeth, R.W. (1995). *Employer Turnover,* Cincinnati, OH: South-Western.

Iles, P. and Salaman, G. (1995). Recruitment, selection and assessment, in J. Story (ed.) *Human Resource Management: A Critical Text,* pp. 209–234, London: Routledge.

IRS (1997). The state of selection: an IRS Survey, *Employee Development Bulletin,* Vol. 85, pp. 8–18.

IRS Employment Review 749 (2002). *Focus of Attention,* pp. 36–41, London: IRS.

IRS Employment Review 792a (2004). *Recruiters March in Step with Online Recruitment,* pp. 44–48, London: IPS.

Legge, K. (1995). *HRM: Rhetorics and Realities,* Basingstoke: Macmillan Business.

Marchington, M. and Wilkinson, A. (2005). *Human Resource Management,* London: CIPD.

Phillips, J.M. (1998). Effects of realistic job previews on multiple organizational outcomes: a meta-analysis, *Academy of Management Journal,* Vol. 41, No. 6, pp. 673–690.

Porter, M. (1985). *Competitive Advantage: Creating and Sustaining Superior Performance,* New York: Free Press.

Porter, K., Smith, P. and Fagg, R. (2006). *Leadership and Management for HR Professionals,* Oxford: Butterworth-Heinemann.

Redman, T. and Wilkinson, A. (2001). *Contemporary Human Resource Management,* Harlow, FT/Prentice Hall.

Rodger, A. (1970). *The Seven Point Plan,* 3rd edition, London: National Institute of Industrial Psychology.

Schuler, R. (1989). Strategic human resource management and industrial relations, *Human Relations,* Vol. 42, No. 2, pp. 157–184.

Schuler, R. and Jackson, S. (1987). Linking competitive strategies with human resource management, *Academy of Management Executive*, Vol. 1, No. 3, pp. 207–219.

Searle, R. (2003). *Selection and Recruitment: A Critical Text,* Milton Keynes: Open University Press.

Sisson, K. and Storey, J. (2000). *The Realities of Human Resource Management*, Milton Keynes: Open University Press.

Smith, M. (2002). Personnel selection research, *International Journal of Organisational and Occupational Psychology*, Vol. 2, pp. 441–472.

Storey, J. (1989). *New Perspectives on Human Resource Management,* London: Routledge.

Storey, J. (1992). *Developments in the Management of Human Resources: An Analytical Review,* London: Blackwell.

Taylor, S. (2002a). *People Resourcing*, London: CIPD.

Taylor, S. (2002b). *The Employee Retention Handbook,* London: CIPD.

Torrington, D., Hall, L. and Taylor, S. (2005). *Human Resource Management*, Harlow: FT/Prentice Hall.

Wanous, J.P. (1992). *Organisational Entry: Recruitment, Selection and Socialisation of Newcomers,* 2nd edition, Reading, MA: Addison-Wesley.

Further Reading

Robertson, I. and Smith, M. (1999). Personnel selection, *Journal of Occupational and Organizational Psychology*, Vol. 74, No. 4, pp. 441–472.

Useful Websites

www.hrmguide.co.uk/hrm/chap8/ch8-links.html – guide to detailed process of recruitment and selection, particularly interviewing

www.agepositive.gov.uk/agepartnershipgroup/ pages/top_tips_selection.htm – Age Positive's (government-sponsored campaign) advice on tackling age discrimination and promoting age diversity in employment

www.thetimes100.co.uk/theory/theory.php?tID= 349 – *The Times* newspaper resource centre covering, inter alia, business studies teaching materials, particularly case studies

CHAPTER 8

Performance Management and Appraisal

By Liz Kennedy and Keith Porter

Chapter outline

Examining the strategic place of performance management (PM), this chapter looks at the ways in which PM can help an organisation achieve the vertical and horizontal integration of people management and development. It explores the practicalities of implementing PM and determines the purpose of performance appraisal while taking note of the relevant human resource management (HRM) issues that surround PM, such as competences and contingency pay.

Learning outcomes

By the end of this chapter, you should be able to:

◆ Explain the strategic role of PM;

◆ Demonstrate the link between PM and effective people management;

◆ Describe the different components of a PM process;

◆ Compare behavioural and output-based appraisal systems;

◆ Contrast the development and the assessment agendas;

◆ Identify the key factors associated with success in PM.

Introduction

The improvement of corporate and individual performance levels is a key priority for any organisation, but these are difficult to achieve. With greater recognition of the value added by competent and committed staff, performance management is increasingly seen as a key tool in most organisations (IRS, 2001). In this chapter we explore the nature of PM and its role within the organisation, as well as the key processes involved and the factors that contribute to its success or failure.

The strategic context

PM as an approach to effective people management

PM is sometimes mistakenly viewed as an event or activity that is somehow separate from the effective day-to-day management of people (Armstrong and Baron, 1998). There are two main reasons for this: firstly, the tendency to associate PM with performance *appraisal*; and secondly, the perception that PM is 'owned' (and enforced) by HR. Appraisal often conveys to employees' minds images of awkward confrontations at annual review meetings and pointless box-ticking exercises. Among small and medium-sized enterprises in particular, performance appraisal is seen as synonymous with PM.

The key to overcoming this confusion is to view PM not as an independent activity, but as a set of integrated processes aligning several elements of effective people management.

PM therefore needs to be placed very firmly in a management context. As Armstrong and Baron (2005) observe, it is a 'natural process of management' and management involves 'getting things done through the efforts of other people' (Mullins, 2002). So in many respects, PM *is* effective people management. Moreover, there is evidence to suggest that effective people management, enabled by a PM system, will lead to positive HR outcomes, such as employee commitment, competence and flexibility. These will in turn lead to quality and productivity, resulting in organisational success (Guest et al., 2000). As Porter et al. (2006: 13) note, this makes intuitive sense:

> 'Employees who are carefully recruited to suit the organisation and their roles, properly trained and developed, appraised and suitably rewarded, communicated to and involved . . . are more likely to put themselves out, to "go the extra mile" and demonstrate the sort of discretionary behaviours that are seen as crucial differentiators between "world class" high performance organisations and the rest.'

exercise

Make a list of all the ways organisations could maximise people's performance in the workplace.

Performance management and strategic alignment

This discussion about the nature of PM also highlights its role in achieving strategic alignment. This purpose is captured succinctly:

> 'Performance management is a strategic and integrated approach to delivering sustained success to organisations by improving the performance of the people who work in them and by developing the capabilities of teams and individual contributors.'

(Armstrong and Baron, 1998: 8)

One of the distinguishing features of HRM is that it represents a strategic approach to people management. The practical question is how to achieve strategic fit. PM can provide the answer to this question by delivering both vertical and horizontal integration.

The potential of a PM system to support such alignment is illustrated by referring to the matching model of HRM (Fombrun et al., 1984); see Figure 8.1. Here, the key HR interventions of recruitment, reward, appraisal and development are mutually reinforcing and interact in a concerted way to enhance performance. 'Performance' in this case can be interpreted as whatever people need to do to achieve the organisation's business objectives. While there is both an underlying logic of this framework and also an attractiveness to HR practitioners striving to achieve 'strategic alignment' (Holbeche, 2001), the model raises some practical problems:

- How can business strategy be translated into a set of expectations about the ways that each individual must perform so that the organisation's objectives can be achieved?
- How can PM interventions be organised with the overall effect that every employee meets these expectations?

An effective PM system can address these problems.

Performance management systems

It is useful to think of PM as a 'system' (Kast and Rosenweig, 1985) – see Figure 8.1. Here, the PM system is a horizontally aligned (linked and mutually reinforcing) set

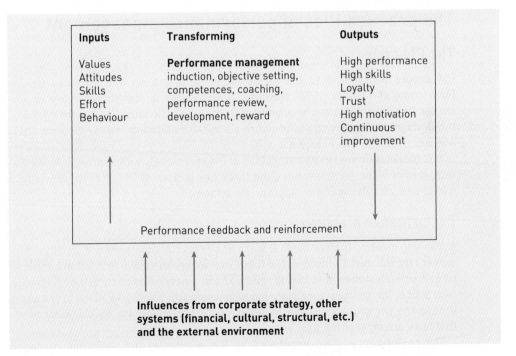

Figure 8.1 PM as a system

of PM interventions that converts existing values, attitudes and behaviours (inputs) into desired outputs, i.e. those values, attitudes and behaviours that are necessary to implement business strategy. The PM system is itself part of a wider organisational system with which it interacts. So, for example, employee reward will be influenced by the prevailing organisational culture and structure, as well as the financial system. This will in turn be influenced by external factors such as labour market conditions and the wider economic environment. But more significantly from the point of view of alignment, the PM system will be designed to ensure that employees' behaviour is directed towards delivering the business strategy.

PM is an *integrated* process that links individual employees and their teams to business objectives. It is *integrative* because an appropriately designed and implemented PM system represents a tool that organisations can use to align people both to the business plan and with each other, in a set of mutually reinforcing interventions, thereby adopting a strategic approach to the management and development of people. Having examined the managerial and strategic context of PM, it is now necessary to look at how PM itself works.

pause for thought

To what extent can a system of PM integrate the objectives of the individual and the organisation?

Why did you reach this conclusion?

The practicalities of performance management

The PM cycle

PM should be tailored to the needs of the organisation and operated flexibly (Armstrong and Baron, 1998). However, it is possible to identify a number of processes that form the basis of any PM system. Conventionally, PM is portrayed as a three-stage cycle involving performance planning, monitoring and review (Armstrong and Baron, 2005). See Figure 8.2.

This model is limited by its association of PM very closely with appraisal. Nevertheless, it is of value as it describes the three key phases of PM, thereby providing a useful basis for designing an appropriate system.

Performance planning

A planning meeting is often the first stage of a PM cycle. Objectives are usually set (or agreed) for the next 12 months, but these may be broken down into (often quarterly) targets or 'milestones' that can be reviewed and amended as circumstances change. In practice, the performance planning discussion will often take place at the same time as the performance review meeting, taking account of any development needs that have arisen over the past year.

The performance plan, negotiated by the employee and their line manager, performs a number of functions:

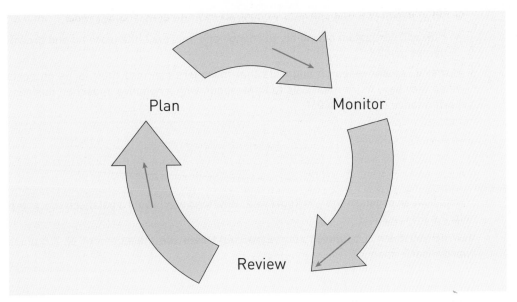

Figure 8.2 The PM cycle

- ◆ It represents a framework for future discussions about performance;
- ◆ It clarifies roles;
- ◆ It forms a basis for assessing progress in the future.

The essential requirement of the plan is the establishment of performance objectives.

Setting performance objectives

Employees may be given project or key task objectives. These should be designed to add value to the business and should not be merely a restatement of the individual's job description. It is important to align individual objectives with corporate strategy so that PM has an impact on business performance. It is conventional to refer to a cascading process, where corporate objectives are translated into functional object-ives, team goals and, finally, into individual objectives. The aim is to establish a 'clear line of sight' between the individual's performance and the success of the organisation as a whole, although the further down the organisational structure, the more difficult it is to establish this link. Some organisations use 'balanced scorecards' in an attempt to create this clear line of sight.

First developed by Kaplan and Norton (1992), **balanced scorecards** are based on the argument that no single measure (e.g. short-term financial gains) provides a good indication of business success. Instead, a balanced selection of objective measures should be used based on the following questions:

- ◆ How should we appear to our shareholders? (the financial perspective)
- ◆ How should we appear to our customers? (the customer perspective)

> ◆ What business processes must we excel at? (the internal perspective)
> ◆ How will we sustain our ability to change and improve? (the learning and growth perspective)
>
> However, recent research suggests that managers can lose their focus on costs when they have more measures to think about, with a negative impact on business performance (Pickard, 2006).

exercise

◆ **Think about an organisation you know well. How (and why) could a balanced scorecard help the HR function?**

◆ **How do you think a balanced scorecard could help the management of Warbings improve performance?**

Organisations usually seek to limit the number of performance objectives set for any individual, encouraging a sharper focus on a number of key goals that reflect business aims. The objectives themselves are usually formulated in line with the well-known 'SMART' model:

> *Specific* – establishing clear expectations for the employee, possibly with the help of *key performance indicators* (KPIs) that help the individual establish when the objective has been met.
>
> *Measurable* – measurable targets allow line managers to differentiate between levels of performance.
>
> *Achievable* – clearly, setting daunting targets will result in demotivated employees. However, by the same token, objectives should be challenging ('stretch objectives'), placing the emphasis firmly on continuous improvement.
>
> *Relevant* – employees' objectives should be relevant to their role and to the needs of the company. This implies the need to prioritise objectives by giving each respective target a weighting.
>
> *Timebound* – setting a completion deadline for each objective allows for monitoring of progress and performance.

Performance planning as communication

Creating a clear line of sight between business goals and individuals' performance objectives is a communication process which, through the sharing of information about company strategy and decisions, makes employees feel trusted and involved and gives them a better understanding of their role (Fletcher, 2004). However, the 'cascading' principle implies top-down, one-way communication that can be viewed as indoctrinating and controlling (Marchington and Wilkinson, 2002). Communication is a two-way process with feedback loops that encourage involvement and reflection at lower levels to be fed back to senior management (Fletcher, 2004). However, research suggests that relatively few organisations have built-in provisions for upward feedback in their performance planning processes (CIPD, 2005).

To what extent do you think that feedback on performance can be damaging?
Your answer should take into consideration organisational and individual aspects.

Competency frameworks

It has been suggested that, 'competencies are now taking a key role in describing the behaviours employees should demonstrate in achieving their goals' (IDS, 2005). By focusing on behavioural goals or competencies (the 'how') as well as on performance objectives (the 'what'), managers can get a more rounded view of an individual's performance. This realisation has lead many organisations to develop competency frameworks that help to align individual behaviour with the organisation's values and business strategy.

Developing management competencies is often the first stage of constructing a suitable framework to cover the whole organisation (IDS, 2001). Competencies are essentially explicit statements of the behaviours required of employees, at different levels and in various roles, to achieve business objectives. As well as promoting vertical integration, once the framework is in place it also provides a vehicle for horizontal integration (Miller et al., 2001). Specifically, a competency framework can support an organisation's HR strategy in the following ways:

- As a basis for recruitment and selection (e.g. competency-based interviewing);
- In performance planning and review;
- As a benchmark against which staff can be developed;
- As a basis for rewarding performance (competency-based and contribution pay).

In performance planning, individuals may focus on a specific number of competencies over the annual planning period, but the annual review is likely to take account of the employee's competency with reference to the whole framework (IDS, 2005).

Competency frameworks should reflect and support company values. Competency development fosters appropriate behaviours, which in turn reinforce organisational values and promote the creation of high performance cultures. The introduction of a competency framework into performance management is likely to be part of a deliberate strategy to bring about cultural change. As ever when implementing organisational change, employee involvement is important to ensure buy-in and staff will typically participate in developing competencies through focus groups and situational interviews, often (expensively) facilitated by consultants (Maloney, 2000). Another advantage of staff involvement is that the language in which competencies are couched is comprehensible to employees.

This leads us to the drawbacks of a competency-based approach to performance management. Woodall and Winstanley (1998) criticise competency frameworks on the following grounds:

- Competencies are static in that they describe the behaviours required by an organisation at a particular point in time and are not responsive to changing business conditions. Competency frameworks therefore require constant maintenance and regular updating to ensure that they evolve to keep up with new demands placed on them.

- ◆ Competency frameworks are bureaucratic and mechanistic. They can become unwieldy, and there have been cases of organisations developing hundreds of competencies (Miller et al., 2001). Thus a competency framework must be focused, providing just enough detail to ensure that competencies are meaningful and fit for purpose.

- ◆ Competencies stifle innovation and flexibility. Prescribing behaviours through a competency framework means that people are less likely to approach their roles creatively and develop original solutions to problems.

exercise

Produce two slides showing the advantages and disadvantages of competency frameworks.

Development plans

The need for the organisation to support employees' own aspirations as well as its expectations of them has highlighted development as one of the key outcomes of PM. Thus one of the benefits of a PM system is seen to be the improved motivation and retention of staff. Personal development plans often form a vehicle for meeting employees' development needs and aspirations.

Development plans and goals are designed to meet individual growth and improvement, as well as meet the performance needs of the job. They encompass new skills needed to meet performance objectives, skills deficits highlighted in the last performance review and development to meet longer-term career aspirations.

Development goals need to be measurable, taking into account how skills and competencies will be acquired and applied in the workplace. Development planning itself often happens at the same time as objective setting and plans are usually included in the same performance agreement (IDS, 2005). It also reinforces the organisation's commitment to supporting employee development, but it should be noted that development can be achieved in ways other than through training.

Monitoring performance: supporting progress

We now turn to the second stage in the PM cycle – the monitoring of performance. The main implication of this is that managers should monitor employees' progress and support them throughout the year. Increasingly, managers are expected to hold either formal interim reviews, where objectives can be amended, or regular one-to-one meetings with employees, but some organisations take this a step further by establishing a coaching culture (Porter et al., 2006).

pause for thought

Can you think of any occasions when individuals might resent their performance being monitored?

Do you think such feelings of resentment would have an impact on their subsequent performance?

Why did you reach this conclusion?

Developing managers as coaches

One of the main functions of these monitoring processes is to provide feedback to people to help them keep on target with regard to their performance plan. One way of achieving this is by line managers taking on the role of coach (Parsloe, 1999; IDS, 2005). Establishing such a 'high performance culture' requires managers to stretch high-potential staff, manage underperformers and motivate 'steady' workers.

For many organisations, creating a coaching culture requires both significant investment in developing managers as coaches and systems that provide incentives for them to focus on the development of employees. Organisations could include the responsibility for employee development in the managers' competency framework and performance objectives to reinforce this developmental focus.

window into practice

Managing underperformance

With staff survey results showing that employees rated their managers' ability to deal with underperformance as 'very poor', a television company decided it was time to tackle the problem. Managers from the company reported that dealing with poor or inadequate performance was one of their most difficult tasks. They particularly disliked dealing with issues that were personal to the employee, or tackling employees who had not received any feedback previously.

A number of interventions were put in place. The management team agreed the standard and level of performance that they were expecting, and clarified this to staff. Team away-days enabled staff to participate in setting team objectives in line with organisational goals, and to review codes of behaviour and ground rules. A revised performance management process made a particular feature of regular one-to-one feedback sessions on an ongoing basis, with clear objectives agreed at each session and followed up subsequently. Rather than relying on an annual appraisal, these regular meetings encouraged better relationships between managers and staff and allowed issues to be raised and resolved before they escalated into more serious performance problems. Focused goals that were reviewed each session took the place of yearly objectives that tended to be overlooked in the day to day work.

By using role plays with actors, managers and staff were trained in how to use these sessions in the most effective way, covering issues of: feedback; dealing with conflict; listening; and questioning skills. Procedures for dealing with discipline and lack of capability were also reviewed.

Overall, performance has improved, with employees reporting greater clarity about their roles and better communications with their managers.

In a recent survey of managers, nearly half of respondents stated that they would prefer to go to the dentist for root canal treatment than appraise their staff.

Why do you think this is?

Performance appraisal

The purpose of performance appraisal

Performance appraisal – or performance review as it is increasingly being called (IRS, 2001) – is at the centre of the PM process. Despite attracting criticism, mainly due to the ineffective way in which it is often carried out, performance appraisal is used as a key element of PM by over 80 per cent of employers (IRS, 2001; Industrial Society, 2001; CIPD, 2005).

While performance appraisal comes in various different forms, it will typically involve a formal review of an employee's work over a set period of time – normally a year. Appraisals tend to have two parts – the first is looking back over the past year to review performance and objectives; and the second part is looking forward to set objectives and targets for the next year and to identify learning and development needs. It provides the opportunity for the employee and manager to sit down and have a dialogue about performance and development at least on a yearly basis.

Key aims for performance appraisal would include the following:

◆ *Improving performance* – in the absence of clear feedback, it is difficult for people to improve, at least in the way the organisation requires. Performance appraisal provides an opportunity for managers to reinforce good performance by praise and recognition. Identifying gaps in performance and providing appropriate learning opportunities also helps to improve performance. Equally important is the clarification of goals, roles and standards.

◆ *Motivating staff* – recognition, knowledge of results, feedback and agreeing SMART goals are all factors that contribute to improving motivation (Locke and Latham, 1990).

◆ *Allocating rewards* – the assessment of performance made in the appraisal interview can form the basis for decisions about allocations of pay and incentives.

◆ *Succession planning and career progression* – identifying those with potential and ensuring that they have the right development opportunities.

◆ *Improving communication between manager and managed* – providing a two-way channel of communication.

pause for thought

What is the main purpose of performance appraisal?

Since it is the subject of so much criticism, why is it commonly used?

While these are all laudable aims, many authors would argue that appraisal often has opposite effects. Taylor (2005) postulates that it can be concluded from the research that performance appraisal is less a panacea and more of a curse. Managers often find the process challenging, particularly when giving critical feedback, and are often expected to do this with little training.

Different approaches to performance appraisal

These can be categorised into two main types – those focused on **output** and those focused on **behaviour**.

Output-based assessment

Output-based assessment has its roots in the Management by Objectives movement originating in the 1950s. Performance is measured in terms of quantifiable results, either in terms of productivity or quality measures or, most commonly on the achievement of a series of specific objectives. With some jobs, such as salespeople, it is relatively easy to identify clear measures of performance that are intrinsic to the achievement of the role, but for others those aspects of the job which are most easily measured are often not the most significant. If this is the case, then employees can be encouraged to focus on the measurable, but less important aspects of their roles. What gets measured is often what gets done.

In a recent CIPD survey, 62 per cent of respondents used objective setting as part of their appraisal process (CIPD, 2005). This involves the appraisee and appraiser jointly agreeing objectives that are specific and measurable, and then reviewing the achievement of these objectives at the next appraisal session. Setting targets in this way not only encourages participation in the process but is a powerful way to increase motivation (Locke and Latham, 1990). The main criticisms of objective-based assessment revolve around the perceived difficulty of setting meaningful objectives for particular jobs; the relevance of these to the totality of the role; and the difficulty of using this approach to compare individuals one with another.

Behavioural assessments

It could be argued that the way a person fulfils their job role is as important, as the results that they achieve. An assessment of employee behaviour is therefore seen by many as an important aspect of an appraisal process. This will involve identifying the criteria that are important for the effective performance of the job, then rating the individual against those criteria. An appraiser would use evidence from direct observation of the employee, or by reports from others, to make a judgement about the appraisee's performance, and rate him or her accordingly.

A variety of different rating schemes are used but despite efforts to improve objectivity, behavioural assessment sometimes remains less objective than the output-based approaches. See the box below.

Behavioural and numerical rating scales

Numerical – individuals are rated on a number of different criteria and given a score on a scale from best to worst. Typical discussions are around whether to have odd or even scales, e.g. 1–5 or 1–4.

Intervals with **descriptions** – as above, but the scales are given verbal descriptions, e.g. outstanding, very good, good, fair, unsatisfactory, too early to judge.

As above, but directly related to **job requirements**, e.g. consistently exceeds requirements, occasionally exceeds requirements, meets requirements, fails to meet requirements.

Behaviourally based scales – in this case, the key dimensions of the job are broken down into aspects of behaviour that relate to effective performance. Each of these is then rated, often using a numerical scale, for example:

Managing performance

1. Agrees objectives and standards with teams
Regularly   1   2   3   4   5   Rarely
2. Uses coaching skills and tools to improve performance
Regularly   1   2   3   4   5   Rarely

There are advantages and disadvantages to both output and behaviour approaches. Because of this, organisations are increasingly moving towards a combination approach, involving the results-based approach of objectives with the development-based approach of the use of competencies (IRS, 2001; Fletcher, 2004). This is more likely to succeed in ensuring that performance expectations are based on a more rounded picture of the role.

Self-appraisal

An increasingly common approach to assessment involves a combination of downward-appraisal (manager-led) and self-appraisal (IRS, 2001; CIPD, 2005). Self-appraisal allows the appraisee to comment on their own achievements and contribute to their performance plan for the next period. This two-way process encourages participation and commitment, and allows the appraisee to take greater ownership of the process.

Multi-source appraisal: 360°

The use of multi-source feedback is growing, partly as a response to flatter organisational structures, and also in an attempt to introduce more consistency and breadth into the process. Evidence from a number of sources is more likely to provide a balanced picture of an individual's strengths and development needs. Multi-source feedback can range from simply asking peers or other managers to make comments, with examples, on an individual's performance, to the more sophisticated 360° feedback systems. These have grown in popularity, particularly for managerial staff, and look to continue to do so (Fletcher, 2004).

Common problems

Making a judgement about another person's performance, and giving them that feedback honestly is something that most people find challenging; they will often take steps to avoid, or to dilute, any critical feedback. Overcoming this is a critical challenge. Other common problems that occur with appraisals include:

◆ Lack of regular feedback – instead of tackling difficult issues at the right time, feedback is stored and given in one piece at the appraisal time;

- ◆ Collecting comprehensive evidence about performance – appraisers do not always work with the staff they are appraising, making it sometimes difficult to collect evidence about performance;

- ◆ Lack of follow-up;

- ◆ Time pressures;

- ◆ It is often viewed as a tedious routine;

- ◆ Filling out the forms and dealing with the paperwork becomes more important than the motivational aspects of the process;

- ◆ Focus on the negative – a large proportion of time in the appraisal spent talking about the things that have gone wrong rather than accentuating the positive aspects of performance;

- ◆ Inadequately trained appraisers;

- ◆ It can be complex to administer.

360° skills surveys

The popularity of 360° or multi-input feedback has increased as organisations seek ways of creating more open environments, with a greater emphasis on continuous performance improvement. This process provides a snapshot of an individual's current impact and an assessment of their performance based on the perceptions of the members of their role set. It is particularly useful for development purposes.

QAS is a thriving and dynamic organisation, providing a range of address management and data accuracy solutions to organisations worldwide. Voted the most fun company to work for in the *Sunday Times* Best Company Awards of 2001, the challenge was to improve managerial proficiency – without losing the fun.

QAS strongly believes in growing its own talent. The vast majority of QAS managers joined as graduates and have grown and developed along with the company, many of them on a fast and steep career trajectory. Early in 2001, the company realised that, with international expansion plans in full swing, the depth of managerial capacity might prove to be a limiting factor on growth.

Making extensive use of 360° surveys and feedback, the bespoke management development programme that was implemented over the next two years was aimed at producing measurable improvements in managerial capability.

Key managerial competencies appropriate for QAS were defined by a team of managers and ratified by the board. A 360° management skills survey questionnaire based on these competencies was developed. The questionnaire had 47 questions, with a 1–5 rating scale, and three free-form questions at the end. A pilot group of 30 managers each selected ten people to complete the questionnaires using a combination of their managers', their peers' and their direct reports' feedback. They also completed a questionnaire themselves. Each manager had a review session, where individual development plans were agreed, based on the results of the survey. Common themes arising from the aggregated feedback were used to design six training modules, which were delivered over a period of a year. In addition, managers worked on their individual plans in a series of action learning sets.

continued

Three months after the completion of the formal part of the programme, the managers took part in a repeat 360° survey to evaluate any change in the perception of their competency. Aggregated scores showed an improvement in 42 out of the 47 questions, while over two-thirds of the managers showed significant improvements – particularly in the areas they had highlighted in their development plans. Generally, participants reported that the 360° feedback was the most valuable part of the programme: not only was it revealing to see themselves as others saw them, but it enabled clear and focused development objectives to be set, which could be followed up during the rest of the programme.

Issues in performance management

Success factors in performance management processes

What makes the difference between a system that is regarded by all as a waste of time and one which delivers key benefits to the business and to individuals?

The 2004 survey on PM by the CIPD revealed a strong degree of consensus among respondents about the key issues associated with a successful system. Top of the list was management buy-in: it is seen as essential that line managers own the system and are well trained in how to use it. Most respondents felt that PM is only successful if it forms a 'continuous and integrated part of the line manager/employee relationship' (Armstrong and Baron, 2005).

Other important elements are:

- Alignment with business goals and objectives;
- Integration of the goals of the organisation with those of individuals;
- Objectivity and the importance of providing quantifiable measures of performance;
- Effective communication of the aims of the process;
- Regular evaluation of its effectiveness;
- A process that is simple and easy to use increases the likelihood of success;
- Effective follow-up with ongoing feedback;
- An explicit link to a personal development plan.

Critics of PM point to lack of consistency as a problem area (Grint, 1993) and organisations are increasingly using different techniques to attempt to overcome this. These include:

- Increased emphasis on line manager training and ongoing coaching;
- The provision of more objective feedback on performance;
- More input into the appraisal process by staff, including a greater emphasis on self-assessment;
- Scrutiny of managers' assessments by their peers;
- Increased use of multi-source feedback.

Cultural and structural fit

Organisations differ in structure and culture and, to be successful, PM systems need to reflect this. A large bureaucratic organisation, where consistency and formal rules are important, will probably need a more formal system. A more organic, project-orientated, organisation in a fast-moving environment will need to have a system that allows for change and flexibility.

Some commentators argue that the traditional hierarchical structure of management is no longer a feature of many organisations (Kettley, 1995). Instead, flexible teams and cross-functional projects are a reality of organisational life. With increasing de-layering, it is not always clear who is directly responsible for an individual's appraisal. The wider span of managerial control often gives them an unrealistic number of employees to appraise. Solutions to this include appointing 'performance managers' or 'team leaders' to undertake appraisal and ongoing feedback for staff and to act as a support for developmental purposes. Peer appraisal may also be seen as a solution.

Staff expectations and values will have implications for the type of PM system chosen and for the way it is operated. For example, a sales company where output is not only crucial but easily measured will be comfortable with a system that is based on quantifiable measures. According to Fletcher (2004), professional groups which are characterised by a high degree of independence, and where some elements of the work are less easy to quantify in any meaningful way, will require a more developmental, less hierarchical approach with a greater emphasis on quality.

---

pause for thought

How do you feel about being assessed by your tutor?

Do you feel the same way about being peer assessed?

Account for the differences, if any, in your feelings between the two methods of assessment.

The aims of PM fall into two main categories – assessing the past and improving the future. This leads us to a conflict at the heart of PM systems. Termed the evaluation agenda or the development agenda, writers such as Taylor (2005) argue that it is not possible to successfully fulfil both aims within the same process. The main reasons for this lie in employees' attitudes towards appraisal. If employees perceive the process to be evaluative, they are less inclined to be open about their performance gaps and development needs, feeling that this will count against them in the assessment process. The mutual trust that is necessary for an honest appraisal of strengths and weaknesses will be further undermined when an individual perceives that this will be used to inform decisions about rewards or redundancy. Fletcher (2004) argues that it is mainly top management who want the appraisal to be primarily assessment driven, while appraisers and appraisees want it to be development led. He suggests that the process is more likely to be successful if it is defined as development led, as this will be more acceptable to both appraisers and appraisees and will provide a strategy for improving performance. He also challenges the efficacy of appraisal as a vehicle for comparative assessments of individuals. In the CIPD survey (2005),

71 per cent of the sample agreed that the focus of performance appraisal should be developmental.

Many organisations overcome any difficulty by clearly distinguishing between these two aims, and by having separate meetings at different times, one to focus on development and one for the purpose of assessing the individual in order to allocate rewards. Fletcher (2004) proposes that the most effective method combines a results-orientated appraisal with a competency-based appraisal, allowing measurement of targets and goals to be combined with a focus on personal development.

Contingent pay

It is by no means essential for a PM system to include performance-related pay – indeed in the CIPD survey, only 42 per cent of all respondents had contingent pay, dropping to 29 per cent for the public sector. The IRS survey on PM (2001) reported a third consecutive yearly fall in the use of merit pay systems.

exercise

What are the arguments for and against using appraisal to link pay to performance?

Contingent pay is seen as desirable by organisations because it is fair and equitable to reward people differentially for their different contributions; it raises the importance of performance and by linking this to contribution, it motivates people to perform better. Yet according to the IRS Management Review (2001: 37), 'the slowdown in the take up of individual merit schemes has coincided with a mounting body of research that suggests performance pay does not actually deliver what its advocates claim.' Armstrong and Baron (2005: 106) question the relationship between contingent pay and motivation, quoting studies that show a negative rather than a positive impact.

However, if people are to be paid differentially in accordance with their contribution to the organisation, then an *accurate* and *fair* assessment of that contribution needs to be made. It is really important for organisations to have a robust performance management system in place before attempting to introduce any kind of contribution-based pay scheme. Employee satisfaction with the reward system depends on their estimate of the fairness of the process, and the accuracy of the measurement of their contribution, particularly in comparison to others. Often managers feel they are operating in a transparent and unbiased way, while employees feel the reverse.

While the 1980s and 1990s were dominated by the rise of performance-related pay schemes, in many organisations these are now being revised and converted into contribution pay schemes. Performance-related pay typically provides increases in the form of basic pay or a cash bonus usually linked to the achievement of agreed objectives. Contribution pay, on the other hand, includes an assessment of competency (inputs) as well as an assessment of performance (outputs), thus giving a more holistic picture. This gives a more balanced approach to pay and performance management, linking pay, career development and performance improvement to rewarding staff for their contribution to personal and business objectives.

Summary

In this chapter, we have explored the strategic role of PM systems in aligning both the efforts of teams and individuals with business objectives and the key HR interventions of reward, development and appraisal with each other. Our examination of the PM cycle has shown that appraisal is one vital but problematic element in a PM system and that to be effective, appraisal systems must be adapted to meet the structural and cultural needs of the organisation. Different approaches to appraisal are discussed in some detail, focusing on the increasing use of multi-source appraisal. The tension in appraisal between assessment and development was also highlighted, as were the issues associated with using appraisal as a vehicle for linking pay to performance. Finally, we considered the value of appraisal training for managers and their staff.

exercise

At the moment, Warbings does not have a PM system.

1. Make a case for the introduction of a performance management system into Warbings.
2. Which factors would you need to take into account when developing the system?
3. Which components would you include in the PM system?

Review Questions

You may wish to attempt the following as practice examination style questions.

8.1 How can a PM system help an organisation achieve both vertical and horizontal integration of people management and development?

8.2 What is the role of competencies in PM?

8.3 How can organisations ensure that line managers are more effective in managing the performance of their staff?

8.4 What are the pros and cons of having a direct link between PM process and pay?

8.5 What are the key success factors for PM?

8.6 What is the role of self-appraisal in PM?

References

Armstrong, M. and Baron, A. (1998). *Performance Management: The New Realities*, London: IPD.

Armstrong, M. and Baron, A. (2005). *Managing Performance: Performance Management in Action*, London: IPD.

CIPD (2005). Survey report, *Performance Management*, September.

Fletcher, C. (2004). *Appraisal and Feedback: Making Performance Review Work*, 3rd edition, London: CIPD.

Fombrun, C.J., Tichy, N.M. and Devanna, M.A. (1984). *Strategic Human Resource Management*, New York: Wiley.

Grint, K. (1993). What's wrong with performance appraisal? A critique and a suggestion, *Human Resource Management Journal*, Spring, pp. 61–77.

Guest, D., Michie, J., Sheehan, M. et al. (2000). *Effective People Management: Initial Findings of the Future of Work Study*, London: CIPD.

Holbeche, L. (2001). *Aligning Human Resources and Business Strategy*, London: Butterworth-Heinemann.

Incomes Data Services HR Study 706 (2001). *Competency Frameworks*.

Incomes Data Services HR Study 796 (2005). *Performance Management*.

Industrial Relations Services (2001). Performance management revisited, *IRS Management Review*, 20 January.

Industrial Society (2001). Managing performance, *Managing Best Practice 86*, at: www.theworkfoundation.com.

Kaplan, R. and Norton, D. (1992). The Balanced Scorecard – measures that drive performance, *Harvard Business Review*, January–February, pp. 197–221.

Kast, F.S. and Rosenweig, J.E. (1985). *Organisation and Management: A Systems Approach*, 4th edition, New York: McGraw-Hill.

Kettley, P. (1995). Is Flatter Better? Delayering the Management Hierarchy, Institute of Employment Studies, IES Report No. 290.

Locke, E.A. and Latham, G.P. (1990). *A Theory of Gaol Setting and Task Performance*, Englewood Cliffs, NJ: Prentice Hall.

Maloney, K. (2000). History repeating, *People Management*, July, pp. 23–25.

Marchington, M. and Wilkinson, A. (2002). *People Management and Development*, 2nd edition, London: CIPD.

Miller, L., Rankin, N. and Neathey, F. (2001). *Competency Frameworks in UK Organisations: Key Issues in Employers' Use of Competencies*, London: CIPD.

Mullins, L.J. (2002). *Management and Organisational Behaviour*, 6th edition, London: Prentice Hall.

Parsloe, E. (1999). *The Manager as Coach and Mentor*, London: CIPD.

Pickard, J. (2006). Scorecard system might not be so balanced, says research, *People Management*, April, p. 5.

Porter, K., Smith, P. and Fagg, R. (2006). *Leadership and Management for HR Professionals*, London: Butterworth-Heinemann.

Taylor, S. (2005). *People Resourcing*, 3rd edition, London: CIPD.

Woodall, J. and Winstanley, D. (1998). *Management Development: Strategy and Practice*, Chapters 4 and 5, Oxford: Blackwell.

Further Reading

Industrial Relations Services (2003). Performance management: policy and practice, *IRS Employment Review 781*, August.

Kearns, P. (2000). *Measuring and Managing Employee Performance*, Marlow: FT/Prentice Hall.

Purcell, J. et al. (2003). *Understanding the People and Performance Link: Unlocking the Black Box*, research report, London: CIPD.

Useful Websites

www.cipd.co.uk – the official website of the Chartered Institute of Personnel and Development – the lead body for HR professionals

www.dti.gov.uk – links to Department of Trade and Industry information on business performance and productivity

www.incomesdata.co.uk – Income Data Services studies on performance management and competency

www.irseclipse.co.uk – access to Industrial Relations Services reviews on HRM issues, including PM

www.teachernet.gov.uk – resources for teaching in PM and appraisal

www.theworkfoundation.com – access to studies on individual and business performance, including the Industrial Society past papers

PART 4
Reward

CHAPTER 9

Through a Glass Darkly: problems and issues in reward

By Angela Wright

Chapter outline

The aim of this chapter is to explore some current developments in reward management and to discuss some key issues and questions around the effectiveness of reward systems. It discusses aspects of reward strategy, in particular the relationship between employee commitment and reward and the interrelationship between motivation and reward. It considers some aspects of market and internal equity issues and examines current developments in pay structures and pay systems and employee-centred reward, especially flexible benefits.

Learning outcomes

By the end of this chapter, you should be able to:

- Discuss reward strategy concepts, the relevance of motivation theory and aspects of employee commitment;
- Identify salary market issues;
- Explain some of the developments in employee-centred reward and in pay structures.

Introduction

Pay and benefits form one of the largest items of expenditure in any organisation and yet in many organisations there is a lack of evidence as to whether the particular pay and benefits practices are adding value or merely adding to costs. There is also often a lack of openness and transparency and poor levels of understanding of the way pay is managed. At the academic level, there is less specific research about the range of activities now termed 'reward management' than there is for some other aspects of people management. As Milsome (2005) summarises from the Reward Management Symposium 2005, reward practices are rarely based on evidence as to what produces good organisational outcomes and what does not. It is just as unusual for practices to be evaluated for their effectiveness.

Some strategic aspects of reward

Reward is underpinned by a mix of theoretical perspectives, drawn from different academic disciplines, principally economics, psychology and industrial relations, as well as the comparatively new perspectives drawn from human resource management. However when considering the strategic place of reward and its impact, the literature and theories of business strategy are of key importance. Within the strategy literature, reward features rather lightly and this has led to the growth in the US of quantitative studies looking for associations between high performance in organisations and specific human resource management (HRM) practices.

Reward strategy may be characterised as comprising the future imperatives of the organisation's approach to pay and benefits. The CIPD (2006), drawing on earlier work, identifies the key characteristics of a written formal statement of strategic intent for reward which:

- Defines broad objectives for reward;
- Is a framework for use by managers in making reward decisions;
- Is long term;
- Has clearly planned goals based on business objectives;
- Is flexible and able to be adapted when business circumstances change.

Lawler (1995) advocated that reward approaches should be tailored to fit the strategic business 'compass' of the specific organisation as a way of promoting change and enhancing performance. However, the CIPD (2006) reveals that only a minority of organisations has a formal reward strategy. Why do so few employers not adopt such a strategic approach to reward? One possible explanation is that there is no business strategy to align to, or, if there is one, it is so weak that it is not worth aligning a reward strategy to, reflecting perhaps the realities and complexities of modern organisations. However, reward could be treated in some organisations as part and parcel of human resource (HR) strategy.

Regardless of what organisations formally commit to writing, the idea that reward might have potential to positively influence organisational performance is compelling. One of the key problems is that the interrelationships between reward and other HR practices are difficult for researchers to determine. Gerhart (2000) concludes from his analysis of various studies assessing the influence of reward on corporate performance that there is evidence of relationships between organisational performance and pay strategy, but it is difficult to determine their precise nature. While key outcomes such as job satisfaction, recruitment/retention and employee performance seem to be associated with reward, the numerous US studies do not permit reward – as an influence on organisational performance – to be isolated from other causes.

pause for thought

Why do you think Gerhart concluded that it was difficult to determine the precise nature of the relationship between the way an organisation performs and its pay strategy? Do you think this relationship is important? Why did you reach this conclusion?

Theoretical perspectives

Best fit or contingency theory

This view suggests there are no universally good reward practices – what is appropriate in any one organisation is what works for that organisation. The contingency view suggests that HR practices need to achieve a 'best fit' by taking into account the circumstances and goals of the company. But, as Boxall and Purcell (2000) argue, there are many problems with this type of approach when we begin looking at practical situations, and the theory could be criticised as being too simplistic. Certain bad practices can be identified, which would add little to any organisation.

Best practice

The best practice school of thought proposes that certain HR practices are related to organisational success, regardless of the organisation's business context or strategy. But this approach has been criticised by Boxall and Purcell (2000) for providing uplifting, simple messages, while lacking credibility. What is 'best' in one set of circumstances will often not work in another, and it stretches credibility to assume that what works best for a multinational oil company can be applied to the local corner shop.

To what extent can reward practices be integrated into and with other HR practices in an organisation known to you?	**pause for thought**

Pfeffer (1998) proposes that there are 'golden rules' in reward policy and practice, which hold good across all organisations. These essential rules in crafting a reward strategy are:

- Include 'large dose' collective reward;
- Accept that pay is not a substitute for a 'high trust' environment, 'fun' and 'meaningful work';
- Openness and transparency are vital, with a positive message about equity;
- Employers should use means other than pay to signal company values and to focus behaviour;
- Employers should use pay as only one element in building employee commitment.

Huselid (1995) and Macduffie (1995) suggest there are 'bundles' of HR practices that help to drive organisational performance, but the elements in the bundles may vary according to business sector. There is little evidence of particular pay or reward practices consistently appearing in these 'bundles', but in all the US studies performance-related pay tends to feature. The rationale for the universal applicability of these practices is that they lead to superior performance, since they draw upon the discretionary effort of individual employees. Marchington and Grugulis (2000) question the validity of such work.

In the search for the bundle of HR practices (including reward practices) that may or may not be associated with higher corporate performance, much of the earlier research has focused on policies and practices. Pfeffer (1998), among others, has indicated that 'shared compensation' schemes, for example long-term all-employee share schemes and gain-sharing schemes, are associated with higher productivity or performance. Few organisations opt for a gain-sharing arrangement (CIPD, 2005) under which employees themselves are fully involved in devising the (sometimes) modest bonus scheme, which rewards productivity improvements.

In order to achieve sustainable organisational improvements, Purcell's (2003) work identifies the importance of releasing the 'discretionary' efforts and voluntary co-operation of employees. The place of specific reward practices in supporting these developments is not clear. The role of front-line managers is seen as critical in translating all people management and development policies (including reward) into practice, and eliciting discretionary behaviour from individual employees. Hutchinson and Purcell (2003) further show that the crucial difference between low-performing and high-performing organisations comes from front-line leaders. CIPD's (2006) survey finds most of the respondents do not rate highly the reward decision-making or communication skills of their line managers, with only one-third of respondents saying they feel managers receive sufficient training in reward skills. Purcell and Hutchinson's later work (2007) shows that the day-to-day reward activities carried out by line managers are largely unregulated by their organisations, although such rewards, even though they may be at the symbolic rather than tangible level, are highly valued by employees.

Cox (2000) raises the idea of 'best process' as a central concept in which the emphasis is more on the quality of relationships between management and employees than with the actual reward practice applied. Essential elements of employee involvement and participation are seen as crucial, particularly in pay system development.

Also of relevance to reward is the newer research area of employee engagement, although this overlaps with more established areas of employee commitment and organisational citizenship behaviour. Robinson et al.'s (2004) study shows that the management of pay and benefits features in the spectrum of factors affecting employee engagement, but does not disentangle reward from the other aspects of HR practice and management.

West et al.'s (2005) study on rewarding customer service demonstrates a strong relationship between employee commitment and reward, and a relationship between employee satisfaction and commitment and reward.

Communication and transparency

Openness and a positive message about equity are vital to the effectiveness of managing pay. Writers, including Pfeffer (1998), support this view. The general principle of openness and transparency of pay policies and practices is also a key requirement under equal pay legislation (see Chapter 10), but few organisations would claim to have transparent pay systems. Apart from the legal rationale, there are other reasons for employers to think seriously about making pay transparency a much stronger focus of their policies:

- Pay delivers a strong message, quite separate from its purely monetary value. If time and expense have been applied to designing a reward system then employees must understand it if it is to influence their behaviour.

- Some studies have shown that employees misunderstand pay relationships. For instance they tend to overestimate the pay of lower level jobs and underestimate the pay of those in higher-level jobs. If pay differentials between one level of role responsibility and another are underestimated by employees, their motivational value is reduced.

- Employees whose organisations are open about pay tend to express greater satisfaction with their pay and the system used to determine it.

Salary market issues

Much has been made of the 'new pay' school of thought (Zingheim and Schuster, 2000), arguing that internal equity should no longer be a priority for employers and that 'market value' should instead predominate. Vocal critics of that controversial manifestation of internal equity in practice – job evaluation – suggest that notions about a job as a distinct concept to the individual job-holder is an outmoded concept in the context of a flexible, market-orientated approach to pay. Instead, new pay writers (Lawler, 1995) advocate a much stronger focus on competencies and skills as well as on salary market rates. One central problem in this is the 'pay market'. In classical terms the market does not operate unless people can move around between organisations freely. This may be too simplistic a view of the complexities of the modern labour market. Gomez-Mejia and Balkin (1992) observe that while the myth persists that the market wage can be accurately and scientifically measured, in fact there is a wide range of market pay rates available for each occupation.

This process of pay comparability takes into account earnings for similar level posts in comparable organisations or in the economy generally, in setting an appropriate level of pay, but this is not the same as the operation of a true market. What the 'right' pay level may be will depend on a number of factors, not least those people with whom employees themselves choose to compare themselves. Heneman and Judge (2000) conclude that there is insufficient evidence concerning the focus on particular 'referents' (i.e. who they choose to compare themselves with) to the exclusion of others.

For pay practitioners, the market and pay surveys are virtually synonymous. Surveys of course are useful, and as IDS (2005) shows there are increasing sources of pay data at the disposal of employers, mostly at a considerable cost. Salary surveys are of course subject to the same statistical quality criteria as other sample surveys. Some, it must be acknowledged, are of dubious quality. The checklist below lists some of the key questions that reward practitioners need to ask when assessing the potential value of any survey.

Checklist of pay data quality

How are data collected?

- *Recruitment salary surveys.* Are these simply surveys of people applying for jobs through a recruitment agency? If so, what evidence is there that the data are representative of people already in post – whose pay may be higher or lower than those active in the job market?

- *Sample surveys.* How is the sample derived? Is it structured, representative, opportunistic?

Sample sizes and job matching:

- Is sample size mentioned?

Check for company size in sample:

- How many small companies/large companies? Large companies tend to have higher pay than smaller ones so it is important to use a survey which has an appropriate and comparable set of organisations.

Job matching is vitally important; job titles alone give a poor degree of matching:

- What job matching techniques are used?
- If job evaluation is used, is the system used relevant for the organisation?
- If a basic ranking scheme is used for job matching, how relevant is this to the organisation?

Check participants/repeat participants:

- Some turnover in participants is inevitable but a sample that is completely different one year to the next can prompt questions about how useful the previous year's participants found the survey results in practice. (Some surveys are only available to those organisations that supply data.)

Table 9.1 is an extract from the government's *Annual Survey of Hours and Earnings*, a survey which has the advantage of a sample which is representative of the workforce, but which is perhaps less useful in providing useable data on executive pay levels.

Pay, motivation, reward and recognition

Few senior managers doubt that *money motivates*. From a theoretical point of view, however, the underpinning for such confidence is mooted. Academics' work on performance-related pay (PRP) has taken a largely sceptical stance, stressing both theoretical deficiencies and the preponderance of studies showing mediocre

Table 9.1 Extract from pay survey (annual pay – gross (£) for all employee jobs[a]: UK, 2006)

Description	Code	Number of jobs[b] (thousand)	Median	Annual percentage change	Mean	Annual percentage change	Percentiles									
							10	20	25	30	40	60	70	75	80	90
All employees		19,700	19,496	2.9	24,301	3.9	5,880	10,002	11,799	13,392	16,355	23,031	27,209	29,779	32,615	42,048
Managers and senior officials	1	3,083	33,423	3.7	46,057	6.1	15,406	21,000	23,211	25,250	29,444	38,400	45,323	49,837	55,188	77,635
Corporate managers	11	2,628	34,887	3.3	48,470	6.3	16,269	22,192	24,525	26,643	30,583	40,226	47,495	51,844	57,698	81,378
Managers and proprietors in agriculture and services	12	455	26,000	2.3	32,116	1.6	12,780	16,851	18,544	20,038	23,015	29,695	33,866	36,534	39,937	52,947
Professional occupations	2	2,689	31,631	2.8	34,303	2.5	13,169	20,311	23,044	25,124	28,741	34,500	38,032	40,079	43,000	53,392
Science and technology professionals	21	709	34,057	3.4	36,507	3.1	20,480	25,513	27,034	28,568	31,281	36,904	40,188	42,378	45,328	54,159
Health professionals	22	175	47,688	1.7	57,067	-0.6	x	23,608	27,466	33,044	40,251	57,021	73,163	81,132	91,919	111,668
Teaching and research professionals	23	1,257	29,731	0.8	28,421	1.4	8,378	16,785	19,583	22,015	26,333	32,320	34,807	36,499	38,250	43,359
Business and public service professionals	24	548	31,111	3.2	37,678	5.5	16,278	20,648	22,952	25,000	28,179	34,648	39,776	43,458	46,911	60,596
Associate professional and technical occupations	3	2,926	24,644	2.3	26,492	1.9	10,867	15,909	17,701	19,274	22,104	27,154	30,068	31,859	34,033	40,512
Science and technology associate professionals	31	443	24,057	1.6	25,401	1.8	12,706	16,821	18,185	19,518	21,790	26,580	29,366	30,764	32,687	38,796

Table 9.1 continued

Description	Code	Number of jobs[b] (thousand)	Median	Annual percentage change	Mean	Annual percentage change	Percentiles									
							10	20	25	30	40	60	70	75	80	90
Health and social welfare associate professionals	32	977	21,661	4.1	21,199	4.3	8,538	13,065	14,758	16,298	19,173	23,792	26,120	27,488	29,043	32,611
Protective service occupations	33	351	31,003	2.0	31,352	1.9	19,856	24,521	25,812	26,695	28,488	33,568	36,875	38,375	40,017	43,724
Culture, media and sports occupations	34	220	22,757	-1.0	26,991	-2.5	4,805	12,086	14,359	16,568	19,608	25,687	29,414	32,536	35,731	46,013
Business and public service associate professionals	35	936	26,153	1.8	30,592	1.4	13,032	17,631	19,196	20,675	23,504	28,917	32,535	34,694	37,234	46,905
Administrative and secretarial occupations	4	2,704	15,219	3.9	15,867	3.7	6,453	9,109	10,464	11,700	13,672	16,915	18,889	20,043	21,472	25,452
Administrative occupations	41	2,174	15,485	3.7	16,095	3.8	6,715	9,591	10,995	12,139	14,018	17,196	19,126	20,250	21,630	25,388
Secretarial and related occupations	42	531	13,847	3.1	14,933	2.9	5,539	7,831	8,832	9,828	11,945	15,585	17,747	18,981	20,529	25,831
Skilled trades occupations	5	1,627	21,220	2.5	22,050	3.0	11,006	14,506	15,918	17,102	19,228	23,397	25,851	27,320	29,120	33,902
Skilled agricultural trades	51	102	15,944	4.3	15,802	4.9	7,926	11,982	12,497	13,358	14,579	17,006	18,290	19,008	19,979	x
Skilled metal and electrical trades	52	909	23,820	2.5	24,659	2.7	14,182	17,572	18,826	20,009	21,825	25,848	28,309	29,728	31,286	35,984
Skilled construction and building trades	53	311	21,204	3.6	22,221	5.0	12,866	15,960	16,991	18,073	19,652	23,000	25,290	26,450	28,062	32,317
Textiles, printing and other skilled trades	54	304	15,171	1.5	16,166	1.1	6,399	9,747	10,658	11,697	13,359	17,210	19,072	20,141	21,936	26,392

Occupation	Code	Number	Median (£)	Annual % change	Mean (£)	Annual % change	10	20	25	30	40	60	70	75	80	90
Personal service occupations	6	1,558	10,992	3.2	11,667	3.2	3,993	6,230	7,041	7,841	9,433	12,716	14,431	15,362	16,424	19,656
Caring personal service occupations	61	1,253	10,590	2.9	11,122	3.1	3,949	6,210	6,977	7,717	9,176	12,239	13,876	14,811	15,743	18,442
Leisure and other personal service occupations	62	306	12,956	2.5	13,903	4.6	4,209	6,300	7,488	8,602	10,920	14,865	17,253	18,564	19,933	24,354
Sales and customer service occupations	7	1,463	8,535	1.0	9,956	0.3	3,329	4,679	5,223	5,775	6,985	10,325	12,113	13,211	14,417	17,919
Sales occupations	71	1,189	7,903	-0.3	9,422	-0.7	3,167	4,456	4,944	5,436	6,526	9,495	11,245	12,186	13,384	17,065
Customer service occupations	72	274	12,206	3.7	12,274	4.4	4,575	6,343	7,144	8,082	10,314	13,788	15,497	16,355	17,222	19,737
Process, plant and machine operatives	8	1,503	19,274	2.6	19,934	2.6	10,748	13,529	14,529	15,568	17,398	21,354	23,484	24,700	26,174	30,074
Process, plant and machine operatives	81	882	19,059	1.9	20,069	2.8	10,906	13,346	14,308	15,171	17,010	21,230	23,594	24,908	26,690	30,689
Transport and mobile machine drivers and operatives	82	621	19,528	3.4	19,742	2.3	10,252	13,882	15,013	16,015	17,874	21,484	23,347	24,431	25,654	29,008
Elementary occupations	9	2,146	11,129	3.9	11,870	3.4	2,548	4,277	5,201	6,284	8,701	13,369	15,684	16,980	18,507	22,188
Elementary trades, plant and storage related occupations	91	691	15,517	2.6	16,185	2.7	8,313	11,082	11,944	12,685	14,100	16,919	18,711	19,789	20,964	24,712
Elementary administration and service occupations	92	1,455	7,829	4.4	9,820	4.2	1,995	3,260	3,938	4,519	6,035	10,191	12,775	14,399	16,119	20,643
Not Classified	:															

a Employees on adult rates who have been in the same job for more than a year.

b Figures for Number of Jobs are for indicative purposes only and should not be considered an accurate estimate of employee job counts.

KEY – The colour coding indicates the quality of each estimate: jobs, median, mean and percentiles but not the annual percentage change.

The quality of an estimate is measured by its coefficient of variation (CV), which is the ratio of the standard error of an estimate to the estimate.

Source: adapted from Office of National Statistics, *Annual Survey of Hours and Earnings* (2006).

Key	
	CV <= 5%
	CV > 5% and <= 10%
	CV > 10% and <= 20%
x = unreliable	CV > 20% or unavailable
.. = disclosive	
: = not applicable	
- = nil or negligible	

effectiveness in practice. Indeed, Sisson and Storey (2000) claim that, should one ignore the substantial body of evidence casting doubt on the links between pay and performance, the case for PRP is very plausible. Reward practitioner studies (for example, CIPD (2006)) continue to show the value that managers place on the ability to reward performance, within their organisations (Armstrong and Barron, 2005). The CIPD's and other studies show that performance pay remains in use in many organisations.

Theoretical support for performance pay is equivocal. Research casts doubt about the motivational effectiveness of using pay linked to performance. There remains a polarisation of views – managers, HR specialists and consultants 'believe' in what they may regard as the self-evident and practitioner-led case for PRP but most academic writers are sceptical of the value of the practice. Even at its best, however, performance pay may gain only employee compliance, not their long-term commitment. For example, performance may be more effective in helping to build immediate sales of a specific new product than in longer-term new product development generally.

Drawing on Legge's (1995) work, Perkins and Sandringham (1998) argue that instrumental approaches such as performance pay are essentially negative and may not lead to the sort of attitudinal change that is necessary for a 'strategic' level of commitment and high performance. There is as yet little systematic evidence of the specific role reward can play in attitudinal change.

Assumptions that money is the main motivator relate back to Taylorist scientific management principles of the early twentieth century, in which workers were set narrow tasks and paid under a 'piecework' arrangement for work done or output achieved.

From the motivation perspective, pay and benefits form *extrinsic* motivation; that is, they are external to the individual. Such rewards can include praise and promotion prospects as well as monetary rewards.

Both process - and cognitive-motivation theories are relevant to a discussion of reward. Maslow's *hierarchy of needs* and Herzberg's *two-factor theory* models are well known (if somewhat discredited, Rynes et al., 2005), but the *process theories* of motivation have attracted more attention. These theories focus on the psychological processes involved in motivation, and on individuals' perceptions of their working environment. For example, *expectancy theory* – devised by Vroom (1964) and extended by Porter and Lawler (1968) – emphasises that pay and benefits may motivate people if there is a direct relationship between effort and reward, but individuals must be able to control the factors which influence the level of that reward. It leads reward practitioners to incorporate the principle of *line of sight* in the design of pay systems, where employees can see clearly that they can control the criteria which will lead to better rewards. See Figure 9.1.

Basic formula

$F = V \times I \times E$

– F is the Force of the individual's motivation

– V is the Valence or value the individual perceives the outcome to have

– I is Instrumentality – the extent to which performance is seen by individuals to be linked to rewards which they value

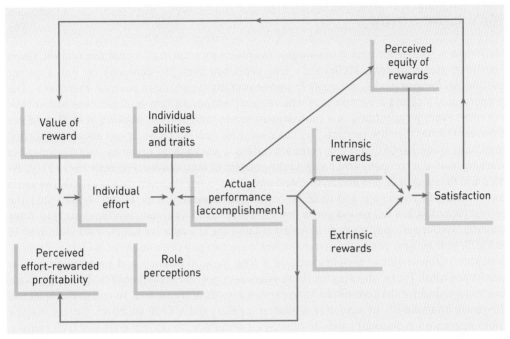

Figure 9.1 Expectancy theory
Source: Huczynski and Buchanan (2001)

The degree of motivational value of a reward is heavily constrained in the eyes of its potential recipient by a number of factors. Both *expectancy theory* and *equity theory* can help us to understand these situational factors. Under Adams's equity theory (1965), employees are seen to compare their reward with others in relation to their input and to determine whether they are equitably rewarded, relatively under-rewarded, or over-rewarded.

Organisational justice theories (Greenberg, 1987) are potentially of considerable relevance to the management of reward. Perceived fairness can be considered from three points of view:

◆ **Distributive justice** – the perceived fairness of the outcome.

◆ **Procedural justice** – fairness of how the rewards are allocated or decisions made.

◆ **Interactional justice** – relating to the nature of the interpersonal relationships.

Bowen et al. (1999) has shown the direct relevance of *fairness* in reward decisions to the quality of service provided by employees to the organisation's customers. On the other hand, the work of Folger and Konovsky (1989) show that although perceptions of *distributive* justice are associated with employee levels of pay satisfaction, it is *procedural* justice that is more strongly associated with employee commitment.

Locke and Latham's (1990) *goal setting theory* suggests that individuals are more likely to achieve agreed goals that they believe are achievable. This led to the development of the SMART concept in setting performance goals – SMART goals are Specific, Measurable, Achievable, Realistic and Time-bound.

Mini case study: 'McDonaldising' pay

McDonald's, notable for paying low wages, maintains its edge in a competitive market. David Fairhurst, vice-president, McDonald's UK, explained that the company is 'not a career destination for everybody', although 75 per cent of managers start as 'crew members'. The proportion of McDonald's employees who regard their pay as 'fair' is 30 per cent higher than the retail average, according to a comparative survey, and pride in working at McDonald's is 6 per cent higher than the average. The basic wage for new staff is at, or just above, the normal minimum wage (NMW), and the company offers a package of rewards including flexible working, with the company emphasizing the concept of *total reward*. For both 18- to 21-year-olds and those aged 22 and above, the McDonald's current minimum rate is exactly the same as the NMW (£4.25 an hour and £5.05 an hour, respectively). But for 16- to 17-year-olds, the lowest rate of £4 is a full pound above the state's 16- to 17-year-old development rate. After training, McDonald's pay rates rise incrementally: the top rate for hourly paid staff over 18 is £8.70. In their first year, all crew members have two pay reviews. After an initial 21 days' probation, crew member benefits include a free meal allowance and paid holidays (four weeks pro rata). Those who stay for three years also get additional benefits. There is private healthcare, and, for the committed, long service awards at three, five, 10 and even 15, 20 and 25-yearly intervals (those who stay a quarter-century get a £750 voucher). Others may be more interested in discount cards on holidays, computers, shoes, holidays and DVD rentals, and even a 15 per cent discount from HSS, a tool hire outfit.

Two performance reviews in the first year are designed to promote people quickly, provided they can convince restaurant managers of their abilities. There is also an additional bonus system for high-performing teams – any restaurant that figures in the top 10 per cent in a league table run by the director of operations wins a 50p-an-hour bonus.

60 per cent of staff is under 21. For 25,000 of its UK workforce, McDonald's is a first job and a first taste of non-academic learning. When critics scoff at the way the company celebrates those who 'graduate' from its programmes, it is possible that these initiatives are perceived differently by teenagers who may be staying in a fancy hotel for the first time. Moving into management job roles can attract a salary of over £30,000.

Fairhurst sees reward as extending to 'values issues' such as recognition, citizenship, personal growth and respect. Everything the company does, he argues, is aimed at affirming these values. These can be relatively trivial things – ensuring the use of 'please' behind the counter, for example, or name badges emblazoned with 'proud of you'. Innovations include a 'family contract', which enables different members of the same family to take shifts for each other.

> 'Reward is only rewarding if it is meaningful to individuals,' Fairhust says.
> 'We do our utmost to ensure that the behaviours that deliver great customer service get noticed and rewarded.'

(Adapted from: Fast Forward, *People Management*, 9 February 2006, and McDonald's fights 'McJob' tag, *People Management*, 23 February 2006, p. 19)

Based on your reading of this case study, and the theories on motivation and organisational justice:

* What is the company seeking to achieve?
* What is your assessment of how well the rewards meet those aims?

Developments in pay structures

Pay structures are developing as employers seek a balance between the highly flexible approaches which typically lack transparency and the more defined structures, which may be difficult to operate in an active salary market climate. Other key factors affecting current developments are *equal pay for work of equal value* and the link between career and pay systems. There are four main types of pay structure:

- **A spot salary structure** – in which there is a single rate of pay for the job and no range of pay through which individuals can progress their pay. Such a system has the advantage of transparency but relies critically on those setting the rates to make the appropriate choice in the context of a moving pay market.

- **A narrow-banded or graded salary structure** – in which there is a restricted level of pay progression – typically on the basis of assessment of individual performance, or pay progression may be service-related. Such systems are easy to understand but with long-serving staff run the risk of a high proportion of people being stuck at the top of the structure and feeling they have no way of progressing their pay

- **Broad-banded structures** – in which the range of pay in a band is significantly wider than in a conventional graded structure. The band width may be 100 per cent or even more. Broad bands or grades make it difficult to explain to people why some earn more than others (and this has dangers from an equal pay perspective). However, they give greater scope for employees to recognise individual performance or competencies, and to respond flexibly to salary market conditions.

- **Job family systems** – in which there are separate pay structures for different occupational groups. These seem simpler to explain to employees; they are responsive to the specific pay market for the respective occupations, and they help in linking pay to career progression. But, again, there may be equal pay dangers where different occupational groups are gender segregated, as is likely in UK organisations, and they may lead to 'silo' thinking and competition rather than co-operation between functions in the organisation.

An e-reward survey (e-reward.co.uk, 2006) claimed that *career families* are the latest manifestation of grade structure development: just 6 per cent of respondents had them while 17 per cent had job families. Career families consist of jobs in a function or occupation, such as marketing, operations, finance, information technology (IT), HR, administration or support services, which are related through the activities carried out and the basic knowledge and skills required, but in which the levels of responsibility, knowledge, skill or competency needed differ. In a career family structure the various career families are also identified and the successive levels in each family are defined by reference to the key activities carried out and the knowledge and skills or competencies required to perform them effectively. Typically, career families have between six and eight levels as in broad-graded structures, although some families may have more levels than others. Unlike job family approaches, career family structures have a common grade and pay structure. Jobs at the same level in each career family are deemed to be the same **size**, and the pay ranges in corresponding levels across the career families are the same. In effect, a career structure is a single graded structure in which each grade has been divided into families.

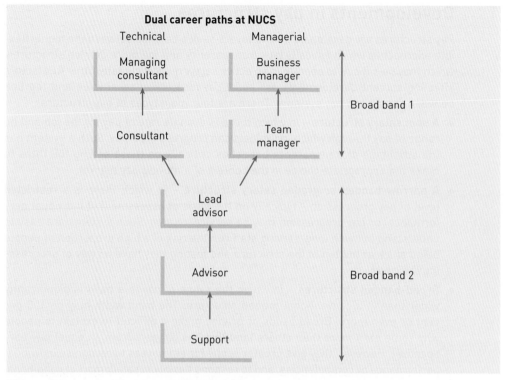

Figure 9.2 Norwich Union: career family pay structure
Source: adapted from *IDS HR Study 814*, January 2006

Norwich Union Central Services (NUCS) designed a new pay structure following a merger. The company wanted a simpler approach than its previous system, aiming to make career progression more transparent and give employees a clearer view of where they fitted into the organisation. The career family structure was developed and includes 22 separate job families – from chauffeurs to switchboard staff.

There are three elements to the pay system – career families, broad salary bands and the use of generic roles/groups. Within the majority of career families jobs are aligned to one of seven generic groups – managing consultant, business manager, team manager, lead adviser and support – see Figure 9.2.

Broad salary bands are used. The salary market is surveyed and for each generic group in each family, a salary entry point, 'low point' and 'high point' are set, as shown in Table 9.2.

Towards a more employee-centred approach to reward

In the last quarter of the twentieth century pay determination in the UK became increasingly individualised, although as Brown et al. (1998) suggest, there often continued to be a standardised approach to the setting of pay and benefits in many organisations, even though collective bargaining with trade unions had been reduced. At the same time there was a growing acknowledgement that employers may need to respond to the increasingly diverse needs and lifestyles of today's workforce.

Broad band	Generic group/level	Market salary guides at 1 April 2005		
		Entry point	Low point	High point
1	Business manager/managing consultant	26,800	33,500	45,000
	Team manager	18,400	23,000	30,000
	Consultant	17,350	21,700	29,000
2	Lead advisor	13,200	16,500	19,600
	Advisor	10,080	12,600	14,500
	Support	9,250	11,300	12,000

Table 9.2 Example of a career family at NUCS: facilities management

One way of meeting the needs of diverse lifestyles in the context of a more individualised approach to pay and benefits is to offer a flexible benefits programme. These have been in existence in a small number of organisations for some years but the pace of growth of such schemes seems to have been modest, with the CIPD reporting (2007) that just 8 per cent of UK organisations have schemes. Such schemes range from the small scale, similar to those that are now termed 'voluntary benefits schemes' (IRS, 2005) – whose cost and extent is minimal – to much more substantive schemes in which employees get a significant level of choice as to the benefits they receive. This may include 'buying ' or 'selling ' holiday entitlement; extending medical insurance or pension benefits; and the possibility of choosing a range of lower cost benefits.

Mini case study: Flexible benefits at AstraZeneca

AstraZeneca implemented a total reward package system incorporating flexible benefits, when UK company Zeneca (formerly part of ICI) merged with Swedish firm Astra. The new company, which employs 10,000 people in the UK, brought together two financially and culturally disparate reward systems by this means. The 'total reward' scheme encompassing flexible benefits is called AZAdvantage. Under it, employees are allocated a fund comprising a reference salary and a budget for spending on various benefits.

An employee can opt to change the mix of salary and benefits as they wish. Although all staff are given core benefits, including annual leave, private healthcare and pension, they are also able to choose from a menu of other benefits, so their package is individually tailored.

The range includes lifestyle options such as extra holiday and retail vouchers; health benefits such as dental cover; financial options such as enhanced retirement benefits; and other options, including insurance.

Each benefit has a pricing structure and offers savings for the employer either through tax and national insurance efficiencies or through corporate discounts. The scheme is administered via an intranet site and a service centre run by the company's consultants.

(Adapted from Manocha, 2002)

Flexible benefit plans also have the advantage of involving employees in selecting the benefits that best suit their current *and* future lifestyles. Various quantitative studies (Hong et al., 1995; Baughman et al., 2003; Dale-Olsen, 2005; Tsai, 2005) indicate that benefit programmes may have positive effects on productivity, motivation and employee retention. Hence it might be argued that offering people a choice over which benefits to receive could have further positive business outcomes (Barringer and Milkovich, 1998). Organisations may also be able to limit benefit costs and exert greater cost control with a flexible programme compared with a standardised package. The Employee Benefits survey (2003) indicates self-reported positive outcomes from organisations that had such schemes. These outcomes include:

- Showing employees the value of their benefits;
- Aiding recruitment;
- Improving retention;
- Harmonising benefits;
- Reinforcing company culture;
- Improving/maintaining staff motivation;
- Aiding 'employer of choice' status;
- Reducing/removing status symbols;
- Reducing/containing the cost of reward.

Although there is little academic research in this area, Barber (1992) reports improved employee satisfaction with benefits and Hillebrink et al. (2003) report potential motivational effects from the possibility that flexible schemes offer the opportunity to 'buy time'.

As with other aspects of reward, there is at present no systematic evaluation of whether flexible benefits add organisational value and are worth the work involved in setting up and maintaining schemes. Considerable research is needed in this and other areas of reward.

pause for thought

'Through a glass darkly.' How does this phrase relate to remuneration systems? Why did you reach the answer you did?

Summary

In managing pay and reward in organisations, gaining trust, commitment and employee engagement within particular situational contexts is vital, but the factors that critically influence this complex set of relationships are only partially understood. Current issues in reward focus on developments in managing – as well as designing – reward systems, but some long-standing problems such as gender pay inequality are still to be solved.

Review Questions

You may wish to attempt the following as practice examination style questions.

9.1 What do you understand by the term reward strategy? How would you set about devising a strategy for an organisation?

9.2 In what circumstances can pay motivate?

9.3 Devise a PowerPoint slide show to explain to senior managers the benefits of greater openness and transparency about pay.

References

Adams, J.S. (1965). Inequity in social exchange, in L. Berkowitz (ed.) *Advances in Experimental Social Psychology*, New York: Academic Press.

Armstrong, M. and Baron, A. (2005). *Managing Performance: Performance Management in Action*, London: CIPD.

Barber, A.E., Dunham, R. and Formisano, R. (1992). The impact of flexible benefits on employee satisfaction: a field study, *Personnel Psychology*, Vol. 45, pp. 55–75.

Barringer, M.W. and Milkovich, G. (1998). A theoretical exploration of the adoption and design of flexible benefit plans: a case of human resource innovation, *Academy of Management Review*, Vol. 23, No. 2, pp. 305–324.

Baughman, R. et al. (2003). Productivity and wage effects of 'family-friendly' fringe benefits, *International Journal of Manpower*, Vol. 24, No. 3, pp. 247–259.

Bowen, D. et al. (1999). How being fair with employees spills over to customers, *Organisational Dynamics*, Vol. 27, No. 3, pp. 7–23.

Boxall, P. and Purcell, J. (2000). *Strategy and human resource management*, Palgrave Macmillan.

Brown, W. et al. (1998). The individualisation of employment contracts in Britain, research paper for the Department of Trade and Industry, Centre for Business Research Department of Applied Economics, University of Cambridge.

CIPD (2005). *Reward Management Survey* 2005, London: CIPD.

CIPD (2006). *Reward Management Survey* 2006, London: CIPD.

CIPD (2007). *Reward Management Survey* 2007, London: CIPD.

Cox, A. (2000). The importance of employee participation in determining pay system effectiveness, *International Journal of Management Review*, Vol. 2, No. 4, pp. 357–375.

Dale-Olsen, H. (2005). Using linked employer–employee data to analyze fringe benefits policies: Norwegian experiences, Institute for Social Research, Norway, paper presented at Policy Studies Institute Seminar, July.

Employee Benefits/MX Financial Solutions (2003). Flexible benefits research 2003, *Employee Benefits*, April, pp. 4–9.

Folger, R. and Konovsky, M.A. (1989). Effects of procedural and distributive justice on reactions to pay raise decisions, *Academy of Management Journal*, Vol. 32, No. 1, pp. 115–130.

Gerhart, B. (2000). Compensation strategy and organisational performance, in S. Rynes et al. (eds.) *Compensation in Organisations: Current Research and Practice*, San Francisco, CA: Jossey–Bass.

Gomez-Mejia, L.R. and Balkin, D.B. (1992). *Compensation, Organizational Strategy and Firm Performance*, Cincinnati, OH: South-Western Publishing.

Greenberg, J. (1987). A taxonomy of organisational justice theories, *Academy of Management Review*, Vol. 12, pp. 9–22.

Heneman, H.G. and Judge, T.A. (2000). Compensation attitudes, in S. Rynes et al. (eds.) *Compensation in Organisations: Current Research and Practice*, San Francisco, CA: Jossey-Bass.

Hillebrink, C. et al. (2003). Choosing time or money: a study into employees' decision-making regarding flexible benefits, paper presented at the HRM Network Conference, Twente, Netherlands, November.

Hong, J.-C. et al. (1995). Impact of employee benefits on work motivation and productivity, *International Journal of Career Management*, Vol. 7, No. 6, pp. 10–14.

Huczynski, A. and Buchanan, D. (2001). *Organizational Behaviour: An Introductory Text*, 4th edition, Harlow, Essex: FT/Prentice Hall.

Huselid, M. (1995). The impact of human resource management practices on turnover, productivity and corporate financial performance, *Academy of Management Journal*, Vol. 38, No. 3, pp. 635–672.

Hutchinson, S. and Purcell, J. (2003). *Bringing Policies to Life: The Vital Role of Front Line Managers in People Management*, Executive Briefing Report, London: CIPD.

IDS (2005). *Directory of Salary Surveys 2005/06: IDS Executive Compensation Review*, London: Incomes Data Services.

IRS (2005). Voluntary benefits: saving in the workplace, *IRS Employment Review*, Vol. 818, Pay and Benefits, 25 February.

Lawler, E. (1995). The new pay: a strategic approach, *Compensation and Benefits Review*, July–August, pp. 14–22.

Legge, K. (1995). *Human Resource Management: Rhetoric and Realities*, Basingstoke: Macmillan.

Locke, E.A. and Latham, G.P. (1990). *A Theory of Goal Setting and Task Performance*, Englewood Cliffs, NJ: Prentice Hall.

Macduffie, J. (1995). Human resource bundles and manufacturing performance: organizational logic and flexible production systems in the world auto industry, *Industrial and Labor Relations Review*, Vol. 48, No. 2, pp. 197–221.

Manocha, R. (2002). Pick 'n' mix, *People Management*, 7 November, p. 45.

Marchington, M. and Grugulis, I. (2000). 'Best practice' human resource management: perfect opportunity or dangerous illusion?, *International Journal of Human Resource Management*, Vol. 11, No. 6, pp. 1104–1124.

Milsome, S. (2005), Symposium report, Reward Management, 13 July, organised jointly by e-reward and CIPD.

Perkins, S.J. and Sandringham, S. (eds.) (1998). *Trust, Motivation and Commitment: A Reader*, Oxford: Strategic Remuneration Research Centre.

Pfeffer, J. (1998). *The Human Equation: Building Profits by Putting People First*, Boston: Harvard Business School Press.

Porter, L. and Lawler, E. (1968). *Managerial Attitudes and Performance*, New York: Richard Irwin Inc.

Purcell, J. et al. (2003). *Understanding the People and Performance Link: Unlocking the Black Box*, research report, London: CIPD.

Purcell, J. and Hutchinson, S. (2007). *Rewarding Work: The Vital Role of Line Managers*, Change Agenda, London: CIPD.

Robinson, D. et al. (2004). The drivers of employee engagement, IES Report 408, London: Institute of Employment Studies.

Rynes, S. et al. (2005). Personnel psychology: performance evaluation and pay for performance, *Annual Review of Psychology*, Vol. 56, pp. 571–600.

Sisson, K. and Storey, J. (2000). *The Realities of Human Resource Management*, Buckingham: Open University Press.

Tsai, M.-C. (2005). Evaluating sociologists in Taiwan: power, profession and passerby, Department of Sociology, National Tapai University, Taiwan.

Vroom, V. (1964). *Work and Motivation*, Chichester: Wiley.

West, M. et al. (2005). *Rewarding Customer Service? Using Reward and Recognition to Deliver Your Customer Service Strategy*, research report, London: CIPD.

Zingheim, P. and Schuster, J. (2000). Total rewards for new and old economy companies, *Compensation and Benefits Review*, Vol. 32, No. 6, pp. 20–23.

Further Reading

Corby, S., White, G. and Stanworth, C. (2005). No news is good news? Evaluating new pay systems, *Human Resource Management Journal*, Vol. 15, No. 1, pp. 4–24.

Forth, J. and Millward, N. (2000). The determinants of pay levels and fringe benefit provision in Britain, discussion paper No. 171, National Institute of Economic and Social Research.

Guest, D. (2002). Human resource management, corporate performance and employee wellbeing: building the worker into HRM, *Journal of Industrial Relations*, Vol. 44, No. 3, pp. 335–358.

Pfeffer, J. and Veiga, J.F. (1999). Putting people first for organisational success, *Academy of Management Executive*, Vol. 13, No. 2, pp. 37–48.

Rynes, S. et al. (eds.) (2000). *Compensation in Organisations: Current Research and Practice*, San Francisco, CA: Jossey-Bass.

Wright, A. (2004). *Reward Management in Context*, London: CIPD.

Zingheim, P.K. and Schuster, J.R. (2000). *Pay People Right!: Breakthrough Reward Strategies to Create Great Companies*, San Francisco, CA: Jossey-Bass.

Useful Websites

www.e-reward.co.uk – information and guidance on rewards, especially business-focused reward strategy

www.eoc.org.uk – downloadable reports and guidance on pay equality

www.incomesdata.co.uk – gives an index of topics covered in IDS journals and research

www.ons.gov.uk – downloadable data such as the *Annual Survey of Hours and Earnings*

CHAPTER 10

Gender Equality and Pay: someday, will my pay be equal?

By Angela Wright

Chapter outline

This chapter seeks to review the key issues for human resource (HR) specialists of a profound and far-reaching problem. As Chapter 4 shows, diversity and equal opportunities policies may be little more than 'empty shells' – a policy on paper that has little effect in practice. An analysis of pay by gender in an organisation can show just how far, or not, equality initiatives have gone in challenging and changing traditional career and pay relationships. The chapter looks at sources of gender pay inequality and examines the ways in which the gender pay gap may be measured and alleviated. It covers some of the lessons from the legal developments on equal pay, picking up on the kinds of pay systems that are likely to be most unequal, and discusses how such inequality may be rectified.

Learning outcomes

By the end of this chapter, you should be able to:

◆ Identify the main causes of gender pay inequality;

◆ Describe some of the trends in pay and gender in the UK;

◆ Summarise some of the key legal developments;

◆ Explain some aspects of pay systems that lead to inequality;

◆ List some measures that employers can take to reduce pay inequality.

Introduction

In 2006, the latest in a series of government-sponsored studies of the causes of gender pay inequality was published. The Women and Work Commission, like its predecessors, produced a lengthy report with numerous recommendations, but will it lead to any change in a pattern of pay inequality, which seems durable even in the face of increasing legislation? Although many HR practitioners may be fully in tune with the issues of diversity and equal opportunities in employment, equal pay may not be central to the concerns of many managers. The systemic problems of unequal pay in UK pay systems, particularly in the public sector, is a vulnerability which is now forcing its way up the organisational agenda, in part because of some high-profile multi-million pound legal settlements.

Measuring the equal pay gap

The Office for National Statistics (ONS; statistics.gov.uk) compiles and publishes the national level data on pay and gender, principally in the *Annual Survey of Hours and Earnings,* previously the *New Earnings Survey.* The gender pay gap is worked out as the difference between the median earnings of men and women, because the median is less influenced by outlying values in the pay distribution than is the arithmetic average (or mean). The data for 2005 show the gender pay gap between the pay of men and women working full time is 13 per cent measured using *median* hourly pay rates; and 17 per cent measured using *mean* hourly pay rates. The data are based on median hourly earnings, excluding the effects of overtime, since that is the measure that best offers a like-for-like comparison, as a far higher proportion of men than women work paid overtime hours. It should also be noted that the hourly rates used in the calculation are 'effective' hourly rates calculated by ONS – they cover the whole workforce, including the salaried higher paid, and *not* just those people who are paid by the hour.

The *Annual Survey of Hours and Earnings* further shows that men begin to earn more than women soon after they enter the labour market, and the pay gap rises with age. In 2005, the mean gender pay gap for full-time workers aged 18–21 was 3.7 per cent. For those aged 40–49, the age group for whom the gender pay gap is largest, the mean gender pay gap was 21.7 per cent. See Figure 10.1.

A number of studies show that the UK has a poor record on equal pay compared with other European countries. The Women and Work Commission (2006) suggests the key to reducing the pay gap lies in measures to balance work and family and notes that countries such as Sweden and Denmark, that have cultures which promote work-life balance (see also Chapter 21), have lower gender pay gaps than the UK, while having similarly high levels of women's participation in work. However, no country has yet achieved full gender equality in pay and employment.

Sources of pay inequality

Gender pay inequality is a pervasive problem in UK reward. As Joshi and Paci (1998) argue, although higher pay for men is just one of the many ways in which pay levels differ between individuals, it is, in comparison with other factors, a very durable

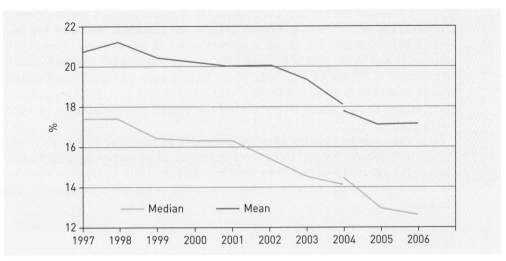

Figure 10.1 Gender pay gap trends, UK 1997–2006
Source: Office of National Statistics

feature. Indeed, Forth and Millward (2000) show the durability of the gender dimension, over a period that saw both significant changes in pay determination arrangements and substantial rises in labour market participation by women. As the Women and Work Commission (2006) points out:

> 'In the 30 years since the Equal Pay Act, major changes in the UK's economy and society have increased the opportunities available to women. It has become more socially acceptable for women to work. In 2005, 70 per cent of women of working age were in employment, compared to 60 per cent in 1975 (Labour Force Survey). Women's education levels have increased and as the traditionally male jobs in the manufacturing sector have disappeared, jobs in the service sector, which are seen as more accessible to women, have expanded. Women are having fewer children and giving birth later in life. Women are more likely to establish a career before having a family and to re-establish themselves at work more easily afterwards. Women are also more likely to work when they have young children than in previous decades; 56 per cent of women whose youngest child was under five were in employment in 2005 compared to 91 per cent of men whose youngest child was under five. The main growth in women's employment rates in the 1990s was among women with very young children (Labour Force Survey). Despite these changes there are still significant barriers to equal pay.'

The concentration of women in lower-paying occupations, known as *occupational segregation*, contributes to the overall gender pay gap. Women tend to be paid less than men within occupations, not climbing the career ladder to the same degree as men. This is known as *vertical segregation* and the barriers to moving up in a profession are also referred to as the *glass ceiling*.

The occupational segregation of women into a narrow range of low-paid jobs or careers, together with the low pay and status of part-time work, are identified as principal causes of the pay gap (see Chapter 14). However, there is also discrimination within pay systems and as a result of some pay practices. The Equal Pay Task Force (2001) estimated the extent of discrimination in pay systems to amount to between 25 and 50 per cent of the total national pay gap between men and women, which stood at 17 per cent in 2005, when factors such as the different pattern of work of women is taken out of the reckoning. Walby et al.'s (2002) econometric study estimated that about 29 per cent of the overall pay gap was the result of discrimination.

Even when women have the same qualifications as men they tend to earn less. Purcell (2002) found that just three years after graduation women were earning, on average, 15 per cent less than their male counterparts, with salary gaps observed even between men and women graduates working in the same occupations. See box below.

Causes of the gender pay gap

♦ Differences between men and women in the jobs they do – *occupational segregation*;

♦ 'Women's jobs' being under-valued;

♦ Length of work experience and the number of interruptions to the work experience of many women;

♦ Part-time employment experience;

♦ Qualifications and skills;

♦ Travel to work issues;

♦ Other factors include discriminatory treatment of women at work and the inaccessibility of training.

(Adapted from Women and Work Commission, 2006)

---

pause for thought

Think about an organisation known to you.

♦ How much occupational segregation by gender can you observe?

♦ If there are part-time workers in the organisation, are they mainly women?

♦ Do you think there are any pay or benefit consequences of your observations?

♦ Why did you reach this conclusion?

exercise

Do you think there is likely to be occupational segregation at Warbings?

Why did you reach this conclusion?

Some lessons from the legal developments on equal pay

Equal pay for women and men is one of the few areas of pay that is regulated. The law in this area dates back to the Equal Pay Act, which was introduced in 1970, and also within European law which contains the founding principles of the European Union (EU). Many of the high-profile legal cases which have taken place over the past three or four decades have been taken under European law, which is directly applied in the UK legal system (see also Chapter 13). Under both European and domestic law, employers are obliged to pay *equal pay for work of equal value* to women and men. The direct applicability of EU law as part of domestic law in England, Wales and Scotland stems from the European Communities Act 1972, when Britain joined the then Common Market. The effect of this is that UK tribunals and courts must, wherever possible, interpret domestic law in accordance with EU law. In circumstances when EU law has direct effect, it takes precedence over domestic law.

On equal pay, the key element of European law is Article 141 (previously Article 119) of the Treaty of Rome, establishing that the European Community stipulates that men and women should receive equal pay for equal work. Any individual can rely on A141 in bringing an equal pay case.

In domestic law, the Equal Pay Act 1970 gives an individual a right to the same contractual pay and benefits as a person of the opposite sex in the same employment, where the man and the woman are doing:

◆ Like work; or

◆ Work rated as equivalent under an analytical job evaluation study; or

◆ Work that is proved to be of equal value.

Because the UK labour market is segregated by gender, women and men tend not to work in the same jobs. Hence equal pay for work of equal value, not 'like work', is of critical importance. However studies by Morrell et al. (2001) and Brett and Milsome (2004) indicate that many employers have a poor understanding of the concept of equal value and its translation into pay practice. With diverse pay arrangements the process of judging comparability may be difficult because jobs/roles may be flexible and the perceived contribution to the organisation variable (Wright, 2004). It may be argued that the concept is fundamentally flawed, since it relies on an acceptance that comparing the value of jobs that are dissimilar is practicable and systematically possible. Various legal judgements and the work of the independent experts give some guidance in this area (see below), but for many aspects of practical pay management and policy there is no hard and fast guidance about what employers must or must not do to satisfy the requirements of the equal pay legislation.

Legal developments since the end of the 1990s have focused on the problems of a cumbersome tribunal process, and the introduction of the Equal Pay Questionnaire under the Employment Act 2002 was designed to make it simpler to unearth unjustified differences between women and men on an individual basis, prior to any legal action.

In the more than 30 years of the operation of the legislation there have been a number of important cases. Below is a summary of some of the key cases, whose judgements have given guidance on practice.

In assessing equal pay for work of equal value – whose pay should be compared?

Can people only compare with current employees? In the *Macarthys v Mrs Smith [1980]* case, it was established by the European Court of Justice (ECJ) that a woman can bring an equal pay claim under European equal pay law, comparing herself with a man who had previously held her post. The Court of Appeal had previously held that the Equal Pay Act did not allow a claim to be brought where the comparator was no longer in employment.

One of the early equal pay for work of equal value cases which showed the potential of the new law to compare across previously rigidly 'male' and 'female' demarcation boundaries was *Ms White and Others v Alstons (Colchester) Ltd, 1987*. In this case women sewing machinists were found to be engaged on work of equal value to male upholsterers and awarded equal pay. One of the main difficulties with the equal pay legislation is that the concept of equal value is not formally defined in either EU or domestic legislation. The Equal Pay Act provides that when a claimant claims equal pay on grounds of equal value, a comparison should be made between the claimant's work and that of the named comparator 'under such headings as effort, skill and decision'. This broad definition leaves many areas of doubt.

Equal value claims can be made using comparators paid under different grading systems, collective agreements or job evaluation schemes. The question of whether two jobs are of equal value involves a weighing and balancing between the features of the claimant's and comparator's jobs, thereby allowing comparisons between quite different types of jobs. The EOC (www.eoc-law.org.uk) gives examples of claims between very different jobs, which have been successful at tribunal or settled in favour of the claimant(s), including:

♦ Primary school classroom assistant with a library service driver messenger;

♦ School nursery nurse with a local government architectural technician;

♦ Wholesale news distribution clerical assistant with a warehouse operative;

♦ Cook with a shipboard painter;

♦ Head of speech and language therapy service with the head of a hospital pharmacy service;

♦ Nursing home sewing room assistant with a plumber;

♦ Motor industry sewing machinist with an upholsterer;

♦ Canteen workers and cleaners with surface mineworkers and clerical workers.

Equal value and the use of job evaluation

Job evaluation is a process used in pay setting that puts a value to the organisation of different jobs. It is important for employers wishing to defend themselves against an equal pay claim, since if there is an unbiased scheme used for this purpose and it gives a higher value to a job done by a man than to one done by a woman, the woman will not be able to take a valid claim for equal value to an employment tribunal. However, it is important to recognise that all job evaluation schemes contain implicit values and these may well be biased against the sort of roles or jobs women do. If the organisation has strong job segregation by gender, questions about professed impartiality of the job evaluation method used may be raised. In some legal cases this issue has been considered. In *Bromley v H* and *J Quick Ltd [1988] IRLR 249 CA*, the study commissioned by the employers used the paired comparisons method (that considers jobs on a 'whole job' basis), rather than split into various factors to provide a rank order of benchmark jobs. Jobs not evaluated in this process were then slotted into the rank order on a 'felt-fair' basis in line with the general level of expectation as to the value of the job. The claimants and comparators had not been chosen for the paired comparison exercise but instead had been slotted into order on a 'felt-fair' basis. The Court of Appeal held that the method used for the study was not analytical (that is, the jobs had not been considered under various factors or headings). This aspect is considered important since there may be more tendency for people to think in terms of the person holding the job (and hence their gender) when rating jobs on a whole job basis rather than rating under different factors.

Tribunals can appoint independent experts to help them in assessing the comparative value of the claimant and comparator jobs. The expert may assess the jobs against a simple low–moderate–high scale. In the first equal value claim referred to an independent expert, *Hayward v Cammell Laird [1984] IRLR 463 ET*, the expert used a small number of factors to compare the work of the claimant (a cook) with that of her comparators (a shipboard painter, carpenter and heating technician), as follows:

- Skill and knowledge demands;
- Responsibility demands;
- Planning and decision-making demands;
- Physical demands;
- Environmental demands.

In contrast, in the *Enderby and Others v Frenchay Health Authority and Anor [1993] IRLR 591 ECJ* case, when comparing a large number of speech therapist jobs with clinical psychologists and hospital pharmacists the team of independent experts used a large numbers of factors, as follows:

- Knowledge;
- Knowledge base;
- Development;
- Experience;
- Responsibilities;
- Patients/clients and the provision of a service;
- Managing work of self and others;
- Plant/equipment/resources;
- Teaching/training/mentoring;
- Mental demands;
- Concentration/accuracy;
- Physical demands and environment;
- Physical effort;
- Working conditions;
- Hazards;

- Decision making and initiative;
- Complexity and analysis;
- Freedom to act;
- Communications/relationships.

Each factor had five levels and each job was assessed and then scored against a scale as in a job evaluation scheme. However, as Armstrong and Baron's (1995) survey shows, the usual number of factors used in a job evaluation scheme is between three and eight, since a large number of factors increases the chance that certain attributes in different jobs are recognised under more than one factor, thereby potentially double-counting that attribute. Too few factors and there is a risk of missing important attributes. Both too many and too few factors carry potential equality risks.

In *Eaton Ltd v Nuttall [1977] IRLR 71 EAT*, the importance of objectivity in the job evaluation was emphasised. Here, the company job evaluation exercise led to the setting of pay grades, where management decided where in the pay range the individual job was to be placed, using their own judgement as to how much responsibility was involved in each job. This amounted to a subjective, rather than relatively objective judgement.

Evaluating just a few 'benchmark' jobs and then slotting in the other jobs in the organisation into the pay structure on the basis of the benchmarked jobs has been a common practice. In *Bromley v Quick [1998] IRLR 249 CA*, the job evaluation process used by the study employers was flawed not just because it used a whole job method but also because no evaluation of the claimant's and comparator's jobs had taken place in the process. Instead, they had been ranked against the benchmark jobs.

How equal is 'equal'?

A number of cases have considered the question of 'what amounts to equal?'. Whether a claimant must have either a direct equivalent in points scored, or a greater number of points to be considered 'equal', or whether 'equal' should be assessed in broader terms, is problematic. Case law indicates that small differences in score will not necessarily prevent the jobs from being equal. In *Worsfold v Southampton and South West Hampshire HA ET/18296/87* and *Lawson v South Tees HA ET/17931/87*, the independent expert found a small points difference of less than 5 per cent between the claimant and comparator jobs. In the tribunal's view, work is not of equal value where there is 'an overall measurable and significant difference' between the demands of the respective jobs. The tribunal concluded that there was no measurable and significant difference between the jobs, and their conclusion was supported by the evidence of the independent expert, who said it was unlikely in a company setting that the job score difference between them would have led to any difference in grading.

Material factor defence

To explain why a comparator, although doing equal work, is paid more than the applicant the employer may use the 'material factor defence'. To be successful this factor must be significant and depict a relevant reason why there is a difference in pay. To succeed in such a defence the employer needs to show that the material factor accounts for the *whole* of the difference in pay.

Objective justification

In circumstances where a particular pay practice results in an adverse impact on substantially more members of one or other sex, the ECJ has introduced a test of objective justification. This means that the employer must be able to justify the pay practice in question objectively, in terms unrelated to gender.

Burden of proof

Under both domestic and EU law, the burden of proof falls on the claimant to establish that they do work of equal value to their chosen comparator and that they receive less pay. However, if the pay system lacks transparency (as many do), the principle established in *Brunnhofer v Bank der Österreichischen Postsparkasse AG [2001] IRLR 571 ECJ* was that if the claimant gives evidence that the average pay of, for example, women is less than for men undertaking equal work, then the burden of proof switches.

Back-pay for successful claimants

In the case of *Mrs Levez v T H Jennings [1999]*, Mrs Levez had won her equal pay for like work claim but the Equal Pay Act only allowed her to claim back-pay for two years. Following a decision of the ECJ, the Employment Appeal Tribunal decided that the two-year limit was contrary to European law and ruled that the limit for back-dating awards should be extended to six years.

Examples of the effects of successful equal pay claims

window into practice

The public sector, with its large complex organisations and multiplicity of pay systems, has been particularly vulnerable to equal pay claims. In local government, the 1997 national collective single status agreement provided for the establishment of 'single status' terms for manual and white-collar staff, with a new harmonised package of conditions of service, a new minimum wage and provision for local grading reviews based on equal pay for men and women doing equivalent work. Although the agreement stipulated that implementation would take place at local level, it did not schedule a timetable for completion. Councils were faced with negotiating local pay structures in a context of budget constraints, and progress in implementing single status was very slow.

Failure to make progress in implementing local pay and grading left councils exposed to trade unions taking equal pay cases to employment tribunals. Claims have come almost exclusively from women on former manual grades, such as cooks and home helps. These posts are typically held by women, who traditionally had no eligibility for bonuses or overtime payments. However these jobs had been rated as of equal value to mainly male-dominated posts such as gardeners, refuse drivers and road workers, which were eligible for significant bonuses and other basic pay additions. As a consequence of these equal pay claims, many councils are struggling to fund the new job-evaluated local harmonised pay structures, in addition to paying compensation for up to six years' back-pay for employees bringing equal pay claims.

continued

Some 12 local authorities in the North East of England have paid compensation totalling more than £100 million to settle equal pay claims, according to the North East Regional Employers' Organisation. For example, around 3,000 women, including cleaners, care assistants and catering workers, employed by Cumbria County Council won claims for equal pay with male colleagues in similarly graded posts. About two-thirds of equal pay cases in local government do not *reach* a tribunal, but are settled by agreement under the auspices of ACAS. To try to protect against claims being taken to employment tribunals, councils may make compromise agreements.

In the NHS a new pay system, Agenda for Change, is being rolled out nationally. This is aimed at delivering equal pay for work of equal value, underpinned as it is by a job evaluation scheme, specifically designed for the NHS with equality to the fore. However, the new system does not provide back-dating. Around 3,000 women staff working for the North Cumbria Acute Hospitals NHS Trust, including nurses, clerical officers, catering assistants, domestics, sewing machine assistants, porters and telephonists, have won an equal pay for equal value case dating back eight years.

(Adapted from Incomes Data Services (2006a) and *Municipal Journal* (2006))

pause for thought

Consider the reasons why unequal access to bonus schemes or overtime payments may be discriminatory. Can you think of any circumstances in which they may be argued to be a *'genuine material factor'*?

What kinds of pay system are most unequal?

Legal judgements have given relatively little guidance about those pay practices most likely to be discriminatory and much of the academic research in this area is inconclusive. Grimshaw and Rubery (2001) argue that the emergence of more flexible pay practices that developed in the UK in the wake of the decline in collective bargaining (Cully et al., 1998) influences the prevalence of gender pay inequality. The emphasis on performance pay during the 1980s and its continuation within UK organisational pay practice in the twenty-first century seems to be a prime contender for perpetuating inequality. However, the evidence on this is very patchy (Wright, 2004), with some studies showing that women can do better out of performance pay than men, because performance pay is used by employers to encourage sustained performance in the current post and women may be promoted less frequently than men, especially when they reach the 'glass ceiling' (Women and Work Commission, 2006). Brett (2006) highlights the view that even pay systems which are not inherently biased but that rely on managers making discretionary judgements can be discriminatory in practice: this can be a surprising finding for employers when they monitor pay decisions that they may firmly believe to be unbiased.

In December 1999, ACAS lost a tribunal case against its own women staff, complaining that its service increment scheme (where pay increased according to length of service) discriminated against women, who on average had shorter service within the organisation than men (Incomes Data Services, 2002). The revised pay system

Grade	Job Examples		Entry £pa	Step 1 £pa	Step 2 £pa	Step 3 £pa	Step 4 £pa	Step 5 £pa	Step 6 £pa
12	Administrative assistant	National	11,220	11,425	11,631	11,837	12,043	–	–
		London	15,122	15,327	15,533	15,739	15,945	–	–
11	Administrative officer	National	13,006	13,370	13,713	14,077	14,441	14,784	15,149
		London	16,908	17,272	17,615	17,979	18,343	18,686	19,051
10	Helpline staff, office supervisor	National	16,361	17,001	17,604	18,245	18,885	19,488	20,129
		London	20,263	20,903	21,506	22,147	22,787	23,390	24,031
9	Conciliator, office manager	National	21,739	22,519	23,254	24,034	24,814	25,549	26,330
		London	25,641	26,421	27,156	27,936	28,716	29,451	30,232
8	Senior advisor/conciliator, conciliation manager, resource manager	National	28,436	29,236	29,990	30,791	31,592	32,346	33,147
		London	32,338	33,138	33,892	34,693	35,494	36,248	37,049
7	Assistant director	National	35,799	37,276	38,666	40,144	41,621	43,011	44,489
		London	39,701	41,178	42,568	44,046	45,523	46,913	48,391
6	Regional director	National	48,048	49,158	50,204	51,213	52,426	53,472	54,583
		London	51,950	53,060	54,106	55,217	56,328	57,374	58,485

Table 10.1 Pay structure for ACAS staff, 2002

Source: *IDS HR Report 852*, March 2002, p. 14

it put in place (see Table 10.1) became something of a model for other public sector organisations to follow when seeking to achieve greater pay equality. At the Welsh Assembly, a new pay structure, that reduced the length of time for people to progress via annual increments through the pay ranges, has contributed to reducing the gender gap from 10 per cent to less than 4 per cent (Simms, 2005). This followed an equal pay review that found the main reason for the pay gap was the slow career progression of staff. Progress up the pay scale was dependent on performance, and women taking time out would return on the same pay point in the pay scale and therefore fail to progress. This system seemed fair but it could take up to 20 years for someone to progress from the minimum in the pay band to the maximum. Negotiations between management and trade unions resulted in the development of new six-point pay bands, allowing staff to progress more rapidly to a target rate of pay for their band. In addition, staff returning to work after career breaks, including maternity leave, return at the pay scale point they would have reached had their service not been interrupted by the break.

The question of the circumstances in which length of service can be considered a genuine material factor is the subject of legal cases. In the case of *Cadman v Health and Safety Executive*, the ECJ ruled (Incomes Data Services, 2006b: 20) that employers will have to objectively justify service-related pay structures which lead to women being paid less than men doing equal work. This is where the disadvantaged worker 'provides evidence raising serious doubts' as to whether recourse to the criterion of length of service is, in the circumstances, appropriate to attain the legitimate objective of rewarding experience which enables the worker to perform his or her duties better.

exercise   Summarise the reasons why rewarding length of service can be an equal pay issue. Recommend what should be done by organisations that wish to reward experience but not discriminate against their staff on the basis of gender.

What can be done about the problems of unequal pay?

Wajcman (2000) argues that inequality is entrenched within organisations and Liff and Cameron (1997) further contend that because inequality arises through the totality of patterns of social interaction, it cannot be rectified by conventional HR equality initiatives. Nevertheless, the three committees of enquiry – the Equal Pay Task Force (2001), Kingsmill (2001) and the Women and Work Commission (2006) – set up by the UK government to investigate and report on the gender pay gap, suggest a range of measures that organisations, as well as government, can take to increase equality. The Women and Work Commission, while recognising (2006: IX) that 'the complex and interrelated nature of the causes of the gender pay gap means . . . sustained action (needs) . . . to be taken by a range of players', among other measures asks employers to consider the issues the Commission raises and to take action that will have most impact on women's pay and opportunity. To that end it has recruited some private sector companies to pilot a range of projects and also wants the public sector to be an exemplar of practice. The Commission disappointed some in not recommending that employers must be obliged to undertake an equal pay review or audit (other than in the public sector), while the earlier studies – Equal Pay Task Force (2001) and Kingsmill (2001) – recommend that voluntary audits could be instrumental in revealing the reasons for gender pay differences at organisational level, allowing employers to take remedial action. As the CIPD (2006) found, employers have seemed reluctant to examine gender pay differences in their organisations, some apparently believing there are no problems for them to solve. The window into practice below summarises two major UK companies' experiences of their equal pay auditing processes.

The EOC has produced a *Tool Kit* (eoc.org.uk), a checklist which gives guidance to employers on which variations in pay by gender are considered inequitable, biased by gender or unlawful. This stops short of giving detailed advice on exactly which pay differences are inequitable and which can be treated as merely coincidental in a flexible market-driven pay environment (see also Chapter 9) where no two people can expect to be treated exactly equally.

Equal pay reviews at BT and Nationwide

When **BT** conducted its first equal pay review in 1998, the organisation was already seen as an example of best practice. 'But that review taught us some very basic things and we changed many of our HR practices as a result,' said Caroline Waters, director, people and policy at BT Group.

The company restructured its non-management grading system, and introduced a skills-based system, to reduce traditional differences between, for example, engineering and clerical grades. This encouraged greater movement of men and women across these disciplines.

BT also increased the pay minima for management grades. The company found that by focusing pay expenditure on the lower end of the pay scales, some of the equal pay issues were solved.

Managers responsible for pay reviews were trained in understanding the principles of equal pay. After every pay review BT conducts an audit and, since 2002, has set aside a budget of £4 million to address any equal pay issues that arise. The company works closely with the unions on its equal pay policy.

The company has also addressed barriers to women's career progression by increasing access to flexible working and supporting women on courses to help break down occupational segregation.

BT benefits from being seen to be a fair employer as it is more able to attract the most talented people. In addition, the high (98 per cent) return rate after maternity leave saves about £5 million a year in recruitment costs.

Another major employer, **Nationwide**, undertook its first equal pay review in 2001. This found that basic pay structures were reasonably formalised and unbiased, but the discretionary decisions were problematic from the perspective of equal pay. Nationwide identified a 9 per cent gender pay gap. On delving deeper and looking at the elements of flexibility within pay systems, such as starting salaries, performance review scores, promotions and *ad hoc* pay increases, the company found variances it was largely unaware of because they had developed on a piecemeal basis. Nationwide addressed the problem by putting more controls around *ad hoc* pay, and providing more information, training and support to help managers to make the right decisions. It also trained 'licensed recruiters' within the company and closely monitored performance management scoring. The equitable treatment of part-timers has proved to be a particular challenge, but Nationwide has switched the focus of its assessments from the number of hours an individual works to their productivity and contribution.

'Over time we have seen an improvement, but there is no quick fix,' says Paul Bissell, senior manager of reward at Nationwide.

(Adapted from Simms, 2005)

The Women and Work Commission (2006) looked more broadly at the problem of unequal pay and saw it in the context of a subtle range of inequality of practice more generally in organisations. It recommended that, when managing performance, managers need to focus more on productivity rather than the long hours' culture. However, until society in general moves away from occupations being seen as appropriate for either men or women, progress towards equal pay between the genders may be limited.

Summary

The issues of pay and gender are complex and span a range of issues, from pay to wider employment and social trends. Unpicking the reasons for gender pay differences at organisational level can therefore be a tricky and detailed task. To do so thoroughly involves delving into differences, which superficially may seem unrelated to gender, but at root are indeed gendered.

pause for thought

Consider the changes that can lead to greater pay equality. What needs to happen to achieve this change?

Review Questions

You may wish to attempt the following as practice examination style questions.

10.1   Consider the causes of gender pay inequality.

10.2   What can employers do to lessen problems of pay discrimination?

10.3   Your Chief Executive is rather reluctant for an equal pay review to be conducted in the organisation. Write a short note to him to persuade him this would be good for the organisation.

10.4   After reading the section on transparency and communication in Chapter 9, as well as this chapter, summarise the business case for greater transparency in pay and identify the barriers to achieving this objective.

References

Armstrong, M. and Baron, A. (1995). *Job Evaluation Handbook*, London: CIPD.

Brett, S. (2006). *Reward and Diversity – Making Fair Pay Add Up to Business Advantage*, London: CIPD.

Brett, S. and Milsome, S. (2004). *Monitoring Progress on Equal Pay Reviews*, research paper, London: EOC.

CIPD (2006). *Reward Management Survey 2006*, London: CIPD.

Cully, M., O'Reilly, A. and Millward (1998). *The 1998 Workplace Employee Relations Survey: First Findings*, Department of Trade and Industry.

Equal Pay Task (2001). *Just Pay*, Equal Opportunities Commission.

Forth, J. and Millward, N. (2000). *The Determinants of Pay Levels and Fringe Benefit Provision in Britain*, discussion paper No. 171, London: National Institute of Economic and Social Research.

Grimshaw, D. and Rubery, J. (2001). *The Gender Pay Gap: A Research Review*, London: Equal Opportunities Commission.

Incomes Data Services (2002). ACAS: new pay system aims to ensure progression and guarantee equal pay, *IDS Report 852*, March.

Incomes Data Services (2006a). Equal pay claims make waves across the public sector, *IDS Report 950*, April, pp. 12–14.

Incomes Data Services (2006b). Case watch – appeals, *IDS Diversity and Work*, 29, p. 20.

Joshi, H. and Paci, P. (1998). *Unequal Pay for Women and Men: Evidence From the British Birth Cohort Studies*, Cambridge, MA: MIT Press.

Kingsmill (2001). *Review of Women's Pay and Employment*, London: Department of Trade and Industry.

Liff, S. and Cameron, I. (1997). Changing equality cultures to move beyond 'women's problems', *Gender, Work and Organization*, Vol. 4, No. 1, pp. 35–46.

Morell, J. et al. (2001). Gender equality in pay practices, NOP survey for the Equal Opportunities Commission.

Municipal Journal (2006). £50, equal pay bill, 6 April, p. 1.

Purcell, J. (2002). Qualifications and careers: equal opportunities and earnings among graduates, Working Paper Series 1, Equal Opportunities Commission.

Simms, J. (2005). Just out of reach, *People Management*, 10 March, pp. 27–33.

Wajcman, J. (2000). Feminism facing industrial relations in Britain, *British Journal of Industrial Relations*, Vol. 38, No. 2, pp. 13–20.

Walby, S. et al. (2002). Pay and the implications for UK productivity, London: EOC.

Women and Work Commission (2006). Shaping a fairer future, report presented to the Prime Minister.

Wright, A. (2004). *Reward Management in Context*, London: CIPD.

. . . .

Useful Websites

www.eoc.org.uk – access to Equal Opportunities Commission* reports and guidance on pay equality (e.g. Equal Pay for Equal Value)

 * The Commission for Equality and Human Rights from October 2007

www.eoc-law.org.uk – Equal Opportunities Commission website for legal advisors covering, inter alia, equal pay

www.incomesdata.co.uk – access to Income Data Services reports on equal pay

www.ons.gov.uk – access to the Office for National Statistics survey data such as the *Annual Survey of Hours and Earnings*

www.ec.europa.eu/comm/employment_social/gender_equality – European Union website providing details of European Court of Justice cases, including equal pay, pay discrimination, etc.

CHAPTER 11

Pensions and Human Resource

By Angela Wright

Chapter outline

This chapter examines retirement issues, in particular it discusses the role of human resource (HR), employer and employee in relation to pensions and retirement. It explores pensions within the labour market context, in particular dealing with the implications of the ageing of the workforce. The mechanisms of different basic types of pension, their take-up and the options are discussed and the chapter ends by briefly examining the regulatory environment for pensions.

Learning outcomes

By the end of this chapter, you should be able to:

- Identify the demographic changes posing a challenge for employers;
- Describe different pension systems;
- Discuss the role of HR in relation to pensions;
- Evaluate the advantages and disadvantages of certain types of pension.

Introduction

'For many people management professionals, pensions is not a subject that plays to their core skills and interests' (CIPD, 2002). However, with pensions taking centre stage on the national political scene, pension strikes in the public sector, and many employers radically rethinking their policies and practices on pensions, this is no longer an area to be simply left to the pension specialist. As some employers begin to question the traditional place of pensions in the reward package, and with a fundamental shift in the demographic make-up of the population, there are profound challenges for organisations. HR specialists need more than ever to be aware of the key pension and retirement issues. They need to be able to take a critical view of the media scare stories on pensions and to be aware of the new demands of a radically changed labour market in order to plan to recruit and retain for a future in which there will be far fewer younger people; not to discriminate on grounds of age; and to deal with potential conflicts between age groups.

Labour market context

Implications of an ageing workforce

There are several simultaneous pressures exerting an influence upon the workforce. At the same time as the population is ageing, medical advances mean people are living longer, and most of today's employees have a much longer life expectancy than their own parents. In addition, as the post-Second World War 'baby boomer' generation ages, a slowing birth rate means that fewer younger people are available to replace them in the labour market. In addition, there are fewer people making National Insurance (NI) contributions to pay the current pensioners. Combining these pressures with recent legislation banning discrimination on grounds of age, and concerns about the future affordability of pensions, yields a rich cocktail of HR issues to be considered.

According to the Pensions Commission (2004), drawing on projections from the Government Actuary (GAD), the pattern of the UK's demographic structure will change dramatically over the next 50 years – see Figure 11.1. There will be a negligible increase in the number of 20–64 years olds, but a 78 per cent increase in the number of people over age 65. As a result, the ratio of over 65 year olds to 20–64 year olds will increase from 27 per cent in 2004 to 48 per cent in 2050, with almost all of the increase coming before 2040.

The Pensions Commission (2004) observed in its first report that although people talk of 60 or 65 as being their retirement age, in fact only 53 per cent of women remain in employment by age 59 and only 42 per cent of men are employed at age 64. Just 68 per cent of men and 53 per cent of women aged 55 were employed in 2004. People (especially men) with occupational pensions tend to retire early, while those in manual jobs tend to claim Incapacity Benefit. At the same time as the average male retirement age has been falling, life expectancy has risen significantly. The result is a major increase in the percentage of the average adult male life spent

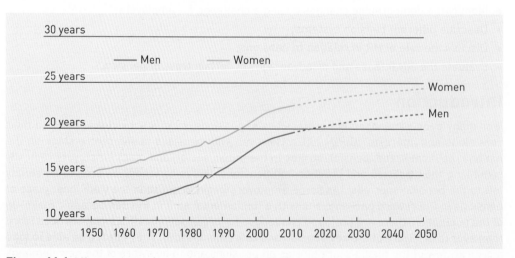

Figure 11.1 Life expectancy for men and women aged 65
Source: adapted from Pensions Commission (2004)

in retirement. In terms of pensions, longer life expectancy means pensions must be paid for longer and therefore cost more to provide. Longer lives put a strong pressure on pensions – if, for example, after a working life of 40 years, people expect perhaps a 25- or 30-year funded retirement, there is no doubt their future affordability is cast in doubt.

The combined effect in the labour market of these trends in longevity and falling birth rate will also of course create some very real people resourcing challenges in the coming years, making the future landscape markedly different from the present one.

pause for thought

Do a falling birth rate and increase in longevity have a negative impact on pension provision? Why did you reach this conclusion?

Employment patterns of older workers

Structural changes in the economy during the last 50 years have had a strong impact on the employment patterns of those later on in their career.

During the 1950s and 1960s the percentage of men aged 65–69 in employment dropped from 48 per cent in 1952 to 30 per cent in 1971 – see Figure 11.2. Then, from the mid-1970s to the mid-1990s, there was a large fall in the employment rate of men aged between 50 and 64. The proportion working fell from 88 per cent in 1973 to 63 per cent in 1995 – see Figure 11.3.

This decline concentrated in two periods. Firstly, during the early 1980s, the decline of manufacturing industry resulted in older male manufacturing workers

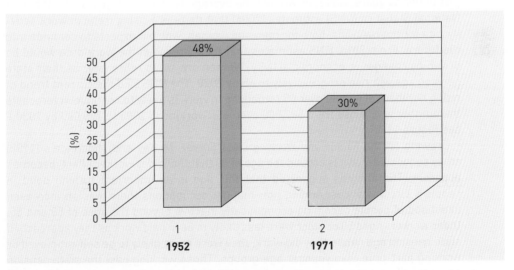

Figure 11.2 Percentage of men aged 60–65 in employment
Source: Pensions Commission (2004)

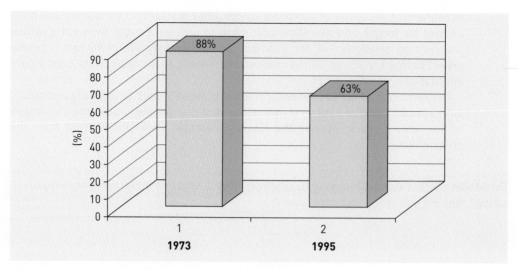

Figure 11.3 Percentage of men aged 50–64 in employment
Source: Pensions Commission (2004)

losing their jobs, many of them never to re-enter the workforce. Secondly, in the early 1990s, there were further manufacturing job losses and also a significant number of redundancies and early retirements in non-manual jobs. Many of these were facilitated by generous early retirement packages from pension funds which were then in significant surplus, enabling organisations to make those employees aged over 50 redundant at little cost to the employer.

In 2004, according to the Pensions Commission, just 21 per cent of men were still working at age 66. The average age of exit from the labour market for men is now just under 64 years, while for women the average is about 61.5 years. The Office of National Statistics (ONS) estimates (2006) that there is a rising trend in work activity rate for the over-50s, both for men and women, which it expects to continue into the future. From 2016, ONS estimates that the increase in the workforce would be driven by changes in economic activity. Women are set to retire later as their state pension age will rise progressively to 65 by 2020. The ONS said the current trend of rising numbers of people over 65 remaining in work is likely to continue. It forecasts the number would rise from 582,000 over-65s working in 2005 to 775,000 by 2020 – see Figure 11.4.

Drawing on the *Family and Working Lives Survey*, McKay and Middleton's (1998) study suggested that it is around the age of 50 that the 'older worker effect' becomes apparent. The analysis suggested that this age is an important turning point in people's circumstances. Among non-manual occupations there was an increased likelihood of people becoming economically inactive beyond the ages of 50 and 55. Older workers aged 50 or older were less likely to be in paid work as they approached state pension age. When they did work, they were more likely to be self-employed or working part-time than younger age groups. Those working past the state pension age were likely to be in temporary jobs, although older people were more likely to be in work if they were better qualified.

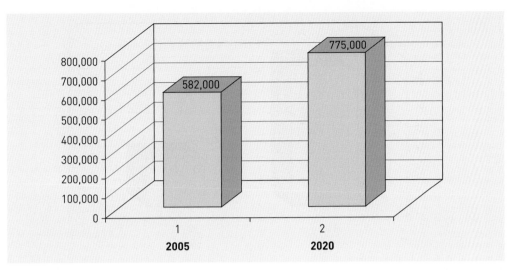

Figure 11.4 People aged 65+ in employment
Source: Pensions Commission (2004)

Age discrimination

Age discrimination may be defined as the rejection of older people as employees, owing to assumptions about the effect of age on the worker's ability to perform, regardless of the factual basis for such assumptions (Sargeant, 2004). For some individuals who are offered generous pension and early retirement terms, age 'discrimination' might be positively welcomed; for others it is as unfair as discrimination on the grounds of race, gender or disability. A CIPD/CIM (2005) survey reports that age discrimination remains a significant problem in the workplace. Fifty-nine per cent of respondents report that they have been disadvantaged by age discrimination at work. New legislation aims to tackle this discrimination and this is likely to affect the pattern of employment in the coming decades.

More retirement matters

Research on retirement ages shows that people currently tend to retire earlier than state pension age, but government policy is that people should expect to retire at a later age. There is, as IDS (2004) reports, a significant degree of resistance to such a development, both among employers and employees. Legally, retirement means 'cessation of service as an employee of the employer in question' (*Vennables v Hornby [2002] EWCA Civ 1277*). Sargeant (2004) explains that there are in essence three types of retirement age; these are:

♦ The *contractual* retirement age, or the age at which employees may be retired;

♦ The *pensionable* retirement age, at which any occupational pension may be taken;

♦ The *actual* retirement age.

These may coincide, and all take place at the same time, or they may occur at different times. Sargeant (ibid.) argues that the age discrimination provision to abolish mandatory retirement age set by employers principally affects contractual retirement ages rather than pensionable age or actual retirement age.

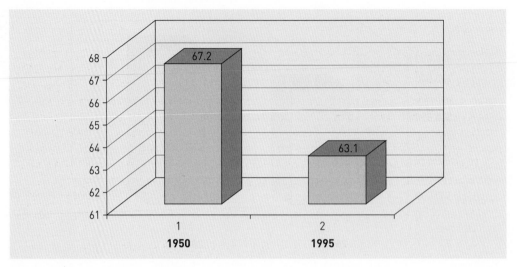

Figure 11.5 Average male retirement ages
Source: Pensions Commission (2004)

The contractual retirement age tends to vary between 60 and 65 years, while the GAD survey (2006) found that the most common pension age for members of private sector defined benefit schemes was still 65, as it had been in 2000.

The average actual retirement age has fallen significantly over the last 50 years, but is now increasing slowly, and could increase further – even without a rise in the number of people working past state pension age. The average male retirement age fell from 67.2 in 1950 to 63.1 in 1995 – see Figure 11.5.

Company pension schemes can, of course, decide the age at which their pensions vest, or when employees become entitled to the benefits. In practice, though, most pension schemes use the same age as that nominated by the State, currently 60 for women and 65 for men. However, the Pensions Act 1995 provides that from the year 2020 both genders will be eligible for their pension from age 65. Women born before 1950 will not be affected by this change, but for those born between 6 April 1950 and 5 April 1955, state pension age will be shifted in monthly steps. In addition, the age discrimination regulations and the Finance Act 2004 encourage employers to make retirement more flexible rather than a 'cliff edge' event. Under the Finance Act 2004, the minimum retirement age will increase from 50 to 55 by 2010.

A CIPD/CIM (2005) report states that there is a significant gap between people's expectations and their realistic prospects about retirement. While 69 per cent of their survey sample anticipates that the age of retirement for the average person in ten years' time will be 66 or older, 80 per cent expect that they themselves will retire by the age of 65.

Other changes in the law include those brought in at **A-day**; 6 April 2006 was the date when new pensions legislation revolutionised the way we think about pensions, and the changes it brings are likely to have a major impact on almost everyone's plans for the future.

Some employers – for example, Nationwide – are seeking to make late or flexible retirement a comparatively more attractive option than earlier retirement.

Flexible retirement at Nationwide

Nationwide has had a flexible retirement policy since the early 1990s, when 2 per cent of employees were aged 50 or over. Now over 11 per cent of employees are in that age group. The Nationwide Pension Fund has a normal pension age of 60. Pensions are reduced for early retirees and increased for people retiring after age 60. Pensions taken at early retirement before age 60 are actuarially reduced, but if the employee chooses to take late retirement after age 60, then their pension is increased by 9 per cent for each year after age 60, if they have contributed to the scheme for at least 36 years. If they have less than 36 years' service, then the actual retirement date will be treated as the normal retirement date and the pension is increased by 5 per cent for each year after age 60.

In Nationwide's *career average* scheme, although the normal pension age is 60, employees can continue to work up to the age of 70, and still continue to be members of the scheme.

(Adapted from IDS (2004) and Millar (2005))

♦ Summarise the main changes in pensions and retirement issues.

♦ Consider how HR specialists could help employees to make more realistic assessments of their future financial realities.

Role of human resource and the employer in the provision of pensions

Across many countries within the Western world, there are increasing debates about who should be responsible for providing employees with a secure income in retirement (Rousseau and Ho, 2000), and these debates are especially pressing in the context of the trends discussed above. What are the appropriate respective roles for the employer, the individual and the State? While each has a role, the Pensions Commission in the UK (2004) has no doubt that the central responsibility should lie with the individual. This has shifted the previous balance, in which large companies and public sector employers took prime responsibility for occupationally linked pensions, the State undertook some aspects of basic pension provision, and individuals provided for themselves on only a voluntary basis.

For the employer, state benefits are a costly item. Research on occupational pensions provided by employers (Taylor and Earnshaw, 1995) shows that employers' motives could be grouped into three categories:

♦ Paternalism, or taking care of the welfare of employees;

♦ Aiding recruitment and retention;

♦ Rewarding employees – enhancing motivation by the provision of a valued benefit.

These factors tend to work together to determine an individual employer's philosophy regarding the provision of pensions. A Confederation of British Industry (CBI)/Mercer (2004) survey found that 73 per cent of employers thought pensions assisted in the recruitment and retention of staff (87 per cent of large employers and 65 per cent of small employers). However, a Pensions Institute report (2004) found that many finance directors in smaller firms were not convinced of the recruitment and retention benefits of providing pension provision. The Employer Task Force on Pensions (2004) concludes that many employers firmly believe that pension benefits are an important tool for attracting and retaining employees, and for many companies it forms an important part of their culture and values. However, such business rationale seems to be based on being seen as *average*, in comparison with competitors, or within the labour market more generally.

There is limited systematic data concerning the recruitment and retention or productivity benefits associated with pension provision. Taylor (2000) found only a weak relationship between pension provision and retention of staff, until employees reach age 50.

pause for thought

Do you think it inevitable that poor pension provision will negatively influence recruitment and retention?

Why did you reach this decision?

Employees and pensions

Employees' interest in pensions appears to be strongly age- and gender-related (Gough, 2004). Research on employee views (Loretto et al., 2001; Gough and Hales, 2003) has shown a preponderance of consumerist opinions, with the university students surveyed by Loretto tending not to see pensions as part of the reward package offered by employers, but rather a personal or individual matter over which they could exercise some choice. Ward (1995) comments that while few people are interested enough, at least under the age of 40, to take positive action about their pension, if they are given the opportunity to have a pension, they will take it.

There is a widespread lack of understanding about pension and retirement issues. The Goode Committee Report (1993) commissioned some research to assess what might be the 'triggers' to people thinking more about pensions. These were:

◆ Concerns about ageing;

◆ Access to a pension scheme;

◆ Major life events such as taking on a mortgage, getting married, becoming a parent, or having increased disposable income;

◆ Perceiving the State pension as inadequate, or under threat;

◆ Observing current pensioners' financial difficulties.

Human resource specialists and pensions

The topic of pensions is not on most HR students' list of favourite subjects. This may be because managerial responsibility for occupational pensions may not even rest with the HR function, but lie with the finance department. Research over the past 20 years has shown few references to pensions in either the strategic or operational priorities for HR. None of the CIPD research on links between people management practices and business performance has highlighted pensions as a high-performance work practice.

As well as funding pension schemes, employers need to consider communicating the benefits of the pension scheme. Some HR specialists may shrink from such activity, fearing that such information provision amounts to giving advice, which only those who are registered with the Financial Services Authority may provide. Many defined-contribution pension scheme providers offer their staff Internet access to their pension accounts.

Oram (2006) suggests that employers' attempts to explain retirement savings options to employees are often greeted with a mixture of disdain, bewilderment and lethargy. Instead, by targeting the diverse interests of different groups of employees, and gathering feedback about various communication strategies, there may be improvements. Employee surveys, and monitoring the take-up of schemes among employees, can also aid communication.

A short guide to different types of pension scheme

State pension

The state pension system in the UK is complex and comprises several parts:

- **Basic pension** – the amount received is related to an individual's NI. For people to receive the full basic pension, a man needs 44 years' and a woman needs 39 years' contributions. This can be reduced if the person has been looking after a child or a sick or disabled person. Women who have had career breaks, even though they have spent most of their lives working, may miss out on the full amount.

  The basic state pension is increased in line with the Retail Price Index (RPI) every year. The system was changed during the 1980s, when it was raised each year in line with national average earnings (NAE), which normally increase faster than prices. This means that over the long term the basic pension is declining relative to earnings. Policy debates continue about restoring this link with earnings.

- **The State Second Pension** – previously the State Earnings Related Pension Scheme – SERPS, this is partly earnings-related and covers people who are not in an employer's or private pension scheme. The amount of pension depends on the individual's pay and the number of years of contributions or credits.

- **Pension Credit** – this is available to pensioners whose income is below a certain level (i.e. it is means-tested).

Occupational pensions

Occupational schemes are provided by employers for their employees, and most require financial contributions from both employer and employee. Less than half the national workforce is in an occupational scheme. The GAD (2005) survey showed that 4.8 million employees were in private sector schemes and 5.0 million in public sector schemes. See Figure 11.6.

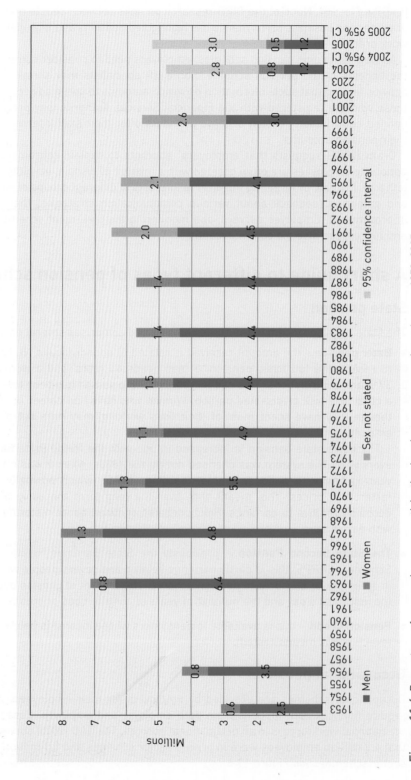

Figure 11.6 Percentage of men and women participating in private sector pension schemes, 1953–2005

Source: Cebulla and De-Beaman (2004)

Defined-contribution schemes

Final-salary or defined-benefit schemes

These have typically been provided by the UK's larger employers. They provide a known pension benefit on retirement, normally calculated by taking into consideration the salary at or near retirement date and the length of service. The pension increases with each year of service, with the commonest rate of growth being 1/60th per year. The employee knows in advance that after, say, 30 years of service, they will receive a pension of 30/60ths of their final pensionable salary. The key advantage is that the employer bears the uncertainty of the ultimate cost of providing the benefit. Around 5 million employees are members of about 38,000 defined-benefit schemes according to the Government Actuary's Department.

In the first few years of the twenty-first century, there was a dramatic downturn in the UK stock market, affecting about half of all final-salary schemes, which then either closed altogether or closed to new members. However, a CIPD (2006) survey reported that changes to schemes continue.

Greenwood (2005) discusses the concerns of employers who have closed their final-salary schemes to new members; in future, they could face age discrimination claims because older employees may be still covered by the more generous final-salary arrangement, while younger employees may be relatively disadvantaged by being refused membership to such schemes.

Some public sector schemes have a different structure to those in the private sector. For example in the local government and other schemes, the pension builds up at a rate of 1/80th of final salary for each year of service. This means that for a 40-year career, a public sector employee will only achieve a pension of half of their final salary, compared with the standard maximum of two-thirds of final salary in a 1/60th scheme. However, the overall pension benefit that public sector employees in these 1/80th schemes receive may be equivalent to a 1/60th scheme, when the tax-free retirement lump sum is included in the reckoning. All schemes are subject to the same tax limits, but public sector schemes may be more generous than some private sector final salary schemes in the early retirement benefits they offer.

The Employer Task Force on Pensions (2004) suggested that 'meaningful employer contributions' are fundamental to a pension scheme's success. The Taskforce emphasised that an occupational pension scheme will have low take-up and be undervalued by employees if the employer pays little or no contribution into it. It recommended a combined employer/employee contribution of around 10–15 per cent, of which two-thirds, it said, should be provided by the employer.

The NAPF (2004) survey shows that average employer contributions to final-salary schemes (16.6 per cent) are more than double the value contributed by them to money-purchase schemes (7.6 per cent).

Public sector pension strikes

In March 2006 more than a million council workers went on strike over plans to penalise some staff for retiring before they were 65. The strike was provoked by government plans to stop council workers benefiting from 'rule 85', a clause in the Local Government Pension Scheme (LGPS) that allows employees to retire early without taking a reduced

continued

pension, as long as their age and the number of years they have worked for local authorities add up to 85. 'Strike action is the only option left to local government workers,' said Unison general secretary, Dave Prentis. 'They want to demonstrate the burning resentment and anger they feel over the government and employers taking away their pension rights.' The Local Government Association (LGA), which represents 500 local authorities in England and Wales, claimed union demands for 'rule 85' to apply to all public sector staff would cost council taxpayers more. 'The changes to local government staff pensions are both needed and necessary,' said Sir Sandy Bruce Lockhart, chairman of the LGA. 'There must be a modern scheme that is affordable, viable and fit for the 21st century. People are living longer and unless action is taken now, the cost to individual council taxpayers and local government will continue to rise.'

(Adapted from Lee (2006))

exercise

- ◆ Summarise the positions of both employers and employees in situations when the employer believes they must reduce pension benefits for current employees.
- ◆ Suggest ways in which such conflicts of interest may be solved.

Career Average Revalued Earnings (CARE) schemes

These have been growing in popularity (NAPF, 2004). They relate the pension to an employee's length of service. However, the resulting benefit is typically lower, because the 'pensionable salary' definition is an *average* of the salary over the length of the employee's career, rather than being based on salary close to retirement, which is typically higher. The pension level would typically be only three-quarters of that under final-salary defined-benefit schemes.

Defined contribution schemes

With money-purchase or defined-contribution schemes, each individual employee has their own separately identifiable pension account, into which their own, and any employer's, contributions are paid. The account is invested and its value is used to provide the pension benefit on retirement. The advantage for the employer here is that their costs are known and stable. The employee bears all the risk related to the ultimate value of the fund. Just over 1 million employees are members of employers' defined-contribution schemes, with the numbers increasing fairly rapidly.

Some schemes have more than one section, in that they offer benefits on different bases to different groups of members. For example, one group of members might be offered benefits on a defined-benefit basis, while a second group might be offered benefits on a defined-contribution basis. Adding to the complexity of these arrangements, some schemes might have different sections in order to offer different levels of the same type of benefit to different members, or simply to account for the benefits and contributions of different groups of members separately.

Re-read the two paragraphs above.

How much risk do you believe it is fair for employees to bear in relation to the funding of their pensions?

Why did you reach this conclusion?

Tesco's career average scheme

In contrast to many other employers, Tesco started a new defined-benefit scheme to provide pensions based on career average earnings rather than final salary. This replaced its money-purchase scheme, which had previously covered part-time employees (final-salary benefits were available to full-time employees). The *Pension Builder* scheme is contributory for employees, with contributions set at 4 per cent of earnings; over a 40-year career, scheme members will build up pension rights worth 60 per cent of average annual career earnings. The annual growth rate is 1.5 per cent of revalued earnings.

Once they have 12 months' service, all new staff over the age of 25 are automatically entered into the new scheme, unless they choose to opt out. Existing staff are also able to join the new scheme. The previous defined-contribution schemes are now closed to new members.

By moving to a career average salary scheme, Tesco aims to strike the right balance between the financial security of its employees, on the one hand, and the needs of the group and its shareholders, on the other. Through the new arrangement Tesco provides what it describes as 'an industry leading benefit' while managing the group's exposure by protecting it from open-ended liabilities. Cost predictability is important to the company; *Pension Builder* uses average salary rather than final salary, and so each year the company knows its funding liability.

(Adapted from *IDS Pensions Bulletin 150*,
November 2001 and *IDS Pensions Bulletin 155*, May 2002)

Stakeholder pensions

Stakeholder pensions are low-cost defined-contributions schemes regulated by the government and provided through pension companies. Employers are not required to set up stakeholder schemes if they employ fewer than five people or they already provide an occupational pension. Under the stakeholder scheme:

◆ Employees can make tax-free contributions from their pay to a defined-contribution (money-purchase) pension scheme;

◆ They are low cost so the pension provider companies cannot make charges to stakeholder members greater than 1.5 per cent of the fund per annum for the first ten years (1 per cent thereafter);

◆ Employers are not required to make contributions to their employees' stakeholder pensions.

There are two types of stakeholder scheme:

◆ **Trust-based schemes** – these are allowed to restrict membership to certain groups, e.g. trade union members, and are governed by normal pension scheme legislation.

♦ **Contract-based schemes** – these are open to all and must have a Financial Services Authority authorised scheme manager.

All schemes must be registered with the Pensions Regulator.

Regulatory framework

A-Day

From 6 April 2006, a number of changes to UK pensions legislation came into force. The previous Inland Revenue rules had effectively set the contours for pension schemes, since they specified the levels of contributions and benefits which could benefit from tax relief. The A-day changes simplify the tax regime, changing some aspects of the tax treatment of pensions.

The principal change is that employees in occupational pension schemes can now continue to work and to draw their pension, if their scheme rules permit. This reform effectively breaks the link between pensions and retirement and could be an important one for employers seeking to make retirement more flexible.

The rules concerning the time when employees can take their pension are also changing – from 6 April 2010, workers cannot take their pensions before the age of 55 unless they retire early as a result of poor health. If employees had the right to retire before 50 on 6 April 2006, that right may be protected.

A new simplified pension system aims to encourage more staff to take out a personal scheme or join an occupational one. The government also hopes that employees' savings will build up more quickly than under the previous rules. Staff can now be a member both of their company pension scheme and a personal retirement fund, something that was not allowed under the old rules.

Before A-day, the maximum amount of money people could save in a pension was linked to their age. Now they can put their entire salary into a pension, up to a limit of £215,000 a year, rising to £255,000 in 2010. From 6 April 2006, the previous annual limits on contributions and limits benefiting from tax relief have been replaced with a single, lifetime cap of £1.5 million.

Age discrimination legislation

The Employment Equality (Age) Regulations 2006 came into force from 1 October 2006, and made a number of changes to the law as it affects retirement and pensions. Although the government aims that pension schemes should be able to operate largely as they did before age discrimination became unlawful, there are significant changes to the regulatory framework as it affects retirement ages – particularly contractual retirement ages (Sargeant, 2004). In summary, some of the principal provisions are:

♦ There is a default retirement age of 65. If an organisation sets a normal retirement age below 65, it will need to be objectively justified. Employees have the right to be informed of their expected retirement date and of their right to request to work longer. This must be done at least six months, but not more than 12 months, in advance of a planned retirement. Employee requests to stay on must be considered using a procedure laid down in the regulations. Failure to follow this procedure could result in compensation of up to eight weeks' pay.

- The age limits on bringing unfair dismissal and redundancy claims are removed, meaning that employees who are over age 65 can bring unfair dismissal claims.

- Pension schemes are exempted from the claims of age discrimination in certain age-related aspects: for example, fixing of ages for admission to the pension scheme; the use of a normal retirement age; age criteria in actuarial calculations; and relating pension benefits to length of service (as in a final-salary scheme).

- In addition, using length of service to calculate other benefits will be lawful if a qualification period of five years or less is used.

Consultation on pension changes

Under the Pensions Act 2004, employers are responsible for providing their staff with relevant information on pension scheme changes and consulting them about changes before they are made.

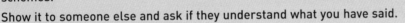

exercise

W

Imagine you are a pensions consultant.

Devise a PowerPoint presentation to explain to the Warbings board of directors the benefits and drawbacks of money-purchase, final-salary and career average pension schemes.

Show it to someone else and ask if they understand what you have said.

Summary

Combined with labour market developments, the increasing cost of pensions has prompted some radical consideration of traditional pension practices. The demographic changes in the labour market put pressure on HR specialists to become acquainted with relevant pension issues in order to adapt HR practices to fit the demands of the new environment.

Review Questions

You may wish to attempt the following as practice examination style questions.

11.1 Draft that part of a recruitment advertisement in which you highlight the benefits of your company's new career average pension scheme.

11.2 'The safe, trusting, if not fully understood, comfort-blanket pensions environment that existed for full-time, white-collar employees in many large companies in the post-war years is well and truly over . . .' (CIPD, 2002). Critically discuss this statement.

11.3 Your company has recently implemented a new normal retirement age of 66 and actively wants to discourage early retirement (even though in the past it has been offered as a way of reducing head count). Prepare for a one-to-one meeting with an employee who wants to take early retirement at age 56. Summarise the key points to be made by both sides.

References

CBI/Mercer Human Resource Consulting (2004). A view from the top: a survey of business leaders' views on UK pension provision, in *The Employer Task Force on Pensions (2004) Report to The Secretary of State for Work and Pensions*, at: www.employertaskforce.org.uk/publications/index.shtml.

Cebulla, A. and De-Beaman, S. (2004). *Employers' Pension Provision Survey 2003*, Department of Work and Pensions, Research Report 207.

CIPD/CIM (2005). *Tackling Age Discrimination in the Workplace: Creating a New Age For All*, London: CIPD/CIM.

CIPD (2002). *Pensions and HR's role: A Guide*, London: CIPD.

CIPD (2006). *Reward Management Survey 2006*, London: CIPD.

Employer Task Force on Pensions (2004). *Report to the Secretary of State for Work and Pensions*, at: www.employertaskforce.org.uk/publications/index.shtml.

Goode Committee (1993). *Pension Law Reform*, London: HMSO.

Gough, O. (2004). Why do employees, particularly women, reject pensions?, *Employee Relations*, Vol. 26, No. 5, pp. 480–494.

Gough, O. and Hales, C. (2003). Employee evaluations of company occupational pensions: HR implications, *Personnel Review*, Vol. 32, No. 3, pp. 319–340.

Government Actuary's Department (GAD) (2005). *Occupational Pension Schemes 2004: The Twelfth Survey by the Government Actuary*, London: HMSO.

Government Actuary's Department (GAD) (2006). *Occupational Pension Schemes: Government Actuary's Report on the Thirteenth Survey of Occupational Pension Schemes in the Public and Private Sector*, London: HMSO.

Greenwood, J. (2005). The final countdown, *People Management*, 5 May, pp. 38–39.

IDS (2004). The average age of retirement must rise, *IDS Pension Bulletin* 176, June, pp. 9–10.

Lee, K. (2006). Council workers strike over pension plans, *People Management*, 28 March.

Loretto, W., White, P. and Duncan, C. (2001). 'Thatcher's children', pensions and retirement: some survey evidence, *Personnel Review*, Vol. 30, No. 4, pp. 386–430.

McKay, S. and Middleton, S. (1998). Characteristics of older workers: secondary analysis of the family and working lives survey, DfEE Research report RR45, London: HMSO.

Millar, M. (2005). Nationwide to allow staff to work until they are 75, *Personnel Today*, 2 June, p. 2.

National Association of Pension Funds (NAPF) (2004). *30th Annual Survey*, London: NAPF.

Office of National Statistics (2006) as cited in A Seager (2006). Government statistician counts on us living and working longer. *The Guardian*, 13 January.

Oram, N. (2006). How to build awareness of company pension schemes, *People Management*, 23 February.

Pensions Commission (2004). *Pensions: Challenges and Choices*, at: www.pensionscommission.org.uk/publications/2004/annrep/index.asp.

Pensions Institute (2004). *Delivering DC? Barriers to Participation in the Company-sponsored Pensions Market*, in Employer Task Force on Pensions (2004) *Report to the Secretary of State for Work and Pensions*, at: www.employertaskforce.org.uk/publications/index.shtml.

Rousseau, D. and Ho, V. (2000). Psychological contract issues in compensation, in S.L. Rynes et al. (eds.) *Compensation in Organizations: Current Research and Practice*, San Francisco, CA: Jossey-Bass.

Sargeant, M. (2004). Mandatory retirement age and age discrimination, *Employee Relations*, Vol. 26, No. 2, pp. 151–166.

Taylor, S. (2000). Pensions and employee retention, *Employee Relations*, Vol. 22, No. 3, pp. 253–259.

Taylor, S. and Earnshaw, J. (1995). An exploration of employer objectives in the provision of occupational pension schemes in the UK, *Employee Relations*, Vol. 17, No. 2, pp. 38–53.

Ward, S. (1995). *Managing the Pensions Revolution*, London: Nicholas Brealey.

Further Reading

Industrial Society (2001). Managing pensions change, *Managing Best Practice*, Vol. 81.

Loretto, W., White, P. and Duncan, C. (2000). Something for nothing? Employees' views of occupational pension schemes, *Employee Relations*, Vol. 22, No. 3, pp. 260–271.

Seager, A. (2006). Government statistician counts on us living and working longer, *The Guardian*, 13 January.

Useful Websites

www.cipd.co.uk/guides – access to Chartered Institute of Personnel and Development guides offering practical insight into key issues such as pensions (published jointly by CIPD and Trade Union Congress, with funding from the Department of Trade and Industry)

www.dwp.gov.uk/publications – access to a range of publications from the Department of Work and Pensions covering research, practical guidance and advice on policy and strategy

www.opas.org.uk – advice and guidance, e.g. on pension schemes, from the independent Pensions Advisory Service

www.napf.co.uk – employer-sponsored National Association of Pension Funds provides surveys, news reports on pension issues and representation of employers' views

www.pensionsatwork.gov.uk – website maintained by the Department of Work and Pensions providing case studies, good practice guidelines, news reports, etc. aimed at employers

www.thepensionservice.gov.uk – website of the Pension Service (Department of Work and Pensions) providing information about pensions and pensioner benefits for employers and employees (e.g. forecasting likely retirement income)

www.thepensionsregulator.gov.uk – website of the Pensions Regulator providing guidance and news updates aimed at trustees, employers and scheme members – focused on good practice

www.employertaskforce.org.uk/index.shtml – website of the Employer Task Force on Pensions (set up from the 2002 Green Paper on Pensions – 'Simplicity, Security and Working and Saving for Retirement'), which is an employer-led body with a mission to increase occupational and private pension provision, providing good practice guides and reports on action research

www.fsa.gov.uk – website of the Financial Services Authority covering regulatory requirements, good practice advice and international perspectives aimed at, inter alia, pension providers and financial advisors

www.hmre.gov.uk – HM Revenue and Customs website with focus on tax issues

www.pensions-pmi.org.uk – website of the Pensions Management Institute, the professional body for those working in the field of pensions and employee benefits, focused on pension scheme management advice, news reports and good practice guidance

PART 5
Relations

Part contents

CHAPTER 12

Employee Relations and Managing the Employment Relationship

By Cecilie Bingham

Chapter outline

The way that an organisation chooses to deploy and manage its workforce is central to the human resource (HR) function. This chapter looks at the ways in which employment relationships are managed. In particular, it examines how different managerial styles and frames of reference will have an impact on the sources of power and its distribution within the workplace. The levels of conflict and the ways it is managed are explored; and the mechanisms for employee voice, specifically the impact this has on the psychological contract, are examined.

Learning outcomes

By the end of the chapter, you should be able to:

◆ Describe the different theoretical perspectives which can be applied to employee relations;

◆ Assess the value of different frames of reference for explaining the employment relationship;

◆ Apply appropriate theoretical concepts to the workplace;

◆ Use theoretical concepts to analyse current employee relations situations.

Introduction

Examining the ways people interact at work, both as individuals and in groups, is at the heart of studying the employment relationship. Such interaction is influenced not just by the perceptions of the individuals and their positions within the organisation but by a variety of different factors, such as the economy, the labour market and the strength of external competitors.

The essence of employee relations

Employee relations is the study of workplace relationships and the way in which the parties to such relationships interact with one another. This will involve individual employees (those who work for others), managers (those who organise and control work processes) and employers (those who own the enterprise in question). It may involve groups or organisations that represent or 'talk for' any of these three main groups. Trade unions, for example, may represent some or all of the workforce, the managers may belong to professional bodies such as the CIPD (Chartered Institute of Personnel and Development), while the employers may belong to an employers' organisation, such as the Engineering Employers' Federation or the Institute of Directors. The relationship does not, of course, take place in a vacuum: the economy and the labour market will have an impact on the relationship, as will rules, laws and codes of practice regulating the workplace. These may originate from within the UK or from Europe or indeed from within the workplace itself, sometimes even as a product of the employment relationship. Depending on the type of organisation, there will be a mixture of customers, competitors, creditors and suppliers, all having an impact on the relationship. The size of the organisation, whether it is a small family-run enterprise or a large multinational conglomerate, whether it is based on one site or many, will have an influence on the way in which the employees are managed and on the ways in which they react to that management. On occasions the courts may influence workplace-based behaviour and so too might the media. In addition to all of these factors, the culture of the organisation, the history of the relationships it has with its employees and the values and expectations of the employees themselves will all have an impact on the way in which the employment relationship is managed and perceived.

Employee relations therefore is about the formal and informal relationships at work. It concerns the ways in which people interact both with one another and with the jobs that they undertake; specifically, it concerns individuals who voluntarily subordinate themselves to the demands of the organisation by exchanging their time, effort and possibly experience and knowledge, for monetary and non-monetary rewards within a regulated work environment. The interaction of the parties involved is crucially affected by the balance of power between them. As Lewis et al. (2003: 6) say, the employment relationship is an 'economic, legal, social, psychological and political relationship in which employees devote their time and expertise to the inter-ests of their employer in return for a range of personal, financial and non-financial rewards.'

Each party to the relationship is influenced by a number of different factors or interests and, in order to understand employee relations as a topic, it is necessary to be aware of the different influences that may affect each of the parties.

pause for thought

What do you think the main concerns of employees are?

Why did you reach this conclusion?

Individual employees work for a number of reasons. Financial reward is perhaps the most obvious, but social status, friendship, professional interest in an area, a sense of achievement, the ability to 'put something back into society' are all other aspects that induce/motivate people to participate in paid employment. Once participating, such motivators influence the expectations that employees bring to the workplace. So, for example, they expect to be treated with respect, paid for the work they do and that the:

- Amount they receive will be a fair reward for the effort that they have expended – and that it will be fair in relation to any remuneration that others they know receive;
- Work they do will be appreciated;
- The workplace will be safe;
- Work expected from them will be within their capabilities;
- Hours that they are required to work will not be excessive;
- Training will be timely and appropriate;
- Holidays will be adequate.

Common expectations that most employees bring to the workplace are listed above. Can you think of any other expectations?

pause for thought

The employers too will have a set of interests that influence them. These may include:

- Making a profit (if it is part of the private sector) while maintaining, if not enlarging, their market share;
- Providing a good service, whether it is part of the private sector or a not-for-profit organisation;
- Providing value for shareholders and stakeholders;
- Deploying the people within the organisation in the most cost-effective way to maximise their time, effort and knowledge for the good of the organisation;
- Ensuring the survival of the organisation;
- Ensuring their corporate social responsibility;
- Maximising any good publicity while minimising any that is bad;
- Operating within the bounds of the law.

Some employers will want to behave ethically, some will not.

In small organisations the employers may well be the managers and have face-to-face interaction with the employees but, in larger organisations, managers are employed to achieve the objectives of the organisation and attached to this role are the concepts of accountability, responsibility and authority.

The employment relationship and human resource management

HRM is regarded as a strategic, holistic way of dealing with the employment relationship; those employed doing so in the light of business planning and development. With HRM there is a move away from centralised personnel departments towards line management control and consequent responsibility for empowering, motivating and regulating those staff for whom they are responsible (Sisson, 1990). (The last decade or so has seen a wide-ranging debate about the nature of HRM and the differences between this and the more traditional aspects of personnel management. John Storey (1992, 1998) clearly delineates the differences and similarities between the two (see Chapters 1 and 3).

David Guest (1987) has examined the academic approaches to HRM and identified two different approaches: the soft and the hard. The former sees employees as an asset to be nurtured and the latter sees employees as a resource to be utilised for the needs of the business. The two are not mutually exclusive; both may be present at the same time depending on the type of employee in question. What is important is the impact that the 'type' has on the employment relationship. Staff who are valued, rewarded, consulted and feel integrated into an organisation are more likely to feel commitment and loyalty to that organisation than those who are treated merely as a resource. Hence the former are more likely to have an employment relationship that is characterised less by 'command and control' mechanisms and more by the four Cs: **C**ommunicate, **C**onsult and **C**are combined with **C**ontrol.

Power and the employment relationship

Power is the degree to which one party can influence, persuade, encourage or force another to do something that they might not otherwise do. The relationship between an employer and an employee can be said to be based around the realities of power, the employee submitting to the control of the employer. Yet in practice the position is not quite that clear cut. The relationship between an employer and an employee is symbiotic. That is, each is dependent on the other and, despite differences, they work together for the mutual benefit of each because it is in the interests of neither to destroy the other. This does not, however, mean that the relationship is one where each has an equal amount of influence and power over the other. The very nature of the relationship is such that the employer, who has the power to hire and fire, to dictate which work is to be done, to control the ways in which the work is to be done, and specify the time in which it is to be done, has the controlling stake in the relationship. Employees, however, are not without power. Their willingness to work, their labour, skills, expertise, knowledge, and availability mean that the employer cannot function without them. While the condition of the labour market (i.e. the supply of those able to work), the degree to which vital skills are available and the legislation in place at the time all play a part in shaping the power balance within the relationship as do the culture and values permeating the organisation.

pause for thought

Do you think the balance of power always lies with the management of an organisation? Why did you reach this conclusion?

exercise

Read the Warbings case study. How would you describe the ways in which power is exercised across the company?

The amount of power that individuals hold can be defined as the degree of influence that one party has over the other in order to achieve their own goals. Individuals may have power because their employer depends on their knowledge, expertise or skills that, on occasion, may be in demand because there are few like them available in the labour market. Sometimes power is achieved by individuals banding together to present a united front to the employer, as when they join a union. In practice the balance of power often means one party subjugating their own desires in order to execute the requirements of the other. Employers share with or delegate power to the managers in the organisation – the amount of power the managers hold will therefore be dependent on their freedom to engage in discretionary behaviour.

Yet there is a balance in the employment relationship. Whoever is in the ascendancy will not want to push the other to such an extreme that the relationship breaks down, leading to the mutual destruction of them both. Indeed on occasions the power of decision making is shared in order to achieve results that are palatable to everyone. Analysis of the power balance can depend on the perspective of those undertaking the analysis; as Gospel and Palmer (1993: 11) say: 'While some people assume that employers always have the real power in industrial relations, others assume that employees, when organised into trade unions, can be as powerful or more so.' Such differing perspectives influence the philosophies behind employment legislation: hence the resulting legislation sometimes promotes collective representation and at other times restricts it. Consequently EU legislation requiring collective representation is sometimes anathema to a UK government and UK employers that prefer to restrict such representation.

Lukes (1974, 1986) and Clegg (1989) develop the notion of power, suggesting that it may be exercised to check, eliminate or enhance certain behaviours, in such a way that the specific values predominate within an organisation, creating cultural norms for each workplace. Such views presuppose that everyone is happy to go along with the dominant values and that individual differences are subsumed in respect of those in power. In many ways it is rather simplistic: individuals, different groups within an organisation, different segments within the same workforce interact with one another and exchange views and information in ways that influence one another's behaviour. The degree of power exercised may change from day to day depending on circumstances, individuals and the market in which they find themselves.

Sources of power (and the ways in which it may be exercised within the workplace) are not homogeneous. French and Raven (1962), in their classic study, delineated five distinct sources of power; two of these sources, expert and referent power, derive from the holder's individual characteristics. The other three, legitimate, reward and coercive power, derive from the holder's position within the organisation.

An individual has **expert power** when they have specific knowledge and expertise that others rely upon, for example an IT specialist in a company of non-specialists. Here the sharing or withholding of specialist knowledge will have a direct impact on the organisation.

Referent power, on the other hand, derives not from expertise, but from the sometimes inspirational, often charismatic, personality of the holder. Such people are liked and respected and others want to do their bidding because they want to please them. In terms of the employment relationship, such people are often able to motivate and persuade their colleagues to undertake difficult tasks, stay late at work and perform duties outside their contract, merely because they are liked and because people don't want to let them down. Arthur Scargill could have been said to exercise referent power when, without a ballot, in 1984–85, he led the miners to strike against pit closures.

Coercive power is in evidence when a compelling argument based on threat is used to encourage obedience: in employee relations terms, this could be displayed by a manager deciding to withhold resources, or perhaps bully colleagues, in order to ensure compliance. The atmosphere created is not one of trust, people often performing to the minimum rather than the maximum standard required because they resent the explicit or implicit threats. Sexual harassment and bullying can be regarded as forms of coercive power. The trade union Unison (2003: 2) says that bullying behaviour in the workplace is an abuse of power that is 'offensive, intimidating, malicious, insulting'. Coercive power in the form of bullying behaviour, even if it is regarded as acceptable in some workplaces, is not acceptable under law. Should cases go to trial they are often settled out of court: in *Kirk v Nacanco*, for example, Kirk eventually received an out of court settlement for £200,000. The company acknowledged that he had been subjected to impossibly escalating production targets coupled with continual criticism both at work and through phone calls at home that contributed to his breakdown.

Reward power is where individuals persuade others to do their bidding in exchange for something that they want. In employment terms, this is epitomised by the pay–work bargain (Farnham 1997: 3), where employees exchange their labour for monetary reward. The reward may not be monetary; it could be promotion, or the opportunity to work on a prestigious project. The strength of the power that a person holds depends on the perception of others that they can actually deliver. Sometimes rewards do not match the expectations of the rewarded and conflict may result.

Legitimate power is where someone's position within the organisation gives them the authority to make decisions and control the activities of others. Line managers therefore have the authority to control the work processes of their subordinates merely because of their position in the organisation. Perceptions, too, are important here. If someone is not perceived as being worthy of the position they hold, their power may be diminished. So, for example, if someone with little experience is brought in to manage an existing sales team the perception of the team may be that the person's inexperience renders them unfit for the job and non-cooperation, conflict and a breakdown in the employment relationship can be the result.

Exercise

Read the scenario below and then answer the following questions:

- Who are the parties involved?
- What are the issues involved?
- How would you describe the balance of power?

In December 2004, airline pilots in the UK threatened not to co-operate with their employers if changes were made to the ways in which they worked. Specifically, they did not want to work the new hours being discussed by transport ministers from the EU that they believed could result in longer hours at work with fewer rest periods. On 10 December, BALPA (the British Airline Pilots Association, the pilots' trade union) took out a number of advertisements in national newspapers explaining its worries: a particular concern was about pilot fatigue and the risks that this posed for the lives of both passengers and air crews. So worried were they that the advertisements said, 'If this European fudge is adopted and we are asked to fly hours we believe to be unsafe we will not take-off.' In addition the union's general secretary, Jim McAuslan, claimed 'Dangerously fatigued foreign pilots will be flying over and landing in Britain, putting at risk communities living around airports.' The union accused the European politicians of trying to impose regulations that were less safe than the existing ones and certainly less scientific. Mr Gramshaw, the chairman of BALPA, and a pilot at Britannia Airways, commenting on the fact that, for a pilot beginning a night flight in Europe, the limit would exceed 12 hours while the existing one in the UK was 10 hours, used emotive language. He compared the long hours to those of junior doctors: 'They kill the patients one at a time. We tend to kill ours hundreds at a time.'

BALPA called for the UK government to veto the proposals and ensure that independent safety experts scrutinised them.

(Sources: case study compiled with information from the TUC *Risks* magazine, *Personnel Today*, *Hansard* and the BBC)

---

exercise

- Look at the Warbings case study and list all of the parties you think are involved in the employment relationship.
- What types of power are in evidence? Don't forget to give examples to back up your answer.
- Is power evenly distributed between the parties?
- Why did you reach this conclusion?

The exercise of power is constrained by circumstance and perception. As the unions in the UK have become constrained by legislative restrictions, and weakened by falling membership, they have looked to a number of different ways to maintain a continuing influence within the workplace. (In autumn 2005, 6.68 million people were union members and the rate of union membership (union density) among employees was 29 per cent. It was higher for women and older employees (Grainger, 2006).) Whereas in the past unions may have asserted their power by means of industrial action, in the twenty-first century this is not always possible. Alternative methods of influence have to be found: sometimes this is via partnership arrangements where the emphasis is on consensual problem solving; at other times it is by a reliance on rules and procedures to help create a fairer employment relationship.

Oxenbridge and Brown (2004) point out that contemporary union influence is no longer as reliant on the mechanisms of negotiation, and hence on the explicit exercise of power. In order to influence the employment relationship, the mechanisms of consultation, partnership and a reliance on procedures are utilised to ensure that they continue to have some sway in the ways in which the employment relationship operates. Other researchers (for example, Jenkins in a paper given at the 2006 International Labour Process Conference) have argued that by entering into partnership arrangements with organisations unions often lose a further degree of power. Indeed long before partnership agreements were in vogue, Flanders (1970: 172) pointed out that managements often maintain control by sharing it.

The Transport and General Workers' Union* is determined to buck this trend of partnership working where it leads to ever-diminishing levels of union influence. It deliberately emphasises the difference between its members' interests and those of management; and rather than develop partnership approaches has declared an interest in being adversarial where necessary.

In his 2003 conference address, Tony Woodley, General Secretary of the Transport and General Workers' Union, stated:

> 'Real change must start at the sharp end – in the workplace . . . We live in a society where workers can be sacked by text message. Where unscrupulous employers close down factories here because it is quicker, cheaper and easier to sack British workers than those elsewhere in Europe. Where poverty pay remains rife, and women and black people are second-class citizens at work. [. . .]
>
> And we have to recognise it – a society where the trade union movement has been able to do too little to help those who need us most. [. . .] How many times have I heard workers say, "why isn't the union doing anything for us?" Even, "what is the point in the union?" And if those who are already our members are saying that, we can only imagine what the attitude is among those millions who aren't in unions.
>
> Why? Because we have taken our eye off the ball, because we are sometimes seen as too close to the gaffer [boss], because we are not delivering satisfaction at the sharp end, in the workplace, we have become almost irrelevant to our members.
>
> That is why we must refocus our time, money and effort on the workplace and industrial priorities of the union, on the T&G becoming once more a fighting back union.
>
> Because fighting back makes a difference to our members.
>
> Some people may misinterpret that as a permanent call to arms, or a programme of endless strikes. That is not the case. What I mean is a T&G that:

Never lets an injustice in the workplace go by without challenging it. Encourages, rather than damps down, the aspirations of working people. When a problem arises, always meets the members before we meet the governor. And, if our members decide they need to fight to secure improvements in pay and conditions, equality, or to save their jobs, gets right behind them one hundred and ten per cent and fights to win.

If we fight we may not always win, but if we don't fight we will surely lose. . . . I have said loud and clear that social partnership is not the way forward for working people. Of course, I don't mean that we stop negotiating, that we stop reaching pragmatic agreements with employers, that we don't have construct-ive engagement, or that we stop respecting companies that respect their own workforce and their unions. But it does mean ending the situation where we look at a company's business plan and demands before we look at our own members' needs and demands.

We want workplace improvements. Concession bargaining must end, our members want real improvements in the workplace.'

* The TGWU merged with Amicus in May 2007 to become Unite

Identify Tony Woodley's view of power within the employment relationship. Give your reasoning behind reaching this conclusion.

pause for thought

Managerial styles

The ways that management behaves within a workplace will depend on the type of power that is exercised, which in turn is affected by the culture and values of the organisation. The ways that employees are treated relate not just to power and perceptions of power but also to managerial styles.

In order to analyse and evaluate current workplace behaviours with their com-plicated set of interrelated activities, there are a number of ways of categorising and sorting the activities associated with managing the employment relationship. Such analysis can be used to predict what is likely to happen in the future if particular managerial styles are adopted.

Allan Fox (1966) organised the ways in which employers and hence managers operated into two main categories. He said that those whose managerial approach was one where management was regarded as a single source of authority without any interference from others, whose management was characterised by a common organisational purpose that was expressed as management's prerogative to man-age, displayed a **unitarist** 'frame of reference'. The managerial perspective in such organisations emphasises loyalty, unity and harmony and assumes that the goals, values and aims of those within the organisation exhibit a high level of congruence – such affinity of ideology legitimises management behaviour. Within this framework conflict is therefore regarded as pathological; should it materialise it is perceived as being due to poor communication or to 'maverick' nonconformist employees. On

Category	Characteristics
Traditionalists	Unitarist Strong managerial prerogative, i.e. management has a *right* to manage Exploitative attitude to the workforce Hostile towards third parties
Sophisticated paternalists	Unitarist Strong commitment to employee well-being Training and development encouraged Third parties discouraged because conditions of work, encouraging loyalty and commitment, are so good that unions are deemed unnecessary
Standard moderns	Pragmatic pluralists Much managerial authority devolved to line managers Unions recognised but employee relations issues are dealt with on a fire-fighting rather than on a strategic basis

Sophisticated moderns	Pluralist
	Consulters
	  Unions recognised and consulted with, although there is a strong emphasis on direct communication with employees
	Constitutionalists
	  Unions recognised, well developed bargaining machinery and procedures

Figure 12.1 Characteristics of managerial styles

the other hand, Fox (1974) categorised the thinking behind those employers and managers willing to share power, and accept that a uniformity of ideology and values throughout the organisation was not necessarily the case, indeed that there might be more than a single 'right' viewpoint in the organisation, as **pluralist**. The distinction however needed refinement and a number of academics have developed the model (Fox, 1974; Purcell and Sisson, 1983). See Figure 12.1 for a summary of these.

Within these frameworks employees may be dealt with in a calculative HRM hard way, or by means of the softer developmental approach. As noted earlier, hard and soft approaches are not always mutually exclusive. Organisations pick and mix the strategies and processes that they think will work best; sometimes this process can be rather *ad hoc*. There is not always a clear line of sight between what an organisation opts to do and ideological purity. Parts of HRM may be adopted, hard and soft strategies may be pursued simultaneously and unions may be recognised in organisations that utilise a number of HRM practices. Arguably, the style chosen will influence whether or not employee relationships are part of the strategic planning within an organisation (Gunnigle et al., 1998).

In general it could be argued that pluralist organisations are associated with a **collective** way of managing, which in many ways is reactive, and not strategic; while unitarist organisations, employing soft HRM, are linked to an **individualistic** way of management and have a tendency to incorporate managing the employment relationship with organisational strategy (Purcell and Grey, 1986; Purcell, 1987).

Traditional indications of collectivism

These include:

- 'The recognition by management of the collective interests of groups of employees in the decision making process' (Purcell and Gray, 1986: 213);
- One or more trade unions recognised for consultation and/or negotiation as well as for representation;
- High density of trade union membership within the organisation;
- Unions have an impact on the employment relationship;
- Formalisation of union arrangements, e.g. time off for trade union duties;
- Agreements between the union and the organisation;
- Communication through representation;
- Possibility of an employer's organisation bargaining for/representing the employer;
- Collective agreements regulating pay and conditions;
- May be adversarial or consensual, as with partnership agreements.

Indications of individualism

These include:

- Individuals are valued and developed for what they bring to the organisation;
- Direct communication with individual employees;
- Performance management and monitoring;
- Individual remuneration packages – such as performance-related pay and/or bonuses;
- Non-standard work packages – such as flexibility around hours or place of work;
- Individuals are assumed to put their own interests first, rather than subordinate their particular needs for the good of others.

pause for thought

Are employees less powerful as individuals than when they act as a group?

Why did you reach this conclusion?

Can you think of any exceptions?

The psychological contract and employee relations

The psychological contract, first discussed by Argyris (1962), describes the implicit, rather than explicit, exchange relationship between employers and those whom they employ. It is concerned with unwritten, unrecorded expectations and perceptions. In the past, for example, job security in exchange for high-quality work could have been perceived as part of the contract. Now, when *beliefs* about job security are sometimes more uncertain, it is not unusual for employees to expect employers to provide them with opportunities for development (Martin et al., 1998). Taylor (2002: 12) talks about a 'growing and widespread lack of satisfaction at work and little advance in any sense of organisational commitment by workers', but points out that the permanent job remains 'very much the overwhelming norm and this is true across every occupational category'.

Each contract will be unique to the individual concerned and will consist of an unwritten 'deal' that indicates the individual's expectations about what they will bring to the relationship and, importantly, of what the employer will give in exchange. As Rousseau said: 'A psychological contract emerges when one party believes that a promise of future returns has been made, a contribution has been given and thus an obligation has been created to provide future benefits' (1989: 123). This can be problematic: if the contract is a matter of perception and unspoken, there is a good deal of room for misunderstanding and the potential for unwitting damage to the employment relationship.

Individuals expect a fair balance in the exchange of services and when this is apparent they honour their part of the contract with commitment and loyalty towards the organisation. If, however, they perceive their expectations as being thwarted, or frustrated in any way, the contract becomes damaged and the employee demotivated.

Managerial styles and frames of reference affect the ways in which employees perceive their psychological contracts. HRM, with the prominence it gives to direct communication, coupled with its emphasis on the individual, taps into the emotional needs of employees and should help promote healthy psychological contracts: high commitment policies leading to positive psychological contracts and hence improved business performance (Guest, 1998; Guest and Conway, 2002a, 2002b, 2002c). Hard management practices treating individuals as resources may lead to damaged contracts depending on the expectations of the participants. Breaches of the contract can lead to drops in productivity, increases in turnover, higher levels of grievances and on occasions an increased commitment to trade unions (Turnley et al., 2004). Aggrieved employees with damaged psychological contracts are more likely to join unions.

exercise

Describe the impact that the increasing surveillance at Warbings has had on the psychological contract of the employees.

Is this a positive change?

Why did you reach this conclusion?

Conflict

The fact that employers and their employees have different requirements from the work process and different perceptions about their needs and requirements sometimes leads to conflict in the workplace.

pause for thought

Think about employer and employee expectations.

How might the apparent differences in expectations lead to conflict?

While, much of the time, co-operation is the norm in the majority of workplaces it should not be forgotten that employers need to maximise the efforts made by employees to ensure that their employment is worth while and that the balance of power, and the ways in which power is exercised, will have an impact on the perceptions of the parties to the employment relationship. Edwards (1995) says this relationship is characterised by structured antagonism – explaining that employees need to be supervised and controlled, and yet need a degree of autonomy in order to perform well. Depending on the managerial style, conflict may be seen as an unusual aberration or a normal expression of differing values and views. In 2004, 904,900 working days were lost in the UK as a result of labour disputes (Monger, 2005). Yet in total there were just 130 stoppages of work – the lowest annual total on record: the high number of days lost was due to the large number of employees involved in just a few disputes. Most of the disagreements were about pay: not just strikes endeavouring to persuade employers to pay more but disputes endeavouring to persuade employers *not to pay less.*

There are a number of mechanisms used by employers to contain, diffuse, prevent and solve conflict. They can include direct and indirect communication (see Chapter 4) and may range from comprehensive procedural arrangements to negotiating with individuals, bargaining with representatives and perhaps introducing partnership arrangements.

The type of management style adopted will have an impact on the ways that conflict is perceived and dealt with. For a traditional unitarist, the possibility of conflict occurring is considered to be unlikely, and so there will be fewer mechanisms in place to diffuse and resolve disputed incidents and disgruntled employees are more likely to show their displeasure by taking time off, changing their employer and/or resorting to the courts. Legally, UK organisations have to provide employees with a means of airing their grievances (with a fair grievance procedure) and a three-stage disciplinary process that complies with the principles of natural justice, but even these are seen by some as unnecessary interference with management prerogative. (The Box on page 229 gives the principles of Natural Justice.)

Those employing HRM practices are likely to use a number of strategies that contribute to making employees feel committed to the organisation and less likely to question the way in which they are treated. Such practices include comprehensive induction programmes to socialise new employees into the culture of the organisation, ensuring they understand their roles, as well as direct communication and teamwork as a means to engage employees and get their buy-in to organisational requirements, together with professional development to encourage loyalty (Marchington and Wilkinson, 2005: 277).

The pluralist framework is more accommodating, acknowledging that a variety of different stakeholders within the organisation will have different views and these are not always likely to show high levels of congruence. Procedures, rules, consultation and negotiation are some of the mechanisms used to resolve differences. According to ACAS, conflict potentially inherent in the employment relationship can be managed successfully (ACAS, 2004/5: 4). Procedures, providing they are perceived as being fair, help to do this. They achieve a number of things, from providing a consistent way of dealing with issues to helping defuse problems by providing a process by which they are managed. Negotiation, too, is often the means by which conflicts of interest are resolved.

Managerial style	Conflict minimising mechanisms							Company examples Can you think of any others?
	Providing information	Involving employees	Open channels of communication	Partnership working	Negotiation and bargaining	Procedures	Clear contracts of employment	
Collective	✓	✓	✓	✓	✓	✓	✓	Ford
Individual	✓	✓	✓		✓ with some individuals	✓	✓	Marks and Spencer
Traditionalist						✓ sometimes – often linked to dismissal of difficult employees	✓ sometimes	Amazon
Sophisticated paternalists	✓	✓	✓	✓ sometimes		✓	✓	Gillette UK Ltd Listawood
Standard moderns	✓ sometimes	✓	✓ sometimes		✓ reluctant fire-fighting	✓	✓	Gate Gourmet London Underground
Sophisticated moderns	✓	✓	✓	✓	✓	✓	✓	Monarch Aircraft Engineering Tesco

Figure 12.2 Managerial styles and methods of dealing with and minimising conflict
Source: © Bingham 2006

The ways of coping with conflict promoted by the Labour Government at the end of the twentieth century and the beginning of the twenty-first have centred around the concepts of fairness, employee voice and alternative dispute resolution, such as workplace-based mediation. Figure 12.2 summarises some of the ways that organisations choose to operate in order to minimise the number of potential disagreements within the employment relationship before things escalate to full-blown disputes or either party resorts to legal remedies.

Procedures

Employers have always used reward as a means of gaining employee compliance but procedures too have played an important part in regulating the relationship, minimising disruption and standardising behaviours. Procedures are sets of organisation-specific rules that provide a framework of processes for handling issues. Such regulations may result from unilateral management decisions, negotiations and/or statutory requirements. In effect, they are a means of restraining behaviour (limiting power) and promoting consistent and fair treatment between the managed and those managing. They clarify relationships and make explicit the processes that the organisation requires its employees to follow; on occasions providing a safety valve and mechanism for the resolution of differences that is fair to all parties yet showing consideration for the employee's point of view and inhibiting bias against him or her. Procedures therefore enable natural and procedural justice; enhancing the psychological contract because they provide a backdrop of fairness around the way that an organisation operates. They institutionalise conflict management and the process of working through a procedure often defuses difficult situations and enables speedier, less emotionally charged resolutions. Procedures may add to the bureaucracy of the workplace and inhibit flexible approaches to individual problems – but with the plethora of legislative requirements impacting upon employment relationships they do promote consistency of treatment, accurate recordkeeping and provide a standardised means of problem solving.

Principles of Natural Justice

That employees know the expected standards of behaviour.

That, should there be allegations against someone, they have the right to:

◆ Be informed of the complaint,

◆ Have the opportunity of stating their case before a decision is reached,

◆ Be accompanied to any hearing,

◆ Be given the outcome in writing,

◆ Be provided with – and informed of – their legal right of appeal.

In many ways these principles are integral to the HRM practices of the four Cs, (**C**ommunicate, **C**onsult, **C**are and **C**ontrol.) Making certain that managers abide by these principles helps ensure healthy psychological contracts. Such principles should be inherent in the ways that employees are dealt with, particularly if their performance is not all that it might be. Employers control employee behaviour by using a number of techniques such as: performance management, training, coaching, mentoring and disciplining. When disciplinary action is considered it is essential that the principles of natural justice be adhered to. Employers abiding by the ACAS code of practice, requiring that normally employees be given an oral warning, a written warning and a final written warning prior to dismissal (most cases, never progress past the first informal warning, if that) will find, provided they tell their employees what is wrong and allow them to answer any accusations, that the principles will have been adhered to. The legislation reinforces this.

Schedule 2 of the Employment Act 2002 lays down the following steps that employers must stick to when taking disciplinary action:

1. Put the events in writing and write to the employee telling them about the alleged misdemeanour and invite them to attend a meeting – there must be enough time for the employee to consider the situation prior to the meeting.

2. Undertake an exploratory meeting where the incidents are discussed and the employee has a chance to put their side of the story: the employer must then take time to consider this evidence: the employee is told of the decision and informed of the right to appeal if disciplinary action is taken.

3. If the employee chooses to appeal they must inform the employer who invites them to a meeting. The employee has to take all reasonable attempts to attend this. If possible the appeal meeting must be held by a more senior manager: the final decision must then be communicated to the employee.

If the offence is classed as a gross misdemeanour, e.g. setting fire to company property, the process may be reduced to two steps – the decision to dismiss communicated to the employee in writing together with details of the alleged misconduct and notifying the employee of their right to appeal. The last stage remains the same.

Sections 10–15 of the Employment Relations Act 1999 also promotes a fair process by giving workers the right to be accompanied by a fellow worker, or trade union rep, when faced with the prospect of formal disciplinary action.

Employee voice

This is based on the principle that employees can enhance the workplace by contributing not just their labour but also their views. (This has echoes of the Farnham dictum that to share power is to regain control.) The recent emphasis on 'high commitment workplaces' (Applebaum, 2002; Applebaum et al., 2000; DTI, 2002) has encouraged organisations to adopt the mechanisms of employee voice by promoting the integration of employees into the processes of decision making and problem solving. The philosophy underpinning the emphasis on employee voice is that hermetically sealed managements who fail to engage with their staff are stifling goodwill, productivity, knowledge sharing and commitment, thereby damaging the psychological contract and failing to meet employee interests within the employment relationship. The mechanisms for voice, on the other hand, are designed to promote all of these. The direct and indirect methods used (see Chapter 4) will depend on the managerial style adopted; for the pluralists, collective representation, informing, consulting and negotiating with unions, staff associations and workplace representatives is the means by which this is achieved. For those with a more unitarist perspective, direct communication in the form of team meetings, appraisals, problem-solving forums and employee surveys is often the way used to engage staff and circumvent discontent.

Legislation plays a part, too, so even traditional unitarist management approaches on occasions adopt more pluralist methods, from listening to an employee grievance or request for flexible working, where the employee is accompanied by a colleague, to health and safety committees making workplace recommendations and representatives consulting about redundancy or business transfers. Similarly, where managements have to recognise trade unions following a ruling from the Central Arbitration Committee they may become reluctant pluralists. Those that pre-empt legislative compulsion and set up their own systems of staff representation discover a mismatch between their unitarist principles and the reality of having to listen to their workforce. Such unitarists on the cusp of pluralism find their management styles changing in order to accommodate or avoid legislative requirements. Information and Consultation Regulations broaden the areas where managements are obliged to inform and consult employees about the business. European Works Councils are required by law (for those businesses with at least 1,000 employees and with 150 employees in no less than two different member states) to consult about European matters affecting the business. Under the Information and Consultation of Employees (ICE) Regulations (2002), an employer must ensure that the timing, method content and level of any consultations are appropriate. It is not acceptable, for example, to consult on something after a decision has been made.

exercise

A recent ACAS policy discussion paper by Grell and Sisson (2005: 1) stated:

'. . . there are particular problems with consultation, stemming from our employment relations history. Like Cinderella, consultation is very much the poor relation – for management it compares unfavourably to communications, while trade unions much prefer collective bargaining.'

What do you think is meant by this?

For pluralists, one of the ways of managing the inevitable conflict that arises within the workplace is to enter into a partnership agreement with trade union representatives. This joint problem-solving approach to management gives employees a say, through their representatives, about the running of the business, and is particularly important in times of change. It does not, however, eradicate conflict and sometimes it results in quite strong disagreements between the representatives and those they represent.

Partnership, when linked to the employment relationship, has no precise theoretical definition or evidence-based practical connotations. The imprecision of the term is a weakness, leading to confusion about what it is meant to imply. It is therefore difficult to disagree with – consequently for many employers and employees the idea of partnership may seem vague and difficult to put into practice. Guest and Peccei (1998) say that organisations operating in a partnership way may well exhibit the following:

◆ Direct participation by employees in decisions about their own work and about personal employment issues;

◆ Participation by employee representatives in decisions about employment issues and about broader organisational policy issues;

◆ Flexible job design, with a focus on quality;

◆ Performance management;

◆ Employee share ownership;

◆ Communication;

◆ Harmonisation;

◆ Employment security.

However all of these categories may well be present in organisations that, rather than practise partnership, exhibit adversarial employee relations such as those associated with parts of the rail industry.

exercise

W

Look at the case study on Warbings.

What methods of employee voice do you think would be most appropriate for this organisation?

What mechanisms promoting employee voice would you recommend the management to adopt?

Information sharing: informing, consulting, negotiating

Where employee representatives are present, employee voice occurs indirectly for individual employees through the processes of joint consultation or collective bargaining. Where there is no system of representation, these processes may occur directly – often even where there are indirect mechanisms, an employer may additionally use direct methods. Negotiation is 'a process of interaction by which two or more parties who consider they need to be jointly involved in an outcome but who initially have different objectives, seek, by the use of argument and persuasion, to resolve their differences in order to achieve a mutually acceptable solution' (Fowler, 1996: 3).

The outcomes of such discussions can please everyone (win-win), no one (lose-lose) or just one party (win-lose). Negotiations about how to divide up resources are known as distributive bargaining, while those concerned with reaching agreement about the ways to solve problems are interest-based bargaining. Before negotiations begin, the parties will have some idea of why they want things to change – see Figure 12.3.

Negotiations occur within the employment relationship at individual and collective levels. They are individual when an employee discusses pay, workload and workflow with the line manager. They are collective, and therefore indirect, when representatives act on behalf of others and negotiate for them. Negotiations typically follow a pattern whereby the participants:

♦ Prepare their own case (including anticipating the position and arguments to be presented by the other side);

♦ Exchange views establishing and confirming what each party wants;

♦ Explore the issues and examine potential outcomes;

♦ Negotiate around such issues and outcomes;

♦ Secure agreement;

♦ Implement the agreement.

There are a number of issues about which negotiations frequently occur; the most recently available statistics are from the Workplace Employee Relations Survey 2004 (see Table 12.1), which show that issues such as pay hours and holidays are

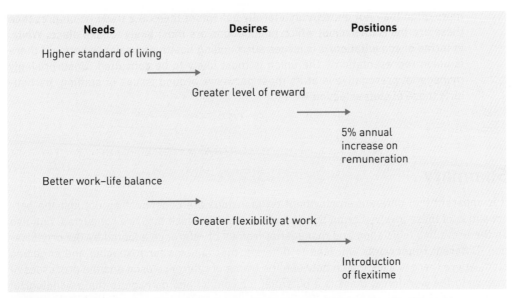

Figure 12.3 Examples showing the pre-negotiation movement from needs to positions
Source: © Bingham 2006

Table 12.1 Joint regulation of terms and conditions[a,b]

Issue	% of workplaces			
	Nothing	Inform	Consult	Negotiate
Pay	70 (16)	6 (10)	5 (13)	18 (61)
Hours	71 (18)	5 (10)	8 (20)	16 (53)
Holidays	71 (19)	9 (17)	5 (13)	15 (52)
Pensions	73 (22)	11 (25)	6 (16)	10 (36)
Staff selection	78 (42)	10 (26)	9 (23)	3 (9)
Training	75 (36)	10 (24)	13 (31)	3 (9)
Grievance procedure	69 (15)	9 (20)	14 (36)	9 (28)
Disciplinary procedure	69 (15)	9 (21)	13 (35)	8 (29)
Staffing plans	75 (33)	11 (26)	12 (34)	3 (7)
Equal opportunities	72 (22)	10 (23)	14 (40)	5 (15)
Health and safety	69 (17)	9 (19)	17 (49)	5 (15)
Performance appraisal	75 (33)	9 (20)	12 (33)	4 (14)

Base: All workplaces with ten or more employees.
Figures are weighted and based on responses from at least 2,007 managers.

Notes:
[a] Managerial respondent was asked 'whether management normally negotiates, consults, informs or does not involve unions' on 12 items. Also asked with respect to non-union employee representatives.
[b] Figures in parentheses relate to workplaces with recognised trade unions and are based on responses from at least 1,004 managers.

Source: Kersley et al. (2005)

more often than not decided unilaterally but where there is a trade union presence these are the issues about which negotiations are most likely to take place. While, in terms of consultation, it is issues surrounding health and safety where – if there is union representation – the union is most likely to be consulted. Unsurprisingly managerial prerogative is at its most pervasive around issues of staffing, particularly those of staff selection.

Summary

It is apparent that different employment relationships are dependent on not just the personalities of those involved or on the type of business in which they are conducted, but also on the prevailing legislation and managerial frames of reference adopted by the organisation. Different frameworks will lead to different mechanisms for managing and engaging staff: where there is a mismatch between the frame of reference used and the processes of managing the workforce, there is a potential for conflict and damage to the psychological contracts of individual employees. By ensuring that systems are perceived as fair, and by endeavouring to give employees an opportunity to 'voice' their opinions, there is the potential for managing conflict within the workplace and creating high levels of commitment and productivity.

Review Questions

You may wish to attempt the following as practice examination style questions.

12.1 Explain the differences between a unitarist and a pluralist frame of reference, giving examples of how each impacts on managerial styles.

12.2 Give details of a sophisticated modern organisation and say why it belongs in this category. How does it differ from a sophisticated paternalist organisation that you are familiar with?

12.3 How do different sorts of power affect the employment relationship? Give examples to illustrate your answer.

12.4 What is the psychological contract? Why is it important in the employment relationship?

12.5 'Natural justice is just an outdated concept, not relevant to twenty-first century employment relationships.' Critically evaluate this point of view.

12.6 Describe five different mechanisms for containing conflict in the workplace and evaluate their efficacy.

12.7 Is partnership partnership? What were the reasons behind your answer?

12.8 Enumerate the stages negotiators usually go through.

References

ACAS (2004/5). Managing conflict at work – lessons from ACAS, *Employment Relations Matters*, Issue 2.

Applebaum, E. (2002). The impact of new forms of work organisation on workers, in G. Murry, J. Bélanger, A. Giles and P.-A. Lapointe (eds.) *Work and Employment Relations in the High Performance Workplace*, London: Continuum.

Applebaum, E., Bailey, T., Berg, P. and Kalleberg, A.L. (2000). *Manufacturing Advantage: Why High Performance Work Systems Pay Off*, Ithaca: NY: Cornell University Press.

Argyris, C. (1962). *Understanding Organisational Behavior*, Homewood, IL: Dorsey Press.

Clegg, S.R. (1989). *Frameworks of Power*, London: Sage.

DTI (2002). *High Performance Workplaces: The Role of Employee Involvement in a Modern Economy*, London: Department of Trade and Industry.

Edwards, P. (1995). *Industrial Relations: Theory and Practice in Britain*, Oxford: Blackwell.

Farnham, D. (1997). *Employee Relations in Context*, p. 3, London: IPD.

Flanders, A. (1970). *Management and Unions: The Theory and Reform of Industrial Relations*, London: Faber.

Fox, A. (1974). *Beyond Contract: Work, Power and Trust Relations*, London: Faber.

Fox, A. (1966). Managerial ideology and labour relations, *British Journal of Industrial Relations*, Vol. IV, pp. 366–387.

Fowler, A. (1996). *Negotiation Skills and Strategies,* 2nd edition, London: IPD.

French, J.R.P. and Raven, B. (1962). The bases of social power, in D. Cartwright (ed.) *Group Dynamics; Research and Theory*, Evanston, pp. 607–623, IL: Row Peterson.

Gospel, H.F. and Palmer, G. (1993). *British Industrial Relations*, 2nd edition, London: Routledge.

Grainger, H. (2006). *Trade Union Membership 2005*, London: DTI.

Grell, M. and Sisson, K. (2005). *Has Consultation's Time Come*, ACAS Policy Discussion Papers No. 2, at: www.acas.org.uk/media/pdf/8/8/AcasPolicyPaper2_1.pdf.

Guest, D. (1987). Human resource management and industrial relations, *Journal of Management Studies*, Vol. 24, No. 5, pp. 503–521.

Guest, D. (1998). Is the psychological contract worth taking seriously?, *Journal of Organisational Behaviour*, Vol. 19, pp. 649–664.

Guest, D. and Conway, N. (2002a). Communicating the psychological contract: an employer perspective, *Human Resource Management Journal*, Vol. 12, No. 2, pp. 22–38.

Guest, D. and Conway, N. (2002b). Pressure of work and the psychological contract, CIPD Survey Report, London: CIPD.

Guest, D. and Conway, N. (2002c). Organisational change and the psychological contract, CIPD Survey Report, London: CIPD.

Guest, D. and Peccei, R. (1998). *The Partnership Company: Benchmarks for the Future*, London: IPA.

Gunnigle, P., Turner, T. and Morley, M. (1998). Strategic integration and employee relations: the impact of managerial styles, *Employee Relations*, Vol. 20, No. 2, pp. 115–131.

Kersley, B., Alpin, C., Forth, J., Bryson, A., Bewley, H., Dix, G. and Oxenbridge, S. (2005). *Inside the Workplace: First Findings from the 2004 Workplace Employment Relations Survey*, at: www.dti.gov.uk/er/insideWP_finalweb_jan_2006.pdf.

Lewis, et al. (2003). *Employee Relations; Understanding the Employment Relationship*, London: FT/Prentice Hall.

Lukes, S. (1974). *Power: A Radical View*, London: Macmillan.

Lukes, S. (ed.) (1986). *Power*, Oxford: Basil Blackwell.

Marchington, M. and Wilkinson, A. (2005). *Human Resource Management at Work*, 3rd edition, London: CIPD.

Martin, G., Stains, H. and Pate, J. (1998). Linking job security and career development in a new psychological contract, *Human Resource Management Journal*, Vol. 8, No. 3, pp. 20–40.

Monger, J. (2005). Labour disputes in 2004, *Labour Market Trends*, Vol. 113, No. 06, pp. 239–252.

Oxenbridge, S. and Brown, W. (2004). Achieving a new equilibrium? The stability of cooperative employer–union relationships, *Industrial Relations Journal*, Vol. 35, No. 5, pp. 388–402.

Purcell, J. (1987). Mapping management styles in employee relations, *Journal of Management Studies*, Vol. 24, No. 5, pp. 533–548.

Purcell, J. and Grey, A. (1986). Corporate personnel departments and the management of industrial relations, *Journal of Management Studies*, Vol. 23, No. 2, pp. 205–223.

Purcell, J. and Sisson, K. (1983). Strategics and practice in the management of industrial relations, in G. Bain (ed.) *Industrial Relations in Britain*, Oxford: Blackwell.

Rousseau D.M. (1989). Psychological and implied contracts in organisations, *Employee Rights and Responsibilities Journal*, Vol. 2, pp. 121–139.

Sisson, K. (1990). Introducing the *Human Resource Management Journal*, Vol. 1, No. 1, pp. 1–11.

Storey, J. (1992). *Developments in the Management of Human Resources*, Oxford: Blackwell.

Storey, J. (1998). Is HRM catching on?, *International Journal of Manpower*, Vol. 16, No. 4, pp. 3–10.

Taylor, R. (2002). *Britain's World of Work – Myths and Realities*, London: ESRC.

Turnley, W.H., Bolino, M.C., Lester, S.W. and Bloodgood, J.M. (2004). The effects of psychological contract breach on union commitment, *Journal of Occupational and Organisational Psychology*, Vol. 3, No. 77, pp. 421–428.

Unison (2003). *Bullying at work*, at: www.unison.org.uk/acrobat/13375.pdf.

Further Reading

ACAS (2004–06). *Employment Relations matters*. All issues of this quarterly publication are useful and can be accessed from www.acas.org.uk/index.aspx?articleid=402.

Hollinshead, G. et al. (2003). *Employee Relations*, 2nd edition, FT/Prentice Hall.

Murry, G., Bélanger, J., Giles, A. and Lapointe P.-A. (eds.) (2002). *Work and Employment Relations in the High Performance Workplace*, London: Continuum.

Healy, G. et al. (eds.) (2004). *The Future of Workplace Representation*, London: Palgrave Macmillan.

Useful Websites

www.acas.org.uk – for ACAS (Advisory, Conciliation and Arbitration Service)

www.acas.org.uk/index.aspx?articleid=402 – for the quarterly issues of *Employment Relations Matters*; currently issues 1–7 can be accessed individually:

Issue 7 – Winter 2006 [399kb]
Issue 6 – Spring 2006 [411kb]
Issue 5 – Winter 2005 [329kb]
Issue 4 – Summer 2005 [254kb]
Issue 3 – Spring 2005 [257kb]
Issue 2 – Winter 2004/5 [380kb]
Issue 1 – Autumn 2004 [310kb]

Note: Adobe Acrobat needed for downloading

www.cipd.co.uk – for general information about employee relations

www.dti.gov.uk – for general information about employee relations, case studies and updates on employment legislation from the Department of Trade and Industry website

www.incomesdata.co.uk – for general information about employee relations, case studies and updates on employment legislation; is useful for legislative updates and information about pay

www.irseclipse.co.uk – for general information about employee relations, case studies and updates on employment legislation in Industrial Relations Services reviews

www.tuc.org.uk – for general information about employee relations, case studies and updates on employment legislation from the Trade Union Congress website focused on protecting workers' rights

www.worksmart.org.uk – for general information about employee relations – TUC newsboard

www.ons.gov.uk – for statistical information relating to employment and the labour market from Office of National Statistics, with focus on economic and population statistics

www.unison.org.uk/resources/docs_list.asp – for general information about employee relations, case studies and updates on employment legislation, focus on news, guidance tips (e.g. how to calculate your pension benefits) from the largest public sector trade union

CHAPTER 13

Law and the Employment Relationship

By Patricia Price and Paul Smith

Chapter outline

This chapter provides an overview of the rights and duties of parties within employment contracts. It is not intended to provide an in-depth legal review but to highlight the core stages of the contractual relationship. The chapter will focus mainly on the contractual relationship and associated individual statutory rights and protections, although other aspects will also be touched upon.

Learning outcomes

By the end of this chapter, you should be able to:

◆ Explain the role of law in the employment relationship;

◆ Explain the legal process of contractual relations at work;

◆ Explain the rights of an individual based on the contractual relationship;

◆ Discuss the importance of employment law for the HR practitioner;

◆ Debate the importance of fair procedures in relation to employment law.

Introduction

Employment law emanating from this country and the EU increasingly impinges on the ways in which organisations select, recruit, deploy, reward and dismiss their employees. Fundamental to the ways in which managers and those they manage interact is the employment contract. This chapter looks at some of the processes surrounding the employment relationship and considers the wider implications that the legislation underpinning the employment relationship has for human resource management (HRM) practitioners and those that manage in the workplace.

Employment law in context

'Any modern economy needs its share of regulation, including employment law. In today's world though, employment law has to be created with an assessment of its impact on the overall employment relationship and organisational suc-cess. Legislators, policy makers and regulators have an obligation to develop proposals that create a framework to support that relationship and its con-tribution to the development of organisations.'

(Simon Marsh, HR Director CIA, interview on 25 May 2006)

HRM involves a number of activities: recruitment and selection, appraisal and pay, and training and development for example. Just *how* these activities are approached, organised and carried out is partly a matter of management choice – management prerogative – although there may also be elements of consultation with employees, or even of joint regulation with trade unions for example. Yet such business decisions are increasingly subject to external regulation in terms of legislation. As Anderman (2000: 1) points out: 'The enormous increase in labour legislation in the past four decades has thrust labour law into the role of widely regulating business decisions.'

Employment protection legislation may be directed at the individual, or may be collective (trade-union based, for example). It may regulate decisions directly, by creating legal obligations for employers for example, or indirectly, by influencing the capacity of trade unions to engage in joint regulation with management through collective bargaining.

Prior to 1970, statutory regulation of the employment relationship in the UK was very restricted. Individual terms and conditions of employment were stated in the contract of employment and in any collective agreements. The law's intervention was limited to basic health and safety protection, the right to limited redundancy payments and the general requirement for employers and employees to honour the contractual terms agreed at commencement of employment. Since 1970, this has changed dramatically. The contract of employment remains of crucial importance and can be enforced in court but, in addition, a whole host of statutory rights in the areas of health and safety, equal pay, unlawful discrimination and unfair dismissal have been added which employers are required to comply with. More recent legislation, much of it originating from the European Union (EU), includes that on working time, family-friendly rights and consultation, and this has continued with, for example, legislation on age discrimination.

'The flowing tide of [European] community law is coming in fast. It has not stopped at high water mark. It has broken the dykes and the banks. It has sub-merged the surrounding land. So much so that we have to learn to become amphibious if we wish to keep our heads above water.'

(Lord Denning, quoted by Peter Winfield
in Porter et al., 2006: 487)

HR practitioners need a knowledge and understanding of developments in employ-ment law in order to both devise appropriate policies and procedures and to provide correct advice to line managers and employees. They themselves also need to know when, and where, to seek more specialist advice.

Employment law and human resource management

Theories and models of HRM make little direct reference to employment law *per se*. Even in the exceptions (e.g. Beer et al.'s, 1984 Harvard model), where situational factors, including laws and societal values, are depicted as an influence, they are not given primacy. In some ways it could be argued that the growth in employment legislation runs counter to the philosophy of HRM and its development from personnel management. Thus, if as Smith (in Porter et al., 2006) argues, HRM as depicted by Storey, Guest and others can be viewed as more strategic, more closely aligned to the needs of the business, more individualistic and more management-driven, less rule-bound and less bureaucratic, then the proliferation of legislation would appear to run counter to this and better suit the 'old' personnel management. Thus HRM aims, such as flexibility in terms of flexible utilisation of labour, are likely to be constrained if not subverted by such recent legislation as that giving part-time employees pro-rata rights (Part-Time Workers (Prevention of Less Favourable Treatment) Regulations, 2000) and workers on fixed-term contracts greater protection (ERA, 1996 and ERelA, 1999).

An alternative perspective would be that the 'good' or 'best' practice resulting from 'soft' HRM (see, for example, Pfeffer's (1998) list of key high commitment human resource (HR) practices) is likely to result in employment policies and practices well above the basic floor or safety net of employment rights provided for by legislation. Whether from a management perspective this would encompass support for trade union recognition, or even some of the family-friendly policy legislation is, however, a moot point.

In addition, Kahn-Freund (1972) points to the different *functions* of law in regulating the employment relationship. Thus, as well as the regulatory and restrictive functions, it also has an 'auxiliary' function whereby the law is designed to promote particular behaviours (for example, consultation, collective bargaining, etc.) towards certain ends. The statutory recognition procedures contained in the Employment Relations Act 1999 provide a good example of this function, as the increase in voluntary recognition arrangements made since the introduction of the act testify.

The reluctance of some UK managers to enthusiastically embrace such developments echoes the reluctance of the Thatcher government to fully embrace the European Social Chapter. The UK could be seen to have been, and possibly still be, uncomfortably perched on the fence between an approach to employment policies based on social partnership and protection embraced by the rest of the EU partners, and the more unregulated free market laissez-faire approach adopted in the US.

Do you think that the law impedes, or facilitates, managerial activity?

Why did you reach this decision?

pause for thought

The employment relationship

The employment relationship involves two principal players: the employer and the employee. In the labour market, employees 'sell' their labour (time, effort, skills, experience, etc.) to the buyers of labour services, the employers. Central to this relationship is the 'contract of employment'; this sets out the duties and obligations of both parties.

In the employment relationship the two parties have certain *commonalities* of interest: they both benefit from the success of the enterprise, but are also likely to have certain *differences* of interest (over pay and conditions, for example). In this, the balance of bargaining power would normally be perceived to lie with the employer, since they have the power to hire and fire (see Chapters 7 and 12). Employment legislation is, however, one mechanism for partially ameliorating the position where employers, via managers, can act as they please. Thus Anderman (2000) argues that such legislation can be viewed as a form of legal regulation of business activity that explicitly or implicitly seeks to strike *a balance* between the interests of management autonomy and the interests of worker protection. Although the statutory duties imposed upon employers are rarely absolute, they usually incorporate some variant of a 'rule of reason' test. Phrases such as 'reasonably practicable', 'reasonable in the circumstance' or 'justification' recur with sufficient regularity to ensure that the aim of worker protection is balanced with another value – the discretion of employers to take decisions in the course of business activity.

pause for thought

What do you think 'reasonableness' means?

Do you think the concept of 'reasonably practicable' is too vague?

Why did you reach this conclusion?

Sources and institutions of employment law

Employment law can originate from a number of different sources, the main ones being common law, legislation or statutes and European law (Nairns, 1999).

Judges make common law when they make decisions about each case – these may set precedents. Legislation or statute law is drafted and enacted by the government. European law has a major impact on national employment law. In the event of a conflict between national and European law, the latter takes precedence and must be followed by our courts.

The main institutions of relevance are the courts (County Court, High Court and European Court) and Employment Tribunals. In general, claims involving breach of the common law or contract are brought in the courts, while claims involving breach of statute are brought in the Employment Tribunals. (See Further Reading for elaboration on sources and institutions.)

The contract of employment

The central importance of the contract of employment to the employment relationship has already been outlined. Within the employment relationship there are a number of different categories of contract that can be entered into such as: full-time employee, part-time employee, part-time worker, agency worker and independent contractor. These categories place different legal responsibilities on the organisation and also provide the person entering into one of these relationships with varying degrees of legal protection.

Defining who is an 'employee'

The employee has certain obligations to the employer, and vice versa. In contrast, people who are self-employed, or who are subcontractors, have a greater degree of autonomy, but also a more direct legal accountability for their actions. It was stated in *Broadbent V Crisp [1974]* (quoted in Nairns, 1999: 76) that 'all employees are workers but not all workers are employees'. The law makes an important distinction between the two groups:

- An employee works under a contract *of* service;
- An independent contractor works under a contract *for* service.

Only employees are covered by most of the available statutory protections. Thus, for example, only employees can make claims for unfair dismissal and redundancy pay. Independent contractors have no such rights. It should be noted, however, that certain employment law statutes have a wider remit – thus discrimination legislation and that on equal pay, for example, covers both employees and independent contractors.

Tests used to determine status

The labels that organisations give to any contractual relationship may not be sufficient to differentiate the true position. What the courts will look at in determining whether a worker is an employee is the substance of the relationship. To do this a number of tests which have been developed over time will be applied. These tests include:

- The Concept of Control;
- The Integration Test;
- The Multiple or Economic Reality Test;
- The Degree of Substitution;
- Mutuality of Obligation.

The concept of control

This relates to the degree of control exercised by the employer; it asks 'who decides' what is to be done. Control used to be the conclusive test but, as work has changed with employees now often having greater autonomy, other tests have been used in addition to this.

The integration test

This test considers the extent to which a person is 'integrated' into the organisation and thus is an employee rather than an independent contractor. It thus focuses on the organisation of work.

The multiple or economic reality test

This was proposed in the case of *Ready Mixed Concrete (South East) Ltd v Minister of Pensions and National Insurance [1968] 2 Q.B. 497* and is a three-part test. A contract of employment exists if:

- The servant (note that servant means *employee*) agrees in consideration of a wage or other remuneration to provide work and skill in the performance of some service for his or her master (note master means *employer*);

- Expressly or implied agreement that in the performance of the service he or she will be subjected to the others' control (see control test above) in sufficient degree to make the other master (*employer*);

- Other provisions of the contract are consistent with its being a contract of employment.

Substitution

When looking at the employment relationship, the courts have to decide whether there is a need for an employee to personally perform the contract. In considering the concept of substitution or absence of obligation, the courts examine whether such an 'absence of obligation' precludes an employment relationship from emerging. This was a central argument in the case of *MacFarlane and others v Glasgow City Council [2001] IRLR 7*. In this case there was *no* written contract; payment was given for each teaching session undertaken. Glasgow Council did however at the start of each term specify in writing that where an individual could not take a session, a substitution could be made but only from a specified list of approved teachers. This requirement among others *limiting* substitution suggested an employee relationship rather than an independent contractor.

Mutuality of obligation

This test has been used in a number of important cases to determine the status of 'non-standard' workers (for example, part time or casual). The first obligation of the employer is to provide work and of the employee to perform work; the second is the obligation of continuity on, both employer (to provide work) and employee (to continue to perform). If both obligations are found to exist, then the person is likely to be an employee and a contract of employment to exist. Thus, in *O'Kelly v Trusthouse Forte plc [1983] IRLR 369*, it was determined that part-time casual catering workers were not employees since the court found that the company were under no obligation to provide work, nor the workers to accept work if it was offered. See also *Carmichael v National Power plc [2000] IRLR 43*.

Agency workers

An organisation may decide that in the short term a skills gap can be covered by bringing in agency workers. The legal status of such individuals is, at the time of writing, difficult to establish. See, for example, the cases of *Bunce v Postworth Limited (t/a Skyblue) [2005] IRLR 557 CA, Motorola Ltd v Davidson and Melville Craig [2001] IRLR 4* and *Frank's v Reuters [2003] IRLR 423 CA*. It is necessary that organisations should remain vigilant as to the amount of time that agency workers are retained. The longer the placement, the more control that an organisation exerts over the worker and the more likely it is that an implied contractual relationship will emerge, and the more likely it becomes that this will be with the end user (i.e. the organisation) as opposed to the agency. An attempt by the EU to formalise the position of agency workers has, at the time of writing, not been finalised.

Write an email to a friend explaining the different tests that can be applied in order to ascertain whether someone is actually an employee.

Summary

In applying worker and employee tests, all aspects of the relationship need to be examined in order to determine whether a contract *of* or *for* service can be established. Courts will use the most suitable tests to reach a decision, examining the degree of control that is exercised, the need for mutuality of obligation, and whether any terms negate the formation of the employer–employee relationship and, most importantly, the need for personal service.

At the Warbings' Leeds depot different drivers are employed on different terms. It is stated in the contracts of all drivers that they are self-employed.

John and Peter have both worked for the company as lorry drivers for four years. John is paid per delivery, although he is guaranteed a minimum of ten deliveries per week. The company provides his lorry, although he must maintain it. He receives no holiday or sick pay and pays his own tax and national insurance. He may substitute another driver when he needs to.

Peter is paid a monthly minimum weekly wage (equivalent to ten deliveries) and, after that, per delivery. He uses a company lorry that the company maintains. He may also substitute a driver, but only with written permission from the company. Peter used to receive his wages net but, recently, the company told him it would be cheaper for both the company and him if he became responsible for his own tax and insurance and he agreed to this.

What tests would you apply to determine whether John and Peter are in fact employees or self-employed?

(Adapted from a case by Lockton, 2006: 24)

Phases of the employment relationship

There are five distinctive phases through which the employment relationship may move:

- Pre-contractual;
- The formation of the contract;
- Rights and duties of the parties to the contract during its lifetime;
- Rights concerning termination of the contract;
- Post-contractual rights of the parties.

At each of these stages the law provides different rights for and responsibilities on the parties involved.

Pre-contractual stage

Once the organisation has identified a skill gap it will make a range of decisions about what kind of skill is needed. It will draw up a set of documents, such as a job description and person specification, and will design advertising and undertake recruitment and selection.

During these processes the organisation must ensure that they do not either directly or indirectly discriminate on the grounds of race, sex, disability, religious belief, sexual orientation and, since October 2006, age. How, then, can this be achieved?

window into practice

Discrimination

The Discrimination Acts define three forms of discrimination: direct, indirect and victimisation. These rights are not based within a contractual framework, therefore they afford protection to applicants at all stages before, during and after termination of any contract.

Direct discrimination occurs where one person is treated less favourably than another, on the grounds of sex or race for example.

Indirect discrimination is broadly defined as *applying a policy criterion or procedure which of itself may not seem discriminatory but operates as a detriment to the person complaining*. It is this aspect of discrimination that is most likely to be breached during the pre-contractual phase. Organisations should therefore review all aspects of job descriptions, personnel specifications, the wording of the job advertisement and information given to agencies, and be prepared to answer the question: 'If challenged, could the organisation substantiate a business case for the policy criterion or practice?' If yes, then proceed; if no, why not, and amend the areas causing concern.

Victimisation occurs where an employer takes action against an employee for having, for example, brought proceedings or given evidence against the employer. A fuller discussion of discrimination, as well as equal pay, can be found in Chapters 10 and 14.

Formation of contract

Contracts in Employment law stem from both the Common Law Principles of Contract and the Employment Statues and Regulations. To create an enforceable agreement:

◆ There must have been a formal offer;

◆ There must be acceptance;

◆ Both parties must have agreed to be legally bound by the agreement;

◆ The agreement must be supported by consideration;

◆ The terms of the contract need to able to demonstrate the binding nature of the relationship.

An offer is normally given in writing by the organisation at the conclusion of the selection process. However, the offer can be made at any time. Verbal offers are lawful and, if accepted, form a binding contract. It is necessary therefore to be extremely careful about words and conduct during all aspects of the recruitment process so as not to give the impression that an offer of employment is being made when it is not.

The offer should be a formal statement setting out the conditions of the relationship. In the first instance, the organisation will need to comply with Section 1 of the Employment Relations Act 1996, which details what information must be given to the prospective employee. At this stage also, the organisation should clearly indicate what express or implied terms have been agreed, such as mobility clauses, confidentiality and restraint of trade clauses. It also needs to be clearly stated what term the contract will be for – whether a fixed term, permanent, or temporary – as well as the rights on monitoring of personal correspondence and computer files such as emails.

The formation in drawing up the relationship is the same for all contracts; the important difference is the degree of legal protection offered to the individual at termination. For an individual to claim full protection under employment legislation, they must be able to demonstrate that the relationship is one of employee and employer.

The parties must demonstrate an intention to be bound by entering into a contract of employment. Under Section 1 of the ERA 1996, the employer must give the employee a written statement of the particulars of employment within two months of the commencement of employment. This statement, while not the contract of employment itself, is accepted by the courts as evidence towards there being an employee–employer relationship. The statement may not cover all the express and implied terms that the organisation may want to incorporate and without further evidence this statement will *not amount to proof of the terms of the contract* that should have been incorporated. (See *Rank Xerox Ltd v Churchill [1988] IRLR 280.*) It may well be that express terms can be derived from a number of documents, such as collective agreements, organisational handbooks and custom and practice of the industry. (For custom and practice to be incorporated, it must be widely known and used within the industry.) It must be deemed as being reasonable and the employee must be able to act in accordance with it. Other evidence supporting the existence of an employer–employee relationship could include an exchange of letters in which an offer of employment and its acceptance had been agreed. Oral contracts are also valid, especially when supported by conduct (such as carrying out duties).

On the employer's side, breach of common law duties is regarded as a 'repudiatory breach of contract' that may enable an employee to resign and claim to have been constructively dismissed, whereas a breach of common law duties by the employee could lead to disciplinary action being taken. See Table 13.1.

Table 13.1 Duties of employer and employee

Common law duties of employer	Common law duties of employee
To pay wages	Work according to the contractual terms
To take reasonable care of the employee	To obey all lawful and reasonable instructions
Not to breach mutual trust and confidence	To give honest and trustworthy service; not to breach confidentiality; not to compete; to act in good faith
	To take reasonable care while carrying out their duties

Handling discipline and grievances

The employee's right to a statement of employment particulars is outlined above. Section 3 of the Act specifies that such a statement must specify any disciplinary rules applicable to the employee, or make reference to suitable documents that do so. The Employment Act 2002 has added a further requirement that the statement must also include information about any procedure applicable to the undertaking of disciplinary decisions. In addition, the statement must also specify to whom an employee can appeal if dissatisfied with any disciplinary decision made.

At present Warbings has no formal disciplinary or grievance policies and procedures. One of the managers argues that they are not necessary.

What answer would you give?

What were your reasons for making this decision?

Rights during the contractual relationship

These rights are determined by the contractual relationship entered into. Individuals who can be classified as employees gain full employment protection, which includes:

◆ Employee status rights;

◆ Maternity/parental leave;

◆ The right to apply for flexible working;

◆ The right not to be unfairly dismissed;

◆ The right not to be unfairly selected for redundancy;

◆ For fixed-term workers, the right not to be discriminated against under the Fixed Term (Prevention of Less Favourable Treatment) Regulations 2002;

◆ Rights under the Transfer of Undertaking Regulations.

Individuals who have non-employee status but who are classified as workers have lesser degrees of protection, the following applying to all workers and not just employees:

◆ Protection from discrimination;

◆ Protection from unlawful deductions from wages;

◆ Protection under the Working Time Regulations;

◆ Protection under the Minimum Wage Act 1998;

◆ For part-time workers, the right under the Part Time (Less Favourable Treatment) Regulations to be treated not less favourably than equivalent full-time employees/ workers.

Employee status rights

All employees and workers are entitled to a written statement of their main terms and condition of service under Section 1 of Employment Rights Act 1996. This must include information on the date of commencement of employment and the details of who the employer is. This information is used, together with length of service, to establish rights during and at the termination of the employment relationship.

Maternity rights

Maternity leave is a complex area and this chapter can only provide an outline of the main provisions. The starting point is the basic statutory rights which are found within Sections 71 to 79 of the Employment Rights Act 1996, which were amended by the Maternity and Parental Leave (Amendment) Regulations (2002). These provide a floor of rights for all female employees on a sliding scale depending on length of service. These rights are:

◆ *Ordinary Maternity Leave* – where a women qualifies regardless of her length of service for 26 weeks of leave (SS71/73 ERA (1996)). When a woman takes leave under this right, she is entitled to return to the same type of job that she was employed in before her absence.

◆ *Additional Maternity Leave* – this takes effect when a woman has been continuously employed for 26 weeks on the fifteenth week before the expected date of delivery. This extra leave is dependent on the woman informing her employer of her intention to return to work as prescribed by S79 ERA (1996).

Organisations may also offer enhanced contractual rights and where this happens the employee has the right to choose the most beneficial terms for her leave (Section 78 ERA (1996), cited in Willey, 2003: Chapter 13).

For many organisations it is the management of the employee during the period of maternity absence that gives rise to litigation. This is an area that requires specific attention and detailed records of employees away on maternity leave. Women are afforded protection not to be treated less favourably while on leave. Contractually, the woman is entitled to the benefits of her employment contract with the exception of wages or salary. Situations that occur while the employee is on leave, such as promotion opportunities, need to be communicated to the employee. Even where the organisation feels that she would not be successful, this is not a defence for not notifying her of the possibility of the position. This was the case of *Visa International Services Association v Paul [2004] IRLR 42*, where a woman on maternity leave resigned and claimed constructive unfair dismissal and sex discrimination.

Working part time after maternity leave

Women may request to return from maternity leave on fewer hours than before. The employer needs to consider any such requests very carefully, for a refusal could lead to a claim for indirect sex discrimination. Where such a request is refused, the employer needs to be able to *objectively justify* the reason for refusal (see, for example, *the case of Sibley v The Girls' Day School Trust Norwich High School for Girls [2003] EAT 1368/01 May*).

Flexible working

The right to apply for flexible working stems first from the Employment Rights Act 1996, supplemented by the Flexible Working (Procedural Requirements Regulations (2002)) and the Flexible Working (Eligibility, Complaints and Remedies) Regulations

(2002). These regulations provide the grounds on which employees who have a minimum of 26 weeks' continuous service and who have parental responsibilities for children under the age of six years (or 18 years where the child is disabled) can apply for a change in their hours of work or the location of work. Specifically, the applicant must:

- State that it is such an application;
- Specify the changes applied for and the date on which it is proposed the change should take place;
- Explain what effect (if any) the employee thinks making the change applied for would have on the employers and how, in the employee's opinion, any such effect might be dealt with;
- Explain how the employee meets, in respect of the child concerned, the conditions as to the relationship mentioned in Subsection 1(b).

Under Regulation 3 Flexible Working (Eligibility, Complaints and Remedies) (2002), the applicant needs to demonstrate that they are the mother, father, guardian or foster parent of the child, or that they are married to, or are the civil partner of, the mother, father or guardian or foster carer who has or expects to have responsibility for the child's upbringing.

Once the application has been received, the employer is required to hold a meeting to discuss the application within 28 days. The employer needs to consider the application and give notice of the decision within 14 days. This must be in writing, giving either permission to a variation of the contractual terms, or refusing, stating the grounds on which that decision has been taken. The organisation's right to refuse is limited to one of the eight reasons laid down under Section 80 G 1(b) of the 1996 Act, as well as such grounds as the Secretary of State may specify in the regulations. These are:

- The burden of costs;
- Detrimental effect on the ability to meet customer demand;
- Inability to reorganise work among the existing staff;
- An inability to recruit additional staff;
- Detrimental impact on quality;
- Detrimental impact on performance;
- Insufficiency of work during the period the employee proposes to work;
- Planned structural changes.

Where an organisation does refuse such a claim, the employee may be able to bring a claim for constructive unfair dismissal under Section 95 1(c) of the Employment Rights Act 1996, as was the case in *Commonation v Rully [2006] IRLR 171 EAT.*

Tribunals and courts will consider the rigour of the investigation and the process undertaken, which might include discussions with line managers of the applicant and other staff members. Quinn and Nathan (2006) point out that organisations can learn a number of lessons from this case, the main one being the need for a paper trail showing the investigation that was undertaken.

A recent study undertaken by the Chartered Institute of Personnel and Development (2005) shows a number of benefits that flow from the operation of the Flexibility

Regulations, the most significant being retention. Take-up was found to be highest in the smaller establishments (i.e. less than 50 employees). The study further suggested that those organisations that have a positive attitude to flexible working practices showed an improved recruitment rate. In any industry where skills are in short supply, this could be a major factor. As with all policies and procedures, the issue is to manage expectations; employees need to feel confident that the operation of these policies will be dealt with equitably.

'Avoid the pitfalls of work-life balance by considering flexible working seriously'

An article by David Gibson in *Personnel Today* (16 May 2006) warns employers that a knee-jerk reaction to a request to work flexibly will undoubtedly lead to the law courts. It argues that men are now starting to exercise their statutory right to request flexible working and quotes a new buzzword 'fambition' to describe fathers seeking to spend more time with the children and less in the office.

Since the introduction of the legislation, 10 per cent of male employees have approached their employers about changing hours, according to a TUC report, *Out of Time*. However, UK managers have tended to look more favourably on requests from female staff, with only 10 per cent of working mothers having their requests rejected out of hand, compared with 14 per cent of men.

Employers must follow a strict procedure when considering an application. Failure to do so can lead to a tribunal or ACAS awarding compensation and insisting the application be reconsidered. More importantly, failure to agree a request for flexible working for a man, where a similar request has been granted for a woman, can lead to a claim of sex discrimination – with uncapped compensation.

Parental rights

These rights were introduced by the Maternity and Parental Leave Regulations (1999) that enacted powers within Section 76 of the Employment Rights Act (1996) Regulations and created a statutory right for employees who have, or expect to have, responsibilities for a child to take a period of absence to care for a child. This right is separate from that which protects a woman who is pregnant. As with the regulation on flexibility, there is a qualifying period of continuous service under Section 210 of ERA (1996). These regulations provide for a maximum of 13 weeks parental leave in respect of each child. There are, however, restrictions on when employees become entitled to this right: these regulations do not apply to children born before 15 December 1999, nor once the child reaches its fifth birthday (or eighteenth if disabled).

Organisations may develop further contractual agreements, but where these do not exist, the regulations are deemed to be a 'fallback' position. The position then is:

◆ Employees **may not** take parental leave of less than one week except in the case of a disabled child;

◆ Employees **may not** take more than four weeks leave in any one year;

◆ Employees **must comply** with a request to provide evidence of the child's age and/or disability;

- Employee **must give** notice of period of leave, clearly indicating the start and end dates;
- The employer **may** postpone a period of parental leave in the case of business needs for a period of six months, but this must be in writing stating the reasons for the delay.

The right to only take parental leave in blocks of one week or more was confirmed by the Court of Appeal in *South Central Trains Ltd v Rodway [2005] EWCA Civ 443*, where it was made clear that this was to be the situation: 'unless the employee had an over riding contractual term either as an express term or incorporated from a collective agreement'.

Dependency leave

This right, unlike flexibility and paternity rights, *does not* have a qualifying length of service. All employees are entitled to take a reasonable amount of time off during his or her working hours within Section 57 A Employment Rights Act 1996. This right is enacted to enable employees with dependants in emergencies to:

- Provide assistance when a dependant falls ill, gives birth, is assaulted or injured;
- Make arrangements necessary for the care of a dependant who falls ill or is injured, or as a result of the death of a dependant;
- Deal with unexpected disruption or termination of arrangements for the care of a dependant;
- Deal with incidents which involve a child at an educational establishment.

Employees can only obtain protection under this right if they inform the employers of the reason for the absence and state the intended time of absence.

Part-time employees or workers

At present, there is no legal definition of a part-time worker. The current position is regulated by the Part Time Workers (Prevention of Less Favourable Treatment) Regulations (2000) (S1 222/1551), in which a part-time worker is deemed to be a person who works under the same type of contract as a full-time worker but for fewer hours. For part-time workers (or employees), access to full employment rights are the same as for full-time workers (or employees). For organisations, therefore, part-time contracts should follow those of full-timers on a *pro rata* basis.

Rights on termination of the contract

Termination of contract can be either by operation of common law, where one side gives notice in accordance with the express terms, or, where the contract is silent, by reference to statute. Termination may also occur where either side is in breach of contract, or where there is an intervening event beyond the control of either party, for example changes in work permit rights, can lead to a frustration of contract.

Employer terminations

To bring a contract to an end the organisation is required to give at least statutory notice as defined within Section 86 ERA (1996). The Employment Rights Act 1996 protects employees with one year's continuous employment at the effective date of termination not to be unfairly dismissed. Employees with less than one year have only a contractual right not to be wrongfully dismissed, unless the dismissal is in breach of discrimination law.

Terminations for employees with over one year's service can only be deemed as *fair* where the organisation can demonstrate that they have operated within Section 98 of the Employment Rights Act for dismissal, or Section 139 if the employee has two years' continuous service and is to be made redundant. What then is a *fair* dismissal? Organisations, under Section 98 ss (2), are permitted to dismiss where it can be demonstrated that the employee no longer has the 'capability, or qualifications to carry out their duties, or that their conduct is such as to breach the contract of employment, or is redundant'.

The dismissal process is now formalised by the enactment of the Employment Rights Act 2002 (Dispute Resolution) Regulations (2004). These stipulate that the employer must operate within the three-stage procedure to prevent claims of unfair dismissal. Failure to follow these procedures may lead to a claim for Automatic Unfair Dismissal. Such a claim shifts the burden of proof from the employee to the employer. Once the employee makes a claim under the Act, the organisation must be able to defend the action to dismiss in line with the test of a 'reasonable employer', that is, 'the dismissal is one within a band of reasonable responses that any other employer acting reasonably would have considered reasonable'. The statute places on the employer a further burden that even where they have the right to dismiss (and could satisfy the band of reasonable responses test), they must be able to demonstrate that they did so after application of the requirements laid down in Section 98 4(a) and (b) of the Employment Rights Act 1996. This means that they have considered that there is sufficient reason for dismissal. In addition, the organisation has to show that it has applied equity to the decision.

The ACAS Code of Practice on 'Disciplinary and Grievance Procedures (2004a)' is of great importance in the management and resolution of disciplinary issues – although breach of this code is not in itself unlawful, it will weigh heavily against an employer if not followed.

In terms of grievances, the basic provisions under the 1996 Employment Rights Act is that the employer has to specify a person to whom the employee can apply if he or she has a grievance and this information should, again, be included in the statement of particulars. Although a formal grievance procedure is not legally required, it is highly recommended for organisations to have one; not only will it give everyone a route to follow when dealing with a claim, and counter claim, it also helps ensure perceptions of fairness.

Finally, under Section 10 of the Employee Relations Act 1999, workers have the right to make a reasonable request to be accompanied during a disciplinary or grievance hearing. A single companion, as designated in the legislation, may accompany a worker.

window into practice

The organisation must be able to:

◆ Defend the dismissal under Section 98;

◆ Have the right to dismiss;

◆ Be able to continue with the dismissal, taking into account all the surrounding circumstances of the breach and the resources of the organisation.

The role of employment tribunals and ACAS

Individual employees seeking to enforce their rights on unfair dismissal, redundancy or claims for discrimination and a number of other matters, do so by application to the employment tribunal. These are independent judicial bodies that seek to deal with employment disputes relatively quickly and inexpensively.

The Advisory, Conciliation and Arbitration Service (ACAS) has a number of roles in relation to employment and industrial relations issues, namely to:

- Promote good practice;
- Provide information and advice;
- Conciliate in complaints to employment tribunals;
- Conciliate in the case of collective disputes;
- Prevent and resolve employment disputes.

In unfair dismissal cases specifically, ACAS-appointed conciliation officers have the statutory duty to explore the possibility of reinstatement or of re-engagement *before* seeking to facilitate a monetary or other form of settlement. Furthermore, under the Employment Rights (Disputes Resolution) Act 1998, conciliation officers have the power – if both parties agree – to draw up a binding settlement in which the employee's complaint of unfair dismissal is resolved through binding arbitration rather than through the employment tribunal system. It was hoped that the involvement of ACAS would decrease the numbers of cases taken to tribunal, but the use of this facility has been low.

Non-renewal of a fixed-term contract

The non-renewal of a fixed-term contract is defined within Section 95 ss 1(b) as a dismissal. A fixed-term contract can be brought to an end either by operation of a predetermined date or by a predictable event (for example, loss of renewable funding.) Where, however, the fixed-term contract is for more than one year, then the employee is entitled to the same rights on dismissal as permanent employees and the three stages laid down in the dispute regulations apply.

Termination of employment by the employee

Within Section 95 Employment Rights Act 1996, an employee has the right to bring the contract to an end by resigning and claiming to have been *constructively dismissed* by the employer. The section places on the employee the burden to demonstrate the conduct of the employer that has led to the exercise of this right. Without pervasive evidence to the contrary, a resignation would operate as a contractual termination.

Since the enactment of the Dispute Regulations, organisations need to read each termination letter closely as it may contain information that indicates a grievance. Where this is the case, the organisation *must* proceed with the dispute regulations.

Litigation for constructive dismissal can arise from a breach by the employer of the common law duty of mutual trust and respect. This can cover any aspect of the contractual relationship, including breaches of discriminatory legislation. In the case of *United Bank v Aktar [1989] IRLR 507*, the employer wanted to rely on a mobility clause to relocate Mr Aktar from Leeds to Birmingham with no financial support for the move, and at very short notice. The Employment Appeals tribunal upheld the right of Mr Aktar to resign and claim constructive dismissal.

Redundancy

The law recognises that the contractual relationship is a fluid one; skills, qualifications and work processes constantly adapt to meet the changing market needs of the organisation to remain competitive. Nevertheless, the organisation has to ensure that employees selected for redundancy have been chosen fairly via due process of procedure, either within the contract of employment, or by regulations set out in the Employment Rights Act 1996. An employee who can show that they have been unfairly selected for redundancy could bring a claim for unfair dismissal. Since the enactment of age legislation, reaching the statutory age of 65 will no longer protect the organisation from using age as a reason for ending the contract. It is also crucial that appropriate consultation takes place with Individuals and if 20 or more are to be made redundant on a collective basis. Employers have to beware of being found guilty of unfair dismissal and failures to consult collectively. (See ACAS booklet on Redundancy Handling, 2004b.)

window into practice

In everyday terminology, redundancy can occur when the employer closes down completely, moves premises, requires fewer people for particular jobs or requires no people for such jobs. Redundancy can also occur when an individual has been laid off or kept on short-time working for a period, as specified in the Employment Rights Act 1996.

In terms of good practice and to prevent engendering a negative psychological contract, it is important for organisations to avoid redundancies if at all possible. Relevant policies and transparent procedures are also vital.

pause for thought

Why do you think it is important for the procedures surrounding redundancy to be transparent?

What were the reasons for you reaching this conclusion?

Rights and obligations after the termination of the relationship

Rights and obligations arise from the terms of the contract that were incorporated at the commencement of the relationship. Organisations can insert restrictive covenants that take effect to protect the business after the termination of the contract. Such covenants are enforceable only if they are reasonable; therefore the clauses need to be carefully drafted and only imposed on employees who are likely to be involved in dealing with confidential information or moving to a competitor. The clauses must be reasonable and no wider than necessary to protect a *legitimate business interest*.

A legitimate business interest has been held to cover customers, suppliers, trade secrets and confidential information. The test as to reasonableness was laid down in the case of *Marshall Thomas (Exports) Ltd v Guinle [1979] CH 227*, where it was held that the:

◆ Owner of the information must believe that its release would benefit a competitor;

◆ Owner must believe that the information is confidential and not public knowledge;

◆ Information must be judged in relation to the knowledge of the industry.

Ex-employees may also be limited in the geographical location of their new job on termination of employment, as in *Hollis and Co v Stocks [2000] IRLR 712*, where a solicitor's contract contained a clause that on termination he would not work within a ten-mile radius of the employer's practice for a period of one year, and this was upheld. The employer cannot however prevent the employee from exercising skills learned while in their employment – this would be deemed to be against public policy. Where the organisation believes that an employee moving to a competitor would cause harm to the business, the contract should contain a right to place an employee on 'garden leave' (i.e. not working) for a period deemed to be reasonable. However, where the employee can demonstrate that the organisation is in breach of contract, it is unlikely that the courts will uphold against the employee.

Right to references

The employer is under no duty to provide the ex-employee/worker with a reference, but where these are supplied the employer has a duty of care to both the ex-employee and to the recipient organisation. The reference should be truthful, honest and within the context of the total work history – see *Bartholomew v London Borough of Hackney [1999] IRLR 246*. Organisations that provide oral references must ensure that these are provided as neutrally and honestly as possible.

Other aspects of employment law

This chapter has focused on the rights and obligations surrounding the contract of employment, along with the individual protections provided by various statutes. Two other aspects of employment law will, however, be briefly touched on: collective aspects and health and safety.

Collective employment law

There are three dimensions to the law relating to collective rights (Willey, 2003), namely: processes of employee relations, industrial action and individual trade union legislation.

The processes of employee relations

These relate to trade unions and their activities, particularly collective bargaining and consultation, and to non-union representation via consultation. Thus, for example, the European Works Council Directive (1994) and its 1997 extension provide for a European-wide information and consultation system to be set up in organisations of a certain specified size. The National Information and Consultation Directive (2002) requires employers with 50 or more members of staff to inform and consult employee representatives about employment prospects and decisions likely to lead to major changes in work organisation or contractual relations.

An employer may choose to recognise a union voluntarily or, under The ERel Act 1999, there is provision for statutory recognition if certain conditions are fulfilled. Recognition of a trade union by the employer is important. It entitles the trade union to involvement in collective bargaining and to disclosure of certain information for such bargaining. It also allows for certain time off for union duties and activities and for the union to be consulted on training issues and opportunities.

Industrial action

This dimension concerns, firstly, the role and liability of trade unions for industrial action and, secondly, the positions of individual workers who take part in industrial action, particularly with regard to dismissal and pay deduction.

Individual trade union membership

This relates to the admission of individuals to, and their exclusion from, trade unions, as well as the rights of individual members of a trade union to participate in the internal democracy of their trade union.

Health and safety

It is of vital importance that a workplace is safe and that employees' well-being is promoted. The main sources of health and safety law are the common law, statute and European legislation. Much of the common law regarding health and safety is contained in the employer's implied term of duty of care. The major consolidating legislation is the Health and Safety at Work Act 1974 (HSWA). The Act applies to all work situations. It imposes a duty on employers to ensure, so far as is reasonably practicable, the health, safety and welfare of their employees and, in addition, imposes certain duties on employees, such as the duty to take reasonable care for the health and safety of themselves and others. Recent years have seen additional legislation introduced to implement European directives.

Regulation of working time

The Working Time Regulations are intended to implement the Working Time Directive 93/104/EC and provisions of the Young Workers Directive 94/33/EC. The legal basis for the Directive was Article 118a EC (now Article 137 EC) relating to health and safety. The Directive states that, 'in order to ensure the safety and health of Community workers, the latter must be granted minimum daily, weekly and annual periods of rest and adequate breaks' and that 'it is necessary in this context to place a maximum limit on working time'. Thus the basic provision includes a maximum working week of 48 hours, averaged out over a 17-week period, though in the UK individuals may opt out of this restriction. Other aspects covered by the Working Time Directive include minimum rest periods and holiday entitlement and limits on night work. The regulations apply to workers in general, although certain categories are excluded.

Summary

To ensure against expensive litigation, as well as to promote good employment practice, employers should:

* Ensure from the outset that the contractual relationship that is entered into is one that will provide the right skills for the length of time that these are needed;
* Regardless of the size of the organisation, make decisions in line with statutory codes. This includes recognising when discipline rules have been broken and dealing with these fairly and consistently;
* Closely monitor the relationship with agency workers so that the accumulations of rights are in line with organisational needs;
* Operate all policies and procedures evenly across the organisation so that compliance and equity are achieved;
* Manage the contractual relationship: increasingly workers/employees are aware of their rights, and are more ready to take action where breaches have occurred.

Review Questions

You may wish to attempt the following as practice examination style questions.

13.1 Why is it important to distinguish between a contract *of* service and a contract *for* service?

13.2 What tests have the tribunals/courts used to make this distinction?

13.3 Outline the common law duties of an employee.

13.4 What is meant by (a) direct discrimination and (b) indirect discrimination?

13.5 Can a woman insist that she works part time when she returns from maternity leave?

13.6 Under what circumstances might the employment contract be terminated?

13.7 What is meant by 'constructive dismissal'?

13.8 What are the different situations that might lead to an employee being dismissed for reason of redundancy?

13.9 Is an employer obliged to provide a reference for an employee?

13.10 What are the sources of health and safety law?

References

ACAS (2004a). *Code of Practice on Discipline and Grievance Procedures*, London: ACAS.

ACAS (2004b) *Booklet on Redundancy Handling*, London: ACAS.

Anderman, S.D. (2000). *Labour Law: Management Decisions and Workers' Rights*, London: Butterworths.

Beer, M., Spector, B., Lawrence, P., Quinn Mills, D. and Walton, R. (1984). *Managing Human Assets*, New York: Free Press.

CIPD (2005). Flexible working: impact and implementation, survey report, London: CIPD.

Kahn-Freund, O. (1972). *Labour and the Law*, London: Stevens.

Lockton, D. (2006). *Employment Law*, London: Cavendish.

Nairns, J. (1999). *Employment Law for Business Students*, London, FT/Pitman.

Pfeffer, J. (1998). *The Human Equation: Building Profits by Putting People First*, Boston, MA: Harvard Business School Press.

Porter, K., Smith, P. and Fagg, R. (2006). *Leadership and Management for HR Professionals*, Oxford: Butterworth-Heinemann.

Quinn, J. and Nathan, D. (2006). Causing a commotion, *People Management*, 23 February.

Willey, B. (2003). *Employment Law in Context: An Introduction for HR Professionals*, Harlow: Prentice Hall.

Further Reading

ACAS (2004) *Code of Practice on Discipline and Grievance Procedures*, London: ACAS.

ACAS (2004) *Discipline and Grievances at Work, Advisory Handbook*, London: ACAS.

ACAS (2004) *Booklet on Redundancy Handling*, London: ACAS.

Daniels, K. (2004). *Employment Law for HR and Business Students*, London: CIPD.

Lewis, D. and Sargeant, M. (2004). *Essentials of Employment Law*, London: CIPD.

Rees, W.D. and Porter, C. (2001). Skills of management (chapter 13), in *Disciplinary Handling and Dismissal*, Thomson Learning (6th edition to be published in 2008).

See also employment law updates in the *People Management* journal, *IDS Brief* and *Personnel Today*.

Useful Websites

www.acas.gov.uk – ACAS guidance on legal issues and good practice

www.cre.gov.uk – Commission for Racial Equality, access to guidance (e.g. race quality, inpact assessment), reports on investigations and research. Can download statutory Code of Practice (2005) on racial equality in employment

www.drc-gb.org.uk – offers guidance on rights and practice, disability, debate papers, progress reports from the independent Disability Rights Commission

www.ets.gov.uk – access to statistics on Tribunal cases, details of procedural changes and advice on responding to claims from the Employment Tribunal website

www.eoc.gov.uk – Equal Opportunities Commission, guidance on best practice, legal advice, research and investigations

www.hse.gov.uk – advice on legislation, reports on investigations and recommendations from the Health and Safety Executive

www.peoplemanagement.co.uk – access to CIPD's flagship monthly publication covering articles, news reports, jobs and legal and best practice advice

www.personneltoday.com – CIPD's topical broadsheets with news and views on HR issues

CHAPTER 14

Equality and Diversity in Employment

By Sue Miller and Kieran Williams

Chapter outline

This chapter looks at the nature of 'diversity' and social identity and how socialisation, cultural norms and perceptual bias can lead to prejudice, stereotyping and discrimination. It considers patterns in the labour market, the discrimination and disadvantage faced by particular social groups, and the key pieces of legislation that have been put into place to combat this. 'Equal opportunities' (EO) and 'managing diversity' (MD) are explained as two different approaches, with a consideration of the rationale for organisational action on equality and diversity issues. Finally, there is an outline of the ingredients necessary for the successful management of diversity, with some suggestions about the future of equality and diversity.

Learning objectives

By the end of this chapter, you should be able to:

◆ Identify different dimensions of diversity and their implications;
◆ Describe the nature of discrimination, the effects of perceptual bias and its impact on social interaction;
◆ Analyse your own personal reaction to difference;
◆ Explain occupational segregation;
◆ List key pieces of anti-discrimination legislation;
◆ Explain 'EO' and 'MD' as two different approaches;
◆ Evaluate an organisation's approach to equality and diversity.

Introduction

We are not alike; we differ from each other in an infinite number of ways, and those individual differences produce a richness that has the potential to add something to life in general and to organisational life in particular – hence the argument that we should value diversity.

♦ Imagine that you are describing yourself over the phone to someone who has never met you.

 – What would you say?

 – What does this tell you about how you see yourself?

 – What does this tell you about how you would like others to see you?

♦ Ask yourself how you differ from the person next to you in a lecture. Your list will differ from that of your neighbour – in itself indicating differences in the importance *you* attach to different characteristics! You could also characterise those differences according to their visibility/non-visibility; whether they are acquired or innate; whether they are differences that are covered by the anti-discrimination legislation; and whether they are a potential source of discrimination and disadvantage.

 – List a range of potential differences between people and classify them as described in the previous paragraph.

The nature of diversity

In the literature a distinction is sometimes made between primary and secondary characteristics, or 'dimensions' (Loden, 1996), with the **primary** dimensions as:

♦ Age;

♦ Gender;

♦ Race;

♦ Ethnicity;

♦ Mental and physical abilities and characteristics;

♦ Sexual orientation.

Characteristics such as education, family status, first language and religion are seen as **secondary** dimensions, and may be considered less significant in terms of their potential to lead to disadvantage in terms of employment opportunities and treatment in the workplace.

A typology is also useful for distinguishing between three sets of characteristics:

♦ Demographic characteristics (the 'social category');

♦ Informational differences (encompassing background, education and knowledge);

♦ Personality and attitudinal differences between people.

While we differ infinitely, and the differences are potentially of use to organisations, there are those categories that have a particular impact on our experience of life and the identity we establish for ourselves. The sociological literature uses the terms 'social group' and 'social identity'. While it is recognised that such groups are heterogeneous, that we all belong to a range of groups, and that we have multiple 'identities', certain characteristics impinge more significantly on the opportunities available to us at work, and on our social interactions. It is argued, for example, that sex and race 'are the two dominant statuses that both support and limit people in their life experience' (Epstein, 1973, cited in Guirdham, 1996: 95). It is significant that discrimination at work on the grounds of race and sex has been the subject of legislation for several decades; more recently there have been added grounds of disability, sexual orientation, religion and age. This demonstrates a recognition that these dimensions are potential sources of discrimination and disadvantage, and that there are sometimes negative reactions to difference – by individuals, organisations and even whole societies.

Before moving on to these reactions and looking at how individuals and groups perceive one another, a consideration of three of the key dimensions of difference and how we define them provides some useful clues to the complexity of social identity.

'Race' is an informal classification of the human species according to hereditary differences, but there are those who reject the term altogether because there is, in fact, little evidence of genetic racial distinctions, with more biological differences *within* so-called 'racial groups' than *between* them (see, for example, the debate on the Social Science Research Council's web forum – raceandgenomics.ssrc.org). Any differences in practice could be seen to be a result of cultural *or* social learning.

Similarly, while sex is a biological characteristic determined at conception, the biological differences between men and women are small, on average, and many would argue that any differences in behaviour and motivation (i.e. gender differences) are the product of social conditioning. (See, for example, Kohlberg's cognitive development theory (1966), Mischel's social learning approach (1966) and Bandura's social-cognitive theory (1986).) More recently, feminist academics have explored these ideas (see, for example, a summary in Chapter Nine of Ritzer and Goodman's *Modern Sociological Theory* (2004)).

Disability, too, can be seen as a relative concept, with different perspectives on how far disability is determined by society. In 1976, the Union of the Physically Impaired Against Segregation (UPIAS) published its manifesto, which introduced the idea of a 'social model' of disability. This model argues that society places constraints and limitations on the individual, so disabling him or her, and is in contrast to the clinical model depicting disability as wholly defined by the medical condition. UK legislation, for example, uses a definition which only focuses on the disabled person and how they may be different from the able-bodied majority. The Act spells out that a disabled person has 'a physical or mental impairment that has a substantial and long-term adverse effect on his or her ability to carry out normal day-to-day activities (Disability Discrimination Act 1995).

Definitions and categorisations are neither absolute nor undisputed, while the context – the society and culture – in which we find ourselves, determines both who we are and whom we are seen to be.

The nature and impact of social interaction

Social perception

Social perception is a complex process – how we make sense of all the pieces of information (i.e. clues) that we receive from people via their behaviour, their words and their non-verbal communication. We have to interpret all these pieces of information and sometimes we rely on short-cuts to do so. Placing people into groups can be a quick and easy way of allowing us to draw conclusions about what they are like – and we may need to do this because we want not only to make sense of what is around us and 'file' it in the filing-cabinets of our minds, but we also need to be able to predict others' reactions if we are going to be able to behave appropriately ourselves. This becomes dangerous when we fail to check our assumptions and start to accept stereotypes – judging people by who they are (e.g. female, red-haired, deaf, etc.) rather than what they do or say.

pause for thought

Think for a moment about the assumptions that you make about people and the way in which stereotyping may affect your interaction with others.

If you were buying a gift for a child that you had never met, would the child's gender influence your choice of present?

Do you associate certain behaviour with particular physical features? For example, do you expect people from the Caribbean to be good dancers or people with Welsh accents to have a good singing voice? Is this fair?

Such stereotypes can become extremely deep-seated and we may not even be aware that they are buried in our subconscious. We tend to seek out confirmation of our assumptions and may ignore information that would prove them wrong (Bodenhausen, 1988).

The process of social perception is 'how we obtain, store and recall information about other people in order to make judgements about them' (Arnold et al., 1995: 234). We are limited in terms of our capacity to absorb information and we are selective in our attention, but we also have learned many ideas and beliefs that we do not want to disrupt by having to absorb new data which may conflict with our existing personal vision of the world – the 'locked-in effect' or 'confirmation bias'.

There is also a great deal of scope for misunderstanding and misinterpretation in the process of perception. As Kolb et al. (1971) comment: 'We are not cameras or tape recorders. We do not take in, with our eyes or ears, exactly what is "out there".' So:

◆ We may make errors about people's intentions and motives – 'attribution errors';

◆ We may ignore others' perspectives and frames of reference;

◆ We may extrapolate from one aspect of their behaviour which we like or dislike to decide about other aspects of their behaviour, personality or performance.

All the time we are making assumptions, using limited information and taking mental short-cuts. It is neither surprising, therefore, that social interaction is fraught with misunderstandings, nor that categorisations according to social groupings occur. We have a tendency to regard all members of a group as sharing traits and behaviours and ignore the differences between individuals. This perceptual bias, of which stereotyping is one manifestation, does not necessarily involve negative assumptions, but by its very nature it involves prejudging people. Such prejudice can then lead to discriminatory behaviour, with damaging impact on inter-group relations, misjudgements, miscommunication, conflict and, in an organisational context, a negative impact on performance.

Socialisation

The attempt to explain the limitations and pitfalls of social perception omits one important element: how we establish our worldview in the first place, and how we learn the contents of our stereotypes. We have already considered the problematic nature of definitions of 'race', 'gender' and 'disability' and how they are not absolute but, rather, defined by the society in which we live. Our experience of family, peer group, education and the media all provide models, rules and frameworks for our attitudes and behaviours. This social learning determines the norms of behaviour to which we subscribe: we have to learn the 'norms' of the society and culture in which we live if we are to survive in it. The process involved is 'socialisation' – defined by Giddens (1993: 60) as, 'the process whereby the helpless infant gradually becomes a self-aware, knowledgeable person, skilled in the ways of the culture into which he or she is born.'

pause for thought

- Are we 'born into a culture' or into a country or a nation? What evidence led you to answer in the way that you did?

- What does it mean to be multicultural?

- Is a multicultural society the same as an integrated one? Why did you reach this conclusion?

One tendency in most societies is towards 'ethnocentricism' – a tendency to evaluate the norms of other cultures in terms of one's own. This is mirrored in organisations where the organisation's culture holds sway or has 'hegemony', as Kirton and Greene (2000) describe it: there are implications for the extent to which difference is accepted and celebrated.

Part of this may be linked to the idea of 'in-groups' and 'out-groups' (Tajfel, 1981; Stangor, 2003). Members of the majority 'in-group' may have the power to influence thinking so that they are seen as 'normal' and anyone who is different is therefore excluded. There are many ways that the majority group keep control (Clements and Spinks, 2006) – stereotyping 'outsiders', attaching labels, exaggerating differences, making jokes, ridiculing cultures, imposing values, etc.

exercise

Think of a time when you have been in a minority outside an 'in-group'. Try to analyse your experience:

- How did the majority group exclude or include you?

- What behaviours helped or hindered you?

- What have you learned from these experiences that may help you to be more sensitive in valuing diversity rather than isolating people who may be different?

Majority groups or cultures may attempt to isolate or assimilate minority cultures, whereas real power sharing may only result from incorporation (National Police Training, 2001, cited in Clements and Jones, 2006).

Interaction in the workplace

So how are these processes seen in the workplace? The term 'discrimination' is widely taken to have negative connotations in connection with discussions of equality and diversity. However discrimination is in itself a neutral concept – we need to make a distinction between different people if we are to choose one for a partner, and when we are to select someone for a colleague or employee. Such discrimination, however, becomes inappropriate in situations relating to employment, training and service delivery if it is based on irrelevant criteria such as their social group membership, or other characteristics that have no bearing on their *ability* to perform the job, undertake the training or use the service provided. It may be deemed not only unfair but also unlawful in many instances; moreover, some discrimination not only involves biased decision making but also actual acts of bullying, abuse or harassment.

Unfair discrimination may be unintentional: the unwitting product of perceptual bias, the application of an unacknowledged prejudice or of a lack of understanding that the perpetrator's 'norms' are not shared by members of other groups. It may be embedded in the fabric of the organisation so that new entrants embrace its culture, including a tendency to disadvantage people with particular characteristics – a facet of institutional racism, sexism and homophobia. Acts of harassment, meanwhile, not only constitute unfair treatment but can be seen as the epitome of anti-diversity behaviour. According to Guirdham, this demonstrates a complete lack of interpersonal skills: 'to discriminate, harass or show prejudice is automatically to fail on any measure of interpersonal skills' (1996: 445). It is interesting, therefore, that attempts to define a 'diversity competency' closely mirror sets of interpersonal skills identified as necessary for the effective management of people, regardless of their cultural backgrounds (Kandola and Fullerton, 1998).

pause for thought

There is an ancient Sioux saying:

'Teach me not to judge a man until I have walked for a day in his moccasins.'

◆ What do you think this means?

◆ How relevant is it for you?

◆ What are your prejudices?

◆ Which do you try to hide from other people?

◆ How do you think your prejudices influence your behaviour?

◆ What do you do to overcome them?

Kandola and Fullerton (1998) note, however, that there are behaviours that individuals can fulfil in order to help them meet the challenges of diversity. In order to overcome the effects of prejudice and bias, it helps to recognise our limitations – to recognise the fact that we subjectively define situations; that we see things through a lens that filters out and distorts some social data; that we are prone to prejudice and to mental short-cuts. As Ross and Nisbett (1991) argue, there is a need to make allowances for such weaknesses and to do this we need to understand which lenses we (and they) are using (Kennedy and Everest, 1991). We generally make every attempt to hide our prejudices and limitations from others, but if we are willing to acknowledge them as inevitable, then it can provide both a sense of relief and a way forward.

Patterns in the labour market

Members of certain social groups are liable to face disadvantage in the labour market. There is differentiation, 'occupational segregation', with some groups being disproportionately represented in certain occupations or sectors (*horizontal segregation*) or at certain levels in organisations (*vertical segregation*).

For example, in 2005 less than 3 per cent of apprentices in construction, engineering and plumbing were female and women represented only 13 per cent of students on FE/HE courses in engineering and technology subjects (Learning and Skills Council, 2005).

In the same year, 100 per cent of the workforce in newspaper and journal publishing was white, together with 86.4 per cent of the workforce in book publishing (CRE, 2005).

Occupational segregation does not only affect women and members of minority ethnic communities, adverse effects are also felt by, among others, people with learning difficulties, older people and people with disabilities. Members of such groups have a tendency to face disadvantage in their attempts to obtain work or training. And, once in employment, they may face disadvantages in terms of status, pay, progression and working relationships. The term 'glass ceiling' is often used in connection with women, referring to the invisible barrier some women may face in reaching the top of their organisations. The earliest citation is from an article by Nora Frenkiel (1984) about magazine editor, Gay Bryant:

> 'Women have reached a certain point – I call it the glass ceiling. They're in the top of middle management and they're stopping and getting stuck. There isn't enough room for all those women at the top. Some are going into business for themselves. Others are going out and raising families.'

Similarly, 'sticky floors', 'glass cliffs' and 'concrete ceilings' may face women who try to make progress in the workplace that may well still be dominated by white, middle-class, middle-aged males.

Amongst FTSE 100 boards in 2005, only 10.5 per cent of directorships were held by women and less than 4 per cent of executive directorships. Nearly a quarter of the boards have no female members (Singh and Vinnicombe, 2005).

One approach to challenging this pattern has been the use of 'positive action' programmes which provide training and development to under-represented groups so that they reach a point where they can apply for a position on an equal basis to others. The appointment is then made solely on the grounds of selecting the best candidate for the post. It is important that all concerned are clear that candidates are not appointed or promoted because of their membership of an under-represented group. That would be positive discrimination and unlawful in the UK.

There are different ideological perspectives of occupational segregation. The economic view assumes a rational labour market; that is, people receive the employment that accommodates their preferences, and which they 'deserve', in terms of their skills and experience that they can offer to employers. Differences in patterns of employment between different groups are simply a matter of merit and choice. Such a 'neo-classical' approach is a simple and incomplete explanation; there is a need, for example, to consider how the worker was limited in acquiring their human capital in the first place, and to look at how their preferences were shaped by the society in which they live. Other factors need to be considered – issues to do with socialisation and social identity; the structures of inequality; and power relations in society. Relevant influences vary according to a particular social group. For women, patriarchy and the norm of the woman as 'homemaker' are phenomena offering some insight.

One particularly significant concept in relation to occupational segregation is 'statistical discrimination': this occurs whenever an individual is judged on the basis of the average characteristics of the group or groups to which he or she belongs rather than on his or her own characteristics. This statistical discrimination happens because employers adopt a 'low-cost' strategy and the judgements (concerning the human capital and likely costs) may have some validity in relation to the group as a whole – but not in relation to many of the individuals in the group. This is why the problem of inequality becomes particularly intractable – employers feel justified in their decision making even though the truth of their judgements and assumptions should be questioned in relation to the group as a whole, and not only in relation to individuals (Anker, 2001).

The rationale for 'equal opportunities' and 'managing diversity'

It is salutary to remember that UK legislation is enacted, policed and upheld by institutions made up largely of people who are white, middle-class, middle-aged males. However, the legislative framework should be taken into account when discussing the context of diversity.

Behind the legislation is the principle that it is unfair to discriminate against people on grounds that are irrelevant to the jobs they are doing, or applying for. Considering gender and race, for example, is irrelevant in relation to most types of work, and making decisions based on these characteristics is both unfair and unlawful. Recruitment and training on the basis of merit is not straightforward, however. Not only 'suitability' but also 'acceptability' can enter into the employment decision, and it may be disguised as an issue of 'merit'. Seemingly objective criteria may be impossible to apply. Moreover, some groups are not in a position to compete effectively in the employment market, because they are already disadvantaged in terms of education and background; they may already be under-represented in particular organisations or occupations because of prior disadvantage and discrimination. The 'positive action' provisions of the legislation are included for this purpose.

Some recent legislation has introduced another dimension to the discussion of diversity. In the past, laws such as the Race Relations Act (1976) made it unlawful to discriminate on the grounds of race or ethnicity. The 2000 Amendment goes further – placing an enforceable statutory duty on public bodies to pay due regard at all times to the need to:

◆ Eliminate unlawful racial discrimination;

◆ Promote equality of opportunity and good relations between persons of different racial groups.

The specific duties in relation to race are echoed in the European Union (EU) Equal Treatment Directives on gender and disability and we can see a change of emphasis towards the requirement for a more proactive and positive approach.

All of this presupposes a philosophy of 'EO'. There is no one universally accepted meaning of 'EO', and there are different stances reflecting different views on the moral and ethical issues involved. They show avariety of views of employment, the nature of disadvantage, and the propensity to discriminate. These views will influence the employers' interpretations of EO and whether there is a responsibility over and above any legal requirement for equal treatment or 'non-discrimination.' Arguably, there is a spectrum of approaches to EO, a number of different 'levels', each of which reflects a different stance and which leads to a different tendency to action.

Straw (1989) provides a simple typology, moving from an interpretation of EO as 'equal chance', where everyone is given the same chance but where no account is taken of the barriers to entry, through a position where EO involves removing barriers to entry to the organisation ('equal access'), through to equal opportunity as 'equal share', where there is access and representation at every level. The latter will involve a more radical programme of action, with a range of positive action initiatives.

There is a move from 'equality' to 'diversity'. The diversity approach, like EO, varies in its application, and some also make a distinction between managing the differences and valuing them – between 'MD' and 'valuing diversity'. But there are a number of accepted differences between diversity and equality. In contrast to EO, diversity is not seen as being legally driven; it does not use positive action; it does not focus on numbers and representation. Instead, diversity focuses on the quality of experience; it promotes pluralism rather than assimilation; and it is the responsibility of managers in every function, not just the human resource (HR) department.

MANAGING DIVERSITY	EQUAL OPPORTUNITIES
◆ ensures all employees maximise their potential and their contribution to the organisation	◆ concentrates on discrimination
◆ embraces a broad range of people; no one is excluded	◆ is perceived as an issue for women, ethnic minorities and people with disabilities
◆ concentrates on movement within an organisation, the culture of the organisation and the meeting of business objectives	◆ concentrates on the numbers of groups employed
◆ is the concern of all employees, especially managers	◆ is seen as an issue to do with personnel and human resource practitioners
◆ does not rely on positive action/ affirmative action.	◆ relies on positive action.

Figure 14.1 How managing diversity is different
Source: Kandola and Fullerton (1998: 167)

Essentially, diversity is concerned not so much with classifying people into various groups, but instead with acknowledging and celebrating the multiplicity of individual differences.

In practice, such an approach may vary from the extreme of creating an environment in which everyone feels valued and accepted, to a more strategic approach where systems and policies are devised to help build skills and capitalise on difference. Increasingly, the impetus is moving away from the moral and the ethical paradigms, and from the need for legal compliance, towards a focus on the contribution to organisational performance.

The business case for diversity was summarised by the Equality Unit of the DTI in 2003. This outlines the benefits for employers who can gain competitive advantages if they are able to recruit from 'the widest possible talent pool' and reminds the reader that businesses taking a positive approach to diversity are likely to be more innovative and have a more positive public image.

In practice, it is arguable whether some of the language and practices traditionally associated with EO have been erased, even in organisations that subscribe wholeheartedly to a diversity approach. There are many examples of organisations that both 'value equality and promote diversity'. This is reflected in the statements in the recruitment advertisements of a number of organisations – for example, the NCH's strapline: 'committed to quality, equality and valuing diversity', and Bexley Council: 'committed to promoting equality and diversity in its employment and service delivery'. The University of Westminster's diversity mission, meanwhile, explicitly involves 'embracing diversity and promoting equality'.

The management of equality and diversity

Kandola and Fullerton (1998: 72–73) provide a useful summary of 11 models for MO. Integrating the best elements of these models, they suggest, results in a strategy web in which each element impacts on all. In this somewhat idealistic state, top management are committed to an organisational vision – there is auditing of needs and an evaluation of progress; effective co-ordination and communication; and clear accountability and objectives. They go on to describe an organisation that is orientated towards diversity and has reached a state where well-managed, valued diversity has become a reality.

M
O
S
A
I
C

where the organisation's:

Mission and values embrace diversity as a key business objective;

where processes which impact on people are

Objective and fair;

where employees understand and are aware of the needs of diversity, and are

Skilled in applying their knowledge and commitment;

where there is

Active flexibility, both in working patterns and in the application of practices in order to meet diverse needs;

where the focus is on

Individuals, not groups;

and, finally, where the

Culture encourages participation and encourages and enables the use of contributions from all staff at all levels.

This model echoes the ten-point plan advocated by the Commission for Racial Equality in its online guidance (www.cre.gov.uk) and has some resonance with change management models, some of which are explored in *Change Architecture* (Carnall, 2003: Chapter 13).

Diversity has relevance in a range of HR processes:

- recruitment and selection
- induction
- training and development
- promotion
- appraisal
- pay and conditions of employment
- harassment, grievances and discipline
- dismissal
- redundancy.

One of the central principles is the need to formalise procedures, to be systematic, transparent and objective, in what are often intrinsically subjective processes. This applies particularly to recruitment and selection, where employers are advised to use objective, competency-based, justifiable, job-related criteria; accompanying job descriptions, person specifications and standard application forms should contain only directly relevant questions. It is hoped that the avoidance of word of mouth recruitment, together with positive attempts to recruit from all sections of the community, will help to widen the pool of applicants and provide a potentially more diverse workforce. Panel interviews using agreed criteria, and trained, aware interviewers, should lead to decisions based on competency rather than acceptability.

There is also a need to have well-communicated policies and procedures to deal with instances of discriminatory or anti-diversity behaviour. Expected standards of behaviour should be clear, and every member of the organisation must be made aware both of how to behave appropriately, and what action to take if they face abuse or harassment.

Unfortunately, the existence alone of policies and procedures is insufficient to bring about a change in diversity or to ensure that an organisation can reap its benefits. Other elements must also be present – top management commitment, evaluation and monitoring and diversity as a business objective.

There is no doubt, however, that the rhetoric sometimes belies the reality. A range of stakeholders play their part in achieving diversity:

- senior managers
- trade unions and trade unionists
- line managers
- individual employees
- customers and suppliers.

We are discussing here the creation of an organisational culture which values diversity and this may rely on a shift in attitudes and examination of underlying values. The challenge to the HR practitioner may be to manage the procedural and management changes, while at the same time creating an environment which challenges attitudes and encourages development.

The future

pause for thought

Imagine you had a crystal ball and could see into the future. What might it look like in relation to diversity? Please consider the following questions in your answer and explain your reasoning:

- Will equality and diversity continue to be areas of concern for HR managers in the twenty-first century?
- Will those from ethnic minority groups, women and people with disabilities remain disadvantaged in the labour market – or will the glass ceiling be smashed forever?
- Will employers remove all the barriers that result in disabled people being absent from many areas of the workforce?
- Will employers continue to discriminate on grounds of age and disability?

We do not know how the future will be, but your answers may tell you something about your own values and perception.

There are, however, a few certainties. The population is ageing, the service sector is growing, markets are continuing to globalise, and society is becoming increasingly disparate.

The skills needed in this globalised, service economy – namely, enhanced interpersonal competency and emotional intelligence – may be key to effectiveness. There are those who would argue that the future has a female bias – that women are more suited than men to modern organisations. Research undertaken by the International Labour Organisation in 2001 found that attributes that have traditionally been associated with women are being increasingly recognised and valued (Wirth, 2001). Tracking companies in the FTSE 100 between 1980 and 1998 reveals a direct correlation between a company's profits and the number of senior female executives in its ranks.

The debate about gender differences, about the nature of those differences, and explanations for them, will continue. Regardless of whether the future needs of the UK economy will favour women over men, it is likely that the ability to communicate effectively will become an increasingly important skill.

The eradication of discrimination and the removal of inequality is an ideal that is unlikely to be completely realised – people will continue to hold prejudices, and to perceive and behave imperfectly. Hopefully, however, organisations will begin to meet the challenges and opportunities presented by multiculturalism, and the workplace of the future will draw on the many benefits to be gained from employing people with different perspectives and different backgrounds. It will be those organisations that truly embrace diversity and multi-culturalism that will have the most promising future.

- ◆ How far do you think Warbings' corporate culture allows for the management of diversity?
- ◆ What aspects of the organisation's people management approach might prove to be obstacles to effective diversity management?

Summary

People are different and understanding the implications of this diversity is central to human resource management (HRM). Socialisation can sometimes create stereotypes, which may lead us to make assumptions based on a person's gender, race, age, etc. Acknowledging our prejudices can help us to find ways of overcoming them.

Patterns in the labour market often reflect this inequality. Certain groups are liable to face disadvantage either in certain occupations or at higher levels within organisations. *Positive action* may be one way of starting to challenge these patterns, by providing training and development to under-represented groups.

This chapter discussed two approaches to understanding and combating prejudice and discrimination – exploring the legal framework for combating discrimination alongside the business case for MD. The legislation is based on a principle that it is unfair to discriminate in employment on any grounds that are irrelevant to the job. The case for valuing diversity, on the other hand, recommends that employers take a more positive approach if they are to recruit and retain the widest range of talent.

There are a number of models for managing diversity and success may require a shift in attitudes as well as the introduction of formal procedures in HRM. For many employers this could involve a radical change in organisational culture, in which HR practitioners will play a key role.

Review Questions

You may wish to attempt the following as practice examination style questions.

14.1 Distinguish between the primary and secondary factors that influence individuals and give examples of each.

14.2 Give an explanation of occupational segregation.

14.3 Describe the differences between 'EO' and 'MD' and clarify how these two approaches might have different impacts on the organisations using them.

14.4 List the areas in HRM where diversity is relevant, and in each case say why it is so.

14.5 Why is it important to address individual perceptions and assumptions when introducing diversity training into an organisation?

14.6 What is ethnocentricism?

14.7 Give details of the legislation that you think has an impact on the ways in which organisations manage diversity.

References

Anker, R. (2001). *Gender and Jobs: Sex Segregation of Occupations in the World*, 2nd edition, Geneva: International Labour Office.

Arnold, J., Cooper, C.L. and Robertson, I.T. (1995). *Work Psychology*, 2nd edition, London: Pitman.

Bandura, A. (1986). *Social Foundations of Thought and Action: A Social Cognitive Theory*, Englewood Cliffs, NJ: Prentice Hall.

Bodenhausen, G. (1988). Stereotypic biases in social decision-making and memory: testing process models of stereotype use, *Journal of Personality and Social Psychology*, Vol. 55, No. 5, pp. 726–737.

Carnall, C. (2003). *Managing Change in Organisations*, 4th edition, Englewood Cliffs, NJ: Prentice Hall.

Clements, P. and Jones, J. (2006). *The Diversity Training Handbook*, 2nd edition, London: Kogan Page.

Clements, P. and Spinks, T. (2006). *The Equal Opportunities Handbook*, 4th edition, London: Kogan Page.

CRE (2005). *Why Ethnic Minority Workers Leave London's Print Journalism Sector*, London: Commission for Racial Equality.

DTI (2003). *Business Case for Diversity and Equality*, Women and Equality Unit, London: Stationery Office.

Epstein, C.F. (1973). Positive effects of the multiple negative: explaining the success of black professional women, *American Journal of Sociology*, Vol. 78, No. 4, pp. 912–935.

Frenkiel, N. (1984). The Up-and-Comers: Bryant Takes Aim At the Settlers-In, Adweek Special Report, *Magazine World*, March.

Giddens, A. (1993). *Sociology*, Cambridge: Polity Press.

Guirdham, M. (1996). *Interpersonal Skills at Work*, 2nd edition, Englewood Cliffs, NJ: Prentice Hall.

Kandola, R. and Fullerton, J. (1998). *Diversity in Action: Managing the Mosaic*, 2nd edition, London: IPD.

Kennedy, J. and Everest, A. (1991). Putting diversity into context, *Personnel Journal*, September, pp. 50–54.

Kirton, G. and Greene, A.-M. (2000). *The Dynamics of Managing Diversity: A Critical Approach*, Oxford: Butterworth-Heinemann.

Kohlberg, L. (1966). A cognitive-developmental analysis of children's sex-role concepts and attitudes, in E. Maccoby (ed.) *The Development of Sex Differences*, London: Tavistock.

Kolb, D.A., Rubin I.M. and McIntyre, J.M. (1971). *Organisational Psychology*, Englewood Cliffs, NJ: Prentice Hall.

Lai Wai-Fong (2001). *Equality and Excellence: The Business Case*, London: Business in the Community.

Learning and Skills Council (2005). Further education, work based learning for young people and adult and community learning – learner numbers in England 2004/05, ILR/SFR08, at: www.apprenticeships.org.uk/partners/frameworks/apprenticeshipsdata/reports20042005/report2.htm.

Loden, M. (1996). *Implementing Diversity*, Burr Ridge, IL: Irwin Professional Publishers.

Mischel, W. (1966). A social-learning view of sex differences in behavior, in E. Maccoby (ed.) *The Development of Sex Differences*, London: Tavistock.

Ritzer, G. and Goodman, D. (2004). *Modern Sociological Theory*, 6th edition, New York: McGraw-Hill.

Ross, L. and Nisbett, R.E. (1991). *The Person and the Situation*, New York: McGraw-Hill.

Singh, V. and Vinnicombe, S. (2005). *The Female FTSE Index 2005*, Cranfield: Cranfield School of Management.

Stangor, C. (2003). *Social Groups in Action and Interaction*, New York: Psychology Press.

Straw, J. (1989). *Equal Opportunities: The Way Ahead*, London: IPM.

Tajfel, H. (1981). *Human Groups and Social Categories*, p. 369, Cambridge: Cambridge University Press.

Wirth, L. (2001). *Breaking Through the Glass Ceiling – Women in Management*, Geneva: International Labour Office.

Recommended Reading

CIPD (2005). *Managing Diversity: People Make the Difference at Work – But Everyone is Different*, London: CIPD.

Daniels, K. and MacDonald, L. (2005). *Equality Diversity and Discrimination*, London: CIPD.

IDS Study 719 (2001). *Promoting Racial Equality*, London: IDS. See also the IDS journal, *Equal Opportunities at Work*.

Kirton, G. and Greene, A.-M. (2004). *The Dynamics of Managing Diversity: A Critical Approach*, 2nd edition, Oxford: Butterworth-Heinemann.

Rubery, J. (2002). Gender mainstreaming and gender equality in the EU: the impact of the EU employment strategy, *Industrial Relations Journal*, Vol. 33, No. 5, pp. 500–519.

Tipper, J. (2004). How to increase diversity through your recruitment practices, *Industrial and Commercial Training*, Vol. 36, No. 4, pp. 158–161.

Useful Websites

www.eoc.org.uk – focus on guidance, advice (e.g. on avoiding gender discrimination), legal implications (including EU dimension), research and recommendations from the Equal Opportunities Commission

www.opportunitynow.org.uk – website of Opportunity Now, a membership organisation representing employers who want to transform the workplace by ensuring inclusiveness for women – guidance on benchmarking, legal issues, good practice, exemplar employers and news items

www.cre.gov.uk – website of Commission of Racial Equality, with wide range of guidance reports, recommendations and research on equality and diversity issues

www.drc.gov.uk – access to guidance, e.g. employers' duties, individual rights, advice on discriminatory practices focused on the central aim of 'a society where all disabled people can participate fully as equal citizens', from the Disability Rights Commission

www.croner.cch.co.uk – access to Croner (commercial service) business compliance information and services, including news reports and practical guides

www.dti.gov.uk – the Department of Trade and Industry website covers equality and diversity policy and initiatives, e.g. countering age discrimination in employment

www.statistics.gov.uk – statistics on population composition/changes and economic activity from the government's National Statisical Office

www.cipd.co.uk – access to the Chartered Institute of Personnel and Development information, reports and recommendations on equality and diversity, e.g. the CIPD Position Paper on Diversity (1996)

www.womenandequalityunit.gov.uk/publications/ FTSE_report_2003.doc (and 2004) – access to government and other publications with a focus on women in work

www.tuc,org.uk/extras/disabledjobs.com – Trade Union Congress advice and help for those with disabilities

Part contents

CHAPTER 15

Training and Learning

By David Simmonds

Chapter outline

This chapter examines the organisational structure, strategies and work processes that have implications for the ways that organisational and individual training and learning occur. It examines specific training initiatives in wider organisational contexts and looks at how training and learning can aid planned change in an organisation's internal and external environments.

Learning outcomes

By the end of this chapter, you should be able to:

◆ Explain the practical implications of organisational goals on training and learning;
◆ Explain current and future performance problems and their training implications;
◆ Understand the responsibility of the training and learning function in addressing skills imbalances;
◆ Evaluate models and roles of training and learning.

Introduction

The area of learning and training at work is both vast and fast-changing. In this chapter, we can only explore some of the more fundamental issues. It is also important to remember that – as a learner – you need to take responsibility for your own learning! Further reading and links to websites will help you to explore this fascinating area.

The chapter has been structured to help you gain an insight into the immense area of learning at work. It begins by exploring the important relationship between training and change. It then looks at some of the organisational characteristics that pertain to training. Models of strategic human resource development (SHRD) are analysed. Finally, the future of training and learning is investigated.

Change: managing it or making it happen?

Change is here to stay! The only thing we can know for sure is that tomorrow is likely to be different from yesterday. This is true for our families, our friends and ourselves. It is certain that there will be changes in our workgroups, our departments and our organisations. There has always been change, since the beginning of time.

What alarms many of us is the phenomenal **rate** of such change. It often seems that we are rushing out of control, as if somebody else has got their foot on the accelerator. There probably has been more change in your lifetime than all the other changes in the history of civilisation put together. We are all in a constant state of change. Literature on the subject seems to suggest that there are two basic forms of change – incremental change and transformational change:

- **Incremental change** often happens slowly or in small stages. Little steps lead eventually to big changes. Let's take an example from the retail sector in the last five years. A shop I know had always sold music cassette tapes. Gradually, they started selling CDs and videos as well. Now, they are introducing DVDs, and since they sell so few audiocassettes these days, these are being withdrawn. Soon, no doubt, they will stop selling videos as well.

- **Transformational change**, on the other hand, usually happens fairly quickly. The build-up to it can – and should – take quite a while, and the subsequent implementation can take place over an extended period. But the change itself is so radical that it is introduced relatively quickly. One example happened at a university. The new vice chancellor wanted to streamline the administrative systems and arrangements. He commissioned some outside consultants to advise the senior management team. Within a very short period of time, through a process known as 'rewiring', the administrative staff were moved from the familiar teams that were previously formed under programme leaders and associated with particular academic programmes. These professional administrators were summarily – and compulsorily – 'reallocated' into new departmental and cross-functional groupings on either an undergraduate or postgraduate basis. The administrators, academics and students alike found the new systems very difficult to operate.

So, what are some of the essential components of change processes, and what are the links to training and learning?

Learning may occur through:

- teaching
- studying
- discussing
- observing
- experiencing
- practising
- committing to memory . . . or not!

Training, on the other hand, facilitates learning directed towards job *performance* and can modify knowledge, skills and attitudes. Training focuses upon *implementation*

– doing things to the required standard; *improvement* – doing things to a new standard; and *innovation* – doing new things.

If training and learning are to do with performance at work, then **performance standards** should identify: the task; the performance criteria; range indicators; and evidence. **Competency** statements outline the ability to perform the activities, within an occupational area, to the levels of performance expected in employment. For example, below are the competencies of an HR practitioner in the area of resourcing and recruitment:

◆ Design, deliver and evaluate changes to organisational structure;

◆ Contribute to the design, delivery and evaluation of work procedures;

◆ Design, deliver and evaluate recruitment procedures;

◆ Design, deliver and evaluate selection procedures;

◆ Design, deliver and evaluate employee reward and benefits procedures;

◆ Design, deliver and evaluate employee support procedures;

◆ Design, deliver and evaluate the delivery of personnel procedures in international contexts (www.i-l-m.com/qualifications/specialist0/level0.ilm).

HR managers clearly have a responsibility for training, but why should individuals and their employers undertake training and development? Here are some reasons for training:

◆ Achieving full job performance;

◆ Development of employee potential;

◆ Improved morale;

◆ Improved quality;

◆ Greater customer satisfaction;

◆ Less waste of resources;

◆ Better utilisation of resources;

◆ Reduced cost and increased productivity;

◆ Reduced need for supervision.

How can we ensure that training is successful?
  To succeed, training must:

◆ Be the appropriate solution to the problem;

◆ Have the support of management and the individual;

◆ Meet correctly identified needs;

◆ Be carried out in an environment favourable to learning.

Organisations wishing to carry out an audit on their training systems should consider a number of questions to ensure that they are relating training with business results:

◆ Is your training linked to your strategic decisions and business goals?

◆ Is it supported by strong leadership?

- ◆ Does it reflect the needs and values of your customers?
- ◆ Does it communicate your organisation's values?
- ◆ Does it help you address customer retention, acquisition, lower costs, less waste, higher speed and greater innovation?
- ◆ Does it build on the core principles of learning?
- ◆ Is it immediately relevant to your organisation?
- ◆ Can you clearly map an individual's path toward human resource development and human resource managements mastery?
- ◆ Does the environment empower employees to use what they learn?
- ◆ Does it lead to measurable results?

Once these questions are answered to the satisfaction of all major stakeholders, then not only will learning take place but both the organisation and the individual will benefit from it.

Systematic training

What is the best way to get started with training and learning? This is the systematic approach to training:

- ◆ **Examine** – identify training needs at the organisational, team and individual levels;
- ◆ **Plan** – plan and design training to meet these needs;
- ◆ **Do** – implement the training plan effectively;
- ◆ **Review** – assess the results of the training.

See Figure 15.1.

This widely reported model is unfortunately not widely implemented. Many organisations often merely repeat previously designed programmes with little or no thought to their relevance, applicability or value.

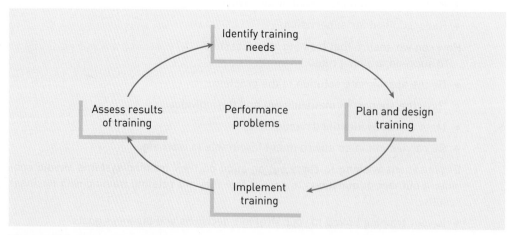

Figure 15.1 Systematic training

Human resource development and human resource management

There has been much discussion (Stewart and McGoldrick, 1996; Simmonds, 2003) concerning the relationship between HRM and HRD. The management of people at work must necessarily include their development. Figure 15.2 is an illustration of the links between HRM and HRD. It shows the various roles and responsibilities of the HRM manager, including the activities normally associated with HRD.

There is no one universally accepted model of the relationship between HRM and HRD. Figure 15.2 illustrates one view of this. McLagan's model (1989) acknowledges the existence of both HRM and HRD. The developmental aspects of the human resource

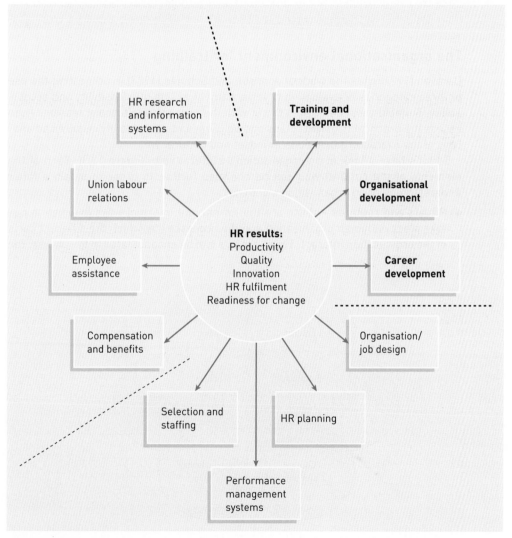

Figure 15.2 A representation of the HR wheel
Source: McLagan (1989)

(HR) function are clearly highlighted in bold, and their links with other aspects of the role of the HR practitioner, and the HR outcomes which should result can be discerned. McLagan has pointed out (1989) that, 'HRD must be the strategic partner with the business in all of the eleven areas of the HR wheel'. If the organisation is going to achieve its strategic objectives, HRD implications of any change need to be given serious consideration at an early stage. The alternative point of view, discussed in Chapter 3, would be that HR is the business partner, of which HRD is a subsidiary function.

exercise

- ◆ **Think about an organisation known to you. How would you describe the relationship between HRM and HRD?**
- ◆ **What is the relationship between HRD and organisational objectives?**

The organisational environment for training

Garavan (1991) cites the work of Johnson and Scholes (1993) in advocating the use of three categories of evaluation criteria, namely: suitability, feasibility and acceptability. Suitability will determine the fit with the organisation's goals; feasibility can assess the practicality of HRD plans and policies; and acceptability requires an analysis of the overall organisational mindset and cultural web.

So let's have a look at an organisation's cultural web (Figure 15.3). Each of the elements of the cultural web can be analysed further in order to obtain a fuller understanding of an organisation's culture:

- ◆ **Rituals and routines** – these are the formal and informal ways in which things take place within an organisation and the processes by which the different parts of the organisation interact. These aspects can be encapsulated in the phrase 'the

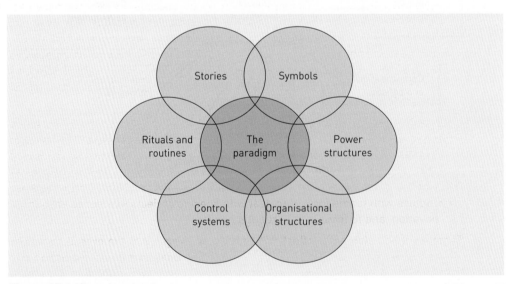

Figure 15.3 The cultural web
Source: Johnson and Scholes (1993: 61)

way we do things around here'. For example, in an organisation like a local authority, much emphasis is placed upon formal committees and their minutes, as well as rituals such as ceremonies and elections.

◆ **Stories** – these are told about the major events and personalities, past and present, and become embedded in organisational 'folklore'. Through constant repetition, stories reflect those aspects of an organisation that people within it see as being particularly important. For example, in a local football club, the stories of heroes passed from one generation to another may be of the great players who typified a style of game where entertainment was seen as more important than results.

◆ **Symbols** – these can indicate who and what is seen to be important within the organisation. Things like the design of offices, the award of company cars and the use of titles can all point to the way in which the organisation views itself. For example, in one hierarchical multinational oil company, a newly appointed manager was given an office with two doors, though his position warranted only one. It took the carpenters less than 24 hours to block off the 'surplus' door!

◆ **Control systems** – the measurement and reward systems are likely to reflect aspects of organisational activity that it is important to monitor or encourage, even if strategy documents, or the chairperson's statements, may stress other issues. The extent of these systems can also indicate how much management within the organisation is centralised or devolved. For example, within most UK universities, academics are expected to engage in teaching, administration and research, but as promotion is largely based on the quantity of an individual's research publications, many feel the 'real' priority lies in this one area.

◆ **Power structures** – indicate which individuals comprise the most important groups within the organisation, the people who take the decisions. The importance of these groups and individuals might not be immediately apparent from the formal organisational structure, so there needs to be an awareness of informal networks. Such power might come from seniority or particular expertise. For example, within the UK electricity generation industry, engineers traditionally had a more prominent role than in other organisations and the priorities of the companies involved reflected this emphasis on engineering. Since privatisation, priorities that are more commercial seem to be reflected in the changing backgrounds of key decision makers.

◆ **Organisational structure** – this is likely to reflect the way that the organisation works, as well as its power structures and important relationships. The levels of hierarchy, the decision-making bodies and what is discussed within them, as well as the information flowing within the structure, will all point towards the priorities of the organisation. For example, an advertising agency may well have a flat structure with teams formed to deal with specific projects in order to encourage innovation, and to focus on the client's needs.

Together these elements reflect and provide an insight into the overall paradigm (at the centre of the Johnson and Scholes' (1993) model) that drives the day-to-day actions of organisational life. Furthermore, the cultural web highlights the way in which the corporate culture is reflected in the formal and informal elements of the organisation. Lying as it does at the centre, the paradigm also tends to preserve and reinforce the key of the cultural web, and this has important implications for managing strategic elements.

It is important therefore to use the web to analyse an organisation's culture so that the implications for training and learning can be ascertained. It is particularly helpful when identifying and analysing training needs. Moreover, it is useful to apply the cultural web to an organisation before, during and after a major organisational change in order to map the ways that the change is affecting different aspects of the organisation. This can offer pointers to the learning that has taken place – and that still needs to take place.

pause for thought

Think of an organisation that you know well. How have the stories that you know about the organisation influenced the ways that you think about it?

In order to be able to identify the importance of training and learning to the success of an organisation, let's look at this example from Marks & Spencer.

Mini case study: Change and learning at Marks & Spencer

The major UK retailer Marks & Spencer has, over time, developed an unusual relationship with its clothing suppliers. It has a huge market share, accounting for about a third of all sales in its sector and has accomplished an enviable reputation for its sophisticated supply chain activities. Courtaulds is one of the top four suppliers to Marks & Spencer. There are a number of key stages in the contracting process:

1. A pre-production contract to the supplier authorising the purchase of raw materials.

2. The full contract, including cost prices.

3. A series of 'alterations to order' with colour and ratio requirements.

This contract management system was integrated with the product development process. However, requests for stock to be distributed to stores was managed separately. This caused problems for both parties. The supplier took most of the risk and bore the cost of maintaining stock in the warehouses and for discounting, or disposing of stock, that did not sell. Moreover, Marks & Spencer would suddenly cancel orders on a range of items in the middle of production. It caused significant problems and involved considerable cost.

Clearly, by 1991 change was needed. After much discussion at Courtaulds, people agreed that the abrupt changes in demand was not because of the fluctuations in the market place, but because the merchandisers in Marks & Spencer were unable to forecast the demand. Courtaulds proposed that, in exchange for a continual feed of sales and stock information from Marks & Spencer, the supplier would adjust their production schedules in line with sales and would assume responsibility for replenishment.

This led to innovations in the supply chain relationship that worked well in the early 1990s. However, by 1997, there were signs that the solutions were no longer effective. A number of factors led to another major crisis: a complete internal reorganisation at the clothing giant;

the launch of 'collections'; offshoring production by the supplier; and an extra six weeks lead time. By 2001, sales volumes were halved and profits reduced.

Eventually, Marks & Spencer started its own investigation. Because the initiative came from within the organisation, it had the advantage of top-level sponsorship. Despite this, even these innovations have so far only experienced partial take-up. Many buying departments are still sceptical of their value. The newly created system is rather less advanced than the one abandoned a couple of years previously. It is a web-based service, rather than feeding the data directly to the supplier as previously. However, Marks & Spencer is now relearning the importance of co-operating with its suppliers. Partnership had been largely abandoned from the late 1990s until 2002. It is now very much a part of the current strategy. The streaming of strategic sourcing is now a joint decision.

Many of the Marks & Spencer merchandisers had become complacent, and accustomed to buying from salespeople without having to consider supply issues. Short-term 'macho-style' recruits to these positions seemed to approach the role with overconfidence and aggression. Managers within the company had also become insular. They were recruited at a young age and stayed within the organisation. Company routines and procedures were deeply entrenched. Staff found it very difficult to accept that change was necessary – or to see what different approaches might look like. There was a very strong devotion to traditional methods that had previously brought great success.

(Adapted from Storey et al., 2005)

The Marks & Spencer case reveals considerable resistance to learning. How many examples can you find?

exercise

Strategic HRD (SHRD)

Commentators have examined the theoretical issues surrounding the role of HRD in organisational strategic planning. Torraco and Swanson (1995) point out that HRD not only plays a strategic role by assuring the competency of employees to meet the performance demands of the organisation, but also serves the additional function of helping to shape business strategy. They suggest that HRD has been a key enabling force in strategies based on product innovation, quality and cost leadership, customised service, or global relocation based on workforce skills. They also argue for the strategy-supporting and strategy-shaping roles of HRD, considering the use of HRD to support business objectives. They examine the relationship between HRD, expertise and strategy, and HRD as a shaper of strategy. In addition, they look at the need for the adoption of a SHRD perspective. Torraco and Swanson highlight the distinctive features of the strategic roles of HRD, which are evident in the business practices of successful organisations, and illustrate these roles with examples from some of today's most innovative companies.

Various organisations value training and development differently. In many organisations, training is implemented, at best, on only an *ad hoc* basis, whereas at the other extreme some organisations fully embrace the learning and development function at a strategic level (McCracken and Wallace, 2000: 434). Figure 15.4 illustrates the various ways that training and development may be viewed and valued in an organisation. On the left, training is only seen in an *ad hoc* or supporting role. The middle model shows HRD as having a mainly reactive supporting role. And finally, on the right, SHRD is valued as having a strong proactive, shaping role. From these different viewpoints, you can contrast the three different kinds of focus; the relative maturity of the organisation; nine diverse aspects of the extent to which training is integrated within the organisation; and the relative strength of the learning culture.

As we can see from Figure 15.4, it is possible to distinguish not only the marked differences between training, HRD and SHRD, but also the paradigms that reflect different types of focus, levels of HRD maturity and strength of learning culture. For SHRD to become a reality, the organisation needs to empower the HRD function to adopt a proactive approach in relation to corporate strategy (Walton, 1999).

To contrast with the model by McCracken and Wallace, Figure 15.5 is that of Stewart and McGoldrick (1996). There are a number of differences between these two models. By critically utilising a number of separate parameters, we can now proceed to formulate an assessment of these two different models of SHRD.

Analysing models of SHRD

Deliberate or emergent?

There is some debate as to whether strategy is deliberate or emergent. Stewart and McGoldrick's model (Figure 15.5) suggests that strategy is deliberate and is the result of analysis, which leads to the development of organisational plans in a linear fashion. McCracken and Wallace, on the other hand, argue that strategy emerges from, at times, unrelated and *ad hoc* decisions as a result of compromise and competing interests. Resource-based strategy (as discussed in Chapter 3), on the other hand, focuses on internal competencies in order to gain competitive advantage. In this approach, HRD becomes a more prominent feature of all HRM activities.

Burgoyne's typology (Stewart 1999) of organisational maturity

In Stewart and McGoldrick's model (1999), HRD is driven by the corporate strategy. It is reactive and can be placed at Level 4 of Burgoyne's (1992) typology of the learning organisation:

- **Level 1** – no systematic HRD development;
- **Level 2** – isolated tactical HRD;
- **Level 3** – integrated and co-ordinated structural HRD;
- **Level 4** – an HRD strategy to implement corporate policy;
- **Level 5** – HRD strategy input to corporate policy formulation;
- **Level 6** – strategic development of the management of corporate policy;
- **Level 7** – strategic leverage of learning and development processes to enhance the core competences of the organisation.

However, in McCracken and Wallace's model, HRD also informs and shapes corporate strategy, and can therefore be placed at the highest point of sophistication and maturity – Level 7 of the typology.

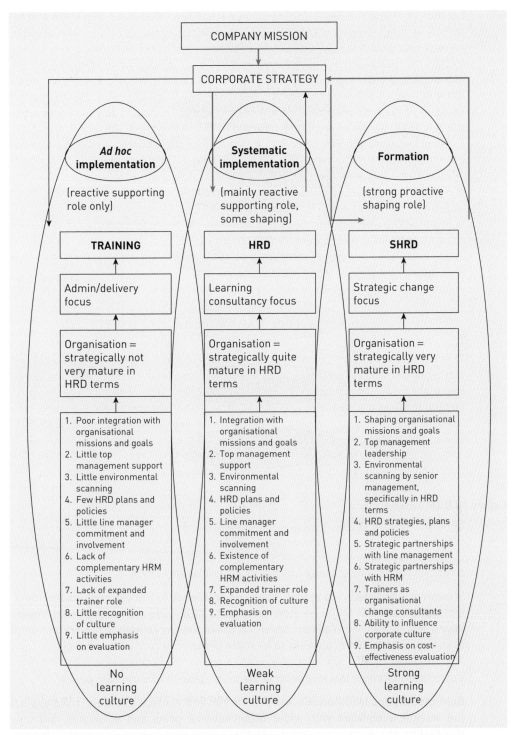

Figure 15.4 Three separate views of the ways in which learning can be aligned with organisational strategy

Source: McCraken and Wallace (2000: 434)

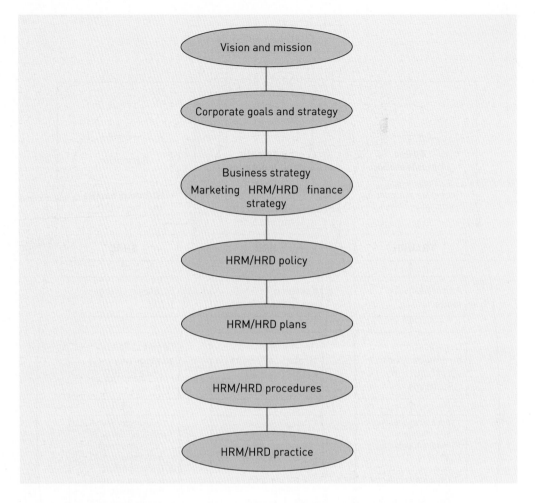

Figure 15.5 HRD model
Source: Stewart and McGoldrick (1996)

External focus for strategy (Johnson and Scholes, 1993)

Stewart and McGoldrick's model makes no reference to the external environment, indicating that HRD might be slow to respond to outside transformational imperatives. McCracken and Wallace conversely make specific reference to environmental scanning. Such a model appears to be more dynamic in relation to change.

Vertical and horizontal integration (Guest, 2002)

Both Stewart and McGoldrick's and McCracken and Wallace's models make explicit the vertical integration with wider organisational goals and strategies, but only McCracken and Wallace's model takes the further step towards horizontal integration with other HRM initiatives. Nevertheless, both Storey (2001) and Harrison (2005) question whether horizontal integration can in fact exist in practice.

Pettigrew's (1982) typology of trainer roles

With Stewart and McGoldrick's model, it can be assumed that the trainer would adopt the role of 'manager' – planning and co-ordinating the training processes and allocating training resources – according to Pettigrew's (1982) typology. Garavan (1991) proposes Pettigrew's 'innovator' or 'consultant' roles, whereas McCracken and Wallace's model goes further in advocating that the trainer adopts the 'change agent' role, where the focus is squarely upon organisational problem solving through learning and development. This appears to be supported by Walton (1999), who observes that the trainer must be able to communicate effectively at the highest levels of the organisation.

Ownership

While Stewart and McGoldrick advocate that HRD practitioners take ownership of the organisation's learning and development, McCracken and Wallace make specific reference to the need for a strategic partnership with line managers. As a result, key stakeholders share in the ownership and implementation of HRD. In this way, the learning and development function becomes embedded in the culture of the organisation as a whole rather than being possessed by the training department.

Lewin's (1951) model of organisational change

McCracken and Wallace clearly see a role for learning and development in the process of organisational change in order to prevent cultural drift into former patterns and practices, whereas Stewart and McGoldrick make no mention of the importance of HRD in influencing corporate culture.

Evaluation and feedback

Overlooking the need for evaluation or feedback, Stewart and McGoldrick imply that training and development is seen as a cost or a luxury rather than as an investment in the long-term prospects of the organisation. McCracken and Wallace, though, refer explicitly to the need for an evaluation of cost-effectiveness. This should focus not only on pay-back investment to achieve short-term tangible results, but also on pay-forward investment to accomplish longer-term intangible results, as proposed by Lee (1996). The rational, linear nature of Stewart and McGoldrick's model allows no feedback into corporate strategy. The forming and shaping function of HRD, as illustrated by McCracken and Wallace, provides the necessary opportunities for continuous improvement and development. They argue against Garavan (1991), who posits a reactive or responsive view of HRD, in so far as it contributes to organisational objectives and is aware of the organisational mission. Their analysis is nearer that of Torraco and Swanson (1995), in that they see HRD as having a role that is pivotal, proactive and strategic.

Unitary or pluralistic approach

Both Stewart and McGoldrick's and McCracken and Wallace's models assume a unilateral approach to organisational mission and vision, and that everyone in the organisation is working towards its achievement. Both models appear to ignore the reality that all organisations comprise a range of individuals working towards a variety of goals, that may be tangential to those of their employer.

Generic or specific considerations

Stewart and McGoldrick present a generic model that could easily be applied to any one of a number of organisational functions, such as marketing, finance or purchasing, while McCracken and Wallace's representation is exclusively HRD orientated.

Summary

It may appear that in effect Stewart and McGoldrick's model is not actually strategic but more operational in approach. Their primary characteristics are, in reality, difficult to achieve. These models lack detail in terms of practical implementation or application. I would therefore recommend instead Walton's (1999) model, where there is an explicit commitment to learning in the organisation's mission and core values. It is supported by corresponding systems, policies, resources, partners, sponsors and stewards. Such collective and collaborative learning produces innovation, creativity, strategic awareness and enhanced job performance. Inevitably, this leads to improved customer satisfaction. Walton insists that learning and development must form a foundational, and holistic, business process rather than being an accidental or tangential postscript.

All these approaches demonstrate the need for the training and development of employees to be undertaken not just on an organisation-wide basis, but also for SHRD to be central to the organisation's accomplishment of its strategic plan. As it addresses its plans in a cycle of continuous improvement, so SHRD will also change and adapt.

---

pause for thought

To what extent do you think training needs to be undertaken on an organisation-wide basis?

So what has all of this to say to us about the way we work, and about the places where we are employed? Well, there is a fundamental connection between work, learning and change. So, let's examine the nature of change in the workplace.

The future of learning at work

Stewart and Tansley (2002: 32) propose a future role for trainers with almost evangelistic zeal:

> 'A key role of the training function in the future will be in the support of knowledge management initiatives and social capital construction. Training specialists need to be involved in disseminating the message throughout the organisation that attempts to manage organisational knowledge must be founded on an understanding of how people learn, how they implement what they learn, and how they share their knowledge.'

They continue:

> 'The building of social capital, a widening client base and the support of knowledge management all imply a shift from the role of training provider to one of learning facilitator. This in turn suggests the need for the adoption of new teaching methodologies in fulfilling the new role of the training function. [. . .] In other words, how training and development are delivered becomes more important than what is delivered. [. . .] Training processes rather than content, then, are more significant in developing the ability to learn, and should therefore be the primary focus.'

So, what are some of the important functions of effective training? Lynton and Pareek (2000) outline three such functions that are less well recognised than that of conducting training sessions: providing guidance and support through, for example, mentoring; helping to design and implement organisational change strategies, through, say, coaching in the workplace; and the leadership, managerial and administrative aspects of preparing an entire training programme.

In a more restricted sense, Burack et al. (1997) look at how the role of management development (MD) is also changing as organisations increasingly merge their strategic goals with HR planning goals, in order to involve staffing and development. They assert that this new pattern of MD focuses on enhancing an organisation's effectiveness while maintaining competitive advantage. They consider the influence that MD has on performance improvement, examining the features of MD approaches adopted by the more successful organisations. Burack et al. (ibid.) propose the application of core competencies and the relationship between these and strategic MD. These writers introduce a general core competency model that reflects the integration of business strategy and HR practices through the progressive building of competencies and their alignment to specific jobs. For a fuller discussion of these issues, refer to Chapter 16.

Such an approach has been developed still further by Noel and Dennehy (1991), who present us with six steps for the introduction of HRD in an organisation:

1. The development of a focused strategic approach.

2. Involvement of top management.

3. The 'refocusing' of course content.

4. The development of 'impactful' learning methods (e.g. action learning).

5. Focused participation of the employees who can provide significant difference.

6. The provision of a learning atmosphere.

They believe that adherence to these steps will help the HRD professional become a significant force for transforming the organisation. This could be very important for most organisations, including those in the public and voluntary sectors.

Sawdon (1999) traces three broad development paths for trainers in the future:

◆ From training to consulting;

◆ From training to learning;

◆ From individual change to organisational change.

Sawdon then arrives at four approaches to training and consultancy:

1. Trainer.
2. Training consultant.
3. Learning consultant.
4. Organisational change consultant.

pause for thought

How do you see the future roles for trainers and developers?

How do trainers themselves describe their roles? Darling and her colleagues (1999) find that, in practice, people describe the roles they carry out in training in one of three broad categories. Table 15.1 summarises their views.

Training roles, and their description, have changed over time. Summarising much of the literature on trainer roles over the past three decades, Walton (1999: 165) provides a most helpful synopsis of the scope and development of trainer roles in this country and the US since the 1970s. In Table 15.2 he offers a useful comparison of traditional and emergent functions.

One of the roles in which trainers can have a major impact is in helping employers to begin the journey towards becoming a learning organisation. Hoffman and Withers (1995: 472) tabulate their comparison (Table 15.3) of traditional training with the learning organisation.

Table 15.1 Trainer roles

Philosophical	Strategic	Operational
◆ Moderniser	◆ Facilitator at organisational level	◆ Facilitator at personal and team level
◆ Stabiliser of chaos		
◆ Creator/supporter of an innovative culture	◆ Integrator	◆ Direct trainer
◆ Leader/supporter of the vision/champion	◆ Internal advisor – organisational development	◆ Internal advisor – personal development
◆ Surfacer of myths and assumptions	◆ Organisational 'confidant(e)'	◆ Coach/mentor
◆ Banner carrier (in conjunction with HR)	◆ Interpreter of people implications of changes in the business	◆ Modeller
◆ Gateway to learning – supporter of lifelong learning – illuminator	◆ Change agent (learning is by definition change)	◆ Manager of learning
◆ Prophet	◆ Influencer	◆ Operational manager, team leader
	◆ Manager of expectations	

Table 15.2 Traditional and emergent development functions

Old		Emergent	
Functional roles	**Interpretive roles**	**Functional roles**	**Interpretive roles**
◆ Direct trainer ◆ Training administrator ◆ Technical instructor ◆ Needs analyst ◆ Programme designer ◆ Transfer agent	◆ Passive provider ◆ Provider ◆ Caretaker ◆ Evangelist ◆ Innovator ◆ Educator ◆ Change agent	◆ Learning and development manager ◆ Contract/partnership manager ◆ Facilitator at corporate university ◆ Internal consultant ◆ Performance consultant ◆ Organisation development consultant ◆ Knowledge manager/intellectual asset controller	◆ Co-learner ◆ Change facilitator ◆ Learning architect ◆ Orchestrator of learning processes ◆ Intrapreneur ◆ Facilitator of strategic processes

Table 15.3 Traditional training versus the learning organisation

Traditional training	Learning organisation
Teaching content	Learning processes
Classroom-focused	Workplace-focused
Teacher-centred	Learner-centred
'Belongs to' training department	'Belongs to' each person
Activity-centred	Outcomes-based
Training specialist	Learning consultants

Applying such an analysis will enable many organisations to embrace organisational learning strategies, rather than having to rely on traditional approaches to training and development. As we focus more on the impact and consequences of their roles in organisations, so we shall see the importance of adopting a contingency approach. Situations and contexts call for adaptability and flexibility. Training professionals need to take the lead here.

The training programme for employees at English Nature epitomises the ways in which individual learning meshes with strategic goals. Walton's (1999) exploration of this process is shown in Table 15.4.

So, we can see from Table 15.4 the links between learning, strategy and change, together with the developing roles for HRD in effecting continuous cycles of performance improvement throughout an organisation.

Table 15.4 An assessment of English Nature as a learning organisation

Feature	Progress so far
Learning approach to strategy	Strategy is reviewed and refined but it is not always seen as easy to change direction.
Participative policy making	Everyone has an opportunity to influence policy; there are tensions between bottom-up and top-down management.
Open information systems	Information is not always readily accessible: a project aims to improve information flow and use.
Formative accounting and control	Government accounting procedures require some control, although the finance team does help other teams to control their own resources.
Internal exchange	Variable. The internal customer ethos is still not fully accepted. Some teams have made considerable progress. Networking is crude.
Flexibility of rewards	Government rules restrict options. Performance-related pay, small special bonuses and flexible working are possible.
Enabling structures	Individuals do move and flexibility is encouraged, but boundaries are seen as fixed in the short to medium term.
Boundary workers act as environmental scanners	Local teams and national partner teams have access to considerable information but to date have not always taken opportunities to influence their environmental scanners.
Inter-company learning	Although there is a liaison with nature conservation groups, in both the UK and abroad, meetings with organisations not involved in nature issues are rare.
Learning climate	There is a history of knowledge-based learning and expectations are high. Process reviews for continual improvement are less common.
Self-development opportunities for all	There are many opportunities to learn and develop, but time and money often limit such activity to key areas of the job.

Using the chart below to help you, assess Warbings in terms of the progress it has made towards becoming a learning organisation. What additional steps do you think the company needs to take to become a learning organisation? Compare notes with a friend; have you reached the same conclusions?

Feature	Progress so far
Learning approach to strategy	
Participative policy making	
Open information systems	
Formative accounting and control	
Internal exchange	
Flexibility of rewards	
Enabling structures	
Boundary workers act as environmental scanners	
Inter-company learning	
Learning climate	
Self-development opportunities for all	

Summary

We have seen how change can be viewed as learning and individual development. The amount and rate of change in work and life roles will continue to have a profound effect on the nature and function of adult development. Training – and trainers – will have a pivotal and foundational role to play in those organisations that seek to embrace an agenda of innovation and creativity. This chapter has explored the organisational context of structure, strategies and work processes that have implications for the ways that organisational and individual training and learning occur. It examined specific training initiatives in wider organisational contexts and looked at how training and learning can aid planned change in an organisation's internal and external environments.

Review Questions

You may wish to attempt the following as practice examination style questions.

15.1 What are the links between learning, development and corporate strategy?

15.2 How can training and development affect national skills shortages?

15.3 Critically evaluate two models of strategic human resource development.

References

Burack, E., Hochwater, H., Mathys, W. and Nicholas, J. (1997). The new management development paradigm, *Human Resources Planning*, Vol. 20, No. 1.

Burgoyne, J. (1992). *Creating a Learning Organisation*, London: Royal Society of Arts.

Darling, J. et al. (1999). *The Changing Role of the Trainer*, London: CIPD.

Garavan, T. (1991). Strategic human resource development, *Journal of European Industrial Training*, Vol. 15, No. 1, pp. 17–31.

Guest, D. (2002). *Managing Excellence and High Performance*, Milton Keynes: Open University Press.

Harrison, R. (2005). *Learning and Development*, London: CIPD.

Hoffman, F. and Withers, B. (1995). Shared values: nutrients for learning, in S. Chawla and J. Renesch (eds.) *Learning Organisations*, Portland, MA: Productivity Press.

Johnson, G. and Scholes, K. (1993). *Exploring Corporate Strategy*, London: Prentice Hall.

Lee, R. (1996). The 'pay-forward' view of training, *People Management*, Vol. 2, No. 3, pp. 30–32.

Lewin, K. (1951). *Field Theory in Social Science*, London: Tavistock.

Lynton, R. and Pareek, U. (2000). *Training for Organisational Transformation*: Volume 2, New Delhi: Sage.

McCracken, M. and Wallace, M. (2000). Towards a redefinition of strategic HRD, *Journal of European Industrial Training*, Vol. 24, No. 5, pp. 281–290.

McLagan, P. (1989). *Models for HR Practice*, Alexandria, VA: American Society for Training and Development.

Noel, J. and Dennehy, R. (1991). Making HRD a force in strategic organisational change, *Industrial and Commercial Training*, Vol. 23, No. 2, pp. 17–19.

Pettigrew, A. (1982). *Training and Development Roles in their Organisational Setting*, Sheffield: MSC.

Sawdon, D. (1999). Making the most of consultancy: perspectives on partnership, in J. Wilson (ed.) *Human Resource Development*, London: Kogan Page.

Simmonds, D. (2003). *Designing and Delivering Training*, London: CIPD.

Stewart, J. (1999). *Employee Development Practice*, London: Pitman.

Stewart, J. and McGoldrick, J. (eds.) (1996). *Human Resource Development: Perspectives, Strategies and Practice*, London: Pearson.

Stewart, J. and Tansley, C. (2002). *Training in the Knowledge Economy*, London: CIPD.

Storey, J. (2001). *New Perspectives on Human Resource Management*, London: Routledge.

Storey, J. et al. (2005). The barriers to customer responsive supply chain management, *International Journal of Operations and Production Management*, Vol. 25, No. 3, pp. 242–260.

Torraco, R. and Swanson, R. (1995). The strategic roles of human resource development, *Human Resource Planning*, Vol. 18, No. 4, pp.

Walton, J. (1999). *Strategic Human Resource Development*, London: Pitman.

Useful Websites

www.trainingzone.co.uk – training professionals network with news reports, research advice and guidance on professional development for trainers from Training Zone.co.uk

www.b.shuttle.de/wifo/ehrd-rev/=index.htm – gateway to research on education in Europe

www.nwlink.com/~donclark/hrd/hrdlink.html – Donald Clark website with news and reports on learning, performance and knowledge links

www.trainersnetwork.org – wide range of items (e.g. online meetings, working from home) from the Trainers Network

www.managementhelp.org – access to the free Management Library, covering a wide range of learning, performance and knowledge issues

www.squarewheels.com – Dr Scott Simmerman's performance management company offering trainer products and services (e.g. team-building games)

www.tip.psychology.org – psychology organisation coverage of learning theory, research on adult learning, articles and course information

www.thiagi.com – the Thiagi Group's source for training games and interactive strategies, including online newsletter and courses

www.trainingmag.com/training/index/jsp – Nielsen's business media information on training publications and courses

www.ibstpi.org – the website of the International Board of Standards for Training, Performance and Instruction, offering research reports, articles and guidance

www.clomedia.com/content/templates/clo_home.asp?articleid=714&zoneid=145 – training media information and guidance

CHAPTER 16

Management Behaviour and Management Development

By Kevin Dalton

Chapter outline

People are the lifeblood of any organisation. Their development is paramount to its success and sustainability. This is even more important in the case of its management. Line managers at all levels need to change and develop beyond the knowledge, skills and attitudes they had when they first accepted the role. This chapter examines the strategic aspects of management development (MD) with particular reference to changing managerial roles and behaviour. It explores the MD cycle and evaluates the different techniques and methods associated with such development. In particular it looks at different learning theories and approaches. Formal and informal MD is explored and the techniques for evaluating MD discussed.

Learning outcomes

By the end of this chapter, you should be able to:

◆ Describe the relationship between what managers do and how they learn;
◆ Explain the importance of a strategic approach to MD;
◆ Assess development needs;
◆ Summarise theories of managerial learning;
◆ Analyse methods of development;
◆ Illustrate issues of evaluation of MD.

Introduction

There is a growing awareness that the managerial role has become essential to business success. Organisations are run by managers who are striving to meet strategic goals, so increasingly their quality is recognised as vital for organisational performance – for its competitiveness, change and renewal. This realisation is leading organisations to look more carefully at their management cohorts – their numbers, their roles, their distribution and how they might be helped to learn in the most effective way. This chapter examines these areas of MD.

Management development

There is now a broad consensus that managers are neither born nor made, but will grow themselves if the organisation provides the right nurturing climate. There is also an emerging appreciation that MD is fundamental to organisational renewal and the management of change – key driving forces for any organisation seeking to survive in the 'white water' conditions of modern business. These concerns merge with the shift towards the new humanism in employment practice, e.g. the shift to lifelong learning; the learning organisation; knowledge management; creativity; and empowerment.

However, despite the surge of interest in MD as a corporate change and individual development tool, there are many criticisms of its effectiveness. As Burgoyne (2001: 33), one of the leading writers in the field, likes to say:

> 'There is no human endeavour to which MD has not been applied. So, we have walking on hot coals, role plays, outdoor adventure and even the pruning of bonsai trees, presented as ways of building the manager of the future.'

The interesting point about all this activity is that there is no proof that any of it works. Very often MD is the focus of management 'fads', political games, impression management and sectional interests. Often it is viewed as a set of discrete and isolated events that may be enjoyable for participants but have limited impact on the behaviours of managers. This has been referred to as the transferability paradox. MD can sometime seem uncoupled from the strategic goals of the organisation.

Definitions

In a field that is still evolving and finding its shape, there is much room for controversy about purpose and process. Some of this is apparent from the jarring descriptions of the nature of MD offered by both theorists and practitioners.

Molander (1986, cited in Beardwell and Holden, 2001: 373) offers the standard definition of the subject:

> 'A conscious and systematic decision–action process to control the development of managerial resources in the organisation for the achievement of organisational goals and strategies.'

However, Mumford has changed his mind on several occasions about what it is all about (1987, cited in Beardwell and Holden, 2001: 373):

'Management Development is an attempt to improve managerial effectiveness through a planned and deliberate learning process.'

However, by 1993 (pp. 5–7) we have Mumford saying:

'Management Development is a continuous ever-changing process where managers often learn through informal, unplanned experience.'

MD is riven with contrasts and contradictions – in terms of the claims made for it, the rhetoric it uses, its purposes and practice:

- At the micro level, MD is often considered to be a tool to improve the performance and potential of individual managers, to identify learning gaps and help to prepare them for future responsibilities. In particular, in times of rapid and chaotic organisational change, MD can be used to help managers adapt to downsizing and de-layering and to find ways of coping with a larger and more complex roles. MD is presented as a vehicle to enable managers to acquire the right profile of competencies for handling organisational complexity and to learn how to update their skills as the environment changes. At the level of individual skills and learning development, 'MD' is really *'manager* development', i.e. developing the qualities needed to manage oneself in relation to others (Harrison, 1997).

- However, taking a more macro view, many commentators believe that MD must go beyond mere individual learning and development. It should also be a vehicle for change. So Varney (1997) talks of MD as a means of organisational renewal, a process for engaging people in continuous collective learning. At its most sophisticated, MD can serve to build a common management culture across the whole management process, developing shared values and a consistent management style, even creating the foundation for organisation development (OD) and a learning organisation (LO).

Some of these divergences are captured by Mabey and Salaman's (1995) taxonomy of latent purposes of MD – see box below.

MD agendas

MD can have various latent functions:

- **MD as *functional performance*** = developing skills/attitudes against a desired profile.
- **MD as *political reinforcement*** = propagating the attitudes and values of top managers to aid higher control and purpose.
- **MD as *compensation*** = for reward of managers who have given good service and as a sign of approbation for rising stars.
- **MD as *psychic defence*** = providing a safety net to relieve the anxieties of managers who need help on the 'slippery' slope of organisational power and politics.

(Adapted from Mabey and Salaman, 1995)

If these conflicting interests are not reconciled in a programme that enjoys a rough consensus of acceptance, different stakeholders will pursue MD programmes for different ends. The outcome will then depend on the balance of political forces, not on the collective needs of the organisation and not on the needs of individuals as systematically assessed using scientific instruments.

A further axis of debate is between those who believe that MD should be concerned with planned, formalised developments (e.g. secondments, special postings, projects) and those who believe that the MD is at its best when informal and concerned with processes. The movement is away from formal, systematic, classroom-based teaching towards experiential learning in which management is seen as a complex web of social and political interactions. Managers are encouraged to learn through doing, reflecting and trying again.

In reality a well-designed and focused MD programme will probably provide a blend of both formal and informal processes, on- and off-job interventions, skills and behavioural and cognitive development. The crucial judgement, for those who have the difficult design decisions, is how to find the most appropriate balancing point within the prevailing circumstances.

Finally, there is controversy and ambiguity around the sub-processes that make up the content of MD as a cognate field of enquiry. What are these and what do they involve? Here, a number of definitions of these sub-processes are offered.

Historically, **management education** has been described as those techniques concerned to improve the learning and knowledge of managers. Management education has always been concerned with the 'professionalism' of management, giving managers the professional expertise, abstract knowledge and techniques to conduct their work more effectively. Typically, the content has been conceptual and academic, helping managers to improve their understanding of the organisational/professional world that they occupy.

Management training is a little different. It is generally considered more specific and short term, concerned with helping managers attain the skills they need to perform their jobs more effectively, e.g. short courses and seminars in specific subjects, such as financial planning, communications, HRM, and decision making. Training tends to be technical, pragmatic, vocational and skills-based rather than conceptual or theoretical.

Managerial self-development is another element within MD, focusing on the organisation of an individual's own personal development plans and career planning; it uses a range of informal and formal methods. Although the individual is required to take the initiative and responsibility for this development, the organisation usually has an interest and tries to ensure that individual plans are aligned with corporate purposes and carried forward in a supportive framework.

Organisational development is both a component of MD and a much larger body of knowledge and techniques about organisational change. OD is concerned with the improvement of organisational structures, culture and systems to help the achievement of organisational objectives. It is often led by action research and focuses on team-based solutions to problems.

Management development and managerial behaviour

The area of MD is in a state of considerable flux. There is uncertainty about what it should include and what it is for. MD programmes are often criticised for being remote from what managers actually do. The assessment of development needs, planning of job moves for development purposes, and training are often divorced from the circumstances of the manager's normal activities. As a result, MD solutions can seem too abstract, neat and logical; they are distanced from the confusing and fragmented nature of management as a lived experience. MD programmes can also seem very prescriptive and procedural, implying that managers need to behave in particular ways and follow certain steps if they want to be effective (i.e. implying that there are 'best practices' in the art of management that are universally applicable).

A major thrust of these criticisms is that MD needs to be located in reality if managers are to become committed to the learning processes and develop through them. From this, it follows that sensitivity to the design of MD and concern for its effectiveness is intertwined with consideration of management as an activity.

exercise

With reference to the Warbings case, list some of the major weaknesses among the managers.

If you were the HR manager, what action would you take to address these?

Management development strategy

A major theme to emerge in MD in recent years has been the growing awareness that development can serve as a strategic tool because it helps to build the talent pool that the organisation needs to survive in a more demanding environment. Traditionally, organisations have regarded MD as a discrete, isolated process, unrelated to wider organisational purposes, priorities and goals. Piecemeal and fragmented activities have typically underpinned a demand-led, menu-driven system of management training in which departments are invited to nominate participants for formal courses that are centrally organised. In these circumstances, the link between the diagnosis of development need, the allocation of resources and the evaluation of results is highly tenuous. The whole process can become a 'sheep dip' – regimented, superficial and more than a little ritualistic.

In fact, MD programmes may fail to provide significant or long-term benefits for a number of reasons:

- Often MD can be overly narrow and technique-driven, focusing on surface skills rather than deeper competencies that the organisation really needs to prosper;
- Sometimes MD can be ineffective because there is no infrastructure; activities are unrelated; or the programme is not focused upon a guiding philosophy of learning and development;
- Often MD programmes, however rational and strategic, become hijacked by sectional interests and operational priorities;

- ◆ MD may also disappoint because it is prescribed as the solution to the wrong problem. Too often, MD is seen as a 'quick fix', a response by senior managers needing to be seen to take action about deep-seated problems.

See the box below.

Burgoyne's levels of maturity of MD

Level 1: No systematic MD – no deliberate MD in structural or developmental sense.

Level 2: Isolated, tactical MD events – isolated and *ad hoc* tactical MD in response to crises and sporadically identified general problems.

Level 3: Integrated, co-ordinated MD interventions around a plan – the specific MD tactics that impinge directly on the individual manager or career structure management are integrated and co-ordinated.

Level 4: MD strategy to deliver corporate strategy – an MD strategy plays its part in implementing corporate policies through managerial HR planning and providing a strategic framework and direction for the tactics of career structure management, learning and education.

Level 5: MD contributes to and helps shape corporate strategy – MD processes feed information into corporate decision making about the organisation's management assets and contribute to forecasting and analysis of the manageability of projects.

Level 6: Corporate strategy is led by the values of learning and development – MD processes enhance the nature and quality of corporate policy making and help to implement it.

(Adapted from Burgoyne, 1988)

In the real world, of course, the organisation of MD is rarely more advanced than Level 4 in this typology. Factors such as career, localised perceptions of 'efficiency', the requirements of outside bodies, the ideologies of top management, the relationship between HRM and line management, and organisational structures, are usually at least as important in determining what goes into an MD programme as strategic processes which relate means to ends. Despite these constraints, some leading organisations (e.g. Motorola, Jaguar and BA) have deliberately tried to create a coherent strategic framework for MD. Of course, details will vary from one organisation to another, but the following themes often apply:

- ◆ **Inter-linkage** – where MD is well established in an organisation, it is often tightly inter-linked with the organisation's other systems and processes. Where MD is working well, it is often a sub-system of a larger HRM system, i.e. there is a clear understanding that MD is located within a framework of inter-connected systems for selecting and identifying, motivating, rewarding and *developing* managers.

- ◆ **Top driven** – where MD is taken seriously, it is owned and guided by senior management. This involves the board demonstrating that managerial learning is a core competency of the organisation. Directors and senior executives will often be the first participants on MD programmes. For example, where 'leadership' is proclaimed as a strategic value, board management will take a close interest in the details of an appraisal scheme that embraces 'leadership' as a core competency, and ensure that these values infuse all aspects of the management process.

◆ **Strategic overview** – a corporate approach to MD means there is an overall review system where each business initiative is carefully assessed in terms of its implications for the role of managers, the profile of experience, and the skills that will be needed in the relationship between learning and organisation. A strategic overview of development also involves cascading learning down the organisation and making learning part of its fabric and direction.

◆ **Partnership** – where MD is successful, ownership is shared between MD advisors/ line managers; individuals/the organisation; and the centre/the periphery. Balancing the conflicting needs of different stakeholders involves MD practitioners in redefining their roles as internal consultants rather than training deliverers. The most important role for the MD advisor is to act as a unifying force, integrating the different interpretations and expectations of various groups into learning programmes that satisfy a wide range of divergent interests.

◆ **MD as OD** – finally, effective MD involves a holistic or systemic approach to development that is intended as a long-term investment in the organisation as a whole. Focusing attention on individual managers will not necessarily bring about transformational change. Where MD acts as a catalyst for organisation-wide change, it is often integrated with OD. This requires the capacity to understand how an entire socio-technical system can be constructed by linking change at the strategic, group and individual levels of behaviour.

MD as a development cycle

If strategy forms the framework of a planned and co-ordinated approach to MD, then it is through the development process that strategic questions about *who* to develop and *how* will be addressed.

Figure 16.1 shows the MD system as a virtuous cycle of information and action. Inputs of information feed into the development process and are brought together in plans and programmes.

Of course, Figure 16.1 is an oversimplification or idealisation of the complex processes of development. These are not really as linear, systematic or clear-cut as here suggested, but this representation does help us to understand the purpose of assessing managers and designing programmes for their development.

Management learning

One of the great debates during recent years has centred upon how managers learn. There are a number of theories of managerial learning. However, a predominant theme is the claim that management is a practical subject and its effectiveness rests on the self-awareness, behaviour and attitudes of practitioners, as much as their specific knowledge and skills. In particular, it requires the capacity to see patterns, themes and the connectedness between often conflicting entities, and to apply general concepts to specific situations. This is the notion of transferability.

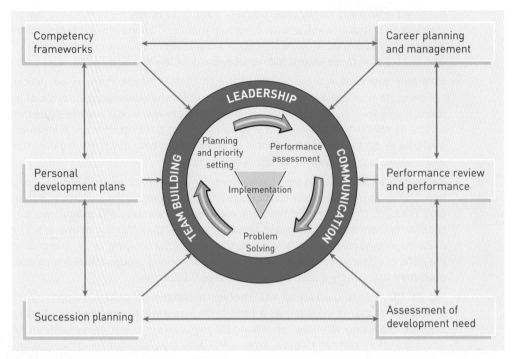

Figure 16.1 MD system

pause for thought

How important do you think it is for managers to reflect on the actions and interactions of those around them?

Why did you reach this conclusion?

These insights form the central concerns of experiential approaches to an understanding of the management process. For example, Weick (1979) talks about learning by 'doing thinkingly', i.e. typically, when faced with a problem, managers do not resolve it with abstract thought; instead, they start to take action, and then as they reflect on the activity, the problem becomes clearer. The CIPD has embraced the concept in its 'Thinking Performer' approach to CPD.

A major proponent of experiential learning is David Kolb, who has researched the learning styles of managers and developed a cycle of learning describing how the individual manager seems to learn, by making sense of his or her experiences. Kolb's cycle consists of four stages, as depicted in Figure 16.2.

This emphasis on 'self-managed' reflective learning is also mirrored in the influential work of Revans (1983) and Knowles (1984), who both stress a questioning approach to learning, e.g. managers need to assess their own learning needs, discovering answers by thinking, discovering answers for themselves, and having confidence in their own critical judgement derived from personal experience.

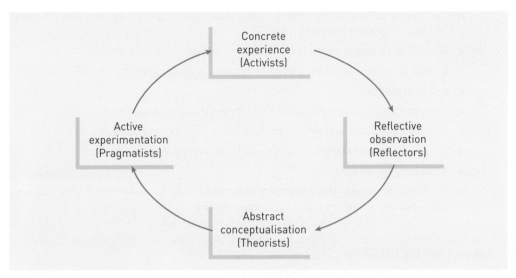

Figure 16.2 Experiential learning cycle
Source: adapted from Kolb (1984) and Honey and Mumford (1996)

**Give an example of when your behaviour changed following a time of reflection.
Why was that?**

In the 1980s, after years of advocating a planned, systematic, formalised system of development, Mumford famously overturned accepted orthodoxy by saying that this was a 'developer's model' not a 'manager's model' of learning. When he asked managers to define the work experiences which they believed had most helped them to learn, they usually mentioned very informal processes – handling crises, walking the floor, watching an acknowledged master at work, being counselled, and contrasting the 'commonsense' of their own organisation with that of another. This, he said, was very good evidence that managers were pragmatic, not theoretical; they learned best when their learning context afforded access to 'real life' situations; and they recognised that they needed to learn something if they were to achieve their personal goals.

Mumford went on to classify several types of learning that he linked to both informal and formal management approaches – learning both 'on'- and 'off'-the-job.

Management development techniques

Self-development

When learners are truly self-managing, they will be self-directed, taking responsibility for their own careers and for growing in self-awareness. As the pressures for performance increase, it may be that only those managers who are truly self-developing will be able to survive. According to Pedler et al. (2001) and Megginson and Whitaker (1999), self-managed learners have:

◆ The ability to diagnose their own learning needs;

◆ A clear picture of what they want to achieve in their career;

◆ Self-knowledge;

◆ The capacity to be honest about their strengths and weaknesses;

◆ An awareness that learning opportunities are all around at work;

◆ Sensitivity to the lessons to be gained from every situation;

◆ A capacity to reflect;

◆ An ability to review their learning processes, and to understand how and why some people are more successful than others.

pause for thought

Ask yourself the following:

◆ What are my strengths and weaknesses?

◆ Do I really know the strengths and weaknesses of my colleagues?

◆ How do I use this knowledge when relating to them?

◆ How much time do I set aside to deliberately reflect on my work?

'On-the-job' techniques

This group of MD techniques is designed within an organisation. Often, these techniques combine both a task and a developmental element.

On-the-job development is most likely to occur when the manager is placed in a challenging situation. Under such circumstances, managers are required to solve problems and to make choices in a dynamic situation under conditions of risk and uncertainty. Exposure to such situations can produce changes in the way the manager approaches problems, handles risks and makes decisions. There are various 'on-the-job' experiences that are said to encourage learning:

◆ **Changes to the job** can take various forms. Moving to a new job is stressful. However, it can also be a period of heightened learning if the manager is aware of the learning potential. In the same way, assignments and project work can be useful for extending experience, broadening horizons and providing an opportunity in which to practise new skills.

◆ **Job rotation** is also a valuable on-the-job opportunity for development. Job transitions require managers to recognise the gap between their current skills and perspectives, and those required by others, and then to find new ways of responding to the challenges involved.

'Off-the-job' techniques

The case for sending managers on training courses is that they can concentrate on learning rather than managing, and can be exposed to new ideas. Management education and training seems to work best when there is a proper balance between dissemination of ideas, critical discussion of concepts and opportunities to apply ideas/concepts in action. It is most effective when it is part of a planned programme that brings together formal and informal methods.

Management education regards development with a wider perspective than management training. It is more knowledge-led and more concerned with attitude change. In some cases this amounts to nothing less than giving the manager a completely new understanding of business processes and organisational life.

MBA courses are perhaps the best-known ways in which managers are educated in a structured way. Traditional MBAs have had a considerable impact on business. Historically, they have been biased to technical, quantitative, analytical skills at the expense of soft skills. However, in recent times there has been an attempt to redress this with more focus on interpersonal, creativity and thinking skills. All the same, there is continuing concern that MBAs produce identikit managers – good at number crunching, good at using business techniques, but without much flair or originality. They often also lack some of the vitally important skills of managing people and leading teams. This is at a time when there is an increasing need for managers with people skills, creative insight, imagination, an ability to think creatively, a philosophy of action, and the will to implement decisions.

Action learning sets are an increasingly important development technique. The underlying assumption of this development technique is that a manager learns by taking responsibility for action rather than by talking about it, or listening to someone else talk about it. Managers, organised in groups of five to ten people from different departments or organisations, are faced with a problem brought by one of the set members. They then work to find a solution by learning from each other in a climate of support and encouragement. The learning set advisor will also help them to reflect upon their learning. When they are working well, action learning sets can encourage people to gain new perspectives; to consider the assumptions involved; to reflect on their thinking; to define problems, make decisions and learn from others' experience; and to improve their critical feedback.

Various writers (Fee, 2001; Margerison, 1991; Mumford, 2005) have suggested key issues that need to be addressed when designing MD courses, for example:

♦ They should start from the managers' perceptions of reality;

♦ They should relate closely to what managers really do;

♦ The teaching/facilitative approach should be participative;

♦ Managers need to be actively interested in the course and not be attending as a 'corporate ritual';

♦ The course programme should be informed by an explicit MD philosophy, which should show an alignment with learning objectives.

pause for thought

Identify a manager or business leader who has been in the news recently.
What inspired or disappointed you about them? And why?

Evaluation

In 2003, UK companies spent £10 billion on corporate training. A large part of this is spent on MD. However, only half of all organisations ever evaluate their training in terms of business impact.

Evaluation is concerned with determining the significance of a programme of development in terms of the social benefit it confers (i.e. does it develop knowledge, skills, and attitudes?) and whether it offers value for money. Evaluation:

◆ Establishes whether the objectives for an event/programme have been achieved. This is called 'validation'. Were the stated objectives met? Were the objectives appropriate in the first place?

◆ Shows the link between learning and performance, e.g. whether a social skills seminar for first-line managers results in different performance in the workplace.

◆ Helps learners by giving them feedback data to allow them to reflect on their performance, identify further learning, and an experience to help them to move on to a larger, more demanding position.

◆ Demonstrates the return on investing in MD. Has the programme really delivered in terms of economy, efficiency and effectiveness? Can realistic links be made between development and payback for the company in measurable terms such as profitability, sales or savings? How has the HR manager, for example, increased staff satisfaction or reduced the amount spent on recruitment advertising?

The process of evaluation in all types of learning and development is always problematic. But in MD, this is particularly so. The development of soft skills, judgement, creativity and thinking, poses methodological problems of evaluation which many busy HR departments have trouble addressing. There is also the problem of distinguishing between one set of influences and another. Management performance is often an amalgam of various forces and it is extremely difficult to differentiate the developmental aspects. There is also the issue of the direct and indirect effects of MD. An MD activity may have limited direct impact on financial performance. However, if there are indirect benefits such as greater flexibility or improved morale, then it is arguable that the activity has been a good investment.

All the same, if an organisation needs to justify its use of resources and derive lessons for the future, it needs to undertake evaluation. This means deciding on a methodology, e.g. whether the evaluation should be only summative (just measuring the final result) or also formative (evaluating development as it proceeds); whether the data needs to be predominantly qualitative or quantitative; whether the evaluation needs to be sophisticated (time-consuming and expensive) or simple, (cheap but relatively shallow). It also means choosing a model of evaluation (either explicitly or implicitly) that will help make sense of the results.

exercise

W

One of the great weaknesses of MD is that this is an area which gives rise to a lot of fads and fashions. However, it also allows scope for real imagination and creative flair. Below are some of the more unusual techniques that have been used by developers to stimulate learners to think about management processes.

continued

W

- Managers are brought into a darkened warehouse that is internally configured into a sort of maze. Managers have to link together and then work as a team to capture a large 'python' somewhere in the labyrinth, in order to develop teamworking and leadership skills.

- To increase their sensitivity to language and the emotional and persuasive power of words, managers are asked to write Japanese 'haiku' poetry and read their efforts to the group (Fee, 2001).

- As an exercise in communication and interpersonal awareness, managers are shown a videotaped scene from a TV soap opera with the sound turned off. Participants are asked to suggest a script based on their observations of body language, gesture and expression (Fee, 2001).

- Samba dancing has been used on management courses to teach improvisation, learning through doing, learning how to learn, and using others as a learning resource (Fee, 2001).

- As an exercise in creativity, teams of managers are asked to design an egg-throwing machine. Again, the focus is on 'process' – how decisions are made and the quality of relationships.

If you were the HR manager for Warbings, how would you convince your sceptical colleagues that these refreshing, progressive and exciting approaches to development were worth supporting?

Summary

Different stakeholders define MD in various ways and many controversies surround priorities and focus, e.g. the macro versus micro view, and informal versus formal methods. MD has various components, including management education, management training and management self-development. A well-designed MD programme may draw on all of these elements. For MD to be perceived as relevant to participants, it needs to start with an appreciation of the contingent nature of management. If MD is conceived as being strategic, it can be a tool for implementing organisational strategy and development, building collective learning, and improving performance.

A strategic approach to MD involves the use of systematic processes, i.e. the development cycle of competency frameworks, performance review and appraisal, assessment techniques, personal development plans (PDPs), succession planning and career development plans. Learning theory allows management developers to design programmes that recognise individual differences in learning, the importance of practise for learning, and the value of creating a climate in which managers take responsibility for their own learning. There are many techniques of MD, both off- and on-the-job, that need to be combined effectively for the objectively assessed development needs of individuals and groups to be met. Assessing the value of an MD intervention is crucial in justifying any investment. Theories and practices of evaluation methodology are varied and diffuse.

Review Questions

You may wish to attempt the following as practice examination style questions.

16.1 'If you develop your managers, you develop your organisation.' This phrase is often cited, but do you agree with it? Specify the conditions under which it is likely to be true.

16.2 How can the HR department contribute to the success of MD?

16.3 'Self-development is the key to successful MD.' Discuss this view and support your answer with reference to an organisation with which you are familiar.

16.4 'Career development for managers is only useful if it fully accommodates individual differences.' Discuss.

16.5 What do you regard as the advantages and disadvantages of MD?

16.6 How does the political culture of an organisation shape its MD?

16.7 'Formal MD has had its day and has nothing valuable to contribute to helping managers to learn.' How would you react to this assertion?

References

Burgoyne, J. (1988). Management development for the individual and the organisation, *Personnel Management*, Vol. 10, pp. 8–14.

Burgoyne, J. (2001). Tester of faith, *People Management*, 22 February, pp. 32–34.

Fee, K. (2001). *A Guide to Management Development Techniques*, London: Kogan Page.

Harrison, R. (1997). *Employee Development*, London: CIPD.

Honey, P. and Mumford, A. (1996). *The Manual of Learning Styles*, Maidenhead: Peter Honey Publications.

Knowles, M. (1984). *Andragogy in Action*, San Francisco, CA: Jossey-Bass.

Kolb, D. (1984). *Experiential Learning*, Englewood Cliffs, NJ: Prentice Hall.

Mabey, C. and Salaman, G. (1995). *Strategic Human Resource Management*, Oxford: Blackwell.

Margerison, C. (1991). *Making Management Development Work*, Maidenhead: McGraw-Hill.

Megginson, D. and Whitaker, V. (1999). *Cultivating Self-development*, London: CIPD.

Molander, C. (1986). Management development, in I. Beardwell and L. Holden (2001) *Human Resource Management: A Contemporary Approach*, London: FT/Prentice Hall.

Mumford, A. (1987). Using reality in management development, *Management Education and Development*, Vol. 18, in I. Beardwell and L. Holden (2001) *Human Resource Management: A Contemporary Approach*, London: FT/Prentice Hall.

Mumford, A. (1993). *Management Development: Strategies for Action*, London: CIPD.

Pedler, M., Burgoyne, J. and Boydell, T. (2001). *A Manager's Guide to Self Development*, Maidenhead: McGraw-Hill.

Revans, R. (1983). *ABC of Action Learning*, London: Chartwell-Bratt.

Weick, K. (1979). *The Social Psychology of Organising*, Wokingham: Addison-Wesley.

Further Reading

Atkinson, S. and Meldrum, M. (1998). Don't waste money on management development, *Organisation and People*, Vol. 5, No. 4.

Buchanan, D. and Badham, R. (1992). *The Expertise of the Change Agent*, Englewood Cliffs, NJ: Prentice Hall.

Burgoyne, J. and Reynolds, M. (1997). *Management Learning*, London: Sage.

Constable, J. and McCormick, R. (1987). *The Making of British Managers: A Report of the BIM and CBI into Management Training, Education and Development*, London: BIM.

Dalton, K. (forthcoming). *A Critical Introduction to Management Development*, London: Pearson.

Dopson, S. and Stewart, R. (1990). What is happening to middle managers?, *British Journal of Management*, Vol. 1, No. 1, pp. 3–16.

Easterby-Smith, M. (1994). *Evaluation of Management Education, Training and Development*, Aldershot: Gower.

Storey, J. (1989). Management development: a literature review and implications for future research, Part 1: Conceptualisations and practice, *Personnel Review*, Vol. 18, No. 6, pp. 3–11.

Strebler, M. and Bevan, S. (2001). Performance review: balancing objectives and content, report 370, Brighton: Institute of Employment Studies.

Syrett, M. and Lammiman, J. (1999). *Management Development*, London: Economist Books.

Walton, J. (1999). *Strategic Human Resource Development*, Englewood Cliffs, NJ: Prentice Hall.

Weick, K. (1995). *Sensemaking in Organisations*, London: Sage.

Useful Websites

www.amed.org.uk – website of the Association for Management Education and Development – a professional network for people in individual and organisational development, covering publications, meetings, services and networks for professionals

www.bam.ac.uk – website of the British Academy of Management, representing management academics and covering research, publications, news, training courses and networks

www.roffeypark.com – Roffey Park Management Institute range of publications, research, learning resources and bespoke development consultancy

www.efmd.org./html/home.asp – network enabling the development of people and organisations through learning and leadership, with a range of publications, conferences and learning groups and services with a focus on business school activities

Organisational Development, Organisational Learning and the Learning Organisation

By Kevin Dalton

Chapter outline

This chapter defines organisational development (OD) and explores the techniques and tools of OD as well as looking at the skills of the OD practitioner. Increasingly, human resource (HR) is becoming focused at the strategic level of change in organisations. The learning and development function is central to this change and human resource management (HRM) is at the forefront of these processes orchestrating and implementing them. We look at some of the theories behind OD and examine the characteristics of the learning organisation (LO) while reflecting on the future for OD. The links between OD and reflective practice are investigated.

Learning outcomes

By the end of this chapter, you should be able to:

◆ Discuss the relationship between management development (MD) and OD;

◆ Describe the philosophy, history and ethics of OD;

◆ Explain techniques, intervention strategies and professional craft of OD;

◆ Illustrate models of organisational learning;

◆ Give details of the link between OD and organisational learning;

◆ Outline theories and practical applications of the LO.

Introduction

MD is concerned with developing the individual, but for many it is also about developing the system of OL. Managers can only achieve their full potential when the conditions for learning are positive. Rigidities in the context of managerial learning inhibit managers from being truly experimental, creative and innovative. An open learning system will have the opposite effect. At the same time, management learning styles shape attitudes, values and behaviours that can decisively influence the culture of learning, either for good or ill. The development of the organisation is closely bound with the development of its managers. Progressive management development is conditional on building a form of organisation that is self-developing and places learning at the centre of all its processes.

Organisational development

The fast-paced, complex nature of change requires organisations to learn to find innovative methods to meet new demands. OD is an influential field of theory and practice that enables organisations to work towards strategies for managing change. OD involves 'whole systems change' and the selective use of interventions that shape the invisible and intangible aspects of organisational processes – values, norms, beliefs, symbols, ideologies, relationships and behaviours. OD embraces a number of techniques to help organisational members address key issues confronting them in times of transition, e.g. managing change; developing leadership skills; building organisational culture and climate; defining vision and strategy; developing business process; and the organisation of work.

Defining OD

OD is a vast field and theorists and practitioners address it from a number of different perspectives. French and Bell's classic study (1984: 17–18) offers a useful definition:

> 'A top management supported, long range effort to improve an organisation's problem solving through an effective diagnosis and management of culture through improved quality of life, team process, group and inter-group dynamics. The focus is on improving the total system with the assistance of a consultant facilitator and the use of techniques of behavioural science and action research.'

OD is fraught with paradox. It is science but also art. It is a toolkit of techniques that contains some fashionable gimmicks, but also well-tested and proven methods derived from social science and systematically evaluated management practice. OD is concerned with small-scale developments (e.g. 'quality of working life' initiatives, person-centred empowerment and team development). It also engages in large-scale strategic management, restructuring and redesign consultancy. The thrust of OD has become somewhat diluted in recent times, as approaches have become absorbed into the mainstream of management processes. At the same time, there is still consensus that for an intervention to be regarded as OD, certain basic criteria need to be satisfied:

♦ **OD is holistic** – most definitions recognise the 'total organisational system' as the target for change. OD is concerned with holistic development. So, while an OD intervention may be targeted at a particular sub-system of the whole (e.g. tasks, structures, strategies or leadership), it is also concerned with the impact of change in one part of the organisation on the totality. This often means progressive interventions to trace inter-linkages as they ripple out from the epicentre of change (e.g. how changing the reward system has implications for leadership and culture change).

◆ **OD is strategic** – it is never a 'quick fix' solution to a particular management problem. The 'total systems' approach requires a fusion between analysis, vision and techniques. All aspects need to be aligned to achieve effective change, which takes time and patience. It involves helping top managers, who are the change architects, to articulate their values and expectations and then move consistently to shift the culture in ways that support desired behaviours that will ultimately have a transformational impact.

◆ **OD is planned change** – so much that takes place in many organisations is reactive, passive or negative. Too many training programmes are entitled 'Managing change'. By contrast, OD focuses upon adaptation and process development, anticipating the need for change and making it happen. OD tends to embrace an incremental approach to change (i.e. a series of small steps, increasing in strides as the momentum builds, add up over time to dramatic change). This is held in opposition to radical and disjunctive approaches, especially if that means following an overarching blueprint for change superimposed and directed from top management. However, the important feature of change that can be characterised as OD is that it is deliberate, systematic and guided by a clear vision for the future.

◆ **OD is participative change** – from its beginnings, OD has always maintained the importance of involving those who will have to live with the consequences of a change programme. OD typically emphasises the participation of a range of stakeholders in diagnosing the organisational problems and empowering them to find solutions that build ownership and commitment to the change. This is the essence of the process consultation model of consultancy and of the action research methodology. This aims to encourage shared meanings and sense-making through guided facilitation and reflection.

◆ **OD is based on behavioural science** – OD is a form of change management guided by the concepts and models of social science. There is no one single theory underlying OD activities, but a variety of contributions from the behavioural sciences, such as: social psychology; group dynamics; organisational analysis; social learning theory; role theory; and personality theories. Behavioural science provides the conceptual tools for analysing and influencing the ideological processes of organisational processes, i.e. the interpretive meanings, cognitive maps and values of different stakeholders within the organisation.

◆ **OD is an educational strategy** – OD is concerned with development through learning. Ultimately it is about 'cognitive restructuring', i.e. shaping how different groups of people construct their realities and relate to each other so that larger organisational goals can be achieved. In the hands of a wise practitioner, OD is about helping people to understand how they think and act and how they might do that differently for the greater good of the whole organisation.

exercise

Design a presentation for your fellow students defining and explaining the importance of OD, highlighting why it is important.

Include organisational examples.

The techniques of OD

OD intervention strategies focus on development of the individual, the group and the organisation, covering a broad and varied spectrum of activities. Here are some of the key techniques.

Process consultation

Process consultation is the quintessential OD technique – see Schein (1987). It is a participative approach in which the consultant acts as observer, counsellor, researcher and facilitator for a group. In this function, the consultant acts to help people share in the process of interpreting issues within the organisation that need to be addressed. He or she encourages them to define what the issues are, what problems are being avoided, and how presenting problems may have their roots in culture and structure. The consultant also acts as a probe; an observer and a challenger helping the group to be aware of process issues so that it can maximise the opportunities for creativity and learning in the future.

Action research/survey feedback approaches

Traditionally, the guiding philosophy of OD has been to make change collaborative. It is about 'listening to the organisation'; listening to the accounts of people at all levels as they define situations; making sense of experience and helping people construct their realities from assumptions, images and stereotypes. This involves a diagnostic or action research approach.

Action research involves the change agent in planning and understanding the change process by being part of it themselves. It is increasingly the key methodology driving OD. It is participative and based on the belief that real change stems from data collected with and from those who will be most involved in the change.

With action research, change is cyclical – as shown in the box below.

The action research process

♦ **Diagnosis of organisational themes to establish the map of issues** – this involves carrying out research with the people concerned. Here, a wide range of issues may be relevant, e.g. How are people motivated? What are the leadership styles? Can anything be said about the relationship between structural and cultural factors?

♦ **Feeding back the results** to those who have supplied the data. Does the diagnosis make sense to them? Can they recognise their experience in the results?

♦ **Discussing the results with wider circles of interested parties** – here, the OD consultant acts as facilitator. What do the data mean for change in the system as a whole?

- ◆ **Action planning** is the next stage. What are the practical consequences of the research findings? What steps have now to be taken to help organisational transition?

- ◆ **Action** involves implementing the OD programme. This is likely to be a blending of techniques, such as envisioning, institutional change, team development, and formal and informal personal development.

- ◆ **Evaluating the action** means having the objectivity and openness to consider tough questions. Has the change been successful? Are there issues here that have not been addressed? Were there problems of initial diagnosis or implementation? Is there a need for another iteration of the cycle, more data gathering, review and action?

(Adapted from French and Bell, 1990)

Team building and team learning

Team building can be used for established long-term groups and also for special project groups. With new teams, the emphasis is on the whole team developing a common framework of understanding and agreeing common goals within which people can work. The facilitator works to help the team move through the various stages of development (see Tuckman and Jensen, 1977).

The team as a whole reflects on recent events to determine the problems and solutions. This critical incident analysis is likely to involve not only 'task' and 'process' issues but also the nature and quality of relationships between team members and between members and the leader.

Interpersonal interactions can be observed as group members try to clarify their objectives and the process of working together. Developers adopt a 'non-interventionist' style. Their purpose is to encourage group members to reflect on how they are reacting to events and building a sense of order in which the group defines roles and rules of behaviour.

At a later stage, the developer will help the group reflect on its experience by raising themes for discussion:

- ◆ How does the group make decisions?
- ◆ What are the problem-solving processes and how rational do they seem?
- ◆ How are people negotiating identities within the team?
- ◆ How are agendas set? Is the team stuck in self-defeating routines of thought so that certain issues cannot be considered and creativity is stifled?
- ◆ What are the micro processes of communication?
- ◆ Why does the group not listen to Jill?
- ◆ Why is Jack always interrupted?
- ◆ Why is Mohammed allowed to dominate the agenda?

Typically, the developer will be acting as a group 'therapist', helping the group to articulate its fears; work though intractable issues; and reach a consensus on the problems facing it.

Organisational mirroring

This is a process by which an organisational group gets feedback from other groups about how it is perceived and regarded. Often it involves bringing together two groups that have a history of conflictual relationships. The objective is to help members of the two groups increase their awareness of the other's activities and reduce a sense of separation.

The technique benefits from the support of an outside facilitator who manages the open space of interaction. The process could involve, for example, both groups producing two lists. The first is, *'the complaints we have about them'*; the second is, *'the complaints we think they have about us'*. The lists are then shared between the two groups. Typically, it emerges that many of the complaints can be resolved quite rapidly because they result from simple misunderstanding and poor communication. The lists of both sides show a lot of congruency, e.g. *'we know what they think about us and they know what we think about them'*. In subsequent discussion, the lists form the basis for an exploration of the causes of submerged feelings, friction and blame. Bringing these issues into the open, in a climate of candour, and mixing the groups in sub-sets to work on contentious problems, then relationships can be improved.

A variation on 'mirroring' is a technique called role negotiation. This can take place between teams and within teams. It involves individuals and teams contracting with each other to change their behaviour. Using 'support and challenge' techniques, participants are asked to say what they want others to do more of, less of, or stay as they are. A follow-up meeting a few weeks later can review progress and set up new contracts if needed.

Strategic management and OD

Although we have concentrated on the 'softer' aspects of OD, increasingly the discipline has to justify itself in terms of tangible, 'bottom line' results. This has involved OD in more 'hard-edged' techniques such as:

- **Strategic management** – helping managers enact their environment (Weick, 1979) and envision the future (scenario planning; future search; vision workshops; and performance gap and strategic choice analyses).

- **Organisational design work** – advising managers how to develop the building blocks of the new organisation (greater differentiation; flattened structures; improved lateral relations; autonomous teams; greater flexibility). It also means micro work (designing interlocking roles; more participative work; and building learning and development into work).

- **Performance management systems** (designing systems which will support the management agenda and give expression to values of equity and fairness; linking systems of performance management with appraisal, quality management, reward, strategy and development).

 pause for thought

- Which techniques of OD have you experienced, heard about or read about?
- How did you respond? And why?

The skills of the OD practitioner

Burke (1998) typified OD competencies as shown in the box below.

Burke's 'typification' of OD competencies

- **The ability to tolerate ambiguity** – every OD intervention begins with a blank sheet of paper and what may have worked well in one setting may not produce similar results elsewhere.

- **The ability to influence** – the OD practitioner needs to have a talent for persuasion and an instinct for influence and negotiation (being able to sell ideas to others and influencing political coalitions in getting commitment to a change).

- **The ability to confront difficult issues** – much of the work of the OD practitioner is concerned with exposing issues that others do not want to acknowledge. This requires intellectual and moral courage.

- **The ability to support and nurture others** – this is the counselling side of the role, i.e. helping managers experiment with new styles of leading; giving encouragement to teams during periods of stressful change.

- **The ability to listen well and empathise** – this is especially true during diagnostic interviews and during mirroring. A related ability is separating your own perceptions and feelings from those of your client.

- **The ability to discover and mobilise human energy** – this is about radiating personal enthusiasm and giving others the confidence to try new ways of behaving.

- **The ability to teach** – this is the facilitative side of the role, e.g. helping people to understand the learning opportunities in a situation; being able to use incidents to challenge existing mindsets; demonstrating the value of alternative approaches.

- **The capacity for vision** – this does not mean that the consultant is doctrinaire in his or her approach or style, but rather it is based on a belief in the value of creating organisations for their people, in a context of learning.

(Adapted from Burke, 1998)

There is evidence that the practice of OD may be changing. There is a trend towards managers becoming internal change agents. For example, a recent Roffey Park survey (2005) defined the essential management skills of the future as:

- Organisational awareness;
- Strategic understanding;
- Self-awareness;
- Knowledge of change management techniques;
- Facilitation skills;
- Micro political skills;
- The ability to manage conflict.

Organisational learning and the learning organisation

The shift of interest towards OL and the LO arises from an increasingly competitive environment, constant change and the need for continual learning. As Edmondson and Moingeon (1998) point out, organisations depend on the learning of individuals and themselves in order to remaining viable over periods of change and uncertainty.

OL

OL is the study of the individual and collective learning patterns and processes aimed at helping organisations develop and use internal knowledge to improve themselves and so become more competitive. OL is more than the accumulation of individual learning efforts. It is possible for individual managers to learn effectively while the organisation does not (e.g. a manager may learn how to serve the customer better without sharing that knowledge with other members of the company). Conversely, organisations may learn in the sense that improvements are made in work design and processes but which leave the social processes of the organisation untouched.

Learning and organisational process

One strand of thinking defines organisations as 'residues of thinking' (Grey and Antonacopolou, 2004). It focuses on deep processes of culture. What are the routines by which organisational knowledge is acquired? Argyris and Schon (1978) talk of the 'master programmes' by which people become mentally conditioned to define and deal with situations. Through socialisation, people develop 'habits of thought' or 'routines' which predispose them to interpret information in particular ways. These 'habits of thought' can prevent recognition of changing conditions and displace effective learning when the routines are 'defensive' and 'closed'. As in 'group think', these blinkers inhibit the reception of new ideas and process is allowed to swamp innovation. Argyris and Schon (ibid.) emphasise that organisational learning is greatly improved when managers develop the sensitivity and reflective insight to recognise self-defeating routines that hinder change and the search for new solutions to old problems.

Another important 'process' model, also developed by Argyris and Schon (ibid.), defines OL as a series of learning loops at different levels, as shown in the box below.

Argyris and Schon's Learning Process Model

Level 1: Single loop learning – sometimes known as 'inner loop learning', this involves problem solving when an error is detected so that operational processes can proceed more smoothly. It is learning how to improve current performance in order to achieve greater efficiencies.

Level 2: Double loop learning – known also as 'outer loop learning', this involves purposeful questions of the value of our actions. Double loop learning involves rising above immediate organisational problems, to enable a re-framing of these issues and embedding them in deeper structures of meaning.

Level 3: Triple loop or deutero learning – this learning is difficult to achieve but can be extremely important for changing paradigms. It implies shifts in ideological models of organisation, challenging purposes, principles and strategies and creating a climate of 'learning how to learn'.

(Adapted from Argyris and Schon, 1978)

This chapter can be associated with Chapter 6, on Knowledge Management. How do you think the two are connected? Why did you reach this conclusion?

pause for thought

Learning and cognitive processes

Much of the literature on OL is concerned with cognition. How we think about the organisation will shape processes of learning and behaving. So Weick (2001) talks about 'interpretive processes' as the key to OL. How people in the organisation 'enact' their environment, i.e. make sense of the opportunities, constraints, threats, etc. facing them will determine how the organisation behaves. This has implications for learning. Enactment that allows too good a fit between organisation and environment may ironically create conditions in which it is difficult to recognise changing circumstances and adapt appropriately.

The 'social action' approach (Silverman, 1970) takes the idea of sense-making further by suggesting that organisational members are engaged in a process of 'socially constructing' their organisation as they continually act and interact with each other.

Consensus on what is 'taken as true' provides the underpinning for organisational action. However, when the pictures of the world held by organisational members become disconnected from objective conditions organisational effectiveness is undermined. Argyris and Schom (1996) suggests that this may be an important source of learning.

Organisations as learning communities

Dixon (1994) has defined the collective learning process based on shared meaning. His representation of an iterative cycle of collective thinking and reflection involves acting, assessing, acting again and building a collective memory of effective action – thus representing OL when it is flowing smoothly and freely. See Figure 17.1.

The learning organisation

The idea of the LO has been developing over the last 25 years. It remains a vague concept and more of a promise than an enacted reality. Much of the writing on the LO is about building normative models for creating change in the direction of improved learning processes (Easterby-Smith, 1997).

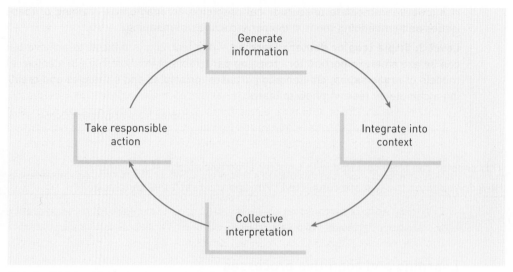

Figure 17.1 The OL cycle
Source: adapted from Dixon (1994)

Another major issue is the plethora of definitions. Here are just two, which may give you a flavour of the field. Senge (1990: 14) defines the LO as:

> '... an organisation that is continually expanding its capacity to create the future. For such an organisation it is not enough to merely survive ... for a learning organisation "adaptive learning" must be joined with "generative learning", learning that enhances our capacity to create.'

Pedler et al. (1997: 3) define the LO as:

> 'An organisation that facilitates the learning of all its members and continually transforms itself.'

Characteristics of the LO

In defining the philosophy and principles of the LO we are faced with the nebulous form of this concept. Nevertheless, it may be possible to distil some consistent features and common assumptions underpinning the LO:

- **Learning and competitive advantage** – organisations have come to realise that competitive pressures require new structural forms that use the mental powers of everyone in the organisation to their full capacity and encourage continual thinking, reflection and learning. Constant updating of organisational knowledge through learning is no longer just desirable but essential for survival.

- **Systematised learning** – the quality and quantity of learning can be increased if it is organised deliberately. Incidental and accidental learning happens all the time, but the value of this can be compounded if it is systematised, and if processes are used to review and share the learning.

- **Shared learning** – learning is best achieved if it is shared with others – through dialogue, team learning and evaluation. Data become information, which becomes knowledge when people act together to discuss the implications, linked to judgements, hunch, intuition, metaphors and symbols which form something new – an idea, a product, a service, new systems or a policy.

◆ **Climate of learning** – It is a management responsibility to build a climate in which learning is valued and people feel motivated to learn. This means replacing an atmosphere of fear, blame, shame and guilt with one of risk-taking, forgiveness and trust. It embraces mistakes. It means developing structures that identify learning processes and explicitly support opportunities for development and learning from past mistakes (i.e. learning 'why' is seen as important as learning 'how'). It also involves recognising and rewarding those who have taken the risk to experiment and create new knowledge, which improves the capability of the organisation.

◆ **Learning across boundaries** – the culture of a LO encourages collaboration across boundaries. It involves drawing on the insights of key stakeholders – customers, suppliers and outsourced workers – as well as people inside the organisation. The aim is to build a self-reinforcing community of learning in which creativity and innovation are valued. Open boundaries between departments, units and companies allow the free flow throughout the organisation of ideas for good practice, product information, customer satisfaction and benchmark data, so that the probability of creative synergies is greatly increased.

◆ **Learning as empowerment** – finally, the LO empowers learners. Sometimes known as 'subsidiarity', it replaces hierarchies with systems of minimum control and facilitates networks of groups and agents who have autonomy to act independently for change. Learning is a central value of the organisation and resources invested in these values help people to become genuinely self-developing innovators. People are encouraged to run their own projects and experience the personal satisfaction of making a real difference within the organisational space they control.

The LO in practice

A number of writers (Garvin, 1993; Lundy and Cowling, 1996; Mumford, 1999, 2004; Lahteenmaki, 2001) have suggested practical forms for realising the spirit of the LO and the implications for management behaviour:

◆ **Leadership** – top managers must drive the learning environment. By their actions they model the behaviour that others will emulate. So, they need to demonstrate openness, questioning, creativity, strategic thinking and their own willingness to learn. Higher levels of management need to show that learning is part of its vision and that creativity and innovation are truly valued.

◆ **Management** – managers need to encourage learning and work to become integrated, as much by behaviour as by exhortation. They must build learning and development into the design of work and act to create a climate in which experience is reviewed and lessons derived.

◆ **Teams** – team leaders need to help members see their activities as part of a learning forum. The key to a sustained learning process is found in collaboration; sharing knowledge and experience; adaptability; and systems thinking. **Action Learning Sets** help members to reflect on experience and learn about interaction, group dynamics and decision making, as well as outcome. Self-managed groups are responsible for an entire project, learning about the complete management process, and have a wider picture of how the organisation works. Quality management systems provide data for joint decision making and team review not its own performance.

- ◆ **Boundaries** – everything possible should be done to learn from others. Customer involvement and 360° appraisals provide vital feedback at all stages of the development process. Joint learning across teams provides a common vocabulary as well as the generalisation of good practices. Attachments to other organisations allow benchmarks to be established and lessons captured that can be brought back to the home organisation.

- ◆ **Self-learning** – people at all levels need to commit themselves to the concept of lifelong learning. This has many implications for the structure of work, not least that it should be linked to planned learning. Within this system, tasks would be designed and delegated so that people can develop. Learning would be seen as part of the work. Learning contracts would be based on maximising learning opportunities. Time would be allocated in daily schedules for reflection, analysis and the generation of new knowledge. Support networks, mentoring frameworks, learning resource centres, local learning cells and customised information technology (IT) all provide an environment for self-managed learning.

exercise

Using the five elements listed above, to what extent could Warbings be described as a learning organisation?

What evidence can you give to support your answer?

Monsanto has produced a 'knowledge management architecture' based on sophisticated electronic knowledge flows and learning forums that are multidisciplinary and project-based. Motorola's TQM system is based on a deliberate attempt to integrate performance standards, customer feedback and quality measures in a continuous learning process. GEC has an institutionalised system of 'town meetings' in which workgroups pool their experience around ideas for change.

There are also some formalised models and tools for learning and change which have been widely applied in corporate settings and can trace their origins, in part, to the LO concept, such as the European Foundation for Quality Management Model, the Balanced Scorecard and the Investor's in People Standard. While serving the useful function of focusing the attention of management on learning, quality and change as inter-connected elements, these models can seem mechanistic and deny the 'process orientation' which is at the heart of the LO project.

More useful, perhaps, are stories of organisational attempts to introduce change which is infused with the values of the LO.

Mini case study: Anglian Water Services plc

Anglian Water is one of the largest water authorities in the UK. In the 1990s, it was decided by top management to try and replace its highly structured, even bureaucratic, culture with one that was more flexible and innovative to help the company respond to a newly deregulated and demanding market.

After much painful restructuring, during which many disparate initiatives were tried, taken up and dropped, the top team decided to move to a 'LO'. In pursuing this ambition, the following initiatives were taken:

◆ Top management attended an 'executive stretch' workshop to embrace the importance of learning and empowerment;

◆ The human resource development (HRD) strategy was revised to proclaim 'learning' as a core value of work at Anglian;

◆ Workgroups were encouraged to suggest ideas for learning projects, which were intended to help workers grow in confidence, experiment with innovative ideas and become accustomed to working in multidisciplinary teams. A number of projects were undertaken, the most ambitious involved work outside Anglian, including renovating a children's hospice and digging a well in Africa;

◆ The company provided facilitation for the team development processes, coaching and mentoring for change roles, intranet learning resources and support for debriefing and disseminating lessons from each learning experience;

◆ A collaborative venture was also established with a local university to augment skills, help with knowledge generation and provide wider learning support networks.

An evaluation after three years showed that there was a lot of support for these initiatives among the workforce but continuing concern about further plans for reorganisation which promised not only further job cuts but also a tightening of central control around business values.

◆ Do you think that these experiments at Anglian suggest a sincere attempt to move towards a LO?

◆ What other innovative ideas would you suggest that Anglian Water introduce in order to become a learning organization?

◆ What factors threaten to derail progress?

(Adapted from Morton (1998) and a lecture by Morton at Roffey Park School of Management)

Summary

In this chapter we have addressed the following:

◆ MD is about developing the individual but it is also about developing the system of OL. Managers are only effective when the context encourages development. MD is therefore a sub-set of OD;

◆ The values and principles on which OD is based (e.g. holistic, planned, strategic, participative change based on behavioural science knowledge and techniques);

- The strengths and weaknesses of the tools and the conditions under which they are most likely to be successful were explored;
- Managers will increasingly use OD techniques and act as practitioners in their own right;
- The link was made between OL and individual learning, through a discussion of process models of OL; cognitive models;
- The LO was outlined in theory and practice by applying it in the real world and by seeing the role of the manager as a facilitator of learning.

Review Questions

You may wish to attempt the following as practice examination style questions.

17.1   How can OD build managerial effectiveness?

17.2   What skills do you regard as key to effective organisational development? Are these the preserve of the specialist consultants or can general managers also act as OD practitioners?

17.3   Why do you think most OD interventions fail to achieve their objectives? Does this mean that the OD approach is flawed or does the onus of responsibility lie with managers in knowing how to make effective use of OD interventions?

17.4   Make a case for your organisation becoming a LO. What are the steps it will need to take?

17.5   'The theory on OL is all very well but it offers little practical assistance to the busy manager?' Do you agree with this proposition?

References

Argyris, C. and Schon, D. (1978). *Organisational Learning: A Theory of Action Perspective*, Wokingham: Addison-Wesley.

Argyris, C. and Schon, D. (1996). *Organisational Learning 2: Theory, Method and Practice*, Wokingham: Addison-Wesley.

Burke, W. (1998). *Organisational Development: A Normative View*, Wokingham: Addison-Wesley.

Dixon, N. (1994). *The Organisational Learning Cycle: How We Can Learn Collectively*, Maidenhead: McGraw-Hill.

Easterby-Smith, M. (1997). Disciplines of organisational learning: contributions and critiques, *Human Relations*, Vol. 50, No. 9, pp. 1085–1113.

Edmondson, A. and Moingeon, B. (1998). From organisational learning to the learning organisation, *Management Learning*, Vol. 1, No. 29, pp. 5–20.

French and Bell (1984). *Organisation Development: Behavioural Science Interventions for Organisation Improvement*, London: Prentice Hall. Also see 1990 edition.

Garvin, D. (1993). Building a learning organisation, *Harvard Business Review*, Vol. 71, No. 4, pp. 78–92.

Grey, C. and Antonacopoulou, E. (2004). *Essential Readings in Management Learning*, London: Sage.

Lahteenmaki, S. (2001). Critical aspects of organisational learning research and proposals for its measurement, *British Journal of Management*, Vol. 12, No. 2, pp. 113–130.

Lundy, O. and Cowling, A. (1996). *Strategic Human Resource Management*, Chapter 8, London: Routledge.

Morton, C. (1998). Waterproof, *People Management*, 11 June.

Mumford, A. (1999). *Management Development*, Chapter 11, London: CIPD.

Mumford, A. (2004). *Management Development: Strategies for Action*, London: CIPD.

Pedler, M., Burgoyne, J. et al. (1997). *The Learning Company: A Strategy for Sustainable Development*, Maidenhead: McGraw-Hill.

Roffey Park Management School (2005). *The Management Agenda*.

Schein, E. (1987) *Process Consultation, Volumes 1 and 2*, Wokingham: Addison-Wesley.

Senge, P. (1990). *The Fifth Discipline: The Art and Practice of the Learning Organisation*, London: Doubleday Currency.

Silverman, D. (1970). *A Theory of Organisations*, London: Heineman.

Tuckman, B. and Jensen, N. (1977). Stages of group development revisited, *Group and Organisational Studies*, Vol. 2, No. 3, pp. 419–427.

Weick, K. (1979). *The Social Psychology of Organising*, Wokingham: Addison-Wesley.

Weick, K. (2001). *Making Sense of the organisation*, Oxford: Blackwell.

Further Reading

Argyris, C. (1999). *On Organisational Learning*, Oxford: Blackwell.

Beckhard, R. and Pritchard, W. (1992). *Changing the Essence: The Art of Creating and Leading Fundamental Change in Organisations*, San Francisco, CA: Jossey Bass.

Blackler, F. (1993). Knowledge and the theory of organisations: organisations as activity systems and the reframing of management, *Journal of Management Studies*, Vol. 30, No. 6, pp. 863–884.

Champy, J. and Nohria, N. (eds.) (1996). *Fast Forward: The Best Ideas on Managing Business Change*, Boston, MA: Harvard Business School.

Cummings, T. and Worley, C. (2001). *Organisational Development and Change*, Cincinnati, OH: South-Western College Publishing.

Dalton, K. (forthcoming). *A Critical Introduction to Management Development*, London: Pearson.

Easterby-Smith, M., Araujo, L. et al. (1999). *Organisational Learning and the Learning Organisation*, London: Sage.

French, W. and Bell, C. (1990). *Organisation Development*, Englewood Cliffs, NJ: Prentice Hall.

Garratt, B. (1987). *The Learning Organisation*, London: Fontana/Collins.

Morton, C. (1998). Waterproof, *People Management*, 11 June.

Pedler, M., Burgoyne, J. and Bodell, T. (1997). *The Learning Company: A Strategy for Sustainable Development*, Maidenhead: McGraw-Hill.

Useful Websites

amed.org.uk – website of the Association for Management Education and Development – a professional network for people in individual and OD, covering publications, meetings, services and networks for professionals

roffeypark.co.uk – Roffey Park Management Institute range of publications, research, learning resources and bespoke development consultancy; useful for articles about contemporary OD

www.seu.au/schools/gem/ar/arp/actlearn.html – useful coverage on OD action research

CHAPTER 18

The Dark Side of Management: the consequences for organisations

By Angela Mansi

Chapter outline

This chapter explains 'the dark side of management' and the phenomenon of management derailment. It considers how so many of the qualities that propel individuals into leadership and senior management roles can, very often, lead to their downfall and possibly destroy the company. It looks at how such managers can wreak havoc on the workforce, resulting in behaviours often seen as bullying and intimidation and, in turn, ruin their own developing careers. It addresses questions posed by psychologists as to why people who are seen as bright, friendly, likeable, enthusiastic and well adjusted can often resort to what is seen as 'strange behaviour' that is sometimes disastrous for an organisation (see Kets De Vries, 1989; Hogan et al., 1994; Furnham, 1998) and considers what type of people 'derail' and what organisations can do to support senior managers.

Learning outcomes

By the end of this chapter, you should be able to:

◆ Describe what is meant by the 'dark side' of personality;

◆ Explain, with examples, the concept of 'management derailment' and how this manifests at work;

◆ Outline the psychological theories underpinning dysfunctional behaviour at work;

◆ Illustrate the development of dark side traits;

◆ Show the harmful consequences of ineffectual management;

◆ Use strategies for managing the 'dark side' of personnel;

◆ Assess their own potential dark side personality traits.

Introduction

Managerial derailment and the 'dark side' behaviours have potentially disastrous consequences for organisations. The higher up the organisation many senior mangers go, the less likely they are to be developed and managed themselves. Often people are promoted for their technical competency and are not developed in interpersonal and management skills for their organisation. They become pressured and, depending on their personality, begin to show signs of dysfunctional behaviours. This chapter will consider and outline what these behaviours are, how they might manifest in the workplace and, more importantly, the negative impact they have on an individual's career, on their fellow workers and the effectiveness of the organisation. It will also indicate some ways in which human resource management (HRM) and organisations can minimise the effects of the dark side of management.

Manager derailment

Research on management has tended to focus on the qualities of leadership rather than on incompetency of managers, and until recently there has been little consensus or empirical evidence regarding the personality characteristics that define effective management and leadership (Hogan et al., 1994, Mansi, 2000). When examining why managers fail, research so far has been inconclusive and speculative. Yet a good manager is considered fundamentally important to effective teamwork and organisational efficiency (Kets de Vries, 1989; Hogan et al., 1994).

Good management is seen as the cornerstone of an effective organisation; when senior management fails, the company is damaged, sometimes beyond repair (Hogan and Hogan, 1997). Enron, Barings Bank and the Disney Corporation (see below) have found, to their cost that some of their most senior executives have been incompetent, untrustworthy and dangerous. This is costly in terms of financial considerations and affects organisational reputation, employee welfare, long-term strategy and external investment. More importantly, bad management can, in the worst case scenarios, cost lives.

The dark side of personality

The qualities that organisations seek in their senior executives – such as ambition, commitment, confidence, enthusiasm and loyalty, the qualities most often associated with leadership – are the very characteristics that can, when exaggerated, lead to their downfall, resulting in 'management derailment'. This occurs when a manager, highly competent in technical abilities, is promoted up to an area that will need completely different skills, such as effective interpersonal skills. In effect, they are promoted beyond their capabilities. A study by Conger found that, 'the very behaviours that distinguish leaders from other colleagues have the potential to produce disastrous outcomes for their organisation' (1990: 44–45).

In the field of organisational psychology personality is defined as 'how other people see us' (Hogan and Hogan, 1997: 9) and that a favourable reputation correlates highly with social acceptance (Furnham, 1998). Certainly, personality is widely

Table 18.1 The dark side of personality

Quality		Dark side
Enthusiastic	becomes	**Volatile** (moody, irritable, unpredictable, volatile, hard to please)
Shrewd	becomes	**Mistrustful** (suspicious, will retaliate, feel misused, cannot take criticism)
Careful	becomes	**Cautious** (paralysed by indecision, afraid to take risks, staid)
Independent	becomes	**Detached** (overly independent and self-focused, lacks engagement)
Focused	becomes	**Passive–aggressive** (stubborn, procrastinates, sluggish)
Confident	becomes	**Arrogant** (demanding, opinionated, self-absorbed)
Charming	becomes	**Manipulative** (ignores own mistakes, takes dangerous risks)
Vivacious	becomes	**Dramatic** (impulsive, takes credit, poor listener, over-committed)
Imaginative	becomes	**Eccentric** (odd ideas, impulsive, unaware of effect on others)
Diligent	becomes	**Perfectionistic** (fussy, critical, stubborn, micromanages)
Dutiful	becomes	**Dependent** (works hard to please superiors, fearful of decision making)

Source: The Dark Side of Personality – Hogan Personality Inventory (1992); reprinted with kind permission of Geoff Trickey, PCL Tonbridge Wells, 2004.

regarded as the sum total of 'those fundamental traits or characteristics of the person, or people in general, that endure over time and that account for consistent patterns of response to everyday situations' (Furnham, 1997: 146). Personality is what we present of ourselves to the world at large, and from this people will form an opinion about us. Personality clearly shapes other people's perceptions of the individual, thus personality concerns reputation.

It is tempting to think that while other people may have particular character traits that are unpleasant to work with, we view our own traits as acceptable and, indeed, our key strengths. Extensive and longitudinal research by Hogan and Hogan (1997), however, found that only 11 per cent of the population do not have any noticeable 'dark side' characteristics. And even that 11 per cent may just be managing them better than the rest. It seems safe to assume, then, that almost everyone has a dark side to their personality. What we might regard as our natural 'charm', others may perceive as cunning or manipulation. While we think of ourselves as being highly diligent and careful, others might perceive us being overly cautious, nit-picking, perfectionistic and micromanaging. See Table 18.1.

While much development occurs at lower levels in the organisational hierarchy, senior management is left very much to its own devices. Some of this is due to the ethos that, 'if they got this far, then obviously they are doing something right'. Another reason is that there is no one able to question, or suggest development, for such senior executives. This has led recently to an upsurge in executive coaching. Generally, incompetent managers are left alone in terms of appraisal, assessment and development, with all the problems this may bring.

The development of the dark side

The 'dark side', or as Jung (1951) called it, the 'shadow side', is that part of our personality, we are either unaware of ourselves, or if aware we usually manage to hide it from others. The 'dark side' is unacceptable to individuals as part of their desired image, and they usually manage to keep it hidden from others in social situations. It is the part of ourselves we prefer not to acknowledge.

Horney (1997) stated that, as children, we first experience situations that are beyond our control and, depending on each individual personality reaction, it is these childhood experiences that lead to the development of anxiety and stress. Furthermore, as children we first develop 'defence strategies' in order to manage the perceived threat from others, thereby alleviating, to some extent, anxiety. Children lack power to deal effectively with stress, fear and anxiety and turn to adults to do this for them. The problem with much childhood development, however, is that the main carers we need to turn to for protection are very often the people who are causing such negative feelings in the first place.

Horney (1937) believed that children learn to hide hostility with defensive behaviours, from which neurotic needs are formed. She classified these neurotic needs under three headings that indicate an individual's styles of reaction when stressed, anxious or threatened. These individual styles of defending ourselves are often displayed inappropriately in our adult relationships so we over-react to perceived threats: '. . . we bring to every experience a style of interacting . . . that we learned in childhood' (Kets de Vries, 2004: 147). We transfer these childhood reactions onto current scenarios and thus affect our working relationships with others.

pause for thought

How do you think that childhood experiences linked to defensive behaviours can influence managerial behaviours? Can you give any examples of this?

The Appendix at the end of this chapter allows you to assess your own dark side personality traits.

Horney identified flawed personality tendencies that showed up in adult relationships as:

+ Moving away from other people: *a need for independence*;
+ Moving against other people: *a need for power*;
+ Moving towards other people: *a need for affirmation and love*.

These three learned styles of defensive behaviour correlate to the dark side behaviours, as shown in the boxes below.

The Neurotic Personality

(moving away from other people and showing a need for independence and solitude)

Volatile
Mistrustful
Cautious
Detached
Passive–aggressive

The **neurotic** style of reacting to stress includes such characteristics as feelings of insecurity, mistrust, hostility, a lack of achievement, emotional instability and social withdrawal. People high on this scale display a lack of control of emotions and social withdrawal. They are often nervous, bad tempered and prone to volatile outbursts. In moving away from people, a person may withdraw, either emotionally or literally, from a stressful situation to defend themselves from neurotic anxiety, and can be seen as isolated and aloof by colleagues who sense the lack of engagement (Kets de Vries, 1989).

The Narcissistic Personality

(moving against other people and trying to dominate them in order to regain some control)

Arrogant
Manipulative
Dramatic
Eccentric

The **narcissistic** style characterises people who are extraverted, energetic and active, with a need for frequent and varied social contact. Such people like to be at the centre of attention, to be seen as entertaining and charming, and enjoy the variety of life. They need to impress others, be seen as charismatic and competent, and perform well in public. Under pressure, however, these behaviours can be perceived as impulsive, unrestrained, smooth-talking, dangerously testing the limits, needing too much attention, and uninterested in other people. When *moving against others*, dark side behaviours include overbearing self-confidence, arrogance, over-competitiveness, self-display, impulsiveness and intimidating others. In this instance, these behaviours are an attempt to reduce anxiety by taking more control of the situation. People with high narcissistic scores can also be seen as manipulative and dramatic by those with whom they work.

The Obsessive Personality

(moving towards others in order to please and placate them)

Perfectionist
Dependent

The **obsessive** scale encompasses such behaviours as being overly eager to please, compliant, over-conscientious, stubborn, fussy, perfectionist and indecisive. Managers may be seen as conservative and conforming and might, under pressure, be seen as being over-compliant and being too eager to please their own manager and thereby avoiding standing up for their subordinates (Hogan and Hogan, 1997). What this scale indicates is the potential for micromanagement, someone unable to delegate, and thus showing that they do not really trust others to do the job as well as them. When *moving towards others*, a person may dissipate their own anxiety by placating the person who makes them feel anxious. They have learned to respond to threats by becoming more compliant and agreeable, and obsessively attempt to create an ordered environment around them, thereby lessening any hostility towards themselves.

These three defensive styles of reacting to other people (**neurotic**, **narcissistic** and **obsessive**) are carried over into adulthood and are the foundation for the development of the underlying theory of the psychometric test to measure for dark sides of personality. These styles of coping when under pressure are very often out of proportion to the situation and are perceived by others as harmful to relationships (Hogan and Hogan, 1997). These beliefs are thought to relate directly to particular manifestations of psychological conditions associated with derailing behaviours (Slusher and Anderson, 1989).

pause for thought

Choose five people from among your work colleagues, family or friends.

◆ How do they each compare to the three personality types – neurotic, narcissistic and obsessive?

◆ How do you know?

◆ How do their personalities affect the way you interact with each individual?

The incompetent manager

While there have been innumerable books on how to be a successful manager, there has been very little written on the incompetent manager. Research had tended to focus on the best qualities of a manager, without considering the personality characteristics that cause them to 'go off the rails'. Moreover, tests look for the optimum measurement of a trait, so if confidence is seen as a key personality trait, then '... the more of it the better!'

Dysfunctional managers have the ability to create a very unhappy workforce, resulting in a lack of trust, job dissatisfaction and increase in levels of stress (Field, 2003). Indeed, 'the perfidious issue of "stress at work" and its more serious cousin the nervous breakdown are often caused by dysfunctional managers' (Furnham and Taylor, 2004: 141). Moreover, the organisation itself can become 'toxic' because of the personality style of senior managers and worse; 'they model dsyfunctionality to young staff' thus perpetuating the problem (ibid.: 143).

One of the most important factors in good relationships between managers and their staff is how trustworthy colleagues perceive their managers to be (Hogan et al., 1994). 'If trust is broken, people are going to feel violated' (Bradford, 2003), a sentiment echoed by someone for whom trust is crucial in their work, a Watch Commander of a national fire service: 'trust is the cornerstone of good teamwork' (Gurney, 2000). Therefore erosion of trust is a threat to organisational effectiveness.

Research shows that, 'the quality of superior–subordinate interactions is one of the cornerstones of successful organisational functioning' (Kets de Vries, 1984: 95), which greatly influences the effectiveness and achievement of group goals (Hollander, 1978).

Studies from the Centre for Creative Leadership (see McCall and Lombardo, 1983) confirm that managers who are seen as incompetent have an adverse impact on their teams by losing the support of colleagues. In the US, for instance, 60–70 per cent of employees in organisations studied stated that the most stressful part of their job was the interaction with their manager (see Hogan et al., 1990). Where there is erosion of trust between workers and manager, the team cohesion will deteriorate, leading to an increase in staff turnover, absenteeism, conflict and safety problems (Kets de Vries and Miller, 1984).

It can, therefore, be seen how the personalities of senior managers are significant in helping to understand why some organisations fail and others succeed (Kets de Vries and Miller, 1984). Bentz found that particular personality characteristics such as moodiness, playing politics, being over-controlling or dishonest, led directly to what he termed 'manager derailment' (1985). According to him, 'derailment' occurs when managers who are technically competent are promoted for perceived personality qualities, but fail in the role for which they have been promoted, either through lack of training or lack of good interpersonal skills (ibid.).

Managers who 'derailed' were seen as:

♦ arrogant

♦ moody

♦ insensitive to others

♦ over-ambitious

♦ cold

♦ over-controlling

♦ selfish

♦ unable to delegate or make decisions, and untrustworthy (McCall and Lombardo, 1983; Lombardo et al., 1988; Hazucha, 1991).

Further research (Lombardo et al., 1988; Hellervik et al., 1992; Peterson, 1993; Hogan and Hogan, 1997) has identified the derailment factors of senior managers. These include untrustworthiness, over-control, exploitation and manipulation, micromanagement, irritability, unwillingness to discipline or confront, and vindictiveness when things do not go their way.

Seemingly friendly and enthusiastic managers who became irrational, impatient and volatile were treated with suspicion and resentment. Needless to say, these had a disastrous effect on work colleagues and, in the long term, on organisational effectiveness and profits (see Kets de Vries, 1989). The following case study highlights this scenario (see p. 340).

exercise

In the following mini case study on Michael Eisner say:

♦ **To what degree has Eisner contributed to the decline of Disney?**

♦ **What kind of a person is Eisner?**

♦ **How do you know?**

Mini case study: the dark side of Michael Eisner – CEO Disney Corporation

◆ Michael Eisner was the CEO of Disney, a post he held for 20 years until September 2005;

◆ The first ten years of his reign were reasonably successful in a financial sense, although they were characterised by major fights between Eisner and other senior executives;

◆ For the past ten years Disney has been declining.

The following is from the business section of the *New York Times*, 11 February 2004:

> *'It is a matter of public record that he is one of the most hated CEOs in America. He has had bitter open quarrels with a number of people, including Stephen Jobs and Roy Disney, brother of the founder. His compensation package is enormous and in his public photos he radiates negative affect whilst at the same time admitting to "seeking vengeance." Mr. Eisner's combative style . . . has forced several talented executives to leave and lead to the recent nasty split with Steven Jobs and Pixar.'*

Eisner was accused of arrogance in attempting to thwart any succession plan for Disney. The report goes on:

> *'Last year Mr. Eisner said he held the name of his successor "in a secret envelope." This year he has a succession plan but it is also secret. Mr. Eisner said he did not like the notion that a successor be designated and groomed in advance, as General Electric did with the changeover from John Welch, Jr. to Jeffrey Immelt. Eisner's arrogance is a given. What is distinctive is his combativeness, his inability to build a team, the view that others are out for vengeance, and a passion for doing things in secret.'*

Professor Robert Hogan analysed psychological data from several media sources. The conclusion on Eisner's dark side was that were he to be measured on his dark side of personality, it is highly likely that he would be: 'a paranoid personality – secretive, suspicious, quarrelsome, combative, and vengeful.' Hogan argues that even with a minimum of data, it is still possible to detect the distinctive features of Eisner's personality, and the dark sides that are causing him to derail.

Research, derived from studies of 360° feedback, demonstrates that the colleagues most likely to be affected by manager derailment behaviours are those subordinate to the manager. Not surprisingly, managers will shape their behaviour more favourably when dealing with superiors, and let their guard down when working with subordinates (McCall and Lombardo, 1983; Lombardo et al., 1988; Kets de Vries, 1989; Kofodimos, 1990; Hazucha, 1991; Hogan et al., 1994).

Even a *perception* of a lack of integrity will affect the manager–subordinate relationship, and commitment to joint goals, which in time can erode the economic health of an organisation (Hogan et al., 1997). Furthermore, research has shown that the integrity of a manager rates as the *single most important* personality factor in determining how a subordinate rates managerial effectiveness (Lombardo et al., 1988; Campbell, 1994; Harris and Hogan, 1992). For this reason, subordinates are considered uniquely placed to be able to evaluate their manager's effectiveness (Hogan et al., 1994).

Some studies of personality affecting group performance derive from studies of airline flight crews. Breakdown in team performance was the primary cause of air transport problems. Furthermore, the flight crew performance, in terms of number and severity of errors made by crew members, is significantly correlated with the personality of the Captain (Chidester et al., 1991). Captains with abrasive, arrogant and cold personalities tended adversely to affect their relationships with colleagues. Consequently, their co-flight deck colleagues (first officers and engineers), as well as their cabin crew, tended to refrain from contradicting them, despite thinking that the Captain's orders or information may be incorrect. This has been detrimental in interpersonal relationships and disastrous in terms of safety and survival.

It is worth noting, however, that the *context* in which the behaviour occurs will influence our perceptions of how 'dark' it is. Research with a national UK fire service (Mansi, 2000), which looked at the management style of Watch Commanders, indicated that while anger was a common reaction to stress or threats, it was *not* seen as a particularly 'dark side' behaviour by others, with comments such as '. . . well, it's what men do isn't it?' or 'that's how we let off steam'. Other studies of fire officers found that context affects individual perceptions of the dark side so that anger is the one emotion that appeared to be culturally sanctioned in this setting (McLeod, 2000). Thus, our working environment shapes how our dark sides are perceived. The same emotional reaction to stress within, for instance, a counselling unit, would be seen as highly hostile and completely inappropriate.

The consequences of dysfunctional management

One major consequence of dark side management styles is an elevated rate of stress among other employees. The seventh Management Agenda Survey (Roffey Park, 2004) showed that over a fifth (22 per cent) of managers had lost trust in their senior executives and, consequently, 74 per cent claimed to be suffering from work-related stress. In the US, the situation is worse; research shows that less than 50 per cent of managers were trusted by their employees (Hogan et al., 1994). Managerial pressure, manifested for instance through bullying, is the most likely cause of people staying off work for longer periods than they might do otherwise (Field, 2003).

More time is lost due to sickness and absenteeism for which poor management practices are blamed than for any other single cause. The Work Foundation (2002) argues in a recent survey that the increase in time off is directly due to poor management, resulting in high levels of sickness and stress and emotional problems.

Moreover, poor management can literally make your blood boil. A report by researchers at Buckingham Chilterns University Collage in 2003 showed that bad managers literally drive up employee blood pressure levels, significantly increasing the chance of a stroke or heart attack (Wagner et al., 2003). The researchers argue that heart trouble would be less of a problem if people had happier relationships with their immediate boss.

How to handle the 'dark side' of management

The 'high flyers' of the corporate world need to be nurtured, so that 'dark side' behaviours are *managed*, rather than suppressed. People do not become 'high flyers' without several potential dark sides to their character. Psychometric testing has found that a significant number of senior executives have very high levels of dark side traits; but they also have the ability to manage their emotional natures, demonstrating emotional maturity and stability.

Psychometric testing is a well-established method that seeks to assess management style and performance. Whereas most of these measure normative personality traits, one test (Hogan Development Survey – HDS) has been designed specifically to measure potential 'dark side' behaviours. This can assist in helping with the development of senior managers through managing their behaviours, rather than rejecting them.

However, in attempting to assess potential dark side characteristics, it would be *inadvisable* for the HDS to be used on its own. The qualities of each scale, when the individual is not stressed, are the very characteristics that are needed to sustain a job at that level. It is only when these are not managed well that the qualities they possess can present problems.

The more dynamic, goal-orientated, creative and focused a manager becomes, the more likely they are to upset someone along their career path. What is needed is to develop a blame-free culture in which ideas can thrive and mistakes learned from. People who are encouraged to initiate change, to see potential in situations, to take risks without being blamed, are less likely to feel defensive and threatened.

exercise

What 'dark side' behaviours does the CEO of Warbings show to his employees?

How could he be helped to manage his dark side more effectively?

These defensive styles of reacting to other people, often out of all proportion to the current situation, are carried over from childhood into adulthood causing immense damage to professional relationships at the individual, the group and the organisational level. However, as Bennis succinctly states: '. . . there is nothing you can do about your early life now, except to understand it. You can, however, do everything about the rest of your life' (1989: 80).

Emotional stability

Impression management is an attempt to influence other people's perception of ourselves in a positive light; for example, when we try to appear our best at selection interviews. Nonetheless, potential dark side behaviours are often undetected at the interview or assessment stage because they 'co-exist with high levels of self-esteem and good social skills' (Harris and Hogan, 1992: 495). If this is so successful that an artificial image is created, it might result in a senior position being given to someone who is actually highly inappropriate, when a more qualified individual is overlooked, resulting in potential future management derailment (Griffin and O'Leary-Kelly, 2004).

Emotional stability, also known as emotional intelligence (EI or EQ), refers to the ability of the individual to be able to deal with their emotional states in a mature, constructive manner. In addition, it refers to the fact that we are aware of how our behaviour and emotional states can impact on other people. We all feel emotional at times but 'emotions felt' are different to 'emotions displayed' and the lack of restraint and self-awareness at such times adds to the manifestation of the dark side of personality at work.

Low emotional adjustment will result in hostile attribution bias towards others, where other people's actions are always interpreted as intentional, malicious and hostile (Dodge et al., 1986). Such people will 'rarely give others the benefit of the doubt: they simple assume that any provocative actions by others are intentional' (ibid.: 47) and thus react accordingly.

To people with high levels of hostile attribution, any added pressure at work will result in quite intense emotional reactions. Understandably, hostility impacts significantly on workplace relationships. Moreover, those with such low emotional adjustment and a neurotic personality will often seek to retaliate, thus contributing to the overall level of aggression in their workplace (Skarlicki and Folger, 1997).

Triggers and solutions

'Good leaders may put pressure on their people, but abusive and incompetent management create billions of dollars of lost productivity each year' (Hogan et al., 1994: 497). Studies in the US show that the failure rate among senior executives has been 'at least 50 per cent' (Shipper and Wilson, 1992; Kets de Vries, 1992). Referring again to the Disney case, one employee is quoted as saying that Eisner '. . . liked to put six bull terriers together and see which five die' (Stewart, 2005: 5).

As dark side behaviours are triggered by intense emotional arousal, stress, tiredness, information overload or feeling threatened in any way, it would clearly be beneficial to both the organisation and the individual if support were shown to those managers who might be more vulnerable at such times (Zillman, 1993; Baron, 2004). Therefore, knowing about individual *potential* dark side behaviours will facilitate such support.

What can be done about such behaviours in senior managers? Can they be changed at all? And will any intervention have a lasting effect on their dark side? Research showed that intensive intervention through effective and *targeted* coaching aimed at derailed managers was the most productive method in significantly changing long-held dysfunctional behaviours. Through a five-year longitudinal study, comprising 370 candidates, it was found that the majority of people were able to change behaviours that were targeted in coaching sessions (Peterson, 1993; Peterson and Hicks, 1995). This study concluded that long-term change needs a long-term intervention, and that there will be a productive and significant commitment to the development of managers if it is carried out over a longer period than current leadership programmes allow (Hogan et al., 1994).

Other strategies to help with the management of dark side behaviours include:

◆ Thorough selection and assessment methods, including testing emotional stability;

◆ Developmental coaching, including interpersonal skills, sensitivity to others and managing diversity;

- Training in self-awareness and assertiveness;
- Effective communication skills, including listening and influencing skills;
- Stress- and time-management techniques;
- The development of effective team skills, including delegating, coaching and motivating;
- Rigorous psychometric testing as part of the career plan, together with developmental feedback;
- Instigating a thorough performance appraisal system that includes everyone in the business – stressing that this is developmental, non-judgemental and explorative;
- Supporting change for individuals, teaching anxiety management and encouraging a climate of acceptance, crucial to developing potential 'high flyers' (McCall, 1998).

Summary

Success at any level requires a certain amount of self-awareness so that particular emotional reactions and behaviours can be managed effectively (Newton, 1995). If apparently well-balanced individuals begin to behave irrationally, this can have disastrous effects on work colleagues and the organisation (see Kets de Vries, 1989). Therefore, it would be both economically and ethically reasonable to offer as much support as possible to raise people's awareness of their style of management under pressure. The results could give some insight into an individual's personality reactions and could help foster greater understanding between colleagues of all ranks. Knowledge of why someone is acting in a particular way can help bring understanding of behaviours.

This chapter has shown how the dark side of personality develops; how it can be seen in senior management; and how damaging it can be to an organisation at many levels. The danger for the workplace is that organisations tend to reflect the personality of their leader – with all the potential for derailment for the organisation, and 'dysfunctional leaders contribute to organizational neurosis' (Kets de Vries, 2004: 193). It must be stressed, however, that without their dark sides, many successful managers would not have achieved so much. Steve Jobs, CEO of Apple, is considered by many to be a genius in terms of his creativity and drive. However, his dark side can be seen in his impatience with closed-mindedness in colleagues and his overconfidence, perceived by others as arrogance. Journalist David Plotnikoff says: '... he exudes arrogance of a blast furnace intensity that people find hard to overlook ... but there is simply no way the Mac could have been born without that' (Campbell, 2004).

An appendix is provided at the end of this chapter, which contains a self-assessment questionnaire for you to examine the 'dark side' of your own personality.

Review Questions

You may wish to attempt the following as practice examination style questions.

18.1 Describe what is meant by 'the dark side of personality' and list some examples of where this phenomena has a detrimental impact on the workplace.

18.2 Explain at least three psychological theories underpinning dysfunctional behaviour at work.

18.3 Critically evaluate the links between childhood coping strategies and managerial behaviours.

18.4 Define management derailment.

References

Baron, R.A. (2004). *Workplace Aggression and Violence: Insights from Basic Research*, in R.W. Griffin and A.M. O'Learny-Kelly (eds.) *The Dark Side of Organizational Behaviour*, San Francisco, CA: Jossey-Bass.

Bennis, W. (1989). *On Becoming a Leader*, Reading, MA: Addison-Wesley.

Bentz, V.J. (1985). A view from the top: a 30-year perspective of research devoted to discovery, description and prediction of executive behaviour, paper presented at the 93rd Annual Convention of the APA, Los Angeles.

Bradford, R. (2003). Kaisen consulting, *The Guardian*, 27 November.

Campbell, D. (2004). Profile of Steve Jobs, *The Guardian*, 18 June.

Campbell, D.P. (1994). Manual for the Campbell Leadership Index, Minneapolis, National Computer Systems, in R. Hogan, G.J. Curphy and J. Hogan (eds.) What we know about leadership: effectiveness and personality, *American Psychologist*, Vol. 49, pp. 493–504.

Chidester, T.R., Helmreich, R.L., Gregorich, S.E. and Geis, C.E. (1991). Pilot personality and crew co-ordination, *International Journal of Aviation Psychology*, Vol. 1, pp. 25–44.

Conger, J.A. (1990). The dark side of leadership, *Organizational Dynamics*, Vol. 19, pp. 44–55.

Dodge, K.A., Pettit, G.S., McClaskey, C.L. and Brown, M.M. (1986). Social competence in children, *Monographs of the Society for Research in Child Development*, Vol. 51, pp. 1–65.

Field, T. (2003). Dignity and decency at work, seminar on work psychology, Douai Abbey, Berkshire.

Furnham, A. (1997). *The Psychology of Behaviour at Work: The Individual in the Organisation*, London: Psychology Press.

Furnham, A. (1998). *The Psychology of Managerial Incompetence*, London: Whurr Publishers.

Furnham, A. and Taylor, J. (2004). *The Dark Side of Behaviour at Work*, London: Palgrave.

Gurney, M. (2000). Unlikely managers – Watch Commanders in the London Fire Brigade, *Management Today*, September.

Griffin, Ricky, W. and O'Leary-Kelly, A.M. (2004). *The Dark Side of Organizational Behavior*, San Francisco, CA: Jossey-Bass.

Harris, G. and Hogan, J. (1992). Perceptions and personality correlates of managerial effectiveness, paper presented at the 13th Annual Psychology in the Defense Symposium, Colorado Springs, CO.

Hazucha, J.F. (1991). Success, jeopardy and performance: contrasting managerial outcomes and their predictors, unpublished doctoral dissertation, University of Minnesota, Minneapolis.

Hellervik, L.W., Hazucha, J.F. and Schneider, R.J. (1992). Behavior change: models, methods and a review of evidence, in M.D. Dunette and L.M. Mough (eds.) *Handbook of Industrial Organizational Psychology*, Palo Alto: Consulting Psychologists Press.

Hogan, R. and Hogan, J. (1997). *Hogan Development Survey Manual*, UK edition, Tunbridge Wells: Psychological Consultancy Limited.

Hogan, R., Curphy, G.J. and Hogan, J. (1994). What we know about leadership: effectiveness and personality, *American Psychologist*, Vol. 49, pp. 493–504.

Hogan, R., Johnson, J. and Briggs, S. (eds.) (1997). *Handbook of Personality Psychology*, San Diego, CA: Academic Press.

Hogan, R., Raskin, R. and Fazzini, D. (1994). The dark side of charisma, in R. Hogan, G.J. Curphy and J. Hogan (eds.). What we know about leadership: effectiveness and personality, *American Psychologist*, Vol. 49, pp. 493–504.

Hollander, E.P. (1978). *Leadership Dynamics*, NY: Free Press.

Horney, K. (1937). *The Neurotic Personality of Our Time*, London: Norton and Co.

Horney, K. (1997). Neurosis and human growth: the struggle towards self-realization, in R. Hogan and J. Hogan (eds.) *Hogan Development Survey Manual*, UK edition, Tunbridge Wells: Psychological Consultancy Limited.

Jung, C.G. (1951). *Aion*, 2nd edition, Princeton, NJ: Bollingen.

Kets de Vries, M.F.R. (1989). Leaders who self-destruct: the causes and cures, *Organizational Dynamics*, Vol. 17, No. 4, pp. 5–17.

Kets de Vries, M.F.R. (1992). Executive selection: advances but no progress, *Issues & Observations*, Vol. 2, pp. 1–5.

Kets de Vries, M.F.R. (2004). Organizations on the couch: a clinical perspective on organizational dynamics, *European Management Journal*, Vol. 22, No. 2, pp. 183–200.

Kets de Vries, M.F.R. and Miller, D.L. (1984). *The Neurotic Organization: Diagnosing and Changing Counterproductive Styles of Management*, San Francisco, CA: Jossey-Bass.

Kofodimos, J. (1990). Why executives lose their balance, *Organizational Dynamics*, Vol. 19.

Lombardo, M.M., Ruderman, M.N. and McCauley, C.D. (1988). Explanations of success and derailment in upper level management positions, *Journal of Business and Psychology*, Vol. 2, pp. 199–216.

Mansi, A. (2000). The dark side of personality in the London Fire Brigade, MSc Organisational Psychology dissertation, City University, London.

McCall, M.W. (1998). *High Flyers: Developing the Next Generation of Leaders*, Boston, MA: Harvard Business School Press.

McCall, M.W., Jr. and Lombardo, M.M. (1983). Off the track: why and how successful executives get derailed, *Technical Report No. 21*, Greensboro, NC: Center for Creative Leadership.

McLeod, J. (2000). Do fire-fighters suffer from stress?, in J. Hartley and A. Branthwaite (eds.) *The Applied Psychologist*, 2nd edition, Buckingham: Open University Press.

Newton, T. (1995). *Managing Stress: Emotions and Power at Work*, London: Sage.

Peterson, D.B. (1993). Measuring change: a psychometric approach to evaluating individual coaching outcomes, paper presented at the Annual Conference of the Society for Industrial and Organizational Psychology, San Francisco.

Peterson, D.B. and Hicks, M.D. (1995). *Development FIRST: Strategies for Coaching and Developing others*, Minneapolis, MI: Personnel Decisions International Corporation.

Roffey Park (2004). *The 7th Management Agenda Report*.

Shipper, F. and Wilson, C.L. (1992). The impact of managerial behaviors on group performance, stress and commitment, in K.E. Clark, M.B. Clark and D.P. Campbell (eds.) *Impact of Leadership*, New York: Center for Creative Leadership.

Skarlicki, D.P. and Folger, R. (1997). Retaliation in the workplace: the roles of distributive, procedural and interactional justice, *Journal of Applied Psychology*, Vol. 82, pp. 434–443.

Slusher, M.P. and Anderson, C.A. (1989). Belief, perseverance and self-defeating behaviours, in R.C. Curtis (ed.) *Self-Defeating Behaviours: Experimental Research, Clinical Impressions and Practical Implications*, New York: Plenum Press.

Stewart, J.B. (2005). *Disneywar: The Battle for the Magic Kingdom*, New York: Simon and Schuster.

Wagner, N., Fieldman, G. and Hussey, T.B. (2003). The effect on ambulatory blood pressure of working under favourably and unfavourably perceived supervisors, *Occupational and Environmental Medicine*, Vol. 60, No. 7, pp. 468–474.

Work Foundation (2002). *Working in Britain Survey*, London: The Work Foundation.

Zillman, D. (1993). Mental control of angry aggression, in D.M. Wegner and J.W. Pennebaker (eds.) *Handbook of Mental Control*, Englewood Cliffs, NJ: Prentice Hall.

Further Reading

Cooper, G.L. and Williams, S. (ed.) (1994). *Creating Healthy Organisations*, Chichester: Wiley.

Fineman, S. (2000). *Emotions in Organisations*, 2nd edition, London: Sage.

Frost, P. (2003). *Toxic Emotions at Work*, Cambridge, MA: Harvard Business Press.

Useful Websites

www.psychological-consultancy.com/contact.htm – Psychological Consultancy Ltd's information on HDS psychometric testing in research training, online assessment and reports on developments

dan@hoganassessments.com – access to information on Hogan Assessment Systems (Drs Robert and Joyce Hogan) – a test-publishing company covering personality research, industry solutions and results and training, with focus on predicting job performance (e.g. Hogan Personality Inventory)

www.thefieldfoundation.org, www.successunlimited.co.uk – Tim Field working for a bully-free world with access to current research and information on all aspects of bullying – the largest website on the subject

www.cipd.co.uk/subjects/dvsequl/harassmt/bully atwork0405.htm – CIPD coverage of harassment and bullying at work

Appendix

Self-assessment: THE DARK SIDE OF PERSONALITY

Try this self-assessment exercise to identify if you may be showing a 'dark side' in your behaviours.

Part 1

Select 6 of the following items that you consider to be among your strengths? Identify these with a tick (✔) in the second column. Now complete the other two columns in the table.

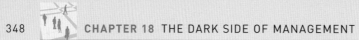

My strengths are:	✔	When stressed, I react by:	What potential 'dark side' might I be showing to others?
1. Strong enthusiasm for people, projects and ideas.			
2. Shrewdness; quick to see if others are taking advantage; difficult to fool.			
3. Careful not to make mistakes or rock the boat; I work in tried and trusted ways.			
4. I am independent and like working on my own; some people think I am shy but I am just concentrating.			
5. I work to my own timetable; I do not like being rushed; I have clear goals; I do not work well with interruptions; I have high standards in my work.			
6. I am confident and talented in my work; I am happy to take the initiative; I have 'vision' in how I want things done.			
7. I am charming and sociable; I can be impulsive at times, yet I work hard at getting what I want; I become bored with routine; I enjoy taking risks.			
8. I am flirtatious, charming and often the centre of attention; I am gregarious, fun-loving and entertaining; I like to be listened to.			
9. I am very creative and can be relied upon to come up with something new; I am seen as visionary, I like to think 'outside the box'; I like to dress/behave differently in my own style.			

My strengths are:	✔	When stressed, I react by:	What potential 'dark side' might I be showing to others?
10. I am conscientious, orderly and attentive to detail; I dislike messiness and am highly organised and hard working; 'If something is worth doing it is worth doing well' is my motto.			
11. I create harmony and if I can help others I always do; I like to feel needed and am happy when praised; good manners are important; I like to fit in with the team.			

Part 2

How to manage your dark side

	Potential dark side	How can I manage this?
1.	Volatile	
2.	Mistrustful	
3.	Cautious	
4.	Detached	
5.	Passive–aggressive	
6.	Arrogant	
7.	Manipulative	
8.	Dramatic	
9.	Eccentric	
10.	Perfectionist	
11.	Dependent	

Part 3

Ways that other people have found helpful

	Potential dark side	How you could manage it?
1.	Volatile	*Stress-management training; learning not to walk away from scenes; staying and talking it through; trying not to get too enthusiastic at beginning then bored; personal development/ coaching.*
2.	Mistrustful	*Cognitive reappraisal of responses when hurt; analysis of why you do not trust others; learn to trust in small ways; give others benefit of the doubt.*
3.	Cautious	*Learn to be courageous at work; challenge procedures; do not dismiss new approaches so quickly; be open-minded to other people's ideas.*
4.	Detached	*Take more interest in colleagues; be less task focused at times; when stressed, tell someone rather than retreat into yourself; learn to engage more often with other people at work; conflict-management training.*
5.	Passive–aggressive	*Assertiveness training; learning to speak up rather than retaliate silently; if interrupted, be calm but firm and tell colleagues they need to wait; learn to be more open when annoyed.*
6.	Arrogant	*Try listening to others more; stand back from the centre of attention; appreciate others' efforts and tell them; learn to take criticism lightly; try to see how your role is only part of the whole; share the credit.*
7.	Manipulative	*Try to adhere to company rules and procedures; let others know you are reliable; be straight-talking; do not play politics; take fewer risks and include others in your decision making; help others to trust you by being honest.*
8.	Dramatic	*Remember not to exhaust others with your dramas; learn to listen to other people's stories; take an interest in colleagues; don't hog the limelight; even if bored, don't keep interrupting others who may be busy.*
9.	Eccentric	*Try to see how your ideas might sound to others; pay attention to your appearance, and to your views; try to work with the team rather than being seen as the odd one out; channel your creativity outside of work, e.g. arts, creative writing, design, photography.*
10.	Perfectionist	*Learn to delegate; micromanage less; learn to let go of the control through anxiety and stress-management techniques; explore cognitive behaviour therapies; develop trust in others; ask others for help at times; learn that at times 'good enough' is fine.*
11.	Dependent	*Learn to trust your own judgement; stick up for colleagues when necessary; flatter the boss less and engage with colleagues more; assertiveness training would help with lack of confidence in decision making; stand up to superiors, in a calm but respectful manner, if you disagree.*

CHAPTER 19

Coaching and Mentoring for Professional Development

By Lisa Matthewman

Chapter outline

This chapter examines how professional development can be supported by coaching and mentoring. The role and extent of coaching within organisations will be explored while the rise of professional development at work, in the form of coaching and mentoring initiatives, will be examined. The historical development of mentoring in the workplace and a model of workplace mentoring will be explained, along with the impact that mentoring can have, while the ways in which mentoring can aid professional development will be explored, specifically focusing on the psychological aspects of relationships. Implementing initiatives and evaluating provisions will follow.

Learning outcomes

By the end of this chapter, you should be able to:

- Differentiate between coaching and mentoring;
- Explain the professional development practices of coaching and mentoring;
- Describe different models for coaching and mentoring;
- Explore how coaching and mentoring might be initiated within organisations;
- Suggest ways in which coaching and mentoring might be evaluated within organisations;
- Explore the future direction of professional development at work.

Introduction

Counselling, coaching and mentoring are similar but there are differences. All three approaches utilise some core counselling skills, such as establishing rapport, building a relationship, reflecting, active listening, questioning, challenging, summarising and providing feedback. Furthermore, each of these relationships could be seen as being based on the establishment of trust, empathy, genuineness and respect. Counselling skills are at the heart of the mentoring and coaching relationship.

Table 19.1 Characteristics of coaching and mentoring

Coaching	Mentoring
Concerned with task	Concerned with implications beyond the task
Concerns skills	Concerns capability/potential
Role of line management	Senior/experienced manager or external provider
Agenda set with coach	Agenda set by mentee
Feedback given to learner	Reflection by mentee
Short-term focus	Medium- to long-term focus
Discussion more explicit	Discussion more implicit

Characteristics of coaching and mentoring

Coaching is specifically related to a skill, task or problem, and involves feedback on performance and questioning to check that learning is taking place. More specifically, coaching is concerned with improving performance and tackling skill deficiencies.

Whereas coaching is concerned with the development of specific skills and performance, counselling focuses on clarification, raising awareness and understanding, and discussing feelings. The coach may define a problem, propose a solution, supervise action, assess performance and give feedback. The counsellor listens and clarifies the problem as proposed by the client, helps the client to explore all aspects of the problem, confronts the client with the implications of different solutions and supports the client as they plan a course of action. Within coaching relationships, the coach knows best; in counselling relationships, the client knows best.

Mentoring, on the other hand, has a focus on development and growth: it deals with individual career-related issues. When mentors use the techniques of the counsellor, they are empowering the mentee to solve their own problems and to deal with their difficulties.

Mentoring involves reflecting on the process of the mentee's development. Questioning techniques are used to stimulate growth, learning and development, as well as to raise awareness. Helping the mentee to raise their awareness and understand their functioning across a broad spectrum of areas is paramount. Table 19.1 summarises the main differences between coaching and mentoring in the workplace.

Coaching in the workplace

There has been an explosion in workplace coaching activity – organisations are starting to accept that coaching has the potential to make a significant contribution to business performance. There has been a huge leap towards harmonising qualifications and professional standards by:

◆ Training standards by ENTO, the relevant standards organisation;

◆ The human resource (HR) professional standards project from the CIPD (Chartered Institute of Personnel and Development);

◆ The International Coach Federation;

◆ The European Mentoring and Coaching Council.

Coaching can improve the performance of an already competent employee by aiding personal reflection and providing constructive criticism and guidance. The coach can share tasks and projects with the individual and ensure that they are challenging enough to stretch the employee's abilities. Coaching is a way of developing performance. Coaching encourages the development of initiative in the learner.

The reasons for introducing coaching are varied and include:

- Improving individual performance;
- Encouraging individual development;
- Dealing with underperformance;
- Fostering a culture of learning and development;
- Motivating staff;
- Accelerating organisational change;
- Demonstrating the organisation's commitment to staff;
- Improving employee retention;
- Helping employees to achieve a better work-life balance;
- Increasing productivity;
- Developing business skills.

Do you think that receiving coaching is ever perceived as a sign of weakness?

Why did you say this?

pause for thought

The coaching process

Coaching can help employees reach their potential while improving the competitiveness and productivity of the business as a whole.

Following a period of instruction, demonstration, observation and feedback, the individual can learn a new set of skills and gradually take more responsibility for a particular task. During this process, there is continuous performance feedback, support and constructive criticism. However this is only possible with a good working relationship. Coaching is often carried out on an informal basis but some organisations have made more formal coaching provisions. The coach essentially creates a learning climate in which an employee can, without any loss of self-esteem, acknowledge gaps in their knowledge, skills or attitudes; recognise how they need to change; and feel that this change is both possible and desirable. The key skills of coaching are listening, reflecting, summarising, challenging and mediating. For the organisation, coaching can help to reduce staff turnover, reduce training costs and improve strategic leadership.

Think about a time you have been coached informally.

What difference did it make to the ways in which you behaved?

pause for thought

Executive coaching

The increase in executive coaching lies in its success in providing structured development and learning for senior managers within the context of business life. Coaching is steadily becoming an essential tool in many organisations' learning and development strategy toolbox and its use by managers is likely to increase in the future. The CIPD confirms (2005) the rise of coaching and illustrates the significant contribution that coaching can make to business.

Organisations use a variety of internal and external practitioners to deliver coaching, including external coaches, specialist internal coaches, line managers and peers, as well as members of the HR department. The majority of coaching delivered by internal staff is primarily by line managers, even though they do not have the perceived neutrality and confidentiality of an external coach. Executive coaching is often reserved for senior level or high-potential employees.

The following case exemplifies the benefits of internal coaching.

window into practice

Basic Health (BH), a private healthcare organisation, is building a pool of internationally accredited coaching managers to help tackle high turnover among its 800 call centre staff. The call centre environment is stressful and many employees leave within a year. The coaching provision aims to reduce attrition and to help people grow organically and move around the organisation. Since introducing the provision, BH has entered the top 100 Best Companies to Work For and has seen more career progression for staff and cross-fertilisation of ideas.

Embedding coaching into organisational culture involves:

◆ A flexible approach to employee development;

◆ Understanding coaching and its benefits;

◆ Champions for the implementation of coaching provision;

◆ Development of a collaborative strategy between all stakeholders;

◆ Ensuring that senior management and executives have personal experience of coaching;

◆ Implementing a monitoring and evaluation process.

Model of coaching at work

The psychology of coaching is a relatively new field of study. It refers to research, theory and practical application of the behavioural science of psychology to the enhancement of life experience, work performance and personal growth. Coaching methods have changed little. Assessment instruments such as 360° feedback and the Myers–Briggs Personality Type Indicator® are also used. These traditional approaches struggle with the complexities of human development. For example, the first step of goal-focused models asks clients to explore a single goal – but often executives have a range of conflicting, sometimes vague, goals and sub-goals. New models, however, are emerging from the field of personal construct psychology (PCP). PCP explores and transforms thinking; it is the psychology of perceptions of options and outcomes. See Table 19.2.

Table 19.2 A model of the coaching process	
Stage	**Coaching method**
Observation	The coach observes the current performance of the employee and helps to clarify areas for development. They help to identify and agree development needs and expectations, and gain commitment to the process.
Analysis	The cause of poor performance is identified and understood. Help is provided to specify performance gaps.
Modelling	The coach demonstrates or explains correct performance, and provides the opportunity to practise in a safe learning environment.
Practice and review	The new behaviour is carried out under guidance and supervision. Performance is evaluated and feedback is given.

Source: adapted from Work Foundation (2003: 24)

exercise

Coaching tends to focus on skills and performance and involves giving feedback to the learner. A coach needs the ability to help others to learn, to know what good performance looks like and to give constructive feedback in a way that is acceptable to the individual they are developing.

Write five bullet points that you would use as a basis for making a business case for coaching as a developmental tool.

The Work Foundation undertook a survey of 221 HR and personnel specialists (2003) and established a set of good practice guidelines for coaching and mentoring – see Table 19.3.

Mentoring in the workplace

Defining mentoring

Mentoring is a particular form of one-to-one relationship between individuals. The archetypal model of mentoring originates from Greek mythology in relation to Homer's *Odyssey* (ca. 800 BC). When Odysseus, King of Ithaca, went to fight the Trojan War he entrusted his son Telemachus to the care and direction of his oldest friend, Mentor. Mentor, his friend and companion, would raise Telemachus to be a worthy successor to his father. It was more than ten years before father and son were reunited. This is the first known example of formal assigned mentoring that appears in literature. Other examples of mentoring can be found in history where people have benefitted from the guidance and support of another individual. Examples include artists, politicians, actors and sports personnel.

Formerly, a mentor was viewed as an older, wiser expert who would be associated with a younger protégé to develop their potential and to support their career development. Mentoring is a way of developing an individual to reach their full potential in a variety of different situations. Helping them to achieve different development

Table 19.3 Practice guidelines for coaching and mentoring

Encourage		Avoid	
Coaching	**Mentoring**	**Coaching**	**Mentoring**
Define coaching and mentoring	Choose mentors as role models	Force the role and responsibilities upon the reluctant or incompetent	Insist
Use coaching to train coaches	Assess mentors' motivations		Impose
HR to undertake training needs analysis of potential coaches	Clear understanding of the role	Use coaching alone as the sole means of training and learning	Denigrate
	Train both mentors and mentees		Put down
			Confuse age with experience
Give time for thinking and reflection	Listen first; advise second	Tell	Assume technical ability is required
Get coaches to meet together for support and to share good practice	Formalise the process	Assume	Expect all mentors to be equally popular
	Establish accountabilities	Dump responsibility	
	Give and receive feedback widely	Keep in the dark	Imagine everything is going well
Set ground rules	Market the scheme through 'satisfied customers'		Pay lip service to the scheme
Establish evaluation strategy at outset			
Discover learner's needs	Ensure commitment by all stakeholders		
Implement coaching at all levels of the organisation			

goals depends on the context and their needs. Mentoring may take place inform-ally or formally, with a more experienced person or a peer, with an individual or even in a group. In all these relationships, mentoring is a process characterised by the mentor helping the learner, or mentee, to discover something new about them-selves and their potential, thus facilitating personal development within the context of the current or a future organisation.

The Industrial Society (1995) pointed out that different definitions, interpretations and terminology have evolved around the subject and that definitions of mentoring should help to convey the nature of the relationship and the process involved. Mentoring is a development strategy, which due to its flexibility can be employed in a number of different situations. As Arnold (1997: 85) notes: 'Mentoring has been defined in various ways, sometimes so loosely that it encompasses almost any harmonious relationship between two people.' It can be varied depending on the context of the relationship and the needs of the learner. Clutterbuck (1997) com-ments that mentoring is a process in which one person (mentor) is responsible for overseeing the career and development of another person (protégé) outside the normal manager/subordinate relationship. Learning and experimentation can occur in this protected relationship. Skills can be developed and knowledge enhanced, which can result in a measurable increase in competencies and effectiveness.

So we can see that mentoring is:

♦ Usually carried out between an individual and a more senior, and/or experienced, colleague unconnected with the individual's immediate workplace;

♦ Concerned with sharing and developing a relationship over time;

♦ A powerful form of professional development for both parties involved; the mentee can discuss perplexing work problems, their feelings and emotions with somebody they trust, admire and respect;

♦ Rewarding for the mentor, who achieves personal development and satisfaction from sharing their wisdom and experience;

♦ Beneficial to the organisation – the mentor's experience and networks help the development of the mentee while other benefits cascade throughout the organisation;

♦ A way of facilitating learning for the mentee, mentor and the organisation.

Reflect on any informal mentoring experiences you have had and explain how these experiences influenced your behaviour?

pause for thought

Provision of mentoring

Mentoring can have many uses in the context of the organisation. These include:

♦ Helping new employees, and others being promoted, not just graduates on a formal development programme, to learn about the culture of an organisation;

♦ Assisting those seeking formal qualifications/membership of professional bodies;

♦ Supporting organisational change;

♦ Aiding staff on secondments, attachments sabbaticals;

♦ Providing special support for women and ethnic minority groups.

In addition, the self-directed approach of management development provisions coincides with the open and experiential learning that can take place in a mentoring relationship.

Initially mentoring provisions were focused upon high-performing managers or new entrants. There was a gradual realisation that all levels of management could benefit from mentoring in relation to employee development and career progression. According to Clutterbuck (1997), mentoring within organisational settings was unheard of until the late 1960s, after which it has become widespread in both the UK and the US, when the value of mentoring increased its popularity as a formal developmental strategy for all employees.

The Industrial Society (1995) conducted a survey of 647 personnel and HR professionals on mentoring policy and practice. It defines formal mentoring as a development method that can be employed in a number of settings to achieve various goals. The survey revealed how widespread mentoring had become in UK organisations by 1995. The findings indicated that very few organisations were using mentoring extensively (6 per cent), but almost half the organisations surveyed had apparently used mentoring to a certain extent. Occasional *ad hoc* mentoring was utilised by 23 per cent of the organisations. Five per cent of the organisations had pilot provisions in operation. But just over a quarter of the organisations commented that they made no use of mentoring at all and did not have plans to do so.

Mentoring has evolved into secondary types of developmental relationships that are characterised by less intensity. Formal mentoring involves organisations (employers or professional bodies) arranging for employees to participate in mentoring provisions or to work with specific mentors as part of an overall provision. Formal relationships are often managed and sanctioned by the HR manager.

Clutterbuck (1992: 3) gives reasons for their popularity of mentoring and comments:

> 'Mentoring, because it allows people to learn in an unthreatening manner, involves relatively little direct cost, and is effective for all sorts of people, is one of the fastest expanding approaches to developing managerial potential.'

As Arnold (1997: 90) comments: 'Mentoring is likely to remain a highly significant aspect of career management in the 21st century. It is very much in line with an emphasis on self-development through personal relationships, and might in a sense be regarded as an extension of networking.' As he notes, those development strategies 'which will prosper in the 21st century will be those that require the least interruption from work whilst also being effective and relatively cheap in helping a person or organisation to access and/or fulfil development needs' (ibid.).

exercise

W

Write a letter to the CEO of Warbings explaining why you think coaching and mentoring could help the organisation become more effective in the market place, giving specific examples of where (and how) both might be introduced.

Model of mentoring at work

Table 19.4 illustrates a 'three-phase model' of the mentoring relationship based on the author's doctoral research. It offers a systematic way of viewing the mentoring process, detailing the focus of each phase of the mentoring relationship and showing specific actions or tasks within each phase. The model offers a systematic view of the developing relationship – although in practice the three phases are not linear but instead overlap. There are limitations regarding the utility of such a developmental model, as each mentoring relationship is unique. However, the proposed three-phase model adds depth to the actions undertaken, and functions utilised for both mentees and mentors. It can be easily adapted for use in counselling and coaching developmental relationships. See Table 19.4.

The model indicates the mentoring process as gradually evolving and changing in focus over time. It highlights how psychological growth and development can result.

Table 19.4 Phase–function model of mentoring relationships

Phase 1 Beginning	Phase 2 Middle	Phase 3 Ending
Defining the problem Characterised by becoming interested, establishing commitment, deciding upon a mentor (selection, reviewing and initial bonding)	Redefining the problem Characterised by building rapport, working together and learning together. Mentor helps mentee to focus on problems and issues and facilitate self-insight and problem resolution strategies in the mentee	Managing the problem Characterised by reviewing and evaluating, developing independence and refining the relationship. Problem resolution is enhanced by the mentee's increased resource utilisation
Actions	**Actions**	**Actions**
Agreement of ground rules (contract/confidentiality) Arranging dates for meetings Establishing realistic goals Seeking opportunities Defining the objectives of the relationship Developing rapport/relationship with mentee (opening up mentee) Scene setting/setting the context Clarification of development needs Clarification of expectations/roles	Negotiating targets Establishing realistic goals Maintaining rapport and mutual respect Continuing to open up mentee Progressing on goals Mutual exchange for both parties (mutual self-disclosure) Setting objectives Action planning Strategy formulation Working on development goals Developing mentee self-reflection/self-insight	Establishing realistic goals Reviewing period of mentoring/reviewing the mentoring process Redefining the relationship Reviewing progress Reviewing objective achievements Summing up progress/achievements Acknowledgement of personal development and progress Two-way mutual exchange of information concerning mutual benefits
Functions utilised as indicated by mentees and mentors	**Functions utilised as indicated by mentees and mentors**	**Functions utilised as indicated by mentees and mentors**
Mutual self-disclosure (sharing experience and history) Listening Establishing realistic goals Acting as a sounding board Passing on know-how and thinking patterns Giving attention to the mentee	All of the functions in phase one, in addition: Encouragement for career advancement Suggesting strategies for achieving career goals Acting as a gateway Acting as a role model Discussion of feelings regarding feelings of competence,	All of the functions in phase one and two

Table 19.4 continued

Encouragement to talk openly/meet objectives	commitment to advancement, relationship with peers and work/family commitments
Conveying feelings of respect	
Providing support and feedback	Presentation of assignments to increase useful contacts/help with promotions
Displaying similar attitudes and values	
Role modelling	Opportunities to learn new skills
Maintaining confidences	Encouragement to complete assignments/meet deadlines
Sharing of ideas	Help to meet new colleagues and contacts
Invitation to socialise	
Discussion of concerns/ feelings of competency	Coaching in work skills
Displaying empathy and concern for feelings	Offering suggestions in relation to work problems
Offering sympathy	Encouragement to try new ways of behaving
	Challenging ideas or behaviours
	Presentation of tasks or assignments
	Sharing resources
	Promoting career interests
	Seeking opportunities/asking for suggestions on work issues
	Providing support and feedback regarding job performance
	Offering feedback regarding professional expertise

Phase one

Initially, during the beginning phase of the relationship, contracting occurs which clarifies both the mentee's and mentor's expectations, facilitates agreement on working goals and identifies how the relationship can be established (logistics of operation). This phase of the relationship is characterised by the mentor listening and using empathy to put the mentee at ease, especially over issues of low confidence and weak communication skills. In particular, mutual self-disclosure occurs which functions to cement the relationship and facilitate its evolution into the next phase of the process. The development of mutual respect and trust building helps to encourage self-disclosure. Here the skills of listening, conveying feelings of respect, displaying empathy and demonstrating similarity are evident.

Phase two

The middle phase of the relationship is characterised by periods of working and learning together. At this stage the mentor is coaching, challenging, encouraging and continuing to listen to the mentee's concerns and issues. Both the mentee and mentor continue to share and learn together mutually. Through continued and increased amounts of mutual self-disclosure and sharing experiences, the mentee becomes empowered and activated to continue learning. Issues are explored; problems resolved; objectives set; and achievements reviewed. The mentor appears to be using all of the functions displayed in the beginning phase, but the focus, in this phase particularly, concerns challenging, coaching and suggesting strategies to achieve development. During this phase, the earlier emotions of anxiety, excitement and enthusiasm turn into frustration, disappointment and satisfaction – particularly in relation to the mentee. The mentee finds this stage exciting but also challenging as they begin to change their mindsets and adapt their behaviours. Innate potential is gradually realised. The mentee develops a level of self-awareness that facilitates personal change, seeing themselves more accurately from the feedback given by the mentor. Such development in self-confidence, grounded in reality, enables both parties to look at alternative ways in which change and development can have a positive impact on the mentee, mentor and the organisation. This phase of mentoring is characterised by growth, change and progress. However, at times there will be resistance to change, strong impulses to revert to old habits and patterns, negativity about doing things differently and frustration at the rate of progress.

The success of the mentoring relationship during this middle phase is facilitated by the degree of relatedness (bond), by mutual self-disclosure or reciprocity, co-operation and commitment to the process. At the core of the process is the mentee's identity or self-concept – self-awareness in relation to strengths, weaknesses, competencies, core values, potential, past experience, current reality and future aspirations is enhanced. Gradually new ideas, learning and options are integrated into the self-concept of the mentee and the mentor because of the mentoring process.

Further, this is a time when the quality of the mentoring relationship becomes important. As new behaviours take effect, a sense of chaos can ensue. Insecurity and confusion can result before any transformation can take place. Gradual increases in responsibility, maturity and self-awareness lead the relationship into the final phase. Perceptions are changed and behaviour is modified. However, at this time there is a danger of not acknowledging the change in the mentoring relationship. If redefinition and review are not conducted, a co-dependent relationship can result. Thus, it is important that a relationship continues with regard to a changed contract, format, content and process.

Phase three

The third phase of the relationship is seen as a reviewing period, whereby the relationship is more equal with regard to power dynamics, exchange of views and mentee growth. At this stage the mentee has achieved as much as they can from the relationship with their present mentor and embraces a new sense of independence. The relationship is celebrated and progression on learning object-ives reviewed. The ending phase of the relationship primarily consists of reviewing, redefining and adapting to the mentee's new-found independence. The mentee has increased resources that can now be utilised and their development has reached a saturation point. It is a time when both mentee and mentor feel satisfied. See the box below.

Characteristics of effective mentoring

The mentor:

- Senior to the mentee in status, age and experience, unless it is a peer mentoring developmental relationship;
- Non-line manager relationship to reduce conflicts of interest;
- Skills and qualities required for mentoring (listening, counselling and coaching skills, analytical decision making and planning techniques);
- Commitment to the development of others;
- Willing to participate in mentoring training;
- Available and able to devote time to developing the relationship.

The mentee:

- Should have potential;
- Willing to learn and develop;
- Open to constructive criticism.

The relationship:

- Mutual trusting;
- Regularly monitored and evaluated;
- Supported by the organisational context.

The activities:

- Encouragement of self-analysis and reflection;
- Learning and development insights;
- Promoting self-understanding;
- Evaluation of strengths and weaknesses;
- Feedback and guidance;
- Development of work-related skills;
- Sounding board;
- Support and guidance;
- Role modelling;
- Apply learning to practice.

exercise

Write an email to an inexperienced first-line manager carefully explaining, with your reasons, why they need to receive coaching rather than the mentoring they have requested.

Show the email to someone else – from what you have written, do they understand the difference between the two?

Implementing mentoring provision

The principles of establishing mentoring provision are not that different from setting up good counselling provision or implementing coaching schemes. Thought needs to be given to the objectives of the scheme and gaining the collaboration of managers and employees. There need to be champions of the scheme and training provided for mentors.

A number of key principles apply to any mentoring provision implementation:

- Ensure top management commitment;
- Adapt the programme to the organisation's development programme;
- Ensure commitment and participation;
- Ensure an acceptance of the time and commitment involved;
- Decide on matching of mentors and mentees;
- Demystify the mentoring programme;
- Ensure confidentiality;
- Ensure monitoring and evaluation.

To be successful a mentoring programme must obtain acceptance and commitment from participants and non-participants alike. The scheme should have empathetic, carefully selected mentors and mentees who understand how to make the most of the developmental opportunity.

Questions to consider when establishing mentoring within organisations include:

- Why would mentoring be beneficial to the organisation?
- Is there someone to champion the provision/organise it?
- What is the mentoring provision designed to achieve?
- Who will be involved in the provision and why?
- What responsibilities will mentors and mentees have?
- Will there be training and support for mentees and mentors?
- How will the provision be evaluated?

Coaching and mentoring case studies – suggestions for practice

Autoglass	Empower
	Encourage self-direction
	Match people carefully
	Focus on the bottom line
BT	Matching process is critical
	Encourage diversity and globalisation
	Audio and video links
	E-mentoring
	Multimedia – but email alone is insufficient
Inland Revenue	Establish aims and strategy
	Pilot scheme and establish firm foundations
	Roll out carefully
	Do not create false expectations for anyone
Microsoft UK	Train mentors and mentees equally
	Continually develop mentors
	Ensure mentors have mentors
Peugeot Motor Company	Communicate aims and purposes to all stakeholders
	Focus on business development and growth
	Allow results to accrue over time

(Adapted from Work Foundation, 2003)

Current issues and new directions

There are a number of issues that concern professional developmental relationships in the workplace.

Training and qualifications

Mentors and coaches, particularly those who operate at senior management level, need to have adequate knowledge of business organisational strategy. When coaches and mentors are dealing with organisational problems, it is paramount that they have been appropriately trained to recognise the issues emerging and suggest appropriate interventions.

Supervision

Supervision for coaches and mentors is a developing area. Supervision needs to be formalised, and it is essential that codes of ethical practice be adhered to in relation to the professional associations of mentoring and coaching. For example, the European Mentoring and Coaching Council and the International Coaching Federation provide professional standards. There needs to be an adequate structure and train-ing mechanism to ensure that there are sufficient professionals who can act as supervisors and thus ensure the quality of the services offered.

Evaluation

There is a lack of in-depth research and information related to effective evaluation of activity in this area, presumably because professional development is difficult to assess. Mentors and coaches need to convince others of their effectiveness through practical demonstrations of their worth so that credible auditing can take place. Real progress will be made when it is possible to demonstrate that an investment in coaching and mentoring activities provides a visible return to the employer. Perhaps the work of Phillips and Stone (2002) in the area of assessing the return on invest-ment of training and development could be used in this context. Provision should be evaluated in relation to availability, accessibility, credibility, accountability and whether the developmental provision is meeting organisational needs.

Ethics

Various ethical issues arising from professional development within organisations must be noted. These include maintaining confidentiality; incompatibility between organisational aims and coaching and mentoring aims; conflict of loyalty of the coach and mentor with those they are developing and the organisation; and manag-ing different roles with the same client.

New directions

As organisations have become flatter in their structure, managers have more con-tact and direct responsibility for larger numbers of people on a day-to-day basis. Organisations are realising that managers need to become stronger in the skills of counselling, coaching and mentoring if they are to engage employee commitment. They will need to adopt a developmental approach that is based on empathy, respect and genuineness. Giving time and attention to employees, being interested in employee well-being and being sincere, open and honest will enrich the manager's ability to develop and lead their employees.

As professional development continues to grow in popularity, it will only be successful if managers and organisations embed such activities into team develop-ment and organisational learning strategies. Linking developmental activity to both individual and business needs will become more important than ever in the future. An organisational culture that encourages engagement in constructive and positive feedback encourages open and honest dialogue, rewards knowledge sharing, and will enhance employee welfare at work. Personal and professional development needs to be viewed as the responsibility of employees, management and the organisation.

Diversity

Embracing diversity is a further area in which coaching and mentoring can develop. Professional development practices need to be sensitive to local and national differ-ences. Professional development solutions need to be tailored to organisational circumstances and cultural appropriateness and thus local managers need to initi-ate and implement them at their own local level.

Summary

This chapter has indicated current issues in coaching and mentoring with regard to training, supervision, confidentiality, evaluation and ethics and explored new directions for professional development. The differences between coaching and mentoring have been outlined. The historical rise of coaching in the workplace was traced and the various reasons why organisations might introduce coaching noted. A simple model of coaching was explained. The developmental activity of mentoring was defined and the chapter further investigated the rise of mentoring activity in the UK. A novel 'Phase–Function model' of the mentoring process was presented and described and the chapter continued to explore how mentoring provision might be developed within an organisation.

Review Questions

You may wish to attempt the following as practice examination style questions.

19.1 What key skills underpin coaching?

19.2 Why has coaching become a popular professional development strategy?

19.3 What is the main purpose for the introduction of mentoring into the workplace?

19.4 Discuss the usability of the Phase–Function model of mentoring.

19.5 What are the main overlapping principles that underpin the implementation of coaching and mentoring provisions?

References

Arnold, J. (1997). *Managing Careers into the 21st Century*, London: Sage.

CIPD (2005). *Training and Development Survey*, London: CIPD.

Clutterbuck, D. (1992). *Everyone Needs a Mentor*, London: IPM.

Clutterbuck, D. (1997). *Everyone Needs a Mentor: How to Foster Talent Within the Organisation*, London: Institute of Personnel Management.

Industrial Society (1995). Managing best practice: the regular benchmark, mentoring report No. 12, London: Industrial Society.

Phillips, J. and Stone, R. (2002). *How to Measure Training Results*, New York: McGraw-Hill.

Work Foundation (2003). Best practice exchange, *Managing Best Practice*, Vol. 111, p. 24.

Further Reading

Clifford, J. and Thorpe, S. (2004). *The Coaching Handbook*, London: Kogan Page.

Clutterbuck, D. and Megginson, D. (1997). *Mentoring in Action: A Practical Guide for Managers*, London: Kogan Page.

Clutterbuck, D. and Megginson, D. (1998). *Mentoring Executives and Directors*, London: Butterworth.

Clutterbuck, D. and Megginson, D. (2005). *Making Coaching Work: Creating a Climate for Coaching*, London: CIPD.

Clutterbuck, D. and Ragins, B.R. (2002). *Mentoring and Diversity: An International Perspective*, London: Butterworth Heinemann.

Klasen, N. and Clutterbuck, D. (2002). *Implementing Mentoring Provisions: A Practical Guide to Successful Provisions*, London: Butterworth Heinmann.

Leibling, M. and Prior, R. (2004). *Coaching Made Easy*, London: Kogan Page.

Parkin, M. (2004). *Tales for Coaching*, London: Kogan Page.

Pelter, B. (2001). *The Psychology of Executive Coaching: Theory and Application*, London: Brunner-Routledge.

Thorne, K. (2004). *Coaching for Change*, London: Kogan Page.

Wray, M. and Parsloe, E. (2004). *Coaching and Mentoring*, London: Kogan Page.

Useful Websites

www.coachingnetwork.org.uk – the Coaching and Mentoring Network portal site offering information on the latest developments in coaching and mentoring and products and services (e.g. courses)

www.cipd.co.uk/subjects/lrnanddev/coachmntor – CIPD coverage of coaching and mentoring research, articles and courses

www.emccouncil.org – website of the European Mentoring and Coaching Council, with guidance on good practice, conferences, news, reports and services

CHAPTER 20

Counselling at Work

By Lisa Matthewman

Chapter outline

When personal life affects professional life – and when professional life has an effect on personal life – employees can become vulnerable and psychological distress can occur. This is when personal development is necessary. Counselling is a way of providing people with the means to help themselves. It aims, in a confidential environment, to help someone see their present situation more clearly and understand fully how they feel about it; in particular to help them grow, change and become more fully functioning. This chapter examines how counselling may enhance personal development. It differentiates between counselling at work and the utilisation of counselling skills and examines the historical development of counselling in the workplace, in particular looking at how the Egan model helps the counselling process.

Learning outcomes

By the end of this chapter, you should be able to:

◆ Explore personal development at work;

◆ Differentiate between counselling skills and counselling at work;

◆ Discuss the historical development of counselling in the workplace;

◆ Justify the applications of counselling in the workplace;

◆ Explain the Egan model of counselling and how it might link to the workplace;

◆ Describe how counselling welfare might be provided within organisations;

◆ Suggest ways in which counselling welfare might be evaluated within organisations.

Introduction

The chapter details the historical development of welfare in the workplace, including the need for counselling at work. The Egan model of helping will be explained and the various types of welfare provision indicated. Specific focus will concentrate on setting up counselling welfare at work and evaluating workplace counselling. Employee assistance programmes will be introduced and current trends and debates in the field indicated, along with future developments in welfare provision.

The chapter ends with a discussion of current issues and ethical debates associated with personal development at work.

Defining personal development

Personal and professional development at work is a vast area. For ease of purpose and understanding, we will differentiate here between personal and professional development. Personal development will refer to counselling in the workplace and professional development will include mentoring and coaching activities. It is acknowledged that there are many types of development in the workplace, and meeting those development needs can take many forms.

Personal development is a process concerned with aspects of the individual: the development of the individual and the ways in which this can be achieved. Personal growth refers to a more generic process to do with the totality of the individual. Within organisations, personal development is facilitated by the use of counselling skills and the provision of counselling at work. In contemporary organisations, personal development is taking on an increased strategic role as emphasis is placed upon employee learning, capability, emotional resilience and adaptability as a means of sustaining employee performance and organisational growth and development.

Counselling skills and counselling work

It is important to differentiate between counselling skills and counselling at work and to highlight the important issues related to their use.

Counselling skills

Counselling skills in the workplace are often used to explore and resolve difficult issues, and to facilitate clear and concise communication channels concerning work-related matters, for example during a meeting. When counselling skills are used to help someone think a problem through, there is an underlying assumption that they have the skills, knowledge and desire to solve the problem themselves but that these abilities are impeded in some way. Counselling skills can be learned and developed on a short training course. They include:

- **Active listening** – to what is really being said and meant rather than simply hearing spoken words;
- **Reflecting back** – being able to show that the listener has heard and understood the speaker's experience;

◆ **Open questioning** – using questioning techniques to probe and facilitate discussion instead of using closed questions that result in yes or no responses;

◆ **Summarising** – the ability to capture the content, feeling and meaning of what has been said during the conversation and over time;

◆ **Empathising** – an ability to see the world from the client's point of view;

◆ **Paraphrasing** – the ability to rephrase what the client is saying briefly; this skill indicates understanding and confirms that the expressed emotions, thoughts and feelings have been noted.

Jane worked for an organisation for many years and contributed to the reorganisation that was to make the company more efficient. She did not, however, get the position that she assumed would be hers. She was reluctant to take the job that was offered to her as in her mind it did not acknowledge all the effort she had put in.

Before a decision was finalised, she became ill. After four weeks' sickness absence for stress she attended the Employee Counselling Service, where she was able to talk freely about her anger and sense of betrayal. She then explored her options in a calmer frame of mind. Being away from the workplace she was able to admit her fears and face her concerns without worrying that there would be consequences.

Aspects of her personal life were contributing to how she felt and after three sessions she felt she had a better perspective on her job and was able to return and discuss her future in a more positive frame of mind.

(Employee Counselling Service – case studies, at: http://www.empcs.org.uk/cs.htm)

Russell et al. (1992) differentiate between various types of helping styles, such as guidance, befriending, using counselling skills and counselling. Counselling skills are defined as the use of communication and social skills in ways consistent with the values and goals of counselling, whereas counselling is defined as the principal use of the relationship to provide someone with the opportunity to work towards living in a more satisfactory and resourceful way.

It is important to be aware that in the use of counselling skills, individual listeners need to know their limitations and be able to refer the person needing help to the relevant services or provisions.

Counselling at work

Counselling in the workplace is concerned with personal development and growth. It may concern relationship problems and individuals usually see managers to get feedback on how they interact with other people. Workplace counsellors are qualified and trained individuals who use counselling skills but who are also knowledgeable about the various psychological theories and therapies that underpin personal development and psychological change. They are also familiar with the organisational context. Counselling can only be provided by people having undergone rigorous training and supervision, while it is not necessary for people using counselling skills to be professional counsellors. Most organisational counsellors in the UK are trained in clinical or counselling psychology (British Psychological Society; BPS) or have acquired advanced therapeutic skills accredited by either the UKCP (United

Kingdom Council for Psychotherapy) or the BACP (British Association for Counselling and Psychotherapy). Being aware of organisational structures, internal policy and channels of communication is essential for good relations with top management.

The manager-as-counsellor uses questioning techniques to raise awareness and it is the individual aspects of counselling which are important.

There are times, however, when the boundary between counselling skills and counselling at work becomes less clear; for example, in the case of an employee who breaks down during appraisal and expresses fears about having the ability to cope with extra responsibilities. Overall, any form of human interaction has the potential for the utilisation of counselling skills and the expression of emotion. Humans are not devoid of emotional expression even in the workplace. Many HR managers may be reluctant to employ listening skills because of fear or anxiety over 'emotional' and 'difficult situations'. See the box below.

Characteristics of counselling

Counselling:

- Is concerned with personal problems;
- Concerns personal relationships;
- Can have an external or internal provider;
- Has an agenda set by the employee;
- Encourages feedback and self-reflection;
- Embraces short-, medium- and long-term focuses;
- Involves discussions that are both explicit and implicit.

Counselling in the workplace

The earliest example of helping relationships in the workplace was provided by the welfare department, which can be traced back to the 1900s. This was when managers and organisational chaplains were encouraged to look after the welfare of their employees. The term **welfare** has connotations of charity and religious guidance. From these early welfare departments evolved the personnel department, where employees would often go for help. Occupational health departments then frequently undertook the welfare function but occupational health nurses were rarely fully trained in the complexities of counselling in the workplace. Over time, the welfare function of the personnel department has been eroded and personnel has now become human resources, with a focus on management functions.

Specialist counselling at work services began to materialise in the 1970s, with Shell Chemicals introducing an in-company counselling service for its 3,000 employees in Cheshire in 1974. Liaison between Mind and the Plessey engineering company was developed in 1975 and external counselling was subsequently provided for the Northampton area. Over time, external types of counselling service for employees, Employee Assistance Programmes (EAPs), developed as a rapidly growing form of workplace counselling. Organisations began to re-brand their services, for example the Inland Revenue Welfare Service, of 30 years' duration or so, called itself an EAP.

In 1977, the Standing Conference for the Advancement of Counselling (now the British Association of Counselling and Psychotherapy) highlighted the need for counselling at work. Since then there has been a rapid increase in the use and application of counselling in the workplace. As the terminology changed, so did attitudes to counselling need and provision. Following organisational trauma, such as in the London bombings in the 1970s and 1980s and more recently in 2005, trauma counselling services have operated, mainly provided by a variety of private consultancies and academic institutions. As organisations began to appreciate the threat of litigation from employees regarding stress, counselling was believed to help mediate against this organisational issue and support employee well-being in the longer term Waldergrave (1992).

Workplace counselling tends to be problem focused, short-term and solution focused. It can be viewed along a continuum, with business-centred goals at one end and person-centred goals at the other. Hence, clients may see managers for personal growth (feeling trapped in their role and unable to progress) or because of a work-related problem or crisis. Managers often work at the interface of personal development. Overall, counselling is primarily a development activity that strives to enable individuals to feel trusted, safe, accepted, understood and secure, so as to encourage self-exploration, self-discovery and self-realisation.

The continuing need for counselling at work

Today, the workforce is not detached from mental illness. It is estimated that one in five employees will suffer from a mental illness at some time in their lives. Stress is regarded as the biggest cause of work absenteeism, with 30–40 per cent of sickness leave related to mental or emotional stress. Overall, it can be assumed that 20 per cent of the workforce is affected by personal problems. Counselling in the workplace is now a well-established professional practice in the UK. It is a defined, task-focused activity with identifiable outcomes. The provision of counselling at work can be varied and has direct cost benefits to organisations in relation to enhancing staff relations and ensuring positive perceptions of the organisation within the eyes of its employees.

window into practice

Kenneth was a well-respected and valued member of staff. He enjoyed his job and for many years did not apply for promotion because it would take him away from customer contact. Eventually he was persuaded to take on a new role that moved him to work under a new manager with a very different style of working. She gave him lists of tasks and deadlines, which she pinned on the section noticeboard. She sat in on some of his meetings and afterwards gave him a list of criticisms. When Kenneth challenged her, she said, 'Look, while you are here you do things my way. If you don't like it – get out.' Kenneth stayed out of her way as much as possible, but his work began to suffer as he lost confidence. At home his wife began to lose patience with his constant moaning about 'that woman' and she persuaded him to talk to a counsellor.

With his counsellor he planned a strategy where he would make a note of the times he felt he was badly treated. He then arranged to meet with his manager and pointed these out. He also explained what he thought was an acceptable way of raising criticism about his work. At first she was defensive, but as Kenneth put his points in a reasonable and constructive way, she had to respond in the same way. There are still tensions but they do now have a working relationship.

The problems that employees experience in the workplace are varied. Problems at home can affect work performance. The associated emotional responses of individuals to personal problems can be varied too. Individuals may turn to counselling in relation to the following two groups of issues:

- **Personal**:
    - burn out
    - depression following bereavement and loss
    - illness and eating disorders
    - anxiety over potential redundancies
    - moodiness and irritability in relation to marital or personal relationship issues
    - family problems
    - mid-life problems
    - issues related to age and life stages (low confidence, mid-life changes in connection to health)
    - substance misuse
    - physical and sexual abuse
    - sexual orientation
    - financial worries.
- **Work-related**:
    - anger following poor performance appraisals
    - alcohol and drug abuse in relation to patterns of absenteeism
    - stress-related sicknesses associated with certain aspects of the employee's job
    - workplace bullying and harassment
    - appraisal and disciplinary interviewing
    - transitional emotions following redundancy (denial, anger and depression)
    - managing change
    - relationships at work
    - pressure of work – too much, or too little, work
    - career change
    - sexual and racial harassment
    - survivor syndrome following organisational downsizing and change (stress-type reactions)
    - post-traumatic stress (stress-type reactions following a traumatic incident)
    - retirement.

Usually the manager or the individual themselves will become aware of a problem and counselling may be suggested or the individual may refer themselves to the counselling service. Certainly, if performance is being affected by psychological ill health, then it falls within the scope of the organisation to make a decision concerning the acceptability of the specific circumstances and to look at other options such as discipline, time off, reduced duties and so on.

The following scenario is typical of the issues dealt with by a workplace counsellor.

Marie is married with two children. She has come to counselling to discuss her emotions as she is going through a very bitter divorce and it is affecting her behaviour with her colleagues – she is irascible and finding it difficult to concentrate on her tasks. Furthermore she is under extra pressure as a colleague has recently left and has not been replaced. This has led to Marie's workload increasing and a lack of line manager support.

What conflicts of interest might arise if managers attempt to counsel their employees?

What influenced you to answer in this way?

exercise

W

Warbings could establish an internal resource pool of people from all levels of the organisation who have been trained in basic listening skills and are available for a proportion of time per week.

What resistance might occur, do you think, from the Warbings' board if such a pool of listeners were proposed?

Applications of counselling at work

Counselling at work can take a variety of forms and serve many functions. Applications include the following.

Redundancy counselling

This is a main area of counselling provision in the workplace. It encompasses advice, information and guidance. Services are usually provided to employees following the initial notice of redundancy and workshops are often held to help individuals deal with the emotional loss of work and to find ways of coping. Job-hunting skills training may be delivered and financial advisors provided in relation to severance packages. The HR managers may be specialists in career development and can help employees to find a way of moving forward towards their next work opportunity.

Pre-retirement counselling

Retirement may be viewed as a process of bereavement or loss. Losing one's job sometimes means that a large part of self-identity is lost and self-worth can be affected. Counselling helps individuals to prepare for retirement and plan for the effects of retirement on their emotions and their life.

Counselling for substance abuse

It is vital that managers are trained to recognise suspected substance abuse and hence encourage the self-referral of employees to the counselling service. (Alcoholism is estimated to cost UK businesses £2 billion per annum.) Managers need to be aware of the different types of specialist support agencies that exist and the treatments available.

EAPs

EAPs are external to the personnel or human resources department and are essentially a short-term counselling and referral agency available to employees and their families. Usually provided by external agencies, they may provide a 24-hour response to any employee with a personal concern or crisis and are supported by a comprehensive referral network of community and private counselling resources. In addition to psychological counselling they can offer specialist services, including career counselling, redundancy counselling, on-site fitness facilities, dietary control, health screening, relaxation classes and stress and health education.

Successful EAPs consist of:

◆ Immediate access to trained qualified counsellors;

◆ Total confidentiality and autonomy from the organisation;

◆ Training of line managers in confronting and referring employees where job performance is affected due to personal problems;

◆ Support for line managers;

◆ Efficient and professional referral capability;

◆ Independent evaluation and quality auditing processes enabling the organisation to assess the value of the service provided and overall credibility;

◆ Adherence to codes of practice developed by professional bodies, such as the Employee Assistance Professionals Association, the UK Standards of Practice and Professional Guidelines for Employee Assistance provisions.

Alker and McHugh (2000: 306) have analysed the reasons for and expectations of introducing EAPs, as shown in Table 20.1.

External programmes can be valuable because they are independent and not part of the organisational system. They could be paramount in helping to challenge

Table 20.1 Reasons for and expectations of introducing EAPs

Assist with	Reduce	Improve	Manage
Policy implementation	Litigation	Success	Change
Downsizing	Costs	Morale	Problem people
Out counselling	Absenteeism	Commitment	Stress
Reactions to crisis	Staff turnover	Performance	Uncertainty
Specific needs or events	Bullying	Profits	Environment
Problem diagnosis	Estrangement	Productivity	
Problem expression	Conflict	Quality	
Problem dissipation	Stress	Images/PR	
Problem solution	Anxiety	Perks	
		Benefits packages	
		Feedback	
		Coping skills	
		Health	

organisational norms, climate and culture. It must be remembered by organisations using EAPs that they are profit-making organisations and sometimes a lack of organisational knowledge, coupled with their recommendations, might hinder the delivery of services, especially if the politics or culture of the organisation are misunderstood. The EAP might be viewed as an interfering inflexible outsider. However, the client should be empowered to challenge the situation.

Stress counselling

Counselling can help to reduce absenteeism and, importantly, to help reduce the 40 million working days lost in the UK every year owing to stress and mental illness. Stress costs industrialised economies around 10 per cent of gross national product (GNP), through sickness absence, ill health and labour turnover. Much of stress at work arises from work overload, job insecurity, poor work role boundaries, poor working relationships, poor individual coping strategies, time pressures and lack of rewards and praise. As employees work longer and more unsociable work hours, propelled by certain organisational cultures, the home–work interface has been eroded, leading to increased pressure for individuals. These factors are often referred to as occupational stressors.

David and Eileen were in a company vehicle returning from a meeting. As they drove down a narrow road, a young child ran out in front of their car and was hit. Eileen, who was driving, was in shock and could not get out of the car. David, dreading what he would see, got out and found the girl lying unconscious and her mother beside her screaming.

People came out of a nearby park and some were angry, claiming that cars always drove too fast and someone was bound to be killed. The police were on the scene first and took David and Eileen into a police car, where Eileen was breathalysed. As this was happening, the ambulance took the child and mother away.

A manager at their company knew about critical incident debriefing and arranged for a session for Eileen and David. This took place three days after the incident. They knew that the child was recovering and that the police were taking no further action. The session helped Eileen in particular, as she was scared that she was having a nervous breakdown. The counsellor helped her to understand and normalise her feelings. David offered to go for a drive with Eileen so that she could see how she felt driving again. Eileen had one further session with a counsellor and while it took her some weeks to recover she was able to work normally.

(Employee Counselling Service – case studies, at: http://www.empcs.org.uk/cs.htm)

An increase in counselling provision to combat stress in the workplace has lead to stress management services aimed at enhancing the psychological well-being and health of employees. Helping individuals to better cope with stress via counselling is a starting point. The counselling provision needs to operate at the individual–organisational interface to help promote healthier organisations. Dealing with the job and organisational sources of stress requires job redesign, flexible working arrangements, a supportive corporate culture and better organisational communications.

Managing stress at work requires a stage by stage approach; the counselling provision in association with the organisation should aim to identify where the problems occur, intervene to change them or find ways of helping individuals to cope and maintain the monitoring and reviewing of progress.

Organisational change and development

Managers help clients to emotionally adjust to changes in the workplace and to deal with issues linked to resistance.

Career counselling

With increased social and economic change, individuals are changing jobs more frequently. Looking at values, interests and current work opportunities is part of the career developmental process. Individuals often need to engage in a process that enables them to recognise and utilise their talents. Managers can help individuals to do this in order to make career-related decisions and manage career-related problems.

pause for thought

To what extent is there a need to take a multi-level approach to well-being programmes – combining interventions aimed at eliminating work-related stress at source?

Why did you reach this conclusion?

Model of counselling in the workplace

A very simple, problem-focused or helping model for counselling in the workplace is that advocated by Egan (1988) and simplified in the box below. This problem-focused model underpins many developmental models; it is not too long, not too expensive, is client-centred and workplace based. The model gives a broad structure to the counselling process. It serves as a map to orientate the manager in the process of helping and to give direction and purpose to counselling interventions. It is pragmatic and problem focused, offering a rational and systematic format. However, it is important to remember that the employer should be the one to define the problem. It is based on three overlapping stages. Stage one involves exploring the current situation by exploring and understanding the problem; stage two refers to the preferred situation or helping the client to create a new world of possibilities to move into; and stage three explores the strategy of how to achieve this.

Problem-focused counselling model

The current situation (exploration by demonstrating understanding)

- ◆ Explores current problems;
- ◆ Listener develops relationship with client;
- ◆ Uses active listening, genuine rapport building;
- ◆ Focuses on establishing trust via empathy;
- ◆ Leads to exploration of feelings, thoughts, behaviours and experiences.

**The preferred scenario (new understandings
and redefinition through challenging)**

- Helps client to see future picture, how things could look, the ideal situation;
- Develops themes, broadens picture, considers patterns and perspectives with client;
- Helps client decide what *they* want to do about situation.

How to get there (resourcing for action)

- How will client achieve ideal?
- What is stopping them?
- What actions will they need to do it?
- Help client see ways to achieve this;
- Collect and exchange information;
- Practical focus to achieve goals;
- Identify strengths of clients;
- Work out specific plan;
- Commit to plan.

However, such a framework can be misleading. Few employees have issues that they can resolve through such a linear progression. A developmental approach will allow for regression as much as it will support advances. Clients need to be encouraged to address deeper issues in order to grow.

When using this model, HR managers may draw upon different theoretical understandings based on their particular training. However, each listener uses counselling skills when building a relationship with the client. This is the basis for change. Respect, empathy and genuineness will help to put the client at ease.

In the next phase of counselling, the client is helped to see their situation in new perspectives and to focus on what they might do to cope more effectively. Strengths and resources are noted. The manager will explore and clarify issues to understand the feelings of the client.

Gradually the client reaches a full understanding of their problem and will want to make decisions. Facilitating the solutions to be taken by the client will be followed by action skills such as objective setting, action planning, solution finding and problem solving. The client is helped to consider possible ways to act, to look at costs and consequences, to plan action, implement it and then evaluate it. Finally, the manager will summarise the progress made and go over any plans for implementing decisions.

Establishing good practice

Qualified counsellors can enable organisations and their employees to explore and where appropriate to develop personal, professional and organisational aspects of life. The benefits of counselling to both the organisation and employee include relief from emotional distress and improved quality of life, less absenteeism and increased work effectiveness.

Counselling at work may be delivered internally, where the listener is an employee of the organisation, or externally, by specialist outside consultants. However, internal counselling is difficult because of issues associated with boundaries and trust. Counselling provision may entail:

◆ Face to face counselling;

◆ Telephone counselling;

◆ Group work;

◆ Referral to specialist;

◆ Information/advice service (debt and legal issues);

◆ Training;

◆ Health awareness training;

◆ Policy consultation.

Internally delivered counselling may include face to face counselling and/or telephone counselling and is usually limited to a fixed number of sessions per employee and/or family members. The counsellor can get to know the organisation and its culture. However, such intimacy can be viewed as a hindrance. The service's proximity to the organisation could be a potential threat to confidentiality, particularly when it is situated on-site and managed by a human resource function. Some managers may feel threatened by such a service in relation to the pastoral element of their managerial role. Furthermore, confidentiality may also be under threat. This is extremely important.

Externally provided services provide face to face counselling and/or telephone counselling that is normally limited to a fixed number of sessions per employee and/or family members. The service provider may have an advice and consultancy function and needs to ensure that there are sufficient numbers of trained and specialist counsellors to serve the client organisation. External providers offer an independence from the client organisation, and with no line manager ties, confidentiality issues are reduced and conflict of interest removed. Critics of external providers claim that this very separateness and independence does not facilitate an understanding of the organisation and its culture, which may be important when working with work-related issues.

pause for thought

Which sort of counselling provision, external or internal, do you think is preferable?

Does the size of the organisation affect your response?

Why did you reach this conclusion?

When an organisation is setting up a counselling service, whether internal or external, managers and counsellors need to be proactive in promoting the service to everyone. During the initial consultation phase, a clear focus on the needs of all stakeholders in the project, including management, trade unions and employees, is essential. Getting the support of top managers is paramount to the success of the service so as to reduce any negative responses from managers or suspicions from employees regarding the motives of the introduction of counselling services to the organisation. Managers may have their own anxieties regarding the introduction of a counselling service as they may see it as disrupting their disciplinary powers and fear that poor performance will not be regulated properly. Such anxieties have to be addressed and areas of responsibility delineated. Counselling may be viewed negatively as it may be stereotypically viewed as only for those with emotional problems or abnormal people. Negative attitudes to the service will have to be challenged in order to gain the trust and co-operation of senior management.

Each stage of the project needs careful consideration. These stages include:

- ◆ Designing, marketing and launching the counselling service;
- ◆ Ensuring complete accessibility;
- ◆ Guaranteeing training of managers;
- ◆ Monitoring and auditing the service;
- ◆ Undertaking thorough evaluations of the service.

The counsellors themselves need to be professionally supervised and committed to continuous professional development, ensuring that they know when to refer clients on to specialist agencies.

There are a number of key principles that apply to any workplace counselling service:

- ◆ The service needs the support of top management (whether it is an internal department or an external consultancy providing the service);
- ◆ A written policy statement of overall philosophy concerning the health and psychological well-being of employees should be available;
- ◆ Managers should be trained (in counselling skills) so as to identify employees with problems and know how to sensitively and constructively refer them to the service or encourage self-referral. Access to the service should be for all levels of staff and regularly communicated and publicised;
- ◆ Counsellors should be qualified and have their own support network and should be members of the Association for Counselling at Work (ACW). A specialist division of the British Association for Counselling and Psychotherapy, the ACW promotes professional standards and provides a forum and mutual support network for individuals and organisations working in this area;
- ◆ Confidentiality, and limitations, of the service should be explicitly stated in in-company marketing of the service;
- ◆ Records should be maintained;
- ◆ Continuation of care should be in operation, including further specialist referral and follow-up;
- ◆ A system should exist for evaluating and auditing the counselling service.

Why is it paramount to get the support of top managers to enable the success of a counselling service?

pause for thought

A counsellor working in the internal counselling service notices that there is a higher incidence of stress-related illness in the marketing department of the company. She is becoming increasingly worried for the individuals concerned, one of whom is becoming suicidal. The company is also involved in a large merger and any failure in productivity in this department would threaten its future. The marketing manager is causing considerable distress to those working under him by systematic bullying. This manager is regarded by senior management as highly effective in relation to productivity and objective achievement. Attempts by employees to alert management to the situation have either been disbelieved or resulted in discrediting the complainant.

What steps should the counsellor take?

Current issues

A number of issues that concern both personal and professional developmental relationships in the workplace are described in the following sections.

Training

It is vital that training is given to all those involved in the delivery of personal development. This training should draw attention to issues of contracting, maintaining confidentiality, recordkeeping, following codes of practice and undertaking professional supervision. Training needs to ensure that it is focused on counselling of individuals *within a workplace context*.

Ethics

Various ethical issues arising from personal development within organisations must be noted. These include maintaining confidentiality, incompatibility between organisational aims and counselling aims, loyalty of the counsellor to those they are developing and the organisation, and managing different roles with the same client. Training on ethical decision making is advised. Being aware that the ethical issues of workplace counselling are different from mainstream counselling practice is important; specialist codes of ethics for workplace counselling should be employed where possible.

Supervision

Supervision is the process of developing the professional practice of those involved in the helping professions. Usually, in order to gauge the effectiveness of their professional practice with clients, the counsellor talks to another counsellor in a formalised setting. Supervisors can ensure that codes of practice are being adhered to. The British Association of Counselling and Psychotherapy provides professional standards. Professional training needs to be highly practical and develop understanding of both the theory and practice.

Evaluation

Organisations want to see a quantifiable return for their investment, a somewhat difficult task when many employers still do not recognise that their employees are a frail resource whose mental health can affect the organisation's productivity and morale. There is a lack of in-depth research and information related to effective evaluation of personal development. Exploring absenteeism rates, sickness leave in relation to stress, staff turnover, morale and communications is crucial. Counsellors need to convince others about their effectiveness through practical demonstrations of their worth so that credible auditing can take place. Progress will be made when it is possible to demonstrate that an investment in such activities provides a visible return to the employer. Research aimed at giving valid evaluations of these areas is inconclusive but should continue to aim at ensuring that formative and summary evaluations of provision take place. Provision should be evaluated in relation to availability, accessibility, credibility, accountability and whether the developmental provision is meeting organisational needs.

New directions

Counselling in the workplace has relied upon the mainstream theories of counselling. Complementing the practical application of development in the workplace with continued academic research will add credibility in this area. Incorporating new psychologies, such as **positive psychology theory** and emotional intelligence, into theoretical developments will ensure that counselling remains a contemporary developmental approach. Positive psychology explores what is right with people rather than what is wrong with them. It attempts to redress the balance by encouraging psychologists to contribute to positive aspects of life, rather than focusing on changing negative ones. The ultimate aim of positive psychology is to enable more people to live lives filled with greater health and well-being (as well as the absence of illness and disease). Counselling in the workplace should endeavour to bridge the gap in research by taking a positive psychology perspective and asking questions about people's strengths and what organisational characteristics can maximise them.

As organisations become flatter, managers have more contact with, and direct responsibility for, larger numbers of people. Consequently managers take on more development roles in the form of counselling, coaching and mentoring. They need, therefore, to become stronger in the skills of counselling, coaching and mentoring if they are to engage employee commitment. Developmental approaches based on empathy, respect and genuineness that give time and attention to employee well-being will enrich managers' abilities to develop and lead their employees.

window into practice

During the first six months of the year, Sheila used all her annual leave in days here and there. She also had a number of self-certificated sick days. Her manager and colleagues were fed up with her unpredictability.

She eventually asked her manager for a day's unpaid leave. He took the opportunity to ask if there was any underlying problem that was causing her sickness absence. Although she was very reluctant to talk to him, she did accept a need to improve her absence record. He agreed to give her the unpaid leave, but set a meeting for two weeks' time when they would review her work. He suggested that before then she should have a confidential talk to someone from the counselling service.

continued

Sheila spoke to a counsellor on the telephone. She explained that her husband was showing signs of dementia and there were days when she could not leave him. She was taking the time off for his hospital appointment. She did not want anyone at her work to know about his condition. The counsellor helped her to think through the pros and cons of talking in confidence to someone at work about her situation and discussing whether they could provide her with some short-term support while she made arrangements for longer-term care.

(Employers Counselling Service – case studies, at: http://www.empcs.org.uk/cs.htm)

Summary

This chapter has defined personal development as a process concerned with developing aspects of the individual. The difference between counselling skills and counselling has been outlined. Counselling skills can be learned and used by anyone to facilitate effective communication, whereas counselling is a process of helping people explore problems so that they can decide what to do about them. This chapter has explored the reasons why organisations set up workplace counselling and employee support. Alternative applications of counselling at work have been described and the Egan counselling model has been explained. The key principles involved in establishing good workplace counselling provision have been noted and areas of current concern and debate have been explored.

Review Questions

You may wish to attempt the following as practice examination style questions.

20.1   What is the difference between professional and personal development at work?

20.2   How can the introduction of workplace counselling benefit the employee, manager and the organisation?

20.3   What resistance might there be to the introduction of workplace counselling?

20.4   List the advantages and disadvantages of both external and internal workplace coun-selling provision.

References

Alker, A. and McHugh, D. (2000). Human resource maintenance? Organisational rationales for the introduction of employee assistance programmes, *Journal of Managerial Psychology*, Vol. 15, No. 4, pp. 303–323.

Egan, G. (1988). *The Skilled Helper*, 6th edition, Pacific Grove, CA: Brooks Cole.

Russell, J.E., Dexter, G. and Bond, T. (1992). *Differentiation between advice, guidance, befriending, counselling skills and counselling*, London: Advice Counselling Lead Body.

Waldergrave, W. (1992). Introduction, in R. Jenkins and N. Coney (eds.) *Prevention of mental ill-health at work*, pp. ix–xiv, London: CBI and Department of Employment.

Further Reading

Cartwright, S. and Cooper, C. (1997). *Managing Workplace Stress*, London: Sage.

Cochran, L. (1997). *Career Counselling: A Narrative Approach*, London: Sage.

Cooper, C.L. and Williams, S. (eds.) (1994). *Creating Healthy Organisations*, Chichester: Wiley.

Cooper, C., Dewe, P. and O'Driscoll, M.P. (2001). *Organizational Stress: A Review and Critique of Theory, Research and Applications*, London: Sage.

Cunningham, G. (1994). *Effective Employee Assistance Provisions*, London: Sage.

Dryden, W. (1996). *Handbook of Individual Therapy in Britain*, London: Sage.

Edworthy, A. (2000). *Managing Stress*, Buckingham: Open University, Press.

Fineman, S. (2000). *Emotion in Organisations*, London: Sage.

Fowler, A. (1999). *Managing Redundancy, Developing Practice Series*, London: Institute of Personnel and Development.

Jones, A. (1994). *Delivering In-house Outplacement: A Practical Guide for Trainers, Managers and Personnel Specialists*, Maidenhead: McGraw-Hill.

Nathan, R. and Hill, L. (1992). *Career Counselling*, London: Sage.

Nelson-Jones, R. (1993). *Practical Counselling and Helping Skills: How to Use the Lifeskills Helping Model*, 3rd edition, London: Cassell Educational.

Nelson-Jones, R. (1999). *Introduction to Counselling Skills: Text and Activities*, London: Sage.

Newell, S. (1995). *The Healthy Organisation*, London: Routledge.

Newton, T., Handy, J. and Fineman, S. (1995). *Managing Stress: Emotion and Power at Work*, London: Sage.

Palmer, S. and Dryden, W. (eds.) (1994). *Stress Management and Counselling*, London: Cassell.

Rees, D.W. and Cooper, C.L. (1996). *How to Assess and Manage Organisational Stress*, Chichester: Wiley.

Ross, R.R. and Altmaier, E. (1994). *Interventions in Occupational Stress: A Handbook of Counselling for Stress at Work*, London: Sage.

Summerfield, J. and Van Oudtshoorn, L. (2000). *Counselling in the Workplace*, London: CIPD.

Winstanley, D. and Woodall, J. (2000). *Ethical Issues in HRM*, London: Macmillan.

Woolfe, R. and Dryden, W. (1996). *The Handbook of Counselling Psychology*, London: Sage.

Useful Websites

www.bacp.co.uk – website of the British Association for Counselling and Psychotherapy, offering publications, research, courses and guidance on professional practice

www.counsellingatwork.org.uk – website of the Association for Counselling at Work, with news, conferences, reports, publications and training aimed at professional counsellors and other professionals using counselling skills

www.eapa.org.uk – professional body (Employee Assistance Professionals Association) for Employee Assistant programmes representing professional interests and offering advice, research, publications and training

www.hse.gov.uk – Health and Safety Executive coverage, e.g. on workplace stress, with reports on investigations, guidance and recommendations

www.isma.org.uk – website of International Stress Management Association, with news, publications, advice, conferences and training

mindout.clarity.uk.net – website for Mind Out for Mental Health campaign to stop the stigma and discrimination surrounding mental health – initiatives (e.g. conferences), news and publications

www.psychotherapy.org.uk – website of the UK Council for Psychotherapy, offering training, events, news, guidance on professional practice and legal advice aimed at practising professionals

www.worklifebalancecentre.org – Work Life Balance Centre website offering surveys, news, publications, courses and case studies

CHAPTER 21

Work-Life Balance

By Carol M. Wood

Chapter outline

There are many different views about work-life balance and it is important not to make stereotypical assumptions about work-life balance issues. The human resource (HR) function has a direct responsibility for developing work-life balance policies; making the business case, ensuring it is implemented fairly and in accordance with relevant legislation. This chapter explores the concept of the work-life balance and examines a number of the issues that may have an impact upon it. It looks at policy development in the workplace and the subsequent ways of implementing work-life balance practices.

Learning outcomes

By the end of this chapter, you should be able to:

- Identify the nature of work-life balance, including the concept of 'leisure time';
- Discuss relevant legislation;
- Identify advantages and disadvantages to the employer and employee;
- Develop and implement relevant policy.

Introduction

The aim of this chapter is not to advocate one particular point of view about work-life balance but to help you to review, reflect and discuss different views and the associated issues.

Work-life balance, like motivation, is a concept that will have different meanings to different people. A line manager should be careful not to make stereotypical assumptions about their staff requirements for work-life balance. The concept of the 'flexible organisation', including flexible ways and times of working, is certainly good for business, in that it enables a business to respond effectively to changes in the market and customer demands. Equally, though, in the twenty-first century people have higher expectations about the quality of their working life and for their life in general, and, for 'flexibility' to be a success, the needs of both the organisation and the individual need to be taken into account.

What does work-life balance mean?

What comes to your mind when you hear the term 'work-life balance'? It could be something you have heard about in the media recently, perhaps concerning the need for employers to operate 'family-friendly' policies on flexible working so that parents are able to juggle their work and home commitments.

Everyone has different motivations and aspirations that they wish to achieve in their life. Work-life balance is about adjustments that can be made to working patterns to enable people to combine work with the other facets of their life. Bratton and Gold (2003: 105) define work-life balance as, 'the relationship between the institutional and cultural times and spaces of work and non-work in societies where income is predominantly generated and distributed through labour markets.' This includes the concept of paid work and also indicates the trend of how our home life and work life can merge. For example, someone accessing their work emails at home could do it at a time convenient to them, say at 10.00pm at night, even though they would not normally be in the workplace at that time.

Some people work mainly from home, and in the 1990s advances in technology were enabling organisations such as British Telecommunications to close some of their offices so that some employees worked from home as 'teleworkers'. Weightman (2004) suggests that increasingly there are fewer distinctions between work and home and that the term work-life balance is also used to describe the problems of separating work from home life.

Personal circumstances and impact on work-life balance

A person's personal circumstances will have an impact on their needs in relation to their work-life balance and also the extent to which they have choice and control over what they do. Look at the following exercise and reflect on the ways in which circumstances influence the work-life balance of individuals.

exercise

A person's personal circumstances will have an impact on their needs in relation to work-life balance and also the extent to which they have choice and control over what they do. Consider the following examples:

- A part-time student with a full-time job;
- A full-time student with a part-time job;
- A recent graduate in their second job;
- A new lecturer with three part-time jobs.

What practical advice would you give each of them, if they complained to you that they felt tired, depressed, tense and anxious?

Issues that impact on work-life balance

Government influence on work-life balance

In 2000, the government introduced the work-life balance campaign (DTI, 2004b). The campaign's aim was: 'To help employers recognise the benefits of adopting policies and procedures to enable employees to adopt flexible working patterns.' Hopefully this would lead to more motivated and productive staff.

In September 2003, the DTI (2004b) launched their *Prosperity for all* strategy to focus on work-life balance issues. The campaign comprises a number of elements:

◆ Continuing to provide support to business for the adoption of new, or further, work-life balance measures;

◆ Continuing to generate and disseminate research and case studies that demonstrate the impact and benefits of work-life balance measures to business and the individual;

◆ Work in partnership with organisations across the country to mainstream work-life balance policies;

◆ Stimulate initiatives on a regional basis;

◆ Review and refine work based on feedback from research, case studies and information from stakeholders.

Employers keen to obtain the best workforce and to be an employer of choice will:

◆ Review good practice;

◆ Identify the business case;

◆ Consult their employees;

◆ Implement a policy on work-life balance, regularly monitoring its impact and developing it further as required.

Gender differences

Proposed reforms of child custody rules following separation and divorce has led to fathers' groups such as 'Fathers 4 Justice' driving demands for fair access to children (Frith, 2004). This means that separated and divorced fathers who want to take an active role in parenting and keep in contact with their children could need flexible working arrangements to enable them, for example, to be able to pick up their children from school.

Jack O'Sullivan, the co-founder of 'Fathers Direct', another campaigning group, is concerned about the potential negative impact on careers: 'Our vision is for fathers to be able to have more flexibility at work without feeling that it sits at odds with their career development' (Carrington and Holmstrom, 2004: 29).

An example of a father working flexibly is Neil Hasson, an HR manager at Lloyds TSB, who along with his team works flexibly to deliver a week's work in 'four chunks rather than five', i.e. a compressed working week. However the point is made that flexible working for men makes some people 'raise an eyebrow', i.e. that it is not considered appropriate. Hasson says, 'There is an awful lot of people who'll think I'm skiving, but I can do the job, my team can do the job, and we are a more effective unit for working this way' (Carrington and Holmstrom, 2004: 32).

A study by Platt in 1997, cited by Bratton and Gold (2003: 104), of employees at Hewlett-Packard showed that while professional men and women both worked on average 50 hours per week, women spent an additional 33 hours on housework and childcare as opposed to 19 hours by men. This means that professional women spend an additional half a 'working day' in non-paid work at home compared to a quarter of a day by men.

In 2000, a Mintel survey found that only one in five families had a stay-at-home mother with a full-time working father. Significantly, the survey also found that working mothers are just as likely as fathers to emphasise the importance of the personal fulfilment/career satisfaction they get from their paid employment and those who work full time are more prone to do so, with 53 per cent (compared with 47 per cent of fathers) stressing this. Full-time working mothers are also considerably less likely than fathers, or part-time working mothers, to say they only work for the money, calling into question the received wisdom that many families with two full-time working parents are having to do so simply in order to pay the mortgage.

A more recent report by Mintel (2003) reported that a work-life balance survey, which questioned 500 *Management Today* readers, found that many men did not want to reduce the amount of time spent at work in order to give more time to their families.

pause for thought

Are those individuals who want to, and do, spend more time at their workplace achieving a work-life balance?

Why did you reach this decision?

Whereas previous surveys showed an increased interest in a better work-life balance, this survey identified that two in five fathers would not exchange improving their career prospects for spending more time with their children.

Generational differences

Leach (2001) refers to Generation X and makes the point that following the dotcom bubble burst, instead of the failed entrepreneurs seeking a new job, they took the opportunity to 'find themselves' by escaping to exotic locations abroad, something which their grandparents could not have done. Leach goes on to say that the younger generation will make every effort to maintain their work-life balance.

Caroline Waters at British Telecommunications discusses the changing attitudes towards work by graduates: 'Five years ago it became clear that our graduates wanted a different contract with employers . . . they wanted to work to live, not live to work, and developing flexible options for them became incredibly important to attracting them' (Carrington and Holmstrom, 2004: 32). This is borne out by the work of Lammiman and Syrett (2004), who found that recent UK graduates specifically sought jobs that would enable them to have sufficient time outside work for other activities.

There is evidence to support the attitude of young people towards working hours compared to older workers in the DTI (2004a) survey that identified that nearly half (47 per cent) of 16–24 year olds have changed their working hours to enable them to pursue other interests, compared to less than four in ten (37 per cent) of adults between 55 and 65.

Emmott (2004) refers to the evidence from the CIPD's 'Living to Work Survey' (2003) that over half the respondents working more than 48 hours per week were satisfied with their work-life balance. The largest group of these people were middle-aged men. Opportunities for flexible working were mainly taken up by women. There was also little difference between respondents working more than 48 hours and those working less than 48 hours with how satisfied they were with regards to their health and relationships.

Michel Syrett* and his co-author Jean Lammiman researched graduate attitudes to work-life balance for their book, *Cool Search*. In an interview, he said:

'In recent years, "family friendly" political agendas have been replaced by "work-life balance" ones, in an attempt to combat the emerging long hours culture. This is where we are today. But the rationale behind this is still way behind the times. Just as family friendly employment policies pre-supposed that in most people's lives there was "work" and "family", and nothing else, so work-life balance schemes pre-suppose that there is "work" and "life", and that the two are wholly separate.

The reality of course is that in an age where you can "work" anywhere and at any time, you can also "live" anywhere and at any time – and that the artificial distinction between the two is increasingly meaningless. Millennials – the new breed of 18–25 year olds that grew up in the 1990s – are at the cutting edge of the debate. Typically, they want high-paid conventional part-time work to subsidise home-based businesses or (even "and") creative leisure pursuits that provide them with the kind of life-style fulfilment that their parents or elder siblings postpone until middle age. Millennials aren't prepared to wait that long. They want this balance now.'

What kind of work are you looking for? How will this affect how you spend your time?

* Interviewed on 11 June 2006.

Flexible working patterns

There is a range of flexible working patterns and the DTI (2004a) define them as follows:

- ◆ **Part time** – government statistics define part-time working as less than 30 hours per week. Part-time workers are entitled to the same treatment as full-time employees, including the same hourly rate of pay.
- ◆ **Job sharing** – two people carrying out the duties of a post that would normally be done by one person. Each person is employed part time but together they cover a full-time post and divide the pay, holidays and benefits.
- ◆ **Staggered hours** – employees have different start, finish and break times. This can help employers to cover longer opening hours but it can also be a good opportunity to offer people more flexibility.

Table 21.1 Flexible working and leave arrangements for non-managerial employees in continuing workplaces, 1998 and 2004

	1998	2004
	% of continuing workplaces	% of continuing workplaces
Flexible working arrangement		
Switching from full- to part-time hours	46	64
Flexitime	19	26
Job-sharing	31	41
Homeworking	16	28
Term-time only	14	28
Annualised hours	8	13
Zero hours contracts	3	5
Leave arrangement		
Parental leave	38	73
Paid paternity/discretionary leave for fathers	48	92
Special paid leave in emergencies	24	31

Base: All continuing workplaces with ten or more employees in 1998 and 2004.

Figures are weighted and based on responses from at least 847 managers.

Source: Kerstley et al. (2005)

- **Term-time only working** – employees remain on a permanent contract, either on a full- or part-time basis, but can have unpaid leave of absence during the school holidays.

- **Flexitime** – giving people a choice about their actual working hours, usually outside agreed core times. This means staff can vary their starting and finishing times each day and sometimes also their break times during the day.

- **Compressed hours** – working a total number of agreed hours over a shorter number of working days.

- **Annualised hours** – employees work on the basis of the number of hours to be worked over a year rather than a week, usually to fit in with peaks and troughs of work.

- **Shift swapping** – employees can negotiate working times to suit their needs and rearrange shifts among themselves or within teams.

- **Flexible working locations** – at home or on the employer's premises.

- **Practical employee benefits** – e.g. childcare, health and fitness facilities and financial packages.

See Table 21.1.

Benefits of working

At a superficial level it is easy to think that most people only work to earn money and that if they could win a large sum of money, then they would no longer work. Brown

(1989) believes that regarding pay as an incentive is much exaggerated and goes on to say that money is the motive for finding paid employment but it is not enough to make sure of good performance in the job. He believes there is a mixture of motivations that make us want to work well, including achieving management approval, personal pride and doing a good job. This has been called *discretionary effort.* Different people are motivated by:

- A purpose in life;
- Work objectives/challenges;
- Sense of achievement, which can develop confidence and self-esteem;
- Structure to the day;
- Social contact;
- Opportunity to use and develop skills;
- Maintaining specialist knowledge;
- Status;
- Working environment outside of the home.

Think of someone you know well. Now consider their individual rights to:

- **Obtain paid work without being unfairly discriminated against;**
- **Have interests and commitments outside of work to help them achieve a more fulfilling work-life balance;**
- **Change from full- to part-time work and vice versa;**
- **Leave work on time without having to justify themselves;**
- **Have a safe system of work without becoming ill due to overwork, such as accidents and stress-related illness;**
- **Have sufficient energy due to not working excessive hours so that they enjoy their work, retain their enthusiasm for it, and achieve their work objectives;**
- **Have sufficient time during the working day to maintain good working relationships with colleagues;**
- **Have enough energy at the end of the working day to look after their home and family and/or pursue other interests, hobbies, studies or exercise;**
- **Separate work from home life and not to be available 24/7.**

What does this tell you about their work-life balance?

The Working Time Regulations 1998

These regulations implemented the Working Time Directive 1993 and became effective on 1 October 1998. They apply to workers over 18 years of age and aim to limit working time, including overtime, to 48 hours per week. This is averaged over 17 weeks, with further opportunities to extend this to 26 or 52 weeks. An individual worker is entitled to opt out of the limit of 48 hours per week. These regulations also give the right for the first time in the UK for every worker to have 20 days' paid holiday (Willey, 2003).

A Confederation of British Industry (CBI) survey found that one-third of UK workers had signed an opt-out agreement (Lister et al., 2004). Emmott (2004) disagrees with the European Union (EU) suggestion that issues related to working long hours are linked to work-life balance and argues that there should be separate policies to reduce long working hours and those that aim to improve work-life balance.

Further, Emmott (ibid.) discusses the difference between voluntarily working long hours and the importance of the control an individual exercises over their work.

The psychological contract

Workplaces that introduce measures to promote the work-life balance improve the commitment and loyalty of their staff, thus enhancing their psychological contracts. Some of the possible benefits include:

- Happy workforce;
- Reduction in sickness;
- Reduction in staff turnover and recruitment costs;
- Reduction in absenteeism;
- Improved performance;
- Improved customer relations/service;
- Improved working relationships with peers and line managers.

For example, it would be a reasonable employee expectation that their employer would allow them time off for unexpected emergency situations related to personal and/or family needs regardless of legislation. Equally, when there is a need for overtime to be worked due to an urgent unforeseen work situation, then the employer would reasonably expect a favourable attitude by the employee to completion of the work by the deadline.

The box below describes the results of a DTI survey (2004a) on work-life balance.

What would people do if they had a better work-life balance?

Activities that employees would most like to pursue, if they had a better work-life balance*	%
1. Spend more time with friends and family	87
2. Go to theatre, cinema or art galleries	70
3. Read more	66
4. Learn a new skill such as a new language	57
5. Play more sport or take up a new sport	56
6. Do some form of voluntary work	44
7. Join a club or hobby group	40

Further findings from the survey showed that:

- 87 per cent of workers think that having interests and commitments outside the workplace helps to achieve a more fulfilling work-life balance;
- 38 per cent of workers between the ages of 35 and 55 feel they spend too much time at work, at the expense of other commitments.

* Random selection of 2,000 adults.

Organisations that are encouraging flexible working recognise the benefits to the business, and Carrington and Holmstrom (2004: 30) refer to two such companies: '. . . BT and Lloyds TSB stress that there is a solid business case for doing so: they are meeting their objectives, are retaining their employees, and have happy workforces'.

Another company that promotes flexible working is Happy Computers; they were voted number 12 in the *Financial Times* (2004) '50 Best Workplaces' and won a special prize in these awards for 'The most favourable response from its employees on work-life balance issues'. By its creative and innovative approach, the working culture enabled its staff to pursue and achieve further career and self-development.

It is important in this context to consider equity motivation theory, where employees make comparisons with other employees on issues related to work–life balance. A poorly drafted or unfairly implemented policy will lead to employee dissatisfaction, and exacerbate a difficult situation that previously existed. A range of work-life balance issues that could lead to perceived unfairness could arise from the following:

- Employees without children;
- Gender;
- Marital status;
- Part-time/full-time/term-time;
- Permanent/subcontractor;
- Non-smokers;
- Discretion by different managers on giving/withholding permission to work at home;
- 'Trust time' – where employees can choose when to work.

Policy development and implementation

The Work Foundation (2003: 2) carried out a survey of 303 organisations and identified that management resistance was the most common (30 per cent) difficulty in implementing work-life balance, especially in larger organisations. The cost of not having a policy and procedures that are implemented fairly should be discussed throughout the organisation. It also reported that work-life balance is often a feature of award-winning organisations and their advice is to:

- Think flexibly – it is possible to offer employees flexibility and choice;
- Make sure that work-life balance policies and practices are aligned with the core business strategy;
- Have a process to handle requests for flexible working;
- Communicate and champion work-life balance policy and practice;
- Think about people as individuals rather than as numbers or a head count. Remember that different working patterns suit different people and can be arranged to dovetail with customer demand;
- Consider the need of all stakeholders and consult with them;
- Recognise the pressure on managers, and make sure that flexible working arrangements are seen as a solution rather than as an additional task.

A policy is only as good as the action it invokes, so it is pointless in developing a policy without the conviction and commitment of both senior and line management. Cultural issues need to be fully explored and decisions made as to how to change culture where necessary – which cannot be done overnight.

Policies and procedures should be developed with genuine consultation with all the stakeholders. There can be no 'one size fits all' approach to work-life balance and each organisation needs to spend time on developing a policy that will fit in with their business strategy and the needs of their employees. Policies also need to be communicated and managers and staff trained in how to apply them. Regular evaluations need to be made and appropriate changes made so that it remains a viable policy that achieves the appropriate action.

exercise

List the ways that a work-life balance could be introduced at Warbings, and some of the consequences.

Summary

This chapter has explored the scope of work-life balance and discussed relevant legislation. Everyone is different and their personal circumstances will impact on their needs for work–life balance. Evidence referred to in the chapter showed that the largest group of people working more than 48 hours per week were middle-aged men and most had chosen to do so. Poor health was linked to long hours only under conditions of low control. There are benefits but also disadvantages to work-life balance, especially if it has been poorly implemented. Management resistance has been identified as the most common difficulty in implementing work-life balance, especially in larger organisations.

Review Questions

You may wish to attempt the following as practice examination style questions.

21.1   How would you define the work-life balance?

21.2   Describe any disadvantages of the work-life balance that might be experienced by line managers and say how these might be overcome.

21.3   Identify six different ways of working flexibly and explain how this may help:
   (a) A young mother
   (b) A person nearing retirement
   (c) A committed athlete
   (d) Someone studying for an MBA.

21.4   Explain what you would include in a work-life balance policy and why.

References

Bratton, J. and Gold, J. (2003). *Human Resource Management Theory and Practice*, 3rd edition, London: Palgrave Macmillan.

Brown, W. (1989). Personnel management in Britain, in K. Sisson (ed.) *Managing Remuneration*, Oxford: Blackwell.

Carrington, L. and Holmstrom, R. (2004). Signs of change, *People Management*, Vol. 3, pp. 29–32.

CIPD (2003). *Living to Work?*, London: CIPD.

DTI (2004a). *Britain's Workers Crave More Time With Friends in 2004*, survey conducted in December 2003 by ACCESS, a division of BRMB International.

DTI (2004b). *The Worklife Balance Campaign*, at: http://164.36.164.20/worklifebalance.

Emmott, M. (2004). How much does long hours working matter?, *Impact*, Vol. 7, p. 5.

Financial Times (2004). Special Report: Best Workplaces, featuring the UK's Top 50 employers and the EU Top 100, 18 April.

Frith, M. (2004). Parents to face fines for refusing access, *The Independent*, 22 July.

Kersley, B. et al. (2005). WERS first findings, at: www.dti.gov.uk/files/file11423.pdf.

Lammiman, J. and Syrett, M. (2004). *Cool Search*, London: Capstone.

Leach, B. (2001). INSIDE TRACK: The work/life equation, *Financial Times*, 9 November.

Lister, R. Davies, J. and Brittin, K. (2004). A review of EU employment developments by law firm Lewis Silkin: time up for UK working-hours legislation?, *Impact*, Vol. 7, pp. 23–24.

Mintel (2000). *Family Lifestyles and the Effect of Work: UK, April 2000*, at: http://reports.mintel.com/sinatra/mintel/reports/3&7243&44839/report/repcode-S162&a.

Mintel (2003). *Worklife balance survey*, at: http://reports.mintel.com/sinatra/mintel/reports/3&7243&44839/report/repcode-S162&a.

Weightman, J. (2004). *Managing People*, 2nd edition, London: CIPD.

Willey, B. (2003). *Employment Law in Context: An Introduction for HR Professionals*, Chapter 11, 2nd edition, London: FT/Prentice Hall.

Work Foundation (2003). Worklife balance, *Managing Best Practice No. 109*, London: Work Foundation.

Further Reading

Coussey, M. (2000). *Getting the Right Worklife Balance*, London: CIPD.

Daniels, L. and McCarraher, L. (2002). *The Book of Balanced Living: Options to Take Control of Your Time, Work and Life*, London: Spiro Press.

Fletcher, W. (2002). *Beating the 24/7*, Chichester: Wiley.

Glynn, C. Steinberg, I. and McCartney, C. (2002). *Worklife Balance: The Role of the Manager*, Roffey: Roffey Park Institute.

Holden, R. and Renshaw, B. (2002). *Balancing work and life*, London: Dorling Kindersley.

Kodz, J. Harper, H. and Dench, S. (2002). *Worklife Balance: Beyond the Rhetoric*, Institute for Employment Studies, Report 384.

TUC (2001). *Changing Times: A TUC Guide to Work Life Balance*, London: TUC.

Useful Websites

www.acas.org.uk – ACAS advice on work-life balance

www.diversity-whatworks.gov.uk – website offering news, contacts and links on equality and diversity in employment in the Civil Service

www.dti.gov.uk/files/file11423.pdf – Department of Trade and Industry initiatives to encourage work-life balance, research and publications

www.employersforworklifebalance.org.uk – employers' forum covering practical initiatives, news and reports

www.flexibility.co.uk – flexibility publication with news, views, reviews, articles and links on the world of flexible work (including cases)

www.homedad.org.uk – website of UK support group for stay-at-home dads (estimated at 189,000), with news, cases, information and advice, publications and features

www.homeworking.com – website for those wanting to work at home, with case studies, news, job search, links and support

www.tuc.org.uk – Trade Union Congress website, with coverage of flexible working, work-life balance (e.g. 'Changing Times'), home working, news, legal advice and reports

www.ft.com/bestworkplaces2004 – *Financial Times* regular survey of best places to work

www.unison.org.uk – website of largest public sector trade union, with focus on workers' rights and opportunities

www.workingfamilies.org.uk – website of Working Families Work Life balance (formerly Parents at Work) campaign, with news, initiatives, support, links, helpline, focused on family-friendly policies at work and quality childcare

www.workliferesearch.co.uk – website of the Work-Life Research Centre, covering current research, news and advice on policy and practice

www.women-returners.co.uk – website of the Women Returners Network, a lobbying organisation offering news, reports, support, job opportunities and links

www.work-at-home.index.net – website offering details of opportunities to work at home

www.worklifebalancecentre.org – website of Work Life Balance Centre, offering research, news, reports, cases and support, focused on family-friendly policies and practice at work and quality childcare

CHAPTER 22

Managing Internationally Mobile Personnel

By Sue Shortland

Chapter outline

This chapter draws on all of the others in the book and illustrates the holistic nature of human resource management (HRM), showing how all aspects of domestic HRM are equally applicable when managing an internationally mobile workforce. In particular, it depicts the influence of culture on international HRM and highlights aspects of people resourcing, training and development, reward and performance management, individual employment relationships, health and well-being.

Learning outcomes

By the end of this chapter, you should be able to:

- Show awareness of the implications of cultural differences and assess their impact on managing people internationally;
- Apply theoretical models of the stages of global organisational development to people resourcing and human resource development (HRD) initiatives;
- Outline the types of training programmes available to international assignees;
- Draw distinctions between the various approaches to rewarding international assignees;
- Outline some individual employment relationship issues of significance in an international environment;
- Consider individual and family aspects of health and welfare and their importance to business success.

Introduction

This chapter examines the HRM implications of – and provides a theoretical framework to underpin – the practicalities of managing internationally mobile personnel. As it takes an international perspective, you may wish to consider the implications for mobility both into and out of the UK, as well as between and among other countries or regions of the globe.

The influence of culture on international human resource management

The term globalisation is used widely as organisations strive to expand their marketplace and become more competitive. Organisations are increasingly becoming more international in their operations to take advantage of new markets, advantages in sources of production, to spread risk and lower cost and to gain competitive advantage through people. International working has become commonplace for the citizens of the industrialised world and, as countries become multi-ethnic, so contact with people from other cultures becomes a regular feature of people's social and professional lives.

International HRM

There are considerable implications of managing internationally for HR managers. Operating across several business environments presents challenges for policy formulation and implementation, together with the requirement to co-ordinate activities across diverse geographical regions. International HRM is therefore often viewed as a discipline in its own right, to reflect the differences between HRM in an international and a domestic context.

International HRM involves striking an appropriate balance between global integration and local adaptation in terms of resourcing, training and developing personnel, reward and performance management, employment relations including communications, and health and welfare. But to set the context for managing personnel internationally, it is important first to consider culture and its impact.

The impact of culture

The concept of **culture** may be subdivided into: **implicit culture**, that is, basic assumptions which produce values and norms, which, in turn, reveal themselves as **explicit culture**, such as dress, food, manners, architecture, lifestyle and so on.

Fundamental assumptions, norms and values form the basis of culture but are 'invisible'. They come together to form the 'visible' – or explicit – nature of culture manifested in the ways noted above.

Cultural dimensions

International assignees not only have to cope with working in the cultures of different countries, but they may also have to come to terms with a different organisational culture. The latter may reflect the local societal culture as well as the culture of the country where the organisation is headquartered.

Managers from different cultures hold varying assumptions about the nature of management, authority, structure and organisational relationships. These assumptions shape different value systems and are translated into a range of management practices, reinforcing the original assumptions.

Hofstede (1994) has analysed culture in numerous countries along four scales, as shown in the box below.

Hofstede's four main dimensions of culture

Power distance – the extent to which a culture accepts inequalities in the distribution of power.

Uncertainty avoidance – the extent to which a culture feels threatened by uncertain situations and so tries to establish rules.

Individualism/collectivism – individualism refers to a loose social framework ('people look after themselves'), while collectivism refers to a tight social framework ('people look after their group and show loyalty to it').

Masculinity/femininity – masculinity refers to assertiveness and the value of money, while femininity refers to equality and the importance of quality of life.

Think about your own culture; how do you think Hofstede would categorise it? Why did you reach this conclusion?

pause for thought

Implications for management

These dimensions of culture can be used to explain, to some degree, the organisational culture of businesses based in countries with different societal cultural backgrounds. For example, France has a relatively high score for power distance. This manifests itself in hierarchical structures where communications are typically made at the top of the organisation and communicated downwards through the various levels in the hierarchy. An expatriate manager from a relatively low power distance country (e.g. Sweden) who is sent to manage an operation in France, would need to be aware that an authoritarian management style is likely to be more respected and effective than a democratic or participative approach. In Germany, for example, the dimension of uncertainty avoidance indicates that Germans are uncomfortable with ambiguity – they prefer explicit rules to govern what they do. The UK, by contrast, has a greater tolerance of ambiguity. A British manager working in Germany will need to be aware that Germans prefer to follow rules more directly than in the UK, whereas British management may follow a more discretionary approach.

Further examples can be drawn from the individualism/collectivism dimension – the US is the most individualist country in the rankings. Employees in the US prefer individual rewards and performance management based around the contribution of individuals. In collectivist countries such as China and Japan, the preferred way of working and rewarding employees is via team-based approaches (e.g. quality circles). Masculinity and femininity also have implications for the working environment – masculine nations value money and achievement (e.g. the US), whereas feminine countries (e.g. Sweden and France) value quality of life. In essence, masculine societies live to work, whereas feminine societies work to live. An American manager working in Sweden may expect employees to work overtime to meet targets as would be the case in the US. Swedes, however, tend to be less driven by the monetary rewards that this might bring, preferring instead leisure time with their families.

The Ulm office of Warbings is headed by a British director. All other employees are local nationals, with the exception of four British sales staff. How might cultural differences impact on the management of the German operation and relationships with the UK head office?

People resourcing

Introduction

Internationally mobile personnel are often known as international assignees or **expatriates**. They are appointed for a variety of purposes, including setting up or opening new operations, managing local subsidiaries, training local people, supplying scarce skills, transferring or maintaining corporate culture, as part of a development programme and/or to gain, transfer and share knowledge. Assignment lengths may be **short-term** or **long-term**. The assignment may be 'out and back' or be part of a **mobile cadre**. Alternatively, assignees may undertake **commuter assignments**.

The international assignment cycle

The recruitment and selection of individuals forms part of a cycle of management of internationally mobile personnel, as shown in Figure 22.1.

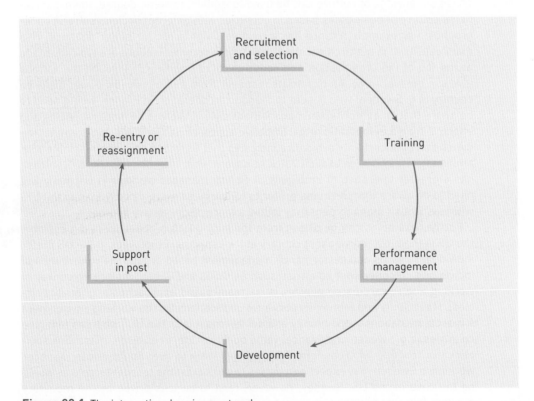

Figure 22.1 The international assignment cycle

The relevance of staged models of global growth

To understand the resourcing, development, compensation and re-entry/re-assignment approaches taken by organisations, it is helpful to see these stages in terms of some of the models of global growth. Perlmutter's (1969) framework, for example, examines four stages: **ethnocentric**, **polycentric**, **geocentric** and **regiocentric**.

At the ethnocentric stage, the resourcing philosophy is to use home country personnel from the organisational headquarters to staff up subsidiaries abroad. The recruitment and selection of internationally mobile personnel is therefore normally carried out in the home country according to local home country practice. This approach is common in the early stages of internationalisation and has the advantage that company culture, rules and policies are transferred and maintained abroad. However, by using parent country nationals in the key foreign positions, this restricts development opportunities for locals, is expensive in terms of compensation packages and the assignees may not be locally responsive.

The polycentric stage takes the opposite approach – local nationals are used to staff key positions, with international assignees used only to transfer knowledge and skills where there are gaps. This approach reduces, if not eliminates, cultural problems and promotes local responsiveness, but the drawback, by contrast, is that a global perspective can be lost. Career opportunities are available for local people and employment costs are not likely to be as high as where there is a significant international assignee population. Local practices with regard to recruitment and selection are used.

In the geocentric approach to resourcing, staff are drawn from worldwide sources and in the regiocentric approach staff are drawn from a regional base. In terms of recruitment and selection, candidates are drawn from worldwide (or regional) talent, thereby creating a pool of senior managers with international experience and global vision. However, there are increased costs associated with these resourcing philosophies in terms of training, development and reward packages. In addition, local immigration laws result in the need for visas and work permits and this can reduce organisations' abilities to fill vacancies quickly. Centralised control is likely to be required to co-ordinate recruitment and selection activities, together with knowledge of local recruitment and selection practices and their cultural implications.

exercise

Warbings has one European office to date, based in Ulm, Germany. The company has assigned a British director and four British salespeople to this office. Comment on how Perlmutter's framework can be applied to this situation and the resourcing implications should Warbings continue to follow this approach in any future European expansion.

International recruitment

To recruit international assignees, various options are available. These include:

- Executive search agencies (headhunters);
- Cross-national advertising (cultural differences in practice must be considered);
- Internet recruitment;
- International graduate recruitment fairs/programmes.

International selection

Once the recruitment process has been completed, the selection of internationally mobile personnel can be carried out. Selection tools include:

- Standardised tests (to give certification of knowledge and skills);
- Interviews backed up by references;
- Psychometric tests (but cultural biases need to be considered);
- Work samples (including simulation of new work duties);
- Biographical data (where personal characteristics are correlated with work success).

Many of these tools can be brought together and used in an assessment centre where candidates undertake group and individual exercises, undergo interviews and perhaps various psychometric tests. It is important that, for international selection, the testers/interviewers are culturally aware as candidates' behaviours and answers reflect their societal cultural background.

The selection process

According to research carried out by UMIST/CBI/CIB (1995), the selection process should include the following steps:

- Create a selection team to reflect the various cultural groups;
- Define the strategic purpose of the assignment;
- Assess the global assignment context;
- Establish selection criteria;
- Define the candidate pool;
- Use multiple selection methods;
- Interview the expatriate *and partner*;
- Make the assignment offer;
- Run appropriate training programmes.

The importance of careful selection

Careful expatriate selection is important to ensure that the best person is selected for the role and that the benefits of diversity are achieved. The process should also ensure that inadvertent discriminatory practice does not take place. In addition, careful consideration of potential assignees' competencies will increase the likelihood of a successful assignment, reducing the numbers of early returns, and thereby improving the cost-effectiveness of international selection and deployment.

International assignee competencies

Organisations seek a number of competencies in their international assignees. These may be grouped into the following areas: strategic skills, professional/technical skills, managerial skills, communication skills and social orientation.

To possess all such competencies is rare and, as such, international assignees who have demonstrated strong ability in the international arena are in great demand.

To attract and retain such talent means that organisations must place significant emphasis on their development initiatives, as well as their reward packages. But these are not enough in themselves and attention must also be paid to support and welfare issues for assignees and their families.

Training and development

Training versus development

Training and **development** are usually discussed together – but it is important to recognise that they are distinct interventions. In the international arena, training concerns providing the tools or the understanding to increase productivity and/or reduce assignment failure. International assignments may be used as part of development programmes to prepare individuals for increased role responsibility and career enhancement as part of organisational strategy to increase competitiveness through people. International HRD is part of the career management of key talent.

International training

Training programmes devised for international assignees (and, increasingly, accompanying partners and family members) may comprise five main elements: briefing; pre-assignment visits; language; cross-cultural awareness; and culture shock.

Briefing

Briefing is the most commonly provided form of pre-departure training given by organisations to assignees, and is frequently offered to accompanying family members too. It usually comprises information delivery via lectures, videos and discussion and is completed within one or two days.

Pre-assignment visits

As part of the preparation process for living and working abroad, organisations may offer pre-assignment visits to the individual (and accompanying partner and, possibly, other family members). Such 'look-see' visits are usually around one week long and enable the employee and family to spend time in the new location to see it first-hand, to arrange housing and schooling.

Language training

Language training is a popular form of support for assignees (and again partners, and sometimes accompanying family members). Being able to speak the local language aids the settling-in process and can improve productivity and proactive local business relationships.

Cultural awareness training

Some awareness of the host country's culture may be gained through briefing but to gain a greater sense of understanding, sensitivity training and field experience is needed. When cultural differences are great, e.g. between the US and Japan, it is generally assumed that cultural awareness training will be particularly helpful in helping assignees (and families) to settle in and in terms of raising productivity.

Culture shock training

Culture shock can have a major impact on assignees and their families and their ability to complete their assignments. It is frequently unexpected. Being unable to cope with local norms and behaviours can result in perceived lack of self-efficacy. Culture shock training is a valuable part of any pre-departure preparation programme to alert assignees to likely experiences and help them develop coping strategies.

exercise

W

Draw up a training programme for Warbings in preparation for its plans to increase its European market share by opening new offices in other European countries.

Human resource development

The development of employees through international assignments has long been regarded as a primary means of ensuring top management in multinational organisations apply a global perspective to the strategic direction of the business. Models of the staged development of organisational growth may be used to determine the likely HRD strategy.

Organisational growth and HRD implications

In the ethnocentric stage, parent country nationals (PCNs) are used to fill key positions in the host country operations. Typically these take the form of relatively long-term expatriate assignments where talent is drawn from the headquarters. The purpose of such assignments is to fill key positions, to manage and control business operations locally. Employees may be assigned as country managers, for example, or as heads of functions for assignment lengths of, typically, three or more years. In terms of development, such assignees should gain local understanding, sensitivity and responsiveness. However, transfers to other countries and repatriation may prove to be problematic as assignees become embedded in local practice.

In the polycentric stage, local nationals are typically used to fill key positions. However, assignees from the home country (or other countries) may be used to transfer knowledge and skills and to train locals. Such assignments therefore tend to be used as needed and are relatively short. Their purpose is, perhaps, more concerned with the development of local personnel than that of the assignee – although assignees do benefit from cultural exposure. Care needs to be taken with the polycentric approach that global vision is not lost locally, as may well be the case if local employees are not developed through international transfers.

A global or regional approach to HRD requires co-ordination at either a central or regional hub. Assignees are developed through international assignments either across the globe or within a regional grouping of operations. Such assignments may well be used to fill skill gaps and train locals, but the transfer of personnel often results from the requirement to develop talent and encourage knowledge sharing. In such assignments, local knowledge is seen with a global perspective and diversity is valued within HRD.

HRD in an international context presents a number of complexities not found in the domestic context. The mix of parent country, local and third country nationals presents a complex picture in terms of arranging international development transfers and secondments, with implications for cross-cultural training and international orientation. Besides the assignees themselves, there are implications for the careers of accompanying partners. Development procedures need to take external and unfamiliar influences into account, with a resulting broadening HRD activity being required in terms of cultural approaches and diversity management.

exercise

Warbings currently employs one senior manager in an international capacity in Germany, heading up the German subsidiary of the company. Comment on the HRD implications of this assignment.

W

International career management

HRD is part of career management. Undertaking this in an international environment provides its own challenges, especially as careers today tend not to follow a traditional 'boundaried' path within a single organisation. Rather, it is more usual for individuals' careers to be 'boundaryless', in that development gained within one organisation is used as a stepping stone to further careers elsewhere. This clearly has cost implications for employers using international transfers as developmental tools in building top talent for the future.

International careers

Foreign assignments have long been recognised as a mechanism for developing the international expertise required for career advancement in multinational organisations, yet the relationship between international assignments and careers remains unclear. Indeed, international careers are increasingly characterised by discontinuity, interruptions and reformulation, with organisational change, corporate restructuring and globalisation having a major impact on career management.

International career management involves helping the assignee to step back from the experience to assess the degree of fit between the skills acquired on assignment and the corporate requirements, to develop strategies for using personal and business experiences and identifying and applying new and enhanced skills.

Mentoring programmes

Mentoring programmes are frequently set up as part of career management for international assignees to facilitate adjustment, thereby ensuring assignees remain in touch with the home country operations and aiding career progression, with mentors advising them of opportunities through regular communication and counselling. For mentoring to be successful, mentors must be willing to serve in this role, be at a senior level and follow communication guidelines. Being appraised on their role can also promote greater commitment to being involved in assignees' career management. There should be replacement arrangements in place should the original mentor leave. Despite emphasis often being given to the role of the mentor in career management, it is important to note that the assignee must be willing to manage their own career – he or she cannot rely (or expect) – others to do this for them.

Re-entry

As part of career management, repatriation programmes need to be strategically managed so as to improve the retention rate of returned assignees and to encourage, by example, the acceptance of international assignments by others. The efficient and effective use of international competencies gained on assignment should be encouraged via knowledge sharing.

pause for thought

Why do you think it is important for the process of re-entry to be systematically well managed?

Give reasons for your answer.

Reward and performance management

Introduction to international assignee compensation

To manage compensation in the international environment successfully involves knowledge of employment legislation and taxation law in the countries of operation, as well as local custom and practice and international trends in reward management. There are two broad staff groups that need to be considered: local nationals and internationally mobile personnel. Compensation practices applied to local employees would typically follow local norms – with market data and local specialised advice needed to ensure that competitive terms are applied and legal requirements met.

Reward management for internationally mobile personnel is usually considered more time-consuming as employers have a range of options and, as the cost of employing such personnel is usually considered to be at least three times that of employing locals, there is greater pressure to ensure effective and efficient methods are applied.

Compensation policy objectives

Individual *ad hoc* negotiation of international terms and conditions is usually time-consuming and expensive and, as a result, it is common practice for written international assignment policies to be devised. Having a formal policy has the advantages of consistency of treatment and administration, cost control, transparency, improved communications and management of expectations. The objectives of any international compensation policy must be to ensure an effective level of acceptance of assignments, as well as employee retention and development, simplicity for ease of understanding by expatriates and other staff along with ease of administration. In addition, the policy should provide a process for long-term management of compensation and be underscored by commitment from home and host management.

Employee expectations

The international assignee will have expectations of the policy too. These include: financial protection (e.g. being no worse off through tax, social security, cost of living), financial advancement (i.e. to have an incentive for the disruption to home and family life of living and working abroad), career development or advancement (on assignment and/or on repatriation) and that family concerns (such as dual careers and children's education) be addressed. Not surprisingly, there is potential for conflict between the expectations of the internationally mobile employee and the employer in terms of the scope and content of the international compensation policy.

Compensation policy components

In general, the compensation policy comprises three main elements: pay (remuneration), various allowances and benefits, and support services (such as training, mentoring and family welfare assistance). The approaches taken to international reward may vary widely, although, broadly speaking, these may be classified into four main types of remuneration policy with the provision of relocation allowances and benefits depending on which is adopted.

- Home-based/salary build-up/'balance sheet' (or a modified version of this approach);
- Host-based or local 'going rate' (or a modified approach such as host-based plus enhancements);
- A global or regionally based 'market rate';
- Individual negotiation/*ad hoc* or better of home/host.

The home-based approach

The balance sheet is by far the most widely used approach to international assignee compensation. Its aim is to ensure that the employee is no worse off than had he or she stayed at home. In theory, the employee is no better off either, as the principle of the balance sheet is not to 'reward' international assignees for the various difficulties they experience, but rather to compensate them for 'losses'. For example, allowances may be paid to compensate for arduous geographical conditions or political instability as a compensatory payment for enduring 'hardship', rather than an incentive paid to encourage mobility to such locations.

Base salary and allowances

The compensation received by international assignees under the home-based approach typically rests on base salary. This is the amount of cash compensation or 'pay' that the employee receives at home. Allowances and benefits are typically related to this (for example, mobility allowances, foreign service premiums, cost of

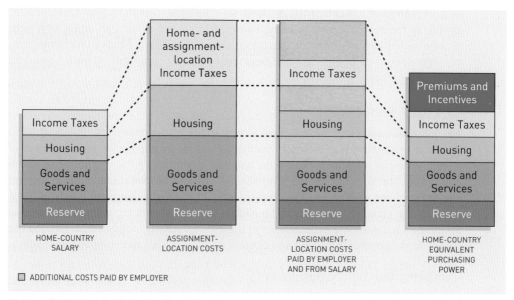

HOME-COUNTRY SALARY	ASSIGNMENT-LOCATION COSTS	ASSIGNMENT-LOCATION COSTS PAID BY EMPLOYER AND FROM SALARY	HOME-COUNTRY EQUIVALENT PURCHASING POWER
	Home- and assignment-location Income Taxes	Income Taxes	Premiums and Incentives
Income Taxes	Housing	Housing	Income Taxes
Housing			Housing
Goods and Services	Goods and Services	Goods and Services	Goods and Services
Reserve	Reserve	Reserve	Reserve

☐ ADDITIONAL COSTS PAID BY EMPLOYER

Figure 22.2 The traditional balance sheet

living allowances (COLA), location/hardship allowances) and it also acts as a reference for the calculation of pension contributions. This is shown diagrammatically in Figure 22.2.

pause for thought

Imagine you have just been posted abroad; would you like your remuneration to reflect that of your colleagues back home, that of your new colleagues, or something else?

Explain why you reached this conclusion.

Delivery of base salary may be made in home or local currency or as a mixture. Foreign service premiums may be paid as a monthly uplift to base pay to compensate for international mobility, although in recent years this practice is being replaced by the provision of one-off mobility premiums (again, a percentage of base salary) but paid once on expatriation and possibly again on repatriation. COLAs are also generally paid to compensate for increased costs of goods and services in the host location. Other allowances typically added into the compensation package include: housing, education, home leave, hardship, relocation/shipping, spouse assistance/dual career allowances and so on.

Taxation

In terms of taxation, the balance sheet is underpinned by the principle of **tax equalisation**. Any additional tax burden is met by the employer but any gains fall to the employer as well.

Advantages and disadvantages

The home-based approach to international assignment compensation presents a number of advantages. It provides equity between assignees from the same home country, it promotes geographical mobility (as employees are no worse off regardless of where they go), it facilitates repatriation and it is clear and straightforward to communicate to employees. However, in terms of disadvantages it can create large disparities between international assignees of different nationalities and between assignees and locals. It is also complex to administer and expensive to operate.

The host-based approach

The pure host-based approach to international assignee compensation treats international assignees exactly as locals in terms of their compensation. The main difficulty with this is that international assignees are not like locals, in that they have particular issues that continue to require employer support. For example, housing and education are two key areas of concern. Other issues include home-leave, as assignees will need to maintain ties with their home country to aid repatriation and taxation.

Pure versus modified approaches

It is rare for international assignees to receive pure host-based terms; rather, a modified approach is usually applied taking into account these special areas of concern. It is certainly the case that assignees may be in jeopardy if a *laissez-faire* attitude is taken and assistance is not provided with tax issues. In some countries, non-payment of local taxes may result in fines or imprisonment, so assistance with tax return preparation is therefore particularly important. Mobility will be impaired if employees are required to move to higher tax jurisdictions, particularly if their net pay is reduced as a result.

Taxation issues

To facilitate mobility, employers may tax equalise or tax protect their assignees. Under **tax protection**, employees will not be worse off – but they can be better off. This too has implications for mobility.

Advantages and disadvantages

The host-based approach to international assignment compensation presents a number of advantages. It provides equity between assignees and local nationals and other assignees working in the same location from different home countries of origin. It is simple to communicate and administer and promotes identification with the host country. It is also a less costly approach for employers, as significantly fewer allowances and benefits are applied. However, it presents a number of disadvantages. Assignees receive different levels of reward should they move from one assignment location to another. It is difficult to persuade assignees to move to low-pay countries or to repatriate from high-pay countries. It also presents potential difficulties in terms of repatriation back into the home country payment system. It therefore does not easily facilitate global mobility.

The Ulm office of Warbings is staffed mostly by local employees, with the exception of the director and four expatriate sales staff. Pay is higher than average and the expatriate staff are paid an additional number of supplements including a 'working abroad bonus', housing allowance, any school fees, and health insurance. Turnover is low and staff recalled to the UK tend to resent their loss of supplementary benefits. How might Warbings' approach to reward be reviewed to support employee mobility to further the company's strategy of increasing its European market share?

Global or regionally based 'market rate'

This approach to international assignee compensation is typically used for globally or regionally mobile personnel (mobile cadre) who move from one assignment to another rather than being repatriated to their home countries. It may also be used when an organisation employs international assignees from numerous home countries in many different host environments. Employers construct special remuneration systems for these mobile employees so that equity is preserved between and among them as they move from one location to another. However, their remuneration bears no link to either their host or their home countries. Such compensation systems are complex to administer and may present communication issues – particularly in terms of areas of concern such as pensions and social security.

Other arrangements

Arrangements such as the use of individual negotiation for compensating internationally mobile personnel may be fraught with difficulty as they are unlikely to be seen to provide equity or promote mobility. It is not uncommon to use a 'better of home or host' approach – with home-based pay used for transfers to developing countries and host-based for transfers into or within the first world. The better of home or host may also be applied to individual elements that comprise the policy – but this again can result in individual negotiation and an increase in costs.

Performance management for international assignees

Attention is frequently focused on individual performance appraisal but this is only a part of the **performance management** process. Stages to be considered within performance management stem from the organisational strategy and include role clarification and setting of direction, goal setting and alignment with strategy, coaching and employee support, and ongoing performance feedback. These steps underpin the performance appraisal from which development plans and reward are generated and future individual goals are devised.

Performance management for international assignees is particularly complex, as individuals' performance is affected by a combination of interrelated internal and external variables. These include: the compensation package, the job requirements, the cultural environment (both organisational and societal) in which the job is carried out, headquarters support and the adjustment of the employee and family in the foreign location (Dowling et al., 1999).

Appraisals

Performance appraisals are complicated by time and distance constraints and by the fact that the assignee may not report directly to anyone on the ground locally. Headquarters' lack of knowledge at local level may also present complications in terms of setting realistic goals and measuring success. In addition, the home country's methods of performance measurement and appraisal processes may be inappropriate at local level due to cultural differences. As a result, organisations may use a variety of approaches, such as combining formal performance appraisal with visits back to the HQ, visits to the host country from HQ, and assessment of results in the local area (Harris et al., 2003).

exercise

What factors should you take into account in assessing the performance of Warbings' British director and the four British salespeople in the company's Ulm office in Germany?

Give reasons for your answer.

Individual employment relationships

This section considers the role of communication and support for assignees while they are at the 'in-post' stage of the international assignment cycle.

International teamworking

Individuals rarely work alone while on international assignments. Increasingly, international assignments require teamworking, particularly within multicultural teams. Such teams may be required on an *ad hoc* basis to complete short-term projects locally or be set up transnationally where projects span national boundaries. Team members may work together, in person, or virtually. Teams may be led by local nationals or by international assignees. They may operate inside the organisation or beyond it, e.g. as part of a joint venture, partnership arrangement or strategic alliance. One of the critical functions of international HRM is to support international teams through communication, training and development.

Teamworking in an international context may be fraught with problems. Teamwork places pressure on hierarchical relationships and may present a challenge to authority – different nationalities' views of power distance are important here. Cultural differences in managing people, e.g. in terms of decision making, leading and communicating, may also present a barrier to success.

Teams therefore need to be supported, particularly through training and cross-cultural team building. Interpersonal skills need to be developed to handle sensitively negotiations and conflict resolution, as well as to use appropriate judgement in local situations.

W

What issues should you consider to improve the effectiveness and efficiency of the Ulm operation of Warbings, bearing in mind the British/German cultural mix of the sales team in Germany?

Flexibility

Flexibility is an important component within the role of international assignees. They may find themselves in an environment where they have much greater autonomy than they had at home and this requires a different approach to management and decision making. Cultural differences are again important to consider here. Having few rules to follow is not easily handled by some societal cultures, yet when working in a country which favours ambiguity over the avoidance of uncertainty requires these people to learn and apply different coping strategies. Take the example of Germany and the UK. Germans are less tolerant of ambiguity than the British. It would follow that, generally speaking, German managers working in the UK would be expected to demonstrate greater flexibility in interpreting procedures and rules than they would in their native land. Similarly, British assignees working in Germany might feel more constrained by rules and regulations applied there.

exercise

W

Consider how you might structure a communications programme for the Ulm office at Warbings to inform the British assignees and the German employees of a programme of change to be instituted throughout the company's European operations.

The psychological contract

The psychological contract comprises perceived reciprocal promises and obligations between the individual and the organisation. Unlike the written contract of employment, the psychological contract is unwritten. It concerns how people perceive fairness. It is informal, is not usually openly discussed and is based on reciprocity. Although the psychological contract does have a transactional element (based upon economic exchange), it is also relational (i.e. based upon interpersonal exchange).

In the international arena, employers sending assignees to work abroad expect them to be committed, to transfer skills, win new business and manage local operations. They expect them to complete the assignment and to demonstrate flexibility and willingness to do what it takes to get the job done. However, a foreign assignment not only impacts on employees but also upon their families. As a result, employees' expectations of the psychological contract tend to extend beyond typical expected returns of pay and benefits, and career development and training. Additional expectations include issues such as housing, career support for partners, good educational support for children, personal security and attention to, and care of, dependent relatives and pets. Where employers pay attention to these issues, the psychological contract is likely to remain intact. Where such issues are disregarded, however, it is likely to be damaged or broken.

The psychological contract is important because it influences performance, extra-role behaviour (i.e. whether individuals will go beyond their role requirements), job satisfaction, organisational commitment and intention to remain with the organisation.

Health and welfare

The health and welfare of international employees and their dependants is a major concern due both to the fact that employers have a duty of care and also because of the impact on productivity and thus international competitiveness. In the current international climate, the threat of terrorism comes immediately to mind, but the reduction of stress and related ill health also needs to be considered in less obvious situations such as culture shock, unaccompanied assignments, remote environments and in family support.

Stress

It is important to start by considering what **stress** is, as from this definition strategies can be developed both individually and corporately to reduce it.

Stress manifests itself when people are unable to cope with the load placed upon them. Stress is therefore a personal issue, in that aspects of life, or the work environment, that present a challenge and enjoyment to some are, for others, too much to bear.

Everyone experiences stress in everyday life, when work and life events place pressure upon them. We all develop coping mechanisms, though, to balance these competing pressures and to escape from them when the need arises. International assignees face an increased number of sources of stress as they try to cope with living and working in a different environment where their usual support strategies, or coping mechanisms, may be unavailable to them. For instance, an international assignment involves finding and moving to new housing, dealing with a partner's career issues and finding new schools for children. Working in an unfamiliar culture where transport and telecommunications systems may be inefficient (and ways of working may be totally different from those at home) are key sources of stress.

Culture shock

The ability to cope in an unfamiliar cultural environment is a key determinant of performance and, ultimately, assignment success or failure. Most individuals will experience what is known as culture shock as they go through a period of adjustment after arrival. Culture shock normally takes the form of a cycle beginning prior to departure with both positive and negative feelings, including excitement and sense of adventure, counterbalanced with emotions of anxiety and fear of the unknown. On arrival, this produces what is known as the honeymoon or tourist phase of the culture shock cycle, characterised by seeing the novelty of the new environment. After a while, this emotion gives way, most typically, to a negative view where individuals commonly report feeling a sense of strain or loss and feelings of incompetency, confusion or rejection. This is the most critical phase of the cycle and when individuals

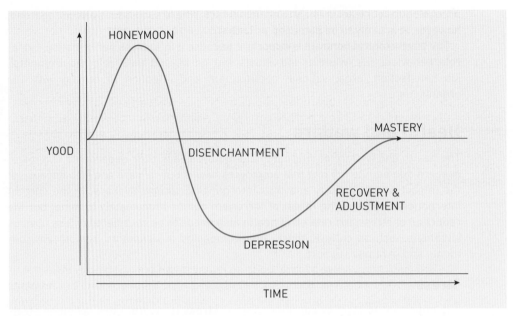

Figure 22.3 The culture shock cycle

or families wish to return home. However, assuming that coping strategies are found, it is usual for a sense of recovery or adjustment to take place followed by mastery of the new environment. This is shown diagrammatically in Figure 22.3. Should a coping mechanism not be found, and the assignee remain in the foreign location, there is a danger of stress-related ill health occurring, such as depression, even alcoholism or drug dependency.

Assignees who have undertaken several assignments may experience little or no culture shock or may move through the stages of the cycle very quickly. Some assignees who have not lived and worked abroad before may also not be affected or experience little culture shock. Everyone is different and therefore it is impossible to predict how long – if at all – each stage in the cycle will take.

It is important to remember that productivity is affected during the early stages of an assignment and the performance management system should take this into account. Training programmes may include awareness of culture shock to help assignees prepare for this eventuality and consider how they might develop appropriate coping mechanisms.

Reverse culture shock

Culture shock also may occur on repatriation. Here it is known as reverse culture shock and is perhaps less expected as employees and families believe that they are returning to a familiar environment. In fact, they have changed as people by adapting to – even embracing – new cultural values. Coming home can therefore present a shock as old friends seem narrow-minded and office practices seem remote from those experienced abroad, particularly if repatriation results in reduced autonomy.

Preparation for repatriation should include training to expect and cope with reverse culture shock, thus reducing the potential for stress and helping to improve the retention of international assignees.

It has been agreed by the UK board that the Ulm office of Warbings in Germany can be more locally responsive and be run more cost-effectively by using local nationals rather than international assignees as sales personnel. It has therefore been decided that the four expatriate sales staff should return to the UK. What programme of assistance might you propose to repatriate these employees? What action might you take to retain them after repatriation?

exercise

W

Unaccompanied assignments

Assignments that involve separation from family members can be very stressful for the individual concerned. Examples include single status short-term assignments, commuter assignments or when children remain in the home country in boarding schools for educational continuity. The mobility strategy used should therefore be considered in the light of health and welfare issues.

Hostile environments

Hostile environments may include parts of the world with severe climatic conditions, be geographically remote, be politically unstable or present a potential threat of kidnapping and/or terrorism. Both actual threat as well as perception of threat can be a source of stress. Although it is unrealistic to prepare for every eventuality, it is possible to reduce the risks to employees working in dangerous locations by interventions at both the individual and corporate level. The use of briefing, backed by security measures, is important. Security consultancies may be engaged and retained to provide updated advice and insurance policies taken out to reduce financial risk. Stress breaks such as rest and relaxation opportunities may be offered to individuals based in hostile environments.

At the corporate level, it is crucial to undertake risk assessments and to research thoroughly the business partners and environments where operations will be based. Individuals working in the headquarters as well as on the ground locally need to be briefed and trained on how to handle crisis situations. It is important to remember that environments that appear 'safe' today can turn into 'hotspots' overnight. It is critically important to keep risk assessments up to date and have contingency plans at the ready.

Family welfare

When employees are asked to live and work abroad, the decision to go impacts not only upon themselves but also upon their families. Attention must therefore be given to family concerns. Two of the major barriers to international mobility are dual careers and children's education. Where possible, and bearing in mind cost constraints, employer support in these areas is particularly valuable to employees.

Summary

In this chapter we have addressed the international assignment cycle through an examination of the key stages of recruitment and selection. The implications of international working in terms of training, development and career management have been highlighted. Focus has been given to reward and performance management to attract and retain people in international positions. Individual employment relations and health and welfare issues have been addressed in relation to maintaining assignees in post. The re-entry aspects of international mobility have also been outlined. Throughout the chapter, the implications of cultural differences have been considered. Self-test exercises have been included throughout for you to apply your knowledge and understanding to the case study of Warbings Office Systems plc.

Review Questions

You may wish to attempt the following as practice examination style questions.

22.1 Discuss the extent to which international assignments are prerequisite to career development for board-level appointments.

22.2 What steps might organisations and assignees take to reduce the impact of culture shock on international assignment productivity?

22.3 To what extent are theories and models of societal culture relevant to both employers and employees in their preparations for international mobility?

22.4 Critically analyse current trends in the use of 'pure' and 'modified' approaches to both home- and host-based expatriate remuneration.

22.5 'Perlmutter's (1969) framework of global growth can be used as a basis for employee resourcing strategy for internationalising businesses.' Critically argue the case for and against this statement.

References

Dowling, P.J., Welch, D.E. and Schuler, R.S. (1999). *International Human Resource Management*, Cincinnati: International Thomson Publishing.

Harris, H., Brewster, C. and Sparrow, P. (2003). *International Human Resource Management*, London: CIPD.

Hofstede, G. (1994). *Cultures and Organizations*, London: HarperCollins.

Perlmutter, H.V. (1969). The tortuous evolution of the multinational corporation, *Columbia Journal of World Business*, Vol. 4, No. 1, pp. 9–18.

UMIST/CBI/CIB (1995). *Assessment, Selection and Preparation for Expatriate Assignments*, London: University of Manchester Institute of Science and Technology, CBI Employee Relocation Council and the Centre for International Briefing.

Further Reading

Armstrong, M. and Baron, A. (2000). *Performance Management*, London: CIPD.

Bartlett, C.A. and Ghoshal, S. (1989). *Managing Across Borders – The Transnational Solution*, Cambridge, MA: Harvard Business School Press.

Dowling, P.J. and Welch, D.E. (2004). *International Human Resource Management*, 4th edition, London: Thomson Learning.

Harris, H. (1999). Women in international management – why are they not selected?, in B. Brewster and H. Harris (eds.) *International HRM: Contemporary Issues in Europe*, pp. 258–276, London: Routledge.

Harzing, A.-W. and Van Ruysseveldt, J. (eds.) (2004). *International Human Resource Management: Managing People Across Borders*, London: Sage.

Hofstede, G. (2001). *Culture's Consequences: Comparing Values, Behaviours, Institutions and Organizations Across Nations*, London: Sage.

Holbeche, L. (1999). International teamworking, in P. Joynt and B. Morton (eds.) *The Global HR Manager*, pp. 179–206, London: IPD.

Jackson, T. (2002). *International HRM: A Cross-cultural Approach*, London: Sage

Joynt, P. and Morton, B. (eds.) (1999). *The Global HR Manager*, London: IPD.

Maund, L. (2001). *An Introduction to Human Resource Management*, Basingstoke: Palgrave.

Mendenhall, M. and Oddou, G. (1985). The dimensions of expatriate acculturation, *Academy of Management Review*, Vol. 10, pp. 39–47.

Mendenhall, M., Dunbar, E. and Oddou, G. (1987). Expatriate selection, training and career-pathing: a review and critique, *Human Resource Management*, Vol. 26, pp. 331–345.

Riusala, K. and Suutari, V. (2000). Expatriation and careers: perspectives of expatriates and spouses, *Career Development International*, Vol. 5, No. 2, pp. 81–90.

Scullion, H. and Linehan, M. (eds.) (2005). *International Human Resource Management – A Critical Text*, Basingstoke: Palgrave Macmillan.

Selmer, J. (2000). Usage of corporate career development activities by expatriate managers and the extent of their international adjustment, *International Journal of Commerce and Management*, Vol. 10, No. 1, pp. 1–23.

Sparrow, P. (1999). International recruitment, selection and assessment, in P. Joynt and B. Morton (eds.) *The Global HR Manager*, pp. 87–114, London: IPD.

Tung, R. (1981). Selecting and training of personnel for overseas assignments, *Columbia Journal of World Business*, Vol. 16, pp. 68–78.

Walton, J. (1999). *Strategic HRD*, London: Prentice Hall.

Useful Websites

www.amanet.org – website of the American Management Association, offering conferences, training, case studies and publications with an international outlook

www.cipd.co.uk – CIPD news and views on international HRM issues

www.croner.co.uk – Croner's publication guides

www.eiu.com – website of the Economist Intelligence Unit, with worldwide news, reports (e.g. worldwide cost of living), reports on economic issues and analyses and forecasts on more than 200 countries and eight key industries

www.eca-international.com – website focused on international HR solutions, with news, reports and analyses on issues such as international comparative salary trends

www.haygroup.com – access to Hay's global management consultancy (88 offices in 47 countries and 7,000 clients worldwide); offers Hay group insights – research reports

www.ilo.org – website of the International Labour Organisation (promoting 'decent work for all'), with publications, meetings, conferences, research and news reports (e.g. global employment trends). Notable campaigns include End Child Labour

www.incomesdata.co.uk – Incomes Data Services reviews and reports on international HRM issues (e.g. international rewards)

www.kpmg.net – website of KPMG global consultants, akin to Hay information services but with focus on taxation issues

www.oecd.org – website of the Organization for Economic Co-operation and Development, with global news, reports on investigation, recommendations and wide-ranging statistical analysis. The OECD is focused on 'a commitment to democratic government and the market economy'.

www.orcworldwide.com – website of ORC worldwide compensation and HR management specialists, with surveys,

compensation solutions, networking opportunities and access to consultancy

www.pensionsworld.co.uk – site of *Pensions World* monthly magazine for pension professionals, offering news, surveys, training courses and seminars, statistical analysis and networking opportunities

www.towers.com – website of global professional services firm Towers Perrin, offering consultancy, surveys, advice, reports and guidance (e.g. how to carry out equal pay audits)

www.shrm.org – website of the US Society for Human Resource Management, offering services and products (with US focus), similar to CIPD in UK

www.watsonwyatt.com – International consultancy, with actuarial base, offering consultancy, survey reports and analyses

Mini case study: Takahe Microelectronics Corporation

Consider the case study vignette of the Takahe Microelectronics Corporation and the report style task based upon it. You may wish to attempt this in the manner of a coursework assignment, drawing upon references in the academic and practitioner literature.

The Takahe Microelectronics Corporation is headquartered in Osaka, Japan and has manufacturing and distribution operations throughout Europe, Asia-Pacific and the Americas. The company's European regional head office is based in London and has responsibility for resourcing within its own region and for contributing towards the company's global career development structure, and corporate performance.

International mobility has been identified as a key driver in the company, achieving a geocentric approach to employee resourcing and in the development of a top international management cadre. The Corporation's key positions in many of the countries where it operates are held by Japanese nationals but it is the company's intention that these positions should be open to its 'brightest and best', regardless of nationality.

The European region has already developed an international cadre programme through which it is recruiting electronics graduates from universities across Europe. To begin their careers with Takahe, these graduates spend their first six months with the company in their local country, before being transferred for a six-month assignment to another country within the region. The intention is that these employees will return home for another six months before being assigned to the Japanese headquarters for a further six months' training and experience. After this period, the employees' careers will be within the European region and they will be expected to be mobile within and between the various European countries where Takahe has its operations. Their careers within the company may also involve further periods in Japan. The graduates recruited to this programme are expected to form the 'backbone' of the company's future managerial staff.

The European region also has an established international mobility experience programme for its existing junior and middle management staff. Under this programme, employees interested in gaining international experience may undertake a two-year secondment programme to another European company location before returning to their home country. Typically, but not always, the secondments are arranged on a reciprocal basis – a manager from Spain, for example, might undertake a secondment to the UK while his or her UK counterpart works in Spain.

In addition to this mobile management cadre, Takahe runs a Japanese 'cultural experience programme' for its existing key middle managers. These managers – who are typically based within one country and are generally not asked to relocate within the European region – are invited to spend two years in Japan working under local conditions to broaden their experience and to gain an understanding of Japanese working practices before returning to their home countries.

The Corporation also uses some European expatriates to head up its European country operations. These posts are typically long-term assignments of up to ten years; for example, a Norwegian is currently running the Corporation's German operation.

Report format assignment task

The European regional head office has been charged with developing an international assignment policy to address these four types of international assignment. Consider and evaluate the approach(es) the European regional head office might adopt in devising a policy in support of desired international employee mobility programmes, together with the underlying rationale(s).

GLOSSARY

360° feedback: The combination of peer, line manager, subordinate, client and self-reviews of performance to provide a comprehensive and balanced appraisal.

Absolutism: Proposition that there are universal truths in morality that apply at all times and in all circumstances.

ACAS: Advisory, Conciliation and Arbitration Service. Independent body promoting harmonious employment relationships; providing advice and helping resolve workplace conflict through conciliation, mediation and arbitration.

Action research/survey feedback: Organisational development technique for collaboration over change by involving those affected in collecting and analysing data and sharing understanding.

Active listening: Skills used to listen to what is really being said and meant rather than simply hearing spoken words; includes giving full attention, openness, honesty.

ACW: Association for Counselling at Work (ACW).

Age discrimination: The judging, often negatively, of older and younger people as employees because of prejudice based on the assumption that age affects the person's ability to perform.

Agency view: A view that a business only has responsibility to its owners or shareholders for whom mangers act as agents – a rejection of any wider social responsibility.

Agency workers: Workers not directly employed but who still have a contractual relationship with the organisation.

Arbitration: A process whereby a dispute is decided by an independent third party.

Attitude: The feelings, opinions and thoughts that affect a person's behaviour; the interaction of values and beliefs; the *affective* domain.

Attribution errors: Mistakes in the interpretation of cues leading to the misunderstanding of the causes of someone else's behaviour.

Balanced scorecard: A measurement system designed by Kaplan and Norton in 1992 that gives managers a comprehensive view of the business.

Behavioural assessments: Performance appraisal on the basis of rating achievement of desired behaviour, e.g. in customer care.

Broadbanded pay structure: A number of grades are compressed into a relatively small number of much wider pay ranges or bands.

Bundles of HRM practices (Huselid, 1995): Proposition that some HRM practices when integrated together can stimulate enhanced organisational performance.

Burn out: A stress syndrome characterised by emotional exhaustion, depersonalisation and reduced personal accomplishment.

Career Average Revalued Earnings Pension: Occupational pension calculated on average earnings over the length of employment.

Chartered Institute for Personnel and Development (CIPD): The professional body for those involved in personnel and human resource management. A source of advice and guidance on 'best practice'.

Coach: Person who gives specialised training and guidance as well as general support and encouragement.

Coaching: A developmentally focused relationship between colleagues or peers that involves specialist skills training and guidance as well as general support and encouragement with the overall goal of improving work performance.

Coaching culture: Overall management commitment to helping staff develop to their full potential.

Collective bargaining: A voluntary process of negotiation between representatives for both the employer and the employees that sets terms and conditions of employment for those they represent.

Commission for Racial Equality (CRE): A body set up by the Race Relations Act (1976) which is working towards the elimination of racial discrimination and the promotion of race equality (Human Rights Commission from October 2007).

Communication: The means by which information and ideas are exchanged between two or more individuals or groups.

Communication fidelity: The degree of sameness between the message intended by the sender and the message understood by the receiver.

Communication strategy: Planning process covering the intended message and the medium for transmission focused on supporting the overall business goals of the organisation.

Communities of practice: Knowledge management activities, e.g. group meetings which spread and apply knowledge.

Commuter assignment: An international assignment serviced by someone who remains at home with their family but commutes on a weekly or monthly basis to work in the foreign location.

Competency: The observable, demonstrable, measurable and evidence-based ability to perform the activities of a job role, to a defined standard, within a given context.

Competency-based pay: Remuneration linked to the skill and expertise of the employees under the scheme.

Competency framework: Identification of a set of behaviours required by employees to achieve business objectives; can also profile top performers in the organisation.

Consequentialist approaches (utilitarianism): Notion that the morality of an act is determined by its consequences and (utilitarianism) people should pursue the greatest good (or happiness) for the greatest number of people.

Contingency or best-fit school: The argument that HRM must be adaptable to what is relevant or fits best with an organisation's strategic and operational requirements.

Contingent (performance) pay: Pay that depends on performance, competency or contribution.

Corporate social responsibility: The responsibilities and relations between an organisation and the community within which it operates.

Critical incident technique: Used in job analysis and by appraisers, it directs the attention of job-holders to those good and bad elements in their jobs that make a difference between overall success and failure.

Cultural display rules: Communication of emotion in socially defined circumstances, e.g. when acceptable to show distress.

Cultural hegemony: The overpowering dominance of deeply embedded values and practices, at a societal or an organisational level, which influence how far those from other traditions can integrate.

Cultural relativism: Notion that morality varies with culture, time and circumstances.

Culture: The common or shared norms, meanings, attitudes values, beliefs and patterns of behaviours in an organisation. There may be a number of sub-cultures within an organisation.

Deregulation: Freedom of the marketplace, removing legal restrictions on the business operation.

Development: Gradual personal growth over time; planned learning events aimed to meet future personal or organisational objectives.

Development Plans: Formal processes, e.g. training to enhance current and future employee performance.

Disability Rights Commission (DRC): Established by the Disability Discrimination Act (1995) and working towards the elimination of disability discrimination (Human Rights Commission from October 2007).

Discipline: Management action against an employee who has not met expected standards of behaviour or performance.

Discrimination: Treating one person less favourably than another because of prejudice against them as e.g. women, or members of a particular ethnic group.

Diversity: Human characteristics that make people different from one another.

Dysfunctional management: Poor decision making or other behaviour (e.g. bullying) which generates problems; often poor standards of conduct or unethical behaviour.

Education: Formal, planned off-the-job learning, usually aligned to qualifications, undertaken at, or with, a college or university.

Emergent strategy: The argument that strategy evolves not from prior planning but from trial and error.

Emotional intelligence: The ability to deal with emotional states (one's own and those of another) in a positive constructive manner.

Empathising: An ability to see the world from the client's point of view and to see the client's subjective point of view.

Employee Assistance Programmes (EAPs): A company-sponsored programme that helps employees cope with personal problems that are interfering with their job performance.

Employee-centred approach: Rewards tailored to the specific needs of employees on individual contracts.

Employment contract: Formal legally binding agreement governing obligations and rights in the work relationship.

Employment rate: The percentage of men/women in various age brackets who are in paid employment at any one time (e.g. by 1995 only 63 per cent of men between ages 50–64 were declared as in full-time employment).

Equal Opportunities Commission (EOC): Set up by the Sex Discrimination Act (1975) and working towards the elimination of sex discrimination (Human Rights Commission from October 2007).

Equal pay: Legal obligation to give the same pay for work of equal value to women and men alike.

E-recruitment: IT-based recruitment, e.g. using websites, cyber agencies, electronic application forms and tests.

Ethics of human rights: Notion that people have basic human rights (cf. Human Rights Act, 1998) to be recognised and respected.

Evaluation: Measurement of the total value and effectiveness of an issues, for example, training and learning; particularly the return-on-investment for the organisation.

Exit interview: An interview designed to discover why someone is leaving an organisation in order that the organisation might capture important information and learn from the leaver's experience.

Expatriates: Internationally mobile personnel who work away from their home countries in a foreign country for a period determined by their employer, after which they may return home, move to another country or remain in their current host location.

Expectancy theory (Vroom 1964): A process theory of motivation which argues that people will direct their effort to behaviours which they can expect to lead to desired outcomes, e.g. where extra effort can lead to a desirable bonus.

Experiential learning cycle (Kolb, 1984): Model of learning from experience applied in management learning to stress the importance of self-managed reflective learning.

Experiential knowledge: Knowledge involving or based on experience, e.g. understanding from custom and usage.

Extrovert/introvert: Personality types: extrovert – outgoing, gregarious, warm; introvert – quiet, reserved, shy.

Family-friendly policies: Policies on flexible working (e.g. hours, place of work) to enable employees to juggle job and family commitments.

Final salary/defined benefit pension: Occupational pension guaranteeing a pension based on length of service and final or 'best' salary.

Flat hierarchical structure: An organisation structure that has only a few levels of management and emphasises decentralisation.

Flexible (cafeteria) benefits: Benefits (e.g. loans, vouchers, gym membership) offered to allow employees some choice in the make up of their remuneration package so it is more suited to their individual needs/circumstances.

Flexible organisation: Notion of the flexible firm (devised by Atkins and Meagre in 1984) as an adaptive organisation which has numerical, functional and financial flexibility in staffing with a limited core group of employees and a larger periphery of those with less job security.

Flexible working hours: A work arrangement that gives employees choice over the starting and ending times of their daily work schedules.

Gatekeeper: A person who *controls* communication by receiving and then re-transmitting the message.

Gender/ethnicity imbalance: Where the workforce fails to reflect the composition (male/female, ethnic) of wider society.

Glass ceiling: The invisible barrier which exists to prevent certain groups from reaching an organisation's upper echelons – the term is often used in relation to women.

Globalisation: Transition of business firms to international operation with worldwide strategies.

Graded salary structure: A sequence or hierarchy of pay levels (grades) into which jobs that are broadly comparable in value/size are placed.

Grievance: A formal complaint by an employee that is processed through a set of procedures.

Groupthink: A term used by Janis (1972) to depict a situation where a close-knit group becomes consensus seeking and pushes aside any consideration of alternative action.

Horns and halo effects: Where interviewers rate candidates as 'good' (halo) or 'bad' (horns) on first impressions which bias their judgement of the candidates' overall suitability for the job.

HRM benchmarking: Systematic comparison with other organisations or best practice models as part of an audit of strengths and weaknesses with the aim of learning and improving.

Human capital: The education and training, abilities, skills and experience possessed by an individual.

Human capital theory: The view that people resources should be seen as an investment and assessed in terms of costs and benefits because they are of value to an organisation in achieving success.

Human resource development (HRD): Organised learning events arranged to improve performance and/or personal growth for the purpose of improving the job, the individual and/or the organisation. HRD includes the areas of training and development, career development and organisation development.

Human resource management (HRM): The holistic and strategic approach used to manage a workforce so that it is aligned with organisational goals. It recognises that individuals are uniquely important to organisational success and give a competitive advantage.

Human resource planning (HRP): Determination of the people resources required by an organisation to achieve its strategic goals.

Implied contract terms: Terms of an employment contract that are not explicit but still binding such as common law duties, e.g. to pay wages.

Impression management: An attempt to influence other people's perception of ourselves in a favourable light, e.g. at selection interviews.

Information and communication technologies (ICT): Use of information technologies-software, hardware and supporting frameworks.

Intellectual capital: Argument that human knowledge can be valued as an asset.

Interpersonal skills: Effectiveness in relating to others, e.g. communication, teamworking

Isolationism: Policy or general view of holding aloof from other groups or countries.

Iterative process: Notion of planning where each successive step builds on the achievement of the previous step.

Job analysis: Systematic collection of information about the ways in which work is performed in order to define jobs and their requirements.

Job description: Systematic listing of components of a job, e.g. tasks and requirements.

Job evaluation: Systematic process for defining the relative values of jobs in an organisation.

Job family structures (career families): Separate grades and pay structures for different jobs or career groups in a function (e.g. accountants) where work activities, competencies are related.

Job preview: A realistic and systematic introduction to the job (warts and all) by various methods, e.g. visits, work experience, website information.

Jungian typology: Carl Jung's (1875–1961) classification of personality types used in some personality tests and based on four different ways of interpreting and responding to reality; thinking, feeling, sensation and intuition.

Key performance indicators (KPIs): Quantifiable measurements of the issues an organisation regards as critical to its success such as labour turnover, return on investment, etc. KPIs differ from organisation to organisation.

Key result areas (KRAs): Focus on elements of the job deemed critical for success in the overall job.

Knowledge: Truths, principles, concepts, constructs and paradigms; information applied within a specific context; the *cognitive* domain.

Knowledge management: Enhancing organisational capability by harnessing the power of information and understanding, creation, dissemination and utilisation of knowledge to fulfil organisational objectives (Murray and Myers, 1998).

Knowledge types: domain/explicit, technical/tacit domain/explicit knowledge is formal, recorded and officially retained, e.g. rules and procedures as against Technical/tacit knowledge which is gained from experience, by doing rather than learned from being taught.

Learning: Changes in knowledge, skills and attitudes shown through behaviour and performance.

Learning organisation: An organisation that continuously teaches and learns from itself.

Line of sight: In the design of pay schemes where employees can clearly see that effort can lead directly to reward.

Locked-in effect: The tendency to cling on to one's established perspective on an issue, situation, etc.

Long-term assignment: An international assignment typically from one to five years in length. The assignment may be 'out and back', i.e. followed by a re-entry to the home country or be part of a series of back-to-back assignments.

Mainstreaming: Incorporating issues to do with equality into all aspects of organisational strategy and policy.

Management development: Planned efforts to enhance the current and future performance of managers through learning programmes.

Management style: The preferred way managers deal with their staff ranging from autocratic to democratic participative.

Manager derailment: Failure of managers to deliver organisational success or maintain legal and ethical requirements.

Managerial escalator: The tendency, over time, for individuals to spend a decreasing proportion of time concerned with their own area of expertise coupled with an increasing proportion of their time organising and managing others.

Maslow's hierarchy of needs (A Maslow 1908–1970): Content or needs motivation theory arguing that people are motivated to strive to satisfy an ascending set of needs from basic physiological to self-fulfilment.

Matching model of HRM (Fombrun et al., 1985): Focus on integrated HRM policies and practice to enhance employee performance and deliver business success.

Material factor defence: An employer defending against an equal pay claim needs to show that the pay difference was for a reason unrelated to gender (e.g. the labour market).

MBTI: Myers–Briggs type indicator – widely used personality inventory based on the Jungian typology.

Mentor: Person delivering mentoring.

Mentoring: A developmentally orientated relationship between colleagues (one experienced and one less experienced) that involves career advising, role modelling, sharing experience and giving personal support to develop personal and professional skills.

Mobile cadre: A group of expatriates taking part in globally (or regionally) mobile series of assignments.

Money purchase pensions: Private pensions purchased by the individual in the market with no employer contribution.

New pay (Zingheim and Schuster, 2000): Notion that internal equity is less important than market value in supporting business objectives.

Non-consequentialist or deontological Approaches: Attempt to establish rationally a set of absolute moral rules, e.g. 'do as you would be done by' (Kant 1724–1804), e.g. 'do not lie or cheat'.

Non-verbal communication: Communication without words, e.g. facial expression, eye and body movements, proximity of two people, the way they listen.

Occupational health/welfare: Department concerned with promoting the health and well-being of employees.

Occupational segregation (vertical and horizontal): The tendency for certain occupations (horizontal segregation) and occupational levels (vertical segregation) to be inhabited by particular social groups.

Older worker effect (McKay, 1998): The argument that from age 50 there is an increased chance of becoming economically inactive, part time, in a temporary job or self-employed.

Open questioning: Skill using questioning techniques to probe and facilitate discussion instead of using closed questions which result in yes or no responses.

Organisation strategy (Chandler, 1962): Creation of long-term goals and action, including allocation of resources, to achieve them.

Organisational development (OD): Concerned with the building of organisational structures, culture, teams and systems to help achieve organisational objectives.

Organisational fit: Managements' view of whether or not someone is suitable for work within the organisational culture.

Organisational justice theories (Greenberg, 1987): Argues that motivation is influenced by perceptions employees have about how fairly and consistently they are treated compared with others.

Organisational learning: The process by which individuals, and whole organisations, develop and use their stock of knowledge.

Organisational mirroring: A feedback process used in organisational development for groups to increase their awareness of each other's activities, problems and issues.

Output-based assessment: In appraisal, performance measured in terms of quantifiable results then targets set for achieving defined output.

Paradigmatic changes: Fundamental changes to the nature of reality.

Paraphrasing: The ability to briefly rephrase what someone is saying, This skill indicates understanding and confirms that the expressed emotions, thoughts and feelings have been noted.

Partnership: An arrangement based on problem solving and consensus where workplace representatives and management work together.

Patriarchy: A social system which leads to the domination of women by men.

Pay gap: The difference in the average rate of pay between one group and another.

Perceptual bias: Errors and distortions in the way we perceive others.

Performance appraisal: Assessment of past and current work performance with a focus on improvement.

Performance management: A 'strategic and integrated approach for delivering sustained success to organisations by improving the performance of the people who work in them' (Armstrong and Baron, 2000).

Performance management cycle: Performance planning, monitoring and review, e.g. annual appraisal process.

Performance monitoring: Regular manager-led reviews of employee performance, e.g. interim appraisal review meetings to check on progress in meeting objectives.

Performance objective: Goals set by the organisation cascading down from corporate objectives to individual targets.

Person specification: Profile, e.g. in terms of competencies, of the person most likely to be successful in performing the job.

Personal development: Process concerned with aspects of developing the individual.

Pluralism: A way of analysing workplace relationships that recognises the legitimacy of often conflicting values held by different groups within workplace. Conflict is regarded as inevitable.

Positive action: Actions and initiatives, mentioned in the legislation, which are aimed at removing obstacles to participation and progress within the labour market by individuals from under-represented groups.

Prejudice: An attitude involving preconceptions about the members of a particular group, often negative.

Prescriptive strategy: The notion that strategy can be deliberately planned in advance.

Problem solving: An ability to use the skills such as active listening, open questioning, empathising, etc., to formulate a concise understanding of an issue, devise and implement a plan of action and evaluate its effectiveness.

Process consultation: A participative organisational development approach which allows a group to share in the process of addressing issues viewed as important by the organisation.

Psychological contract: An unwritten set of mutual beliefs, perceptions and informal obligations between an employer and an employee; the dynamics for the relationship, the context and the practicalities; distinguishable from the formal written contract of employment which identifies mutual duties and responsibilities.

Psychometric approach: The notion that selection is about systematic and objective measurement and assessment and the successful candidate is one who performs best in tests and other hurdles.

Psychometric testing: Systematic assessment and measurement of intelligence, aptitudes and personality.

Redundancy: Official notification and the process of losing current job. Legal termination because of disappearance of job, or reduction in work or change of location of employer's activities.

Reflecting: Skills used to show that the listener has heard and understood something of the speaker's experience or issue.

Repertory grid technique: Used in job analysis to compare key tasks with the competencies needed to carry them out.

Resource-based view of the firm: The notion that an organisation's resources (e.g. people) are a key source of competitive advantage and that the aim should be to maximise resources to create and dominate future opportunities for the organisation.

Retirement: A time, when having experienced a number of years of work, an individual withdraws from the labour market and does not intend to re-enter it.

Reward management: Strategy designed to reward (e.g. pay) employees fairly, consistently and in relation to their value for the organisation.

Reward strategy: Development of objectives for the longer term to implement rewards and support business goals.

Secular concerns: Concerned with worldly affairs rather than spiritual ones.

Selection criteria – validity and reliability: **Validity** – does the test actually measure what it purports to measure (e.g. intelligence)?; **Reliability** – refers to consistency in use.

Self-appraisal: Allows the employee to comment on their own achievements and contribute to a future development plan.

Short-term assignment: An international assignment usually considered to be under a year in length.

Single, double and triple (deutero) loop model: Models of organisational learning: **Single** focuses on doing the everyday job better; **Double** is about questioning fundamentals, e.g. why do the everyday job? **Triple** learning from learning activities to transform the organisation.

Skill: Aptitude to perform a task with ease; usually practical ability; the *psychomotor* domain.

SMART objectives: Specific, measurable, achievable, relevant and time-bound.

Social audit: Inclusion in company annual reports of not just assessment of financial performance but also evaluation of impact on both the environment and the community.

Social identity: The categorisation and self-categorisation of individuals within society according to socio-cultural characteristics.

Social perception: The process of collecting, collating and interpreting information about other people in order to understand them and their behaviours.

Socialisation: The process whereby an individual learns the norms and accepted and expected ways of behaving of the society within which he or she lives.

Socially constructed reality: Selection of specific material in the context of the social norms and expectations of wider society.

Spot salary structure: Single rate of pay for the job instead of a grade or range of pay.

Staff involvement: Management initiatives to gain employee co-operation/commitment through a range of direct and indirect activities with the organisation.

Stakeholder analysis: The idea that many people have a stake or interest in an organisation and their rights and needs must be recognised, not just those of owners or shareholders.

Stakeholder pensions: Low-cost defined contribution pensions regulated by the government and provided through pension companies.

Statistical discrimination: Discrimination against groups of workers on the basis of the perceived characteristics of the group.

Stereotyping: This involves seeing people on the basis of their group identity rather than as an individual who may or may not have the tendency ascribed to their particular group.

Strategic human resource management (SHRM): The alignment of HRM functions, e.g. recruitment with the corporate goals of the organisation to support the achievement of these goals.

Strategic planning: Focus on creating and implementing action on overall, long-term objectives of the organisation.

Stress: Can be the factor that leads to employee strain or ill health (e.g. work overload) or the individual's physical and/or psychological behavioural response.

Summarising: Skill used to capture the content, feeling and meaning of what has been said during the conversation and over time.

Tax equalisation: The same hypothetical tax as the employee would have paid at home is deducted from the home base pay to arrive at a net salary. Allowances, premiums and so on are then added to that amount and the company pays any tax that is assessed by the host location company on the total of the remuneration package that is delivered to the employee.

Tax protection: The employee pays no more tax in the host location that she or he would have paid on company-earned income at home, but could pay less. The company assumes responsibility for any taxes owed to the host location government in excess of the hypothetical home tax.

Taylorist scientific management (F.W. Taylor 1856–1917): Focus on using rational scientific procedures in management with simple effort/reward systems such as payment for goods produced (piecework) in manufacturing.

Team building and team learning: Organisational Development interventions to help groups develop common understanding and goals.

Total reward: An integrated strategic rewards framework (pay, benefits, etc.) to attract, retain, motivate and satisfy employees.

Training: Planned activity directed towards enabling learning at work.

Transactional analysis: Theory of personality focused on interpersonal communication from three key states: Parent, Adult and Child; aims to help people relate better. (Berne, 1964)

Transparency: Reward policies and practices which are open, clear, well communicated and easily understood by employees.

Union density: The unionised workforce expressed as a percentage of potential membership.

Unitarism: A way of perceiving workplace relations that assumes everyone has the same values and beliefs and is working towards the same goals. Conflict is regarded as anathema.

Universal or best-practice school: The proposition that strategic HRM is composed of a single set of HR policies and practices that is suitable for all organisations in all circumstances.

Validation: Measurement of the extent to which training has achieved its purposes.

Virtue ethics: The notion, propounded by Macintyre (1981), of acting as a 'good person' – living a virtuous life.

Walking the talk: Not just rhetoric – ensuring that actual behaviour is consistent with aims, information and claims.

Wellness or welfare programme: A company-wide programme to promote employee health, both physical and psychological.

Word of mouth recruitment: Asking current employees to recommend people known to them for employment.

Work-life balance: The need to deal with equally or balance the competing demands of job and private life (e.g. family caring commitments).

Workplace harassment: Persistent and unwelcome behaviour by an individual or group towards a colleague or co-worker.

Index